The Shofar's *Shabbos Companion*
~ A project from TanenbaumCHAT Wallenberg Campus ~

יום השישי. ויכלו השמים והארץ וכל צבאם: ויכל אלקים ביום השביעי

The Shofar's
Shabbos Companion
ילקוט לשבת קודש

The Greenstein Family Edition

A comprehensive guide to the Shabbos table, from Erev Shabbos to Havdalah. Complete with English translations and transliterations, clear instructions, illuminating and inspiring Divrei Torah, and background information.

A project from

Community Hebrew Academy of Toronto
האקדמיה העברית ע"ש טננבאום

Wallenberg Campus

מלאכתו אשר עשה: ויברך אלקים את יום השביעי ויקדש אותו כי בו שבת מכל מלאכתו אשר ברא אלקים לעשות: סברי מרנן ורבנן

ברכות: ברוך אתה ד' אלקינו מלך העולם בורא פרי הגפן: ברוך אתה

The Shofar's SHABBOS COMPANION
ילקוט לשבת קודש
A project from TanenbaumCHAT Wallenberg Campus

FIRST EDITION - May 2011

The Anne & Max Tanenbaum
Community Hebrew Academy of Toronto
Wallenberg Campus

200 Wilmington Avenue
Toronto, ON M3H 5J8
416-636-5984

ISBN-10: 1460955145
ISBN-13: 978-1460955147

COPYRIGHT NOTICE:

All the Hebrew texts used in this book are from "open-source" online sites. The following English translations have been taken from the "open-source" online site www.zemirotdatabase.org in accordance with their copyright policy: *Kol Mekadesh Shevii, Kah Ribon Olam,* and *Yom Zeh Mechubad.* The transliterations for all of the Zemirot were also taken from the above site. A number of stories included in the text have been taken from previously published and copyrighted material. They have been replicated with permission from the copyright holder and are indicated as such. We are happy to acknowledge their contribution to our project. Other translations and transliterations are original or adapted from existing sources. We have not knowingly used any copyrighted texts.

Staff Supervisors:
Rabbi Yisroel D. Goldstein & Mr. Zachary Isakow

Editors:
Matthew Goodman & Becky Friedman

Teacher Contributors:
Mr. Jeremy Cohen • Rabbi Lori Cohen • Mrs. Esther Friedman •
Rabbi Jay Kelman • Mrs. Tali Lalkin • Rabbi Itai Moryosef •
Rabbi Jeffrey Turtel • Dr. Anna Urowitz-Freudenstein •
Mr. Jory Vernon

Student Contributors:
Rachel Abitan, Idan Bergman, Samuel Buckstein,
Mindy Chapman, Elisheva Friedman, Michali Glasenberg,
Aaron Goldberg, Gabriel Hoffman, Teddy Kravetsky,
Micaela Lechtman, Orli Matlow, Yaron Milwid, Elianne Neuman,
Ari Satok, Josh Seed, Dylan Shaul, Rebecca Silver, Arielle Strasser,
Tzvi Yehudah Tabakman, Ben Welkovics, Zachary Zarnett-Klein

Cover art by:
Tovi Ander

About The Shofar:
The Shofar is a weekly student-run publication at TanenbaumCHAT Wallenberg Campus consisting of Divrei Torah on the week's Parsha. Our student writers display a wide range of ideologies and interpretations, but are united in the task of bringing the Parsha to life and illuminating its many lessons. Alongside our weekly paper, we have previously published a Pesach Haggadah with commentary and a Megillat Esther with original translations, commentary, and Divrei Torah.

Blessings of Gratitude

We would like to express our sincerest gratitude to the myriad of families and individuals within the TanenbaumCHAT community who generously sponsored the publication of this book. It is thanks to them and their contributions that we are able to share this book with you, and the merit of all the ensuing Torah learning is in their name.

The Torah tell us that poles were inserted into small rings which protruded from the sides of the Ark of the Covenant (Shemot 25:14). When the Ark had to be moved from place to place, it was carried by lifting these poles. The Holy Zohar teaches that the poles symbolize those who support Torah. Just as the poles hold the ark when it is lifted, and thus enable it to be transported, so, too, do supporters of Torah keep it raised high and facilitate the spreading of its teachings to Klal Yisrael.

May all who helped support our endeavour, as well as all those in Klal Yisrael who keep the Torah raised, go "m'chayil l'chayil," from strength to strength, and merit to see much happiness, health, prosperity, and joy in their lives.

עֵץ חיים היא למחזיקים בה ותמכיה מאשר
(משלי ג:יח)

It is a tree of life for those who hold it, and its supporters are praiseworthy
(Proverbs 3:18)

Book Sponsorship

In recognition of the importance of Jewish education and support of its future.
In loving memory of our husband and father,
Sydney Greenstein Z"l,
Jean, Michael, & Joel Greenstein

Section Sponsorships

The Roth Family
Shabbos Night
In honour of Cydney Roth's graduation

The Weisberg Family
Shabbos Day
In honour of our children, Alanna and Leni

The Hoffman Family
Bircat HaMazon

The Weissberg Family
Songs
In honour of all the great teachers at TanenbaumCHAT

The Goodman Family
Divrei Torah
Dedicated L'iluy Nishmas Chaim ben Dov Z"l, their beloved father and grandfather,
Harry (Chaim) Farber

Sefer Sponsorships

The Silver Family
Sefer Bereishit
Dedicated L'iluy Nishmas Aidel bas David, Chana Feigel bas Yitzchak, and Shmuel Nachum ben Yosef

The Bloom Family
Sefer Vayikra
In honour of Benjamin, Georgina, and Karly Bloom

The Glasenberg Family
Sefer Bamidbar
In honour of Akiva Yosef Dov Glasenberg, who is enlisting in the IDF (Golani Brigade)

The Weiss Family
Sefer Devarim
In honour of their beloved father and grandfather, Leon Weiss Z"L

Parsha Sponsorships

Laurie Blake
Parshat Vayakhel
In honour of her son, Joey Hadari
Parshat Ha'azinu
In honour of her daughter, Rachelle Hadari

The Cash Family
Parshat Mikeitz
In honour of their children and grandchildren

The Dunn Family
Parshat Nitzavim
Dedicated L'iluy Nishmat HaRav Nachum Yehudah Eliyahu
ben HaRav Shmuel Eliezer Z"L
"Beautiful is the study of Torah with Derech Eretz" (Pirkei Avot 2:2)

The Friedman Family
Parshat Yitro and Re'eh

The Garber Family
Parshat Beshalach

The Gardner Family
Parshat Bo
In honour of our children

The Glasenberg Family
Parshat Vayeishev
In honour of Yonatan Eliyahu Glasenberg
Parshat Naso
In honour of Akiva Yosef Dov Glasenberg

The Goldman Family
Parshat Lecha Lecha
In honour of all the excellent teachers at TanenbaumCHAT

The Grammer Family
Parshat Terumah
In honour of their children, Jonathan, Jake, and Simon

The Hoffer Family
Parshat Metzora

The Hubert-Chandler Family
Parshat Beha'alotecha
In honour of their children, Ariel and Yael

The Klompas Family
Parshat Vayigash

The Markman Family
Parshat Korach
In honour of all the students at TanenbaumCHAT

Brenda Medjuck
Parshat Vayeira
In honour of her mother, Helen Simpson

The Mevorach Family
Parshat Vayeitzei
In honour of all the Mevorach kids, Orry, Dana, and Keren

The Nathanson Family
Parshat Noach
In honour of Logan and Dylan Nathanson, with love

The Roskies-Neuman Family
Parshat Chayei Sarah
In honour of Elianne Neuman and The Shofar staff

The Opler Family
Parshat Va'etchanan
In honour of Arielle Opler

The Rosenstein Family
Parshat Toldot
In honour of Aaron Rosenstein

The Ross Family
Parshat Yitro
In honour of Natan Ross

Mark and Naomi Satok
Parshat Va'etchanan
In honour of their children, Josh, Ari, and Jordana

The Segal Family
Parshat Pinchas
In honour of TanenbaumCHAT

The Shear Family
Parshat Vayishlach
In honour of Sarah Shear

Pearl Schusheim & Moshe Ipp
Parshat Tzav
In honour of their children

The Vernon Family
Parshat Bereishit
In honour of all their children

The Weisbrod Family
Parshat Vayakhel
In honour of all the teachers and staff of TanenbaumCHAT

The Yakobi Family
Parshat Haazinu
In honour of Yasmin Arielle Yakobi

The Zeligson Family
Parshat Yitro
In honour of Taya and Eden

General Donations
Miguel, Beth, and David Singer

Table of Contents

Introductions • הקדמה — 19

Introductory Letters:
- From the Director of Education — 20
- From the Director of Jewish Studies — 21
- From the Vice Principal of Jewish Studies — 22
- From the Vice Principal of General Studies — 23
- From The Shofar's Staff Supervisor — 24

Preface to The Shabbos Companion — 26
Shabbos Kodesh: The Pinnacle of Creation — 28
What Shabbos Means to Me — 43

Stories from the Maggid:
- A Story Postscript — 50
- Yosef Mokir Shabbat — 51
- A Tzaddik's Tears — 53

Shabbos Night • ליל שבת — 55

- Candle Lighting — 56
- Blessing of the Children — 57
- Shalom Aleichem — 58
- Midrash Eishet Hayil, *by Dr. Anna Urowitz-Freudenstein* — 60
- Eishet Chayil — 62
- Kiddush, *by Aaron Goldberg* — 65
- Shabbos Night Kiddush — 67
- Lechem Mishnah, *by Mrs. Esther Friedman* — 70
- Netilat Yadaim and Hamotzi — 72
- Kol Mekadesh Shevii — 73
- Kah Ribon Olam — 76

Stories from the Maggid:
- A Personal and Historical Testimony — 78

- Kah Echsof — 80
- Tzur Mishelo — 81

Shabbos Day • יום שבת 83

Shabbos Day Kiddush	84
Netilat Yadaim and Hamotzi	87
Baruch Kel Elyon	88
Yom Zeh Mechubad	91
Ki Eshmerah Shabbat	93
Yom Shabbaton	95
Dror Yikra	97

Seudah Shlishit • סעודה שלישית 99

Seudah Shlishit, *by Zachary Zarnett Klein*	100
Netilat Yadaim and Hamotzi	101
Atkinu Seudata	102
Bnei Heichalah	102
Mizmor L'David	103
Yedid Nefesh	104

Havdalah • הבדלה 107

The Time In-Between, *by Becky Friedman*	108
Havdalah	110

Bircat HaMazon • ברכת המזון 115

Bircat HaMazon, *by Gabriel Hoffman*	116
Bircat HaMazon	118
The Three Faceted Blessing	131
Borei Nefashot	134

Songs • שירים 135

Acheinu	136
Ana Be'Choach	136
Ani Ma'amin	136

Baruch HaGever	137
Beshem Hashem	137
David Melech Yisrael	137
Esa Enai	137
HaMalach HaGo'el	138
HaRachaman	138
Hineh Ma Tov	138
Im Eshkacheich	139
Ivdu Et Hashem	139
Ki Va Moed	139
Kol Ha'Olam Kulo	139
LeShanah HaBa'ah	139
Mi Ha'Ish	140
Mikolot Mayim	140
Mitzvah Gedolah	140
Od Yishama	140
Oseh Shalom	141
Pia Patcha	141
Shema	141
Tov LeHodot	142
Yibaneh HaMikdash	142

Divrei Torah • דברי תורה — **143**

Bereishit • בראשית

Bereishit
   I am Nothing, *by Matthew Goodman* — 146
   To See the Darkness, *by Becky Freidman* — 147

Noach
   Actions Speak Louder Than Words, *by Elianne Neuman* — 149
   Responding to Failure, *by Matthew Goodman* — 150
   Failure is the Only Option, *by Becky Friedman* — 152

Lech Lecha
   Mission Possible, *by Matthew Goodman* — 154
   Ill-Gotten Gains, *by Becky Friedman* — 156
   Avraham's Legacy, *by Zachary Zarnett-Klein* — 157
   Fair-Weather Husband, *by Yaron Milwid* — 158
   Human Deception, *by Dylan Shaul* — 159

Vayeira
- A Test of Faith, *by Becky Friedman* — 161
- The Ultimate Test, *by Teddy Kravetsky* — 163
- Gratitude Saved the City, *by Matthew Goodman* — 164
- The Value of Hospitality, *by Zachary Zarnett-Klein* — 166
- The Banishments of Hagar, *by Idan Bergman* — 167

Chayei Sarah
- Our Terminal Condition, *by Matthew Goodman* — 169
- Life and Death, *by Teddy Kravetsky* — 171
- But It's Not My Problem, *by Elianne Neuman* — 172
- The Man Behind the Man, *by Yaron Milwid* — 173
- What's In a Name? *by Zachary Zarnett-Klein* — 174

Toldot
- Mercy and Justice, *by Dylan Shaul* — 176
- Like Father Like Son, *by Yaron Milwid* — 177
- To Thine Own Self Be True, *by Matthew Goodman* — 178
- Rivka's Deceit, *by Zachart Zarnett-Klein* — 181

Vayeitzei
- Yaakov's Loving Rebuke, *by Matthew Goodman* — 183
- Heavenward, *by Dylan Shaul* — 186

Vayishlach
- Torah Teachings, *by Ari Satok* — 189
- Yaakov's Struggles, *by Zachary Zarnett-Klein* — 190
- Yaakov and Yisrael, *by Matthew Goodman* — 191

Vayeishev
- Reminders of Home, *by Elianne Neuman* — 195
- The Spirit of the Thing, *by Zachary Zarnett-Klein* — 196
- Sukkot, *by Becky Friedman* — 198
- History in the Making, *by Matthew Goodman* — 199
- Life Altering Decisions, *by Teddy Kravetsky* — 201
- Maase Avot Siman L'vanim, *by Michali Glasenberg* — 203

Mikeitz
- The Revelation of Joseph, *by Elianne Neuman* — 205
- The True Meaning of Chanukah, *by Matthew Goodman* — 207
- Ends vs. Means, *by Becky Friedman* — 211
- Arise Like a Lion, *by Dylan Shaul* — 213
- It's Never Too Late, *by Teddy Kravetsky* — 214

Vayigash
- Little White Lie, *by Becky Friedman* — 216
- Forgive and Forget, *by Matthew Goodman* — 218
- Judah and Joseph, *by Zachary Zarnett-Klein* — 220

Vayechi
- Gam Zu LeTova, *by Matthew Goodman* — 222

The Punishment, *by Elianne Neuman*	226
When Our Thoughts and Actions Wander, *by Rabbi Jeffrey Turtel*	227

Shemot • שמות

Shemot
Even Evil Has Standards, *by Becky Friedman*	230
The Gadol of a Shepherd, *by Matthew Goodman*	231

Vaeira
Fulfilling Our Own Potential, *by Elianne Neuman*	233
You Can't Handle the Truth! *by Matthew Goodman*	234

Bo
Haftorah Huh's? *by Zachary Zarnett-Klein*	236
Prioritizing Mercy, *by Yaron Milwid*	237
A Special Gift, *by Elianne Neuman*	238
Miracles, *by Matthew Goodman*	239

Beshalach
Our Nation's Mood-Swings, *by Becky Friedman*	244
Jump out of bed, sleepyhead! *by Matthew Goodman*	245
Acknowledging G-d, *by Dylan Shaul*	248
Having a Positive Outlook, *by Mindy Chapman*	250
En Route, *by Zachary Zarnett-Klein*	251

Yitro
Catch Me When I Fall, *by Becky Friedman*	254
Kedusha 101, *by Matthew Goodman*	256
The Missing Piece, *by Zachary Zarnett-Klein*	259
Honouring Your Parents, *by Elianne Neuman*	261

Mishpatim
Sensitivity Training, *by Matthew Goodman*	263
Broken Record, *by Becky Friedman*	265
The Bigger Picture, *by Zachary Zarnett-Klein*	267
It's In Your Best Interest, *by Mindy Chapman*	268

Terumah
Valuing All Aspects of Your Life, *by Teddy Kravetsky*	270
The Philosophy of Giving, *by Matthew Goodman*	271
Giving Your Best to G-d, *by Teddy Kravetsky*	273

Tetzaveh
Paying Attention to Details, *by Ben Welkovics*	275
Fleeing from the Spotlight, *by Matthew Goodman*	276
For Glory and Majesty, *by Elianne Neuman*	280
Blot Out My Name, *by Michali Glasenberg*	281
Spreading the Light, *by Mindy Chapman*	282

Ki Tisa
- Counting With a Pleasant Eye, *by Idan Bergman* — 283
- Another Ten, *by Becky Friedman* — 284
- Reward and Punishment, *by Teddy Kravetsky* — 286
- The Coin of Fire, *by Matthew Goodman* — 287

Vayakhel
- Wisdom in Their Hearts, *by Yaron Milwid* — 290
- How to Make Your Own Success Story, *by Matthew Goodman* — 291

Pekudei
- Self-Sacrifice, *by Michali Glasenberg* — 296
- Required Blueprints, *by Becky Friedman* — 297
- The Best of Intentions, *by Matthew Goodman* — 298
- Equal Opposites, *by Aaron Goldberg* — 302
- The First Tzedaka Box, *by Becky Friedman* — 304

Vayikra • ויקרא

Vayikra
- The Need to Change, *by Elianne Neuman* — 308
- Contemplating Torah, *by Matthew Goodman* — 308
- Show the King Your Beauty, *by Becky Friedman* — 310
- Undeserved Cookies Are Tastier, *by Matthew Goodman* — 311

Tzav
- Transcending Time, *by Matthew Goodman* — 316
- Our Father, Our Master, *by Zachary Zarnett-Klein* — 318

Shemini
- Dancing Before the Lord, *by Becky Friedman* — 320

Tazria
- The Bright Side of Life, *by Matthew Goodman* — 323

Metzora
- Desperate Measures, *by Becky Friedman* — 327

Acharei Mot
- Edible Food, *by Idan Bergman* — 329
- Passover: A Story of Social Justice, *by Elianne Neuman* — 330

Kedoshim
- Word Power, *by Rebecca Silver* — 332

Emor
- Hidden in Plain Sight, *by Aaron Goldberg* — 335

Behar/Bechukotai
- Walking with Torah, *by Matthew Goodman* — 337
- We're Free! It's Jubilee! *by Zachary Zarnett-Klein* — 339
- Parent and Child, *by Elianne Neuman* — 339

Bamidbar • במדבר

Bamidbar
- Where have the Leviim gone? *by Michali Glasenberg* — 342
- Changing the World, *by Matthew Goodman* — 343
- A Gift from G-d, *by Teddy Kravetsky* — 344

Naso
- The Nazir and Wine, *by Michali Glasenberg* — 346

Behaalotecha
- Kvetch Much? *by Matthew Goodman* — 348
- Zechariah's Prophecy, *by Zachary Zarnett-Klein* — 350
- Miriam's Sin, *by Elianne Neuman* — 351
- Ascension, *by Becky Friedman* — 352
- Respect and Kindness, *by Teddy Kravetsky* — 353
- We Shall Do and We Shall Listen, *by Rabbi Yisroel D. Goldstein* — 354

Korach
- Religious Authority, *by Samuel Buckstein* — 356

Chukat
- A Mystery Inside an Enigma, *by Mr. Jeremy Cohen* — 358

Balak
- Balaam's Motives, *by Yaron Milwid* — 360

Pinchas
- Why Marry Jewish, *by Samuel Buckstein* — 361

Matot/Massei
- Can-do Attitude *by Becky Friedman* — 363

Devarim • דברים

Vaetchanan
- Love and Rejection, *by Rabbi Jay Kelman* — 366

Reeh
- A Surprise Test, *by Rabbi Jay Kelman* — 368
- Simcha Be'Artzecha, *by Elisheva Friedman* — 370

Shoftim
- The Pursuit of Happiness, *by Teddy Kravetsky* — 374

Ki Teitzei
- Parents and Children: Obligations and Right, *by Rabbi Itai Moryosef* — 376

Ki Tavo
- Ma'aser and Bikurim, *by Zachary Zarnett-Klein* — 377

Nitzavim/Vayelech
- Listening to Hashem, *by Matthew Goodman* — 379

Haazinu
    The Voice of Teshuva, *by Matthew Goodman*   382
    Swansongs, *by Zachary Zarnett-Klein*   384

Holidays • חגים

Sukkot
    HaUshpizin HaKedoshim, *by Matthew Goodman*   386
Chanukah
    Reminders of Home, *by Elianne Neuman*   389
    Sukkot, *by Becky Friedman*   390
    Chanukah's Relevance, *by Idan Bergman*   391
    We Are Miraculous, *by Matthew Goodman*   394
Purim
    The Difference, *by Becky Friedman*   396
    Spreading Awareness, *by Teddy Kravetsky*   398
    The Hidden Face of Hashem, *by Matthew Goodman*   399
    A Day Like Purim, *by Elianne Neuman*   402
    Mishloach Manot, *by Idan Bergman*   404
Pesach
    The Bread of Freedom, *by Matthew Goodman*   406
    Bringing Us Back, *by Becky Friedman*   410
    The Beauty of a Question, *by Ben Welkovics*   412
    The Gift and Responsibility of Freedom, *by Elianne Neuman*   413
    An Act of Faith, *by Becky Friedman*   414
    Sefirat HaOmer, *by Idan Bergman*   416
    In Every Generation, *by Mindy Chapman*   418
    The Seder Plate: A Mystic Centerpiece, *by Zachary Zarnett-Klein*   419
Shavuot
    Visions of G-d, *by Becky Friedman*   422

Introduction
הקדמה

Introductory Letters - מכתבי הקדמה

From the Director of Education

I know of no one who observes Shabbat in any fashion – from the most *halakhic* to the most 'laid-back' – who does not look forward to those magic moments on Friday afternoon when the sun begins to fall toward the horizon. The quality of time seems to change. The cares of the world drop away, and inner and outer serenity take over. The late Abraham Joshua Heschel *ztz"l* famously termed Shabbat as a 'Palace in Time' – just as the Tabernacle stood out, dazzling in its colour and workmanship in the otherwise drab context of the desert, so, too, the 25 hours of Shabbat, dazzling in quality and spirituality, stand out in the time continuum of the otherwise mundane week.

One of the most successful programmes of TanenbaumCHAT in the last decade has been our Shabbaton programme. Now, in any year, some 700 students and staff from both Campuses spend Shabbat together. I would like to think that that our school has given them a precious gift of entry to that beautiful palace…

The team who have put this book together have done something awesome. It is beautifully produced and the material sensitively selected. Like the most delicious *cholent*, the ingredients are many and varied. May it enhance the Shabbat experience for many TanenbaumCHAT students, families, and friends of our school!

Behatzlachah – and *Shabbat Shalom*!

Paul Shaviv

Director of Education

◦∿ *Introduction* ∿◦

∿ From the Director of Jewish Studies

It is a genuine honour and pleasure for me to introduce *The Shofar's Shabbos Companion*, produced by the students and faculty at the Wallenberg Campus. It reflects significant thought and effort and will take its rightful place among past student publications of our School that have served to enrich our lives as Jews.

The Talmud relates that two angels accompany us home from the synagogue on Friday night, one good and one evil. If the home is properly prepared to celebrate the Shabbat, the evil angel is forced to say amen to the good angel's blessing: May it be G-d's will that the home be so prepared next Shabbat. If, however, the home is not properly prepared, it is the good angel who must confirm the same statement from the mouth of the evil angel, laying a curse upon the family.

In the tumult of today's world, we can all easily slip into the habit of "not properly preparing for Shabbat", not simply in terms of a set table and fine clothes, but in preparing our hearts and minds for participating in the beauty and holiness that the Shabbat offers to us all. In short, we need all the help that is available. *The Shabbos Companion*, arising from the sincere efforts of our own friends and colleagues, can only help us to "prepare properly" for the Shabbat. Truly theirs has been a labour of love, reflecting the highest ideals of our School: dedication to Talmud Torah and how it can enlighten and enrich our daily lives as we apply our Judaism to the challenges of contemporary society.

יישר כוחכם!

Samuel Kapustin

Director of Jewish Studies

From the Vice Principal of Jewish Studies

When I was asked to write a letter of introduction to this Shabbat Table companion book, I immediately agreed to do so. This project is very exciting to me for two reasons. First of all, for many years the school has grappled with the idea of producing something like this for the benefit of our staff and students who may be new to the customs and traditions of a Shabbat table, for use at such events as a school Shabbaton. For the most part, this idea stayed on the back burner due to the scope of work it would require. When I saw the proposed project, I was very pleased with the fact that our vision was realized by the wonderful students of the The Shofar committee. This companion will be well-used by our own school community.

Second, it is an absolute pleasure to observe all of the students as they develop this project from concept to print. This particular group of students has shown talents well beyond their years in the development of their publications throughout their years here at TanenbaumCHAT. This includes the weekly "Shofar" on the Parsha and the annual Haggada for Pesach. This is a fabulous culminating endeavour for the senior members of the team, and I certainly look forward to watching them flourish as leaders of our community in the years to come.

To the reader, enjoy the book. It contains countless insights, instructions, and explanations on the beautiful traditions and liturgy of a Shabbat table. Shabbat is meant to be, amongst other things, a time of family, comfort, joy, and familiarity. This is a theme repeated throughout the Zmirot found in this volume. Unfortunately, for some, it is often very unfamiliar, making it uncomfortable. This book will help users of all levels find more meaning and become more familiar with the experience. It will ultimately help you to get the most out of the entire Shabbat experience, each and every week.

Rabbi Eli Mandel
Vice Principal of Jewish Studies

Introduction

From the Vice Principal of General Studies

It is a great privilege to write some introductory words to the first Shabbos Companion. The dedication and hard work by TanenbaumCHAT students and staff is truly inspiring. This is a compilation of the wonderful Divrei Torah that students have written every week. I know that I always look forward to receiving my copy!

Shabbat is a gift to the Jews, and can be expressed in so many ways. The beauty of a day of rest can be best appreciated if we imagine its absence. In atheist Soviet Russia, there was no need for a day to commemorate G-d's completion of the world. People in the "worker's paradise" toiled seven days a week. Each day of the week became virtually indistinguishable from any other. No time was designated to cleanse the mind, spend time with family, or study one's religion. Imagine the effect this had on the hearts and minds of these people.

This is the beauty of Shabbat. We are all able to remove ourselves from our daily grind. We can think of other things, relax, spend time with family, and clear our minds from whatever is bothering us. It is a time set aside each week to learn, talk, laugh, or contemplate. The choices are endless! Go to shul, read a book for pleasure, catch up on your rest, spend time with friends and family, eat good meals, clear your head from the work week.

As you read this companion, look for things that apply to you. It really does contain something for everyone. Whether in a parable, a rabbinic interpretation, or an interesting anecdote, we all can find food for thought in this remarkable work. The key is to read, think, learn, and enjoy!

Jory Vernon
Vice Principal of General Studies

From The Shofar's Staff Supervisor

I feel honored and privileged to be one of the people who introduce the Shabbat Companion to you. This incredible publication is the culmination of three years of hard work by two very special students here at TCW, Matthew Goodman and Becky Friedman. Included in this companion are thoughts and insights on every parsha and the Holidays, which are reprinted from the weekly Shofar publications.

Three years ago, Matthew and Becky assumed responsibility for the student club which is responsible for creating and distributing a weekly Torah thought on the Parsha. I was asked to be the staff supervisor for this student club, and when I accepted, I didn't realize what I was in for. The weekly publication took on a life of its own, a new name, "The Shofar", a brand new look and style, new ways of distribution, and then the beautiful Shofar addition of the Hagadah and Megilat Esther, and, finally, this Shabbos Companion. This club went on to win the "Most Improved Club and Committee" in its first year, and then the "Best Student Committee" in the following year. I continue to be amazed at the incredible work Matthew and Becky produce. What meant the most to me, being the staff advisor and partial editor, was the passion and approach to the holy day of Shabbat.

Shabbat has an aspect that goes beyond the technicalities of the laws. We are commanded to make Shabbat holy and to sanctify it, "for G-d made the world in six days, and on the Seventh day, G-d rested; Therefore G-d blessed the day of Shabbat, and made it holy, and sanctified it" (Exodus 20:11).

People often feel that there are so many laws pertaining to Shabbat that it is difficult to observe properly. The laws of Shabbat are there to help us connect with G-d on a spiritual level. The Talmud in tractate Megilah relates that everyone receives an additional soul on Shabbat. The soul that we have all the time allows us to connect to G-d on a limited, finite level, as Hashem Himself is infinite. The additional soul allows us an increased ability to connect to G-d that is not possible during the six days of work. It gives us a broader channel and greater sensitivity to feel and connect to spirituality and G-d. Therefore, one is encouraged to learn Torah and do the special commandments on this holy day as means of truly connecting to G-d on this very special day.

To Matthew and Becky, I wish you much success is your post-high-school years as you go to the Holy Land to further your self-growth in Torah and Judaism. And, just as this companion will inspire many, I am certain that you will continue to inspire others and reach great heights on personal and communal levels.

To the reader, I hope that you enjoy the words of wisdom and Torah that you will find in this publication.

Rabbi Yisroel D. Goldstein

Preface to the Shabbos Companion
פתח דבר לילקוט לשבת קודש

There is nothing more beautiful in the entire world than the Shabbos table. Families and friends join together to experience a day holier than any other, when the Shabbos bride visits our homes and fills them with immense holiness. We partake in delicious meals and sing heart-warming Zemirot and Niggunim in praise of the special day and of Hashem above. We bless Hashem and we bless our children; we stop, rest, and appreciate what is truly meaningful. We delve into the Torah and share with each other its inspiring words.

For many families, however, this gift is yet an undiscovered treasure. Some of us are unfamiliar with the customs, rituals, and traditions of Shabbos. For many others, Shabbos is indeed an intrinsic aspect of their lives, yet the purpose and deeper meaning behind its practices have yet to be revealed.

Hashem has given us the unique opportunity to publish a companion to the Shabbos table that will help families familiarize themselves with its ways, and inspire those who pursue further insight. It is the product of the efforts of a multitude of teachers and students who have graciously taken the time to contribute articles and Divrei Torah. Its goal is to help illuminate your Shabbos experience through its numerous features.

This book carefully and comprehensively guides you through the different observances associated with the Shabbos table, including Candle Lighting, Night and Morning Kiddush, Hand Washing and HaMotzi, the Blessing after Meals, and Havdalah. It also contains the texts of songs and Zemirot traditionally sung at the table. All of the Hebrew is accompanied by a precise English translation and easy-to-follow, accurate transliterations for those who cannot read Hebrew letters, but would nonetheless like to recite the verses in their original language. Furthermore, interspersed throughout the book are articles that delve deeper into topics related to the Shabbos table and provide further insight into their meaning and applications.

A major aspect of this book is the section of Divrei Torah on the weekly Torah parsha. For the past three years, "The Shofar" committee has distributed a weekly Dvar Torah publication on the Parsha to the TanenbaumCHAT community every Erev Shabbos. The majority of the articles in this book have been compiled from those Divrei Torah. Numerous other Divrei Torah have been written solely for the Shabbos

Introduction

Companion, and likewise grace the pages of our book. It is our greatest hope that you share these Divrei Torah with your family at the Shabbos Table. The Torah's insights on life are all fascinating and beautiful. Our Divrei Torah help unveil some of its teachings; they comment on and interpret a plethora of different stories, laws, and texts.

The successful publication of this book is entirely thanks to the generosity of the numerous families and individuals who financially sponsored its printing. Their contribution is sincerely appreciated, and we are amazed at the sheer number of people who were supportive and encouraging of this endeavour. May they all be blessed for their support of the Torah and go "m'chayil l'chayil," from strength to strength. The cherished guidance and recommendations of Rabbi Yisroel D. Goldstein and Mr. Zachary Isakow were intrinsic to the overall quality and clarity of this book, and we graciously thank them. We would also like to express our deepest gratitude to Mrs. Laurie Blake and Mrs. Frances Bigman of the Development Office for their hard work and effort which ultimately allowed us to publish our project.

We pray that, with the help of The Almighty, this book will inspire you and your families, provide you with deep insight into the marvels of Shabbos and the Torah, and guide you through the observances related to the Shabbos table. May we all merit to see the "yom shekulo Shabbos u'm'nucha l'chayei olamim," the day that is entirely Shabbos and tranquil, for life everlasting, heralded by the coming of the Mashiach.

Good Shabbos!

Matthew Goodman and Becky Friedman
Editors
Nissan 5771 / April 2011

Shabbos Kodesh: *The Pinnacle of Creation*

By Matthew Goodman and Becky Friedman

I. A Gift from Hashem's Treasury

For six days, Hashem created the heavens and the earth and all that is in them, from the rocks to the trees to human beings. On the seventh day, Hashem completed "His work which He had done; and He rested on the seventh day from all His work which He had done" (Bereishis 2:2). Nearly 2300 years later, while wandering in the desert, the Jewish people were commanded to observe one of the most fundamental Mitzvos in the entire Torah. Two months later, this Mitzvah was codified as the fourth of the Aseres HaDibros that were given to three million people at Mount Sinai by Hashem Himself, along with the rest of the entire Torah. This, of course, is the Mitzvah of Shabbos.

Shabbos. The very word drips off the tongue like sweet honey. It graciously invites fond memories, emotions, and feelings that warm our essence and fill our souls with its vast radiance. Jews all over the world, of all denominations and levels of observance, are familiar with it. For hundreds of generations, Jews have carefully guarded it. And we all realize how truly special it is.

Rabbi Aryeh Kaplan (in "Sabbath - Day of Eternity") recalls spending one Shabbos with a poor working man in Williamsburg, New York. He was simple, but very pious; he had few worldly goods, and lived in a dreary, small, cramped apartment. One might have pitied him for being such a pauper, but at his Shabbos table, he sat like a king. He remarked, "I pity people who don't keep Shabbos. I really pity them. They don't know what they are missing. They have no idea at all."

The Torah states, "See that Hashem has given you the Shabbos" (Shemos 16:29). Chazal (the Rabbis of the Talmud) tell us that the verse really alludes to a conversation between Moshe and Hashem, in which Hashem said, "I have an amazing gift in my treasury, and it is called Shabbos. I want to give it to the Jews. Please go tell them" (Shabbos 10b). That man, sitting like a king at his table, truly understood how precious and priceless Shabbos Kodesh is. He knew that it is a gift that comes right from Hashem's treasury.

A cursory look at a real Shabbos quickly ratifies this fact. Every aspect of it is simply beautiful and marvellous. Families and guests join together to eat special meals, sing joyful songs and tunes, bless and thank Hashem for all of His goodness, and share inspiring words of Torah. In a world controlled by productivity and work, we stop and rest, allowing us to fully enjoy what is truly meaningful in life. What a gift!

Furthermore, Shabbos is widely regarded as one of the most fundamental aspects of Judaism, echoing Rambam's teaching that its observance is equivalent to "the observance of all the Mitzvos of the Torah" (Mishna Torah Hilchos Shabbos 30:15).

There seems to be something about Shabbos, however, that surpasses mere fundamentals.

In Lecha Dodi, written by Rabbi Shlomo Alkabetz and sung every Kabbalas Shabbos, we read: "To welcome the Shabbos, let us go, for it is the source of blessing; from the beginning, from antiquity she was honoured, last in deed but first in thought." There are two tremendous teachings based on this verse that display the vast greatness of this holy day. The Eitz Yosef, commenting on the fact that Shabbos is the source of all blessings, says that Hashem renews and illuminates the worlds, upper and lower, through its radiance. Without it, the world would not be able to survive.

Rav Shimon Schwab, in Iyun Tefillah, referring to the latter part of the verse, explains that although Shabbos was not created until the end of Creation, it was first in Hashem's thought. Creation before Shabbos was like a beautiful canopy built by a king, painted and embellished, but lacking a bride. And there is simply no need for a canopy if there is no bride. Shabbos is the bride that Hashem intended to stand under the canopy when He created the world. Shabbos is the final seal of Creation that represents the whole purpose and goal of existence.

There is something inherent in its essence that makes Shabbos the pinnacle of Creation, and without it, the world cannot continue. What is its secret? What truly makes Shabbos so innately special? What makes it the apex of the world?

II. The Fourth Commandment

The Aseres HaDibros (Ten Commandments/Statements) are recorded numerous times throughout the Torah. The first occasion is in Parshas Yisro, when we read of the giving of the Torah to the Jewish people. Gathered around Mount Sinai, three million Jews saw Hashem descend upon it in fire, and He gave them the Aseres HaDibros. There, the fourth commandment reads:

> *Remember (Zachor) the Sabbath day to sanctify it. Six days may you work and perform all your labour, but the seventh day is a Sabbath to the Lord your G-d; you shall perform no labour, neither you, your son, your daughter, your manservant, your maidservant, your beast, nor your stranger who is in your cities. For [in] six days the Lord made the heavens and the earth, the sea, and all that is in them, and He rested on the seventh day. Therefore, the Lord blessed the Sabbath day and sanctified it* (Shemos 20:8-11).

The Aseres HaDibros are later repeated in Parshas Va'eschanan, in the book of Devarim. Moshe reminds the people of the giving of the Torah, and "the day when you stood before the Almighty, Omnipotent G-d in Chorev... and He declared to you His covenant, which he commanded you to perform, Aseres HaDibros" (Devarim 4:10,13). He then re-articulates the words of Hashem. A close reading of the text, however, reveals a number of differences between the Aseres HaDibros in Parshas Yisro and those in Va'eschanan. The most glaring of those differences are found in the fourth commandment:

> *Keep (Shamor) the Sabbath day to sanctify it, as the Lord your G-d commanded you. Six days may you work, and perform all your labour, but the seventh day is a Sabbath to the Lord your G-d; you shall perform no labour, neither you, your son, your daughter, your manservant, your maidservant, your ox, your donkey, any of your livestock, nor the stranger who is within your cities, in order that your manservant and your maidservant may rest like you. And you shall remember that you were a slave in the land of Egypt, and that the Lord your G-d took you out from there with a strong hand and with an outstretched arm; therefore, the Lord your G-d commanded you to observe the Sabbath day* (Devarim 5:12-15).

There are two major divergences between the two texts, among other smaller changes. The first is differing commandments to "remember" and "keep" the Shabbos. The second is the reason given for its observance. Parshas Yisro tells us that it is because Hashem rested on the seventh day, while Parshas Va'eschanan tells us that it is in remembrance of the exodus from Egypt. The commentators give a number of explanations as to why there are variances between the two versions (for example, see Pnei Yehoshua on Bava Kamma 55a and Ibn Ezra on Shemos 20:1). Notwithstanding, the differences still exist, and from them, we can garner tremendous insights into the deeper meaning of Shabbos Kodesh.

On the note of textual differences, elsewhere in the Torah, there is a separate set of "Ten Statements", also repeated twice, given only to Moshe. These Statements differ wildly from those commonly known as Aseres HaDibros, or the Ten Commandments, but the Torah seems to allot them equal importance.

In fact, one of the only commonalities, or the *only* one, depending on how certain verses are interpreted, is the Mitzvah of Shabbos, the fifth commandment in this set of ten:

> *Six days you shall work, and on the seventh day you shall rest; in plowing and in reaping you shall rest* (Shemos 34:21).

In the other instance of this set of ten, Shabbos is listed, depending on how the commandments are enumerated, either second or first:

> *Six days you shall do your jobs, and on the seventh day you shall rest, so that your ox and your donkey may rest, and that the son of your maidservant and the stranger may be refreshed* (Shemos 23:12).

We see that these two iterations of the commandment of Shabbos, though much more succinct, differ from each other significantly, as did the first two. In fact, a parallel may be drawn. The first of these two makes special note of agricultural processes-- "In plowing and in reaping you shall rest." It can be compared to the first version of the commandment in the other set, which explains the mitzvah of Shabbos in the context of G-d's creation of the world. By looking at the two together, we can learn one of the many reasons behind the commandment for Shabbos: just as G-d created the world in six days but refrained from any creative act on the seventh day, on Shabbos, so, too, we must refrain from creative acts, such as plowing and reaping, on the Shabbos.

Similarly, the second two versions of the Shabbos commandment can be compared. In the second of the second set, once again the importance of giving rest to the animals, servants, and strangers is mentioned. In the second commandment of the first set, the mitzvah is explained in the context of the Jewish people having been slaves in Egypt. By juxtaposing these second two commandments, we discover yet another reason behind Shabbos: having been slaves in Egypt, we understand the importance of a day of rest, on which we cannot be compelled to do work. Therefore, we must extend that courtesy to everyone in our care-- servants, strangers, and animals included-- to ensure that they will never be in that same position.

III. A Testimony of Emunah

The desecration of Shabbos is one of the most grievous sins in Judaism. Halachah dictates that one that one who willingly and flagrantly does not keep Shabbos is no longer considered part of the Jewish community (Shulchan Aruch, Yoreh Deah 2:5). Similarly, the Talmud states that one who breaks Shabbos is regarded as if he has denied the entire Torah, for he demonstrates a lack of belief that Hashem created the world. As such, he is classified as an idolator (Chulin 5a with Rashi). It seems, then, that Judaism not only holds Shabbos to be our most important institution, but also sees it as an indication of one's Emunah (belief/knowledge) in Hashem.

This fact is evident from two similar descriptions of the Mitzvah of Shabbos that are found in the Torah. The first is the text of the version of the Aseres HaDibros found in Parshas Yisro, mentioned above, where Shabbos is clearly delineated as a remembrance of Hashem's act of creation. The second is found before the building of the Mishkan, whose text we repeat three separate times every Shabbos: Ma'ariv, Shachris, and Kiddush Rabba. The Torah says:

> *Wherefore the children of Israel shall keep the Shabbos, to observe the Shabbos throughout their generations, for a perpetual covenant. It is a sign between Me and the children of Israel forever; for in six days Hashem made heaven and earth, and on the seventh day He ceased from work and rested* (Shemos 31:16-17).

Both texts relay that our observance of Shabbos demonstrates our belief in Hashem and the fact that He created the world. If Shabbos indeed displays this, then it must be of some fundamental importance in the Jewish faith. Any ritual whose purpose is to serve as a "sign" of Emunah between Hashem and Klal Yisrael must be inherently awesome.

This concept, however, is too difficult to understand on such a simple level. What does Emunah really mean? Why does Hashem need us to believe that He exists and created the world? It is even more difficult to understand how Shabbos embodies Emunah. What aspects of its observances create such a "sign?" How does Shabbos continually refresh and invigorate our connection with and belief in the Creator?

The Rambam, at the very outset of his magnum opus, his compendium of Jewish law known as the Mishne Torah, begins his chapter on Emunah as follows:

> *The foundation of all foundations and the pillar of wisdom is to know that there is a Primary Being who brought into being all existence. All the*

beings of the heavens, the earth, and what is between them came into existence only from the truth of His being (Yesodei HaTorah 1:1).

The Rambam does not describe Emunah as belief in Hashem. He specifically states that the Mitzvah is "to know" that there is Primary Being. The Ma'aseh Rokeach, a commentary on the Mishne Torah by HaRav Elazar Rokeach of Amsterdam zt"l, explains that the Rambam's choice of words was quite deliberate. Our perception of Hashem's existence should be no different from our knowledge of the existence of everything else. Just as I know that I have two hands, so, too, it is a Mitzvah to know that there is a Creator. In fact, the root of the word Emunah is the word Amen, which means "it is true." As such, the most appropriate translation of Emunah is not "belief" or "faith" but rather "conviction."

The Sefer HaChinuch, a systematic overview of all the Mitzvos in the Torah, further quantifies the aspects of the Mitzvah and explains exactly what we are expected to have Emunah in:

We must be convinced that there is one G-d in the world, Who created all that exists, and in Whose power and will everything came to be, that He removed us from Egypt, and that He gave us the Torah (Sefer HaChinuch, Mitzvah 25).

Emunah is something that is meant to be an absolutely intrinsic part of our existence. Our outlook on life as Jews must be infused with the knowledge of Hashem's existence and presence. The Sefer HaChinuch places Emunah as the first of six Mitzvos known as the Sheish Mitzvos Temidios-- the six constant Mitzvos. Unlike the other 607 Miztvot, which are obligatory based on the situation or at certain times of the year, month, or day, the six constant Mitzvos are obligatory constantly, and "should not be absent from one's consciousness for even one second of his life" (Introduction to Sefer HaChinuch).

The reason for this requirement is not because Hashem needs people to be cognizant of Him. A King of flesh and blood may take pleasure in having his people recognize him as their master, for purely egotistical reasons. Hashem, however, is infinite and omnipotent, and personally needs no recognition from His creations. Emunah is something that is entirely in our best interest. It allows us to live with purpose, and it is for this reason that Shabbos' connection with Emunah makes the holy day so holy in the first place. It turns Shabbos into something even greater than a reminder of Hashem. It turns it into a reminder that we live for a reason, and that our existence is inherently meaningful.

Judaism teaches us that the apex of world history will be the coming of the Mashiach. At that time, the world will be perfected, and humankind will live in a state of peace and tranquility, enjoying an immensely powerful connection to and relationship with Hashem. Why, however, is it necessary for the Mashiach to come? What is the point in having all of world history build up to the Days of the Mashiach?

The Maharal writes that the Mashiach must come because this world is not an ends in and of itself. The purpose of the world is to enable us to enjoy the greatest pleasure imaginable. Hashem created us because He, in His tremendous kindness, wanted to share the world's most amazing pleasure. Mesillas Yesharim, the Path of the Just, by HaRav Moshe Chaim Luzzato zt"l, likewise states:

> *Our Sages of blessed memory have taught us that man was created for the sole purpose of rejoicing in G-d and deriving pleasure from the splendor of His Presence; for this is true joy and the greatest pleasure that can be found. The place where this joy may truly be derived is the World to Come, which was expressly created to provide for it; but the path to the object of our desires is this world, as our Sages of blessed memory have said (Avot 4:21), "This world is like a corridor to the World to Come."* (Mesillas Yesharim Chapter 1).

Our lives have a very special purpose, and the years that we have in this world, the corridor to the World to Come, are the playing field in which we work toward that purpose. Life in this world is essentially the opportunity to work on ourselves, become better people, observe the Torah, and contribute to the community. In this way, we "earn" our places in the World to Come and enjoy the greatest pleasure imaginable.

The Sefer Mitzvos HaKatzar, by one of the Tosafists, explains that the belief in the coming of the Mashiach is actually part of the Mitzvah of Emunah. Thus, having Emunah, in part, means that you believe that the world was created for a purpose and that your life has a purpose.

One could easily hold this belief without even considering the Mashiach, as simply understanding that Hashem created you gives you purpose. Every single Neshama (soul) is endowed with unique traits and abilities that are perfectly tailored to allow the soul to achieve its mission here on earth. Emunah means understanding this point and accepting the fact that you are a unique creation of Hashem's, and, consequently, have a very special and important mission that must be completed here on earth. As we go through life, the specifics of our missions become clearer and clearer. For instance, a person with an interest in medicine may decide to become a doctor and realize that his mission on earth is to heal people. A successful and wealthy businessman may realize that his personality traits are suited to allow him to be successful in his field, and his subsequent mission on earth is to use his wealth to help the community at large. Emunah gives us something to work on, something to work toward, and something to live for. In short, it makes our lives meaningful.

And this is all embodied in Shabbos.

How so? The very paragraph that tells us that Shabbos is in remembrance of Creation also commands us to "Remember (Zachor) the Sabbath day." Chazal tell us that we fulfill "remembrance" of Shabbos through positive actions. For instance, Zachor is the root for the Mitzvah of Kiddush and Havdalah, when we publicly distinguish Shabbos from the rest of the week and proclaim it to be a testimony of Hashem's existence and creation of all that exists. It is also the root for the Mitzvah of the three Shabbos meals and the requirement to honour Shabbos, which is done through wearing our nicest clothes, saying special prayers, and singing Zemirot (Shabbos songs).

Essentially, the Mitzvah of Zachor is, for the most part, to verbally convey the greatness and holiness of Shabbos. This also allows the day not just to symbolize but also to express our Emunah. The Sefer HaChinuch explains that one of the ways to invigorate our knowledge in Hashem is to simply talk about it. By consistently mentioning a concept, we allow it to sink deeper and deeper into our hearts, creating a "sign" between us and Hashem.

"The Six Constant Mitzvos" by Rav Yehudah Heimowitz, based on lectures by Rav Yitzchak Berkowitz, tells the following story that aptly embodies this idea:

> Rabbi Shlomo Wolbe, Mashgiach of Yeshivas Be'er Yaakov, once travelled to Rabbi Yechezkel Levenstein, the Mashgiach of Ponevezh, to discuss a difficulty he was having with one of his students. When they were done, Rav Wolbe turned to leave, but Rav Levenstein called him back. "Tell me," he said, "do you know that there is a Creator?"
>
> Rav Wolbe was shocked. He assumed that there must be some hidden depth to Rav Levenstein's question, but he could not understand what it was.
>
> "Yes," he answered after a few moments.
>
> Unsatisfied, Rav Levenstein asked, "Do you REALLY know that there world has a Creator?"
>
> Once again, Rav Wolbe paused, and answered, "Yes, I know that there is a Creator."
>
> "Good," replied Rav Levenstein, "Then go back and tell your students that there is a Creator."

> "It took a long time for me to understand what Rav Levenstein wanted," recalled Rav Wolbe. "Two weeks after this incident, I finally realized what he meant. There are people who go through their daily lives studying Torah, performing Mitzvos, living as all good Jews should, without feeling in the depths of their hearts that there is a Creator. Rav Levenstein was telling me that I should be sure to imbue my students with the knowledge and feeling of Hashem's existence."

Shabbos is the day on which we imbue within ourselves and our families the knowledge of Hashem's existence, a concept that gives our lives special meaning and purpose. That, in and of itself, is something unbelievably amazing, and it saturates Shabbos with a level of holiness that makes it the single most obvious institution in Judaism that embodies everything that we hold dear. We can now understand the text of the Aseres HaDibros found within Parshas Yisro and its underlying message.

IV. A Display of Bitachon

Shabbos does not just embody Emunah. Emunah is a strictly conceptual idea of Hashem and His involvement in the world, and is, therefore, unable to stand alone when attempting to create a proper outlook on life. In needs to be joined with something that brings its concepts into actualization through practical means. The Chazon Ish, HaRav Avraham Yeshaya Karelitz zt"l (1878-1953), in "Emunah u'Bitachon", explains that Bitachon, trust in Hashem, is what actively reflects our knowledge of Hashem's existence.

If Bitachon really is absolutely necessary to making Emunah play an active role in one's life, it is crucial that Shabbos embody it, too. By returning again to the differences in the two texts of the Aseres HaDibros, it becomes clear that Shabbos does just that.

HaRav Yosef Eliyahu Henkin zt"l (1891-1973) in "Perushei Ivra" (Part II, Ma'amar no.1), explains that Shabbos represents two competing concepts that man is charged with balancing: Bitachon, the recognition that everything that happens is in Hashem's control, and Hishtadlus, man's obligation to put in effort to pursue his needs. Hishtadlus is alluded to in the version of the Aseres HaDibros found in Parshas Yisro. There, the Torah tells us that Shabbos commemorates the Creation, and we read at the end of Ma'aseh Bereishis (the description of Creation in the Torah) that "G-d blessed the seventh day and sanctified it, because on it He abstained from all His work, which G-d had created to do" (Bereishis 2:3). This pasuk teaches us that on the seventh day from creation, Hashem ceased from overtly creating the world. From the first Shabbos onward, it would seem that man is in charge, and success is achieved through his endeavours.

The Torah teaches us, however, that truthfully, man is not in control, at all; he controls neither the world nor his success. Everything, in the end, is in the hands of Hashem. As such, the Torah gives us a different reason for the observance of Shabbos in the second text of the Aseres HaDibros, found in Parshas Va'eschanan. There, Shabbos is regarded as a commemoration of Yetzias Mitzrayim, the Exodus from Egypt. Rav Henkin explains that the Jewish people were helpless slaves in Egypt, unable to independently throw off the yoke of severe bondage, and were therefore incapable of performing any Hishtadlus. It was only thanks to Hashem that we were redeemed and freed, and the Jewish people's understanding of this was a display of Bitachon.

This duality, as embodied within the differing texts of the Aseres HaDibros, points to one stunning concept that absolutely transforms and illuminates the meaning of Shabbos. As a remembrance of the Exodus of Egypt, Shabbos reminds us of the trust we have to have in Hashem, that He, in the end, is the Facilitator of all outcomes and the Giver of all things, both wanted and unwanted. As Jews, it is crucial to have Bitachon that Hashem will always do what is best and most right for us. In remembrance of the act of Creation, Shabbos reminds us of the Emunah that we must have in Hashem and of the necessity to perform the proper Hishtadlus so as to allow Hashem's plans to come to fruition.

That Shabbos, the first Shabbos ever, was Hashem's day of rest, and propelled humankind into the spotlight. The Shabbos we have every week is a remembrance of that, and the function of our day of rest is not to re-propel us into a state of illusional grandeur. Rather, it is our chance to declare Hashem's right and proper place in our lives, as the true Master of the Universe. Thus, practically, Shabbos really is a day of absolute Bitachon.

The Torah tells us that "Hashem completed on the seventh day His work that He did, and He abstained on the seventh day from all His work that He did" (Bereishis 2:2). Like Hashem, we, too, stop from any Hishtadlus on Shabbos Kodesh, and treat all of our work as if it has been completed. Rav Shimshon Dovid Pincus zt"l (1944-2001) writes, in "Nefesh Shimshon on Shabos Kodesh", that Shabbos is not just another day of the week. It is a day on which the phone is disconnected, the banks are closed, and it is forbidden to think about problems. Hashem tells us, "All your work is done, and you should know that the whole world belongs to Me."

It is for this reason that we are actually prohibited from talking about work on Shabbos. The Talmud (Shabbos 113a-b) tells us that our speech on Shabbos in general should not be like our speech on a weekday, when we chat idly and discuss business. The Shulchan Aruch (Code of Jewish Law) tells us that, in order to fulfill the Mitzvah of Oneg Shabbos, making the holy day pleasurable, one should consider that all of his work is finished, so that he does not clutter his mind with secular thoughts.

The passage that tells us that Shabbos is in remembrance of the Exodus also enjoins us to "safeguard" (Shamor) the day, and Chazal tell us that this refers to the prohibition of performing Melacha, labour, on Shabbos. This injunction fits perfectly with our newfound knowledge that Shabbos is a day on which we sit back and feel that all of our work is complete and that Hashem is in charge. Obviously, not performing any Melacha means that we should feel that Melacha simply is not necessary on Shabbos. The idea, however, dives deeper than just this.

Rav Shimshon Raphael Hirsch zt"l explains that the forbidden labours on Shabbos represent man's mastery over the physical world. Therefore, if we rest on Shabbos, we make a statement that there is a greater Master over the world than ourselves. By working six days, we proclaim our mastery over the physical world. By resting on the seventh day, we admit that there is a G-d over us.

Similarly, the rest, or Menucha, that results from the lack of work relates a similar lesson, and takes it a step further. Rabbi Shlomo Goldberg, Menahel of Yeshivas Ohr Eliyahu, teaches that there are several other Hebrew words that share the root of the word Menucha, that can give as a deeper glimpse into the true meaning of the word.

First, there is the word Mincha, which means gift. The Sefer HaKesav V'HaKabalah, by Rav Yaakov Tzvi Mecklenburg (1785-1865), explains that Mincha connotes a gift sent from a common person to one to whom he wishes to display reverence. For instance, one of the offerings brought to the Altar in the Temple was called the Mincha offering, as it was a gift that was given to One Whom we revere.

Menucha also shares its root with the word Nichoach, pleasing, which is usually found in the context of the phrase Reiach Nichoach, a pleasing fragrance. Rav Mecklenburg explains that that Nichoach actually implies a feeling of subservience and humility to Hashem.

It is also connected to the phrase 'Lanchosan haderech,' to guide them along the path, which means to lead someone along a path while protecting him at the same time.

Rabbi Goldberg, based on these connections, concludes: "[The true meaning of Menucha is a] state of humility one feels when in the presence of one who will guide him, provide for him, and protect him from all harm. Our Sages described this state as the calm that comes over a person when he finally feels that 'all of his work is done.'"

In short, Shabbos is a day on which we are meant to feel a sense of completion, to the extent that we feel comfortable enough to rest without worrying, without being bothered about work, business, or the mundane. It is meant to instill a feeling of immense Bitachon in Hashem, whereby we profess our knowledge and conviction that everything is safe and secure with the world.

Shabbos gives us the unique opportunity to take our minds off the distractions and worries that so maliciously frequent our lives, and to spend time focusing on the things in life that are truly important. This is, indeed, a very special blessing, and it is articulated in the words of the Navi (Prophet) Yeshayahu:

> *If you restrain your foot because it is the Sabbath, refrain from accomplishing your own needs on My holy day, and you proclaim the Sabbath "a delight," and the holy day of Hashem, "honoured," and you honour it by not engaging in your own affairs, from seeking your own needs or discussing the forbidden – then you will delight in Hashem, and I will mount you astride the heights of the world; I will provide you the heritage of your forefather Jacob, for the mouth of Hashem has spoken* (Yeshayahu 58:13-14).

In fact, as mentioned above, Shabbos is the source of all blessings in the entire world, and its holiness spills into the rest of the week, illuminating it as well. Rav Pincus beautifully writes that Shabbos is a flowing fountain of Bitachon. If we utilize this fountain and draw generous supplies of Bitachon from it for the coming week, then the whole week will be like Shabbos, and we will lack nothing at all.

V. Me'ein Olam HaBa: A Semblance of the World to Come

When the Torah tells the account of the final day of creation, when Hashem ceased from all of His work, it says: "And G-d blessed the seventh day and He sanctified it (vayekadeish oso), for thereon He abstained from all His work that G-d created to do" (Bereishis 2:3). The pasuk is the first time in the entire Torah that the concept of Kedusha, holiness, is mentioned. As such, Shabbos was the first thing in all of creation that received the status of holiness. Moreover, it was a holiness endowed by Hashem Himself.

This idea cannot be fully appreciated, however, if one does not truly understand what holiness is. Indeed, Kedusha is an awfully elusive concept, and very difficult to understand. The word may conjure up the image of an old, quiet, and gentle Rabbi, adorned with a grey beard and immersed in study. It may be associated with the Beit HaMikdash that once stood in Jerusalem and its innermost chamber, the Holy of Holies. Or one might even consider Kedusha to be epitomized by Shabbos itself. Despite this ability to realize that something is holy, or at least to call it so, do we really know what holiness means?

Perhaps it is helpful to first understand what Kedusha is not. Rabbi Shalom Noach Berzovsky (1911-2000), the Slonimer Rebbe, in "Nesivos Shalom", explains that Kedusha is the opposite of Tuma (impurity). Tuma is a Halachic term that refers to a spiritual impurity that can be imparted to people, food, or objects. The highest degree of Tumah is called "Tumat Met," the impurity of a dead body, occuring when a person dies and the soul leaves behind the physical being. The reason why Tumat Met is so virulent teaches us a great deal regarding the underlying meaning of true spiritual impurity.

The Torah tells us that "Hashem G-d formed man from the soil of the earth, and blew into his nostrils the soul of life; and man became a living soul" (Bereishis 2:7). The holy Zohar (3:123b) teaches that when Hashem breathed into the nostrils of man, He "breathed from within Himself" and imparted within us a soul that is a "chelek Eloka mima'al," a piece of Hashem. So long as our Neshama (soul) is safeguarded in our body, there is a powerful connection between our "chelek Eloka" and our physical being, that allows us to elevate life here on Earth. These are lofty concepts, but the fundamental essence of the matter is that the living human embodies connection between the material and the spiritual. When the neshama leaves the body and the connection breaks, the disconnection is called Tuma. Deriving from the same root as "Atimus," blockage, Tuma is when the physical disconnects from the spiritual.

Kedusha is the opposite of Tuma, and is thus the opposite of disconnection. Rabbi Lawrence Kelemen points out a Rashi on the first verse in the book of Vayikra that elaborates on this idea. Rashi reveals that Hashem spoke to non-Jewish prophets such as Balaam in "Lashon tuma," impure language, but He spoke to Moshe using "Lashon chiba," affectionate language. Since Rashi here utilizes affection as the opposite of Tuma, and Kedusha is also the opposite of Tuma, it is only sensible to infer that real holiness is affection, closeness, intimacy, connection.

Rabbi Kelemen also quotes the Ramchal, who, in the

Introduction

aforementioned work "Mesilas Yesharim," wrote that Kedusha is a state in which two things become completely and utterly united, to the point that all else is irrelevant. As King David wrote in Psalms, "My soul clings to You" (Tehilim 63:9).

We see this concept about Kedusha elsewhere, too; marriage, the ultimate form of affection, closeness, and uniting two things (in this case, people), is known in Judaism as Kiddushin, a word which, through no accident, has the same root as Kedusha.

Shabbos, having a Kedusha endowed by Hashem, is the epitome of the connection and affection between Hashem and Klal Yisrael. This is evident from the fact that the two greatest displays of intimacy with Hashem are deeply embodied in the day: Emunah and Bitachon. By serving as a reminder and a strengthener of these concepts, Shabbos allows us to achieve total closeness with the Creator. This is what makes it such a marvelous day. This is what gives it an innate specialness.

Since Shabbos gives us this taste of immense Kedusha, it is referred by Chazal as "me'ein Olam HaBa," a semblance of the World to Come. The Ramban teaches that, just as our six-day work week culminates in Shabbos, so, too, six millennia of our work in this world will culminate in the Days of the Mashiach, a day that is described in the Shabbos insert for Bircas HaMazon (the blessing after eating a meal) as "wholly Shabbos and tranquility, for life everlasting."

Shabbos is a microcosm of the existence anticipated in Olam Haba, a state of the world that, as mentioned previously, is entirely perfect and is the ultimate goal of history – the purpose which we strive to fulfill. Shabbos is a unique opportunity to feel what it will be like to reach those heights.

***

It would be arrogant to say that this essay has exhumed all the profundity of Shabbos Kodesh. In fact, this perspective is only the tip of the iceberg; it skims but the surface of a mountainous layer of depth and insight. As "the source of all blessings" and the semblance of the purpose of existence, there is so much to learn and gain from it. Only so much, though, can be garnered from study. To truly understand the beauty of Shabbos, it has to be experienced in its fullest. There is nothing more wondrous than the Shabbos table, where every single depth of the holy day is unlocked and shared in the singing, blessings, and Divrei Torah. The purpose of this book is to aid your appreciation of the rituals and liturgy for the day, as set forth by the Torah and our Rabbis, may their memories be for us a blessing.

The purpose of this essay is to illuminate a fundamental idea: that the purpose of Shabbos is to create a meaningful, affectionate, and powerful connection with Hashem. Through Emunah, we achieve the knowledge that Hashem exists, and through Bitachon, we actively acknowledge Him as the source of all. Coupled together, as they are on Shabbos, the two themes allow us to form a most amazing relationship with the Creator.

May all Jews, from all walks of life and all backgrounds, be granted the opportunity to achieve closeness to Hashem through the beauty, splendour, and holiness of Shabbos. May we merit to see the days of the Mashiach and the rebuilding of the Beis HaMikdash in Jerusalem, speedily in our days.

Introduction

What Shabbos Means to Me

Shabbos has the power to inspire, illuminate, and enrich the life of every single Jew. We all relate to its marvels differently and connect to the holy day through multiple facets. Some of us find more meaning in concepts; others, in ritual. All of us, however, can agree that Shabbos is a unique part of our tradition. A precious diamond entrusted to us by Hashem Almighty. The following are responses from TanenbaumCHAT Wallenberg students and teachers to the question, "What does Shabbos mean to you?"

***

This past summer, I participated in a pre-college musical theater program in Philadelphia, Pennsylvania. Living on my own, I found myself evaluating my own personal system of values independent from my parents' home. Friday rolled around, and I understood I could not let the evening go by like any other. I asked my parents to find me a Shabbat table in Southeastern Pennsylvania and the surrounding areas, and I found myself in Wynneswood, PA, across from the second cousin of my father's best friend. I felt comfortable, relaxed, and connected to my parents-- though they were hours away-- at the sight of the challah and candlesticks. This moment was profound, for I realized that these symbols of custom are a true constant in my life. I was moved by the hospitality of a couple with whom I had an obscure familial connection, who opened their home and hearts in the true spirit of Shabbat.

- Orli Matlow -

What always first comes to mind when I think of Shabbat is the rush. My family's Erev Shabbat consists of everyone dropping what is on their desks, speeding the entire way home, and then quickly taking a shower, putting on a clean white dress shirt (many times forgetting that last button), running downstairs to grab any handful of food that meets the eye, and saying "Shabbat Shalom" fast enough to get out the door and run to Shul. Now, this weekly habit of ours may seem a bit hectic and quite out of this world, but that is exactly what is so special about it. Hashem commanded us in the Ten Commandments to sanctify the Shabbat, to make it *kadosh* and separate it from other things. Certainly, the above account is one way that we, as a family, separate, or differentiate, the day from the other days of the week in anticipation for Shabbat. As such, the

essence I see in Shabbat, my family's unity and togetherness after this whole rush, reveals itself on this day. We once again become one after being scattered the rest of the week, and, just as the *Shema* says that "Hashem is one," unified in His way, so, too, is my family on Shabbat.
- Idan Bergman -

  The very notion of a day of rest is a beautiful gift that one can easily take for granted. In Soviet Russia, Josef Stalin incorporated a 7-day work week. A designated time for reflection, for not working, for family, or for learning is truly a gift. Each shabbat I try to organize something to do with my family. We all lead such busy lives that getting together is wonderful. Every Friday night we have a wonderful meal together and usher in shabbat with the appropriate blessings. My daughter recites the blessing over the candles, my son over the wine, and they recite the blessing over the challah together. As a father and husband, one of my greatest joys in life is that shabbat enables my family to spend such quality time together every week.
- Mr. Jory Vernon, Vice Principle of General Studies -

  If I had to pick my favourite aspects of Judaism, Shabbos would most definitely be on the top of my list. With commitments to school, work, and family, life can be pretty hectic at times, so to have a day of rest at the end of each and every week is quite comforting. Towards the middle of the week I begin looking forward to Shabbos. What will be I be having to eat? Whom will I be spending Shabbos with this week? Where will I be davening? These are some of the thoughts going through my head. When Friday finally arrives, I can no longer hold back my excitement. Thankfully, the school day goes by quickly, and, soon enough, it's time to head home to prepare to welcome Shabbat HaMalka, the Sabbath Queen. As I listen to the singing during Kabbalat Shabbat, I cannot help but feel a spiritual high. The voices of many soon connect as one, as the prayers of the entire congregation fill the room. This is, in essence, what Shabbos means to me. Not only is Shabbos an opportunity to take a break from a difficult week, but for the 25 hours of Shabbos, Jews throughout the world are connected for a common purpose. It is this unity that makes Shabbos such a special day for me.
- Josh Seed -

Introduction

I started keeping Shabbat many years ago, for entirely the wrong reasons. But as my wrong reasons went away, I still kept Shabbat, because somewhere along the line I'd traded my wrong reasons in for the right ones-- or at least better ones-- without even noticing. And once you start keeping Shabbat, you realize you really can't live without it. Without that one day on which I'm not allowed to think about, let alone do, my school work, I'd die from the stress. Shabbat is my time for seeing my family, especially those parts of it-- such as cousins and grandparents-- that I can rarely interact with during the week. Shabbat is my time for reading the news, since during the week I'm busy reading textbooks. Shabbat's the one time I can go for a walk outside and get a breath of fresh air, rather than hurry from a building to a car and back. Now, Shabbat means so much more to me than an excuse to not practice piano.
- ***Becky Friedman*** -

Shabbat is that one day a week, filled with joy, eagerly awaited for 6 days, when we can all set aside our weekday concerns and distance ourselves from our material possessions. Although, often, it comes off as a day with stifling restrictions, behind the mask of the observance, it is truly a day filled with rest and relaxation; *that* is what Shabbat means to me. In my eyes, Shabbat is a day of enriching our spiritual connection to Hashem and enlightening the world through leisure with family and friends. Regardless of the weather, or the circumstances of the situation, I have a sunny disposition every Shabbat. It is practically impossible to not smile back when someone says "Shabbat Shalom" to you. The nature of the Sabbath is so precious; it awakens new feelings within. So, yes, there are restrictions which limit our actions on this cherished day; however, in return, we are given the opportunity to rest from our weekly endeavours and challenges, and augment our spirituality; that is what I treasure most about Shabbat.
- ***Arielle Strasser*** -

Spirituality, family, rest, love, joining together, friends -- these are only a few of the words that can fully express what Shabbat means to me. Every Wednesday afternoon, I make phone calls to invite people to come over for Shabbat lunch or dinner. On Thursday afternoon, I shop for groceries and cook until late at night, setting the table the next morning. Friday is a special day. From the morning, you can feel the Shabbat spirit. I spend the day relaxing and doing almost nothing until the time for candle-lighting. After my son comes home from Shul and we eat dinner together, the real fun starts. We sing, play, and talk, all the way until Motzei Shabbat.

Shabbat is the only day in the week that we get to be all together; the whole family is able to enjoy quality time with each other. Seeing my kids get ready for Shabbat and hearing my son talk about the Parashat HaShavuah make this day special. Having time to just sit and read and spending good quality time with friends make this day special. When Shabbat is over, we all know that another Shabbat is on the way.
- **Mrs. Tali Lalkin, Ivrit Teacher** -

I always grew up surrounded by Judaism and a Jewish community. My family followed Orthodox law, and I attended a Jewish day school. However, Shabbat at my home only consisted of saying the blessing over the wine and challah, and having dinner with my family. After dinner, we all went and did separate things. At first, Shabbat meant uniting family. I later decided that I wanted more from Shabbat than just the Friday night meal. I started to observe Shabbat to the fullest extent that I knew of. It all changed during Yom Kippur. I met a girl in synagogue who was two years older than me and attended CHAT. During that day, we discussed the food cravings we had, and started to get to know one another. Afterwards, we started to hang out with each other during school and outside of school. Eventually, I got invited to her home for Shabbat. Once I arrived, I met her family, and I got to know each of them during dinner. After a while, I spent countless Shabbats at her home. From all the time that I spent at her house, I found an even bigger connection to Shabbat, unlike before, when I was doing it alone. I felt that Shabbat not only brought together friends and family, but it provided me with meaning and fulfillment in my life that I could not obtain through watching television or going on the internet. I was able to stop and look at the world once a week, recognize the natural beautiful creation of G-d, and maintain relationships with others. Eventually, I lost the temptation to turn on the television or check Facebook. I did not want to anymore. I can now look forward to a day in which I do not have to worry about answering phone calls, finishing homework, or planning out what I have to do tomorrow. It has become a day that I can look forward to, surrounding myself with the people I love, and looking at the world in a different light. To this day, whether I am home or at a friend's house, I still gain more meaning and appreciation for it every Shabbat.
- **Rachel Abitan** -

Shabbos used to be Saturday, and Saturday used to be a day like any other. When I was little, the extent of my knowledge concerning

☙ *Introduction* ❧

Shabbos ended with the family dinners we used to have on Friday nights, which I invariably enjoyed. However, my confined outlook changed when I was around nine years old, when my family switched shuls and started attending every week. We immediately received warm invitations from complete strangers to eat delicious meals and sing mysterious songs at their homes after shul. I was struck not only by the sheer hospitality of these individuals, but also by the foreign yet awe-inspiring actions, prayers and concepts they exhibited. There was something innately beautiful about everything, but at such a young age, I did not quite comprehend what it was. I did, however, know that these people held the key to something special, and I wanted to be a part of it. Upon reflection, I realized what struck me so sincerely: the spiritual feeling of wholeness that these people emanated in their connection with G-d on this uniquely holy day. Over the years, my family has grown in observance and has learned and taken on many mitzvot. It was an arduous and testing journey as we discovered the potential that Judaism has to offer. Judaism has impacted me positively in innumerable ways, and has given me a sense of fulfillment, direction, and meaning. It took us about six years to become shomer Shabbos, and there is still much to learn. Only after so many years of effort can I truly appreciate the meaning of Shabbos. Every Friday night, when my mother lights the candles, a calm embraces our home that elevates the day to greater spiritual heights than the rest of the week. It becomes a time to connect with G-d. It's not Saturday, but Shabbos.
- *Rebecca Silver* -

During the week we are all focused on schoolwork or our jobs. We are all in a rush. When Shabbat comes around, the atmosphere goes from chaotic to peaceful. For me, Shabbat is an irreplaceable opportunity to relax and spend quality time with my family; during the week, there is little time to do that. Although Shabbat may seem restrictive, the peacefulness that Shabbat brings is something I cherish.
- *Micaela Lechtman* -

I remember one Friday afternoon when my boys were young. It was just before candlelighting, and I was already exhausted from the week-- yet I was racing around, cleaning the house, setting the table, and cooking the dinner. But as I was rushing around to create the perfect Shabbat, my boys were being anything but perfect! They were fighting with one another, refusing to get ready or to help in any constructive way. I became increasingly upset, until I felt that there was no other way than to simply

"cancel Shabbat." While I cleared the table and put away the candles, the challah, and the wine, I informed my children that Shabbat was cancelled, and that we would try again the following week; I retreated to my room. About half an hour later, three very contrite little boys came in and whispered in my ear that Shabbat was ready and would I please please please come out and help them to light the candles. They guided me into the dining room, where I saw everything back on the table. As we stood around the table, arm in arm, I realized what a special lesson my boys had taught me about Shabbat. It is beyond our control to create the "perfect" Shabbat, but Shabbat is a beacon of hope for what is possible. That Shabbat, which began in such a difficult manner, became one of the ones that I will always remember. For me, Shabbat is an opportunity for us to experience a window of hope into new possibilities.
- *Rabbi Lori Cohen* -

    A friend of mine once asked me what Shabbos means to me. I thought this should be a simple, easy answer. Little did I know how difficult it is to put the essence of Shabbos on a piece of paper.

    From the outside, looking in, my Shabbos is a routine. I go to shul for Friday night davening, go home, and eat dinner at my mother's house. After dinner, I go to a Mishna Brurah shuir at the BAYT with my father. Afterwards, I come home and go to sleep, only to wake up the next morning to my loud alarm clock that I can't turn off. I get up and get dressed, and walk back over to the BAYT to run a youth group. Afterwards, I go to my father's house for a delicious lunch. When lunch is over (or before it ends), I go back to the BAYT for more learning, until I daven Mincha. After Mincha comes Perchai, then Maariv, and Shabbos is over. Now, that seems like a very short time in which to do a million different things.

    I thought that through, and then I thought to myself, "Is this what Shabbos means to me; a combination of Jewish activities? No feelings about the holiest day of the week?" But, as I was writing this paper, I realized that Shabbos isn't just the sum of all these activities; it's all of them together, and the atmosphere that *is* Shabbos. It's true that we have to follow the 39 Melachot, but there are two ways to look at that. One can look at Shabbos as a painful and very boring 25 hours, as I did when I was younger.

    Or, one can look at these 25 hours as a break from one's life to reflect on it. If one can see the beauty and peace that Shabbos brings, then there is no question that Shabbos is the most highly-anticipated weekly

Introduction

mini-holiday among Jews worldwide. It isn't a time when there's no internet and no electronics and you *have* to-- ugh-- read; rather, it's a time for family, for peace, and for thinking about your life and the changes you can make or ways to improve. Shabbos is a little Yom Kippur every week, only instead of G-d judging you, you judge yourself. And you ask yourself: are you up to par?

- Tzvi Yehudah Tabakman -

Stories from the Maggid: A Story Postscript

By Rabbi Shlomo Riskin

Many years ago, when I was still a very young rabbi with a very young family in Manhattan, I was riding in a taxicab on the way to a lecture. As is my custom, I engaged the driver in conversation. He had never graduated from elementary school. He had raised four children with a wife to whom he was married for over thirty years: one of his children was an engineer, another a lawyer, a third a high-school teacher, and his only daughter a nurse. When I asked him to what he attributed such obvious familial success, he explained to me that as long as his children lived at home, the cardinal family rule was that each and to show up at the dinner table every evening of provide a very good excuse as to why not. These family meals were devoid of television, radio or newspaper; instead, each family member, including himself and his wife, had to recount the most important incident of the day and the most frustrating incident of the day. It was largely as a result of those meals, he believed, that their family loyalty and togetherness was forged, and the strong character of each family member became solidified.

As the taxi driver concluded his description, I burst into tears. What he understood, I had not understood: that every evening meal must be a mini Shabbat meal, with ritual washing, blessing, Torah talk and general discussion. I hope that you will appreciate this.

(From "Around the Family Table: Songs and Prayers for the Jewish Home With Insights and Commentary" by Rabbi Shlomo Riskin, Copyright 2005, Ohr Torah Stone and Urim Publications, Jerusalem, Israel. Reprinted with permission.)

Stories from the Maggid: *Yosef Who Honoured Shabbos*

Talmud Bavli, Massechet Shabbat 119a

There was once a man, by the name of Yosef, who so loved Shabbos that he would honor it with the finest of foods, with fish and meat, never hesitating even if the price was very high.

The fact that Yosef behaved in this manner soon spread through his city, and he became known as *Yosef Mokir Shabbat* (Yosef who appreciates and honors the Shabbos).

In the same city, there lived a very wealthy man, who was also very wicked. The astrologers came to him and told him, "We have seen in the stars that all your wealth will fall into the hands of a Jew called Yosef. Be forewarned and plan how to avoid this."

The man became very frightened, and he sat down to figure a way to prevent his wealth from falling into the hands of the accursed Jew.

Suddenly, an idea occurred to him. This would be the perfect plan! Taking all his wealth, he bought a precious stone. He sewed it into his hat, and smiled, "Let us see the Jew get my wealth now!"

While walking along the banks of a river one windy day, the hat was suddenly blown off his head by a gust of wind. "Stop!" he cried in terror, as the hat sailed into the river. "Someone get my hat for me."

It was too late, however. Though he hired many people to search the river and its banks, there was no trace of the hat or of the valuable diamond that was in it.

The evil man was bitter at the loss, but he said, "At least I have some comfort in my poverty. At least Yosef will not have the stone, either."

That Friday, a group of fishermen were busy at work when they caught the largest and most beautiful fish they had ever seen. Immediately, the same thought struck them all: "Yosef will pay a great deal for this fish to be eaten on Shabbos. Let us go to his home and sell it to him."
Arriving at the house, they told Yosef, "We have caught the most beautiful fish we have ever seen. Would you be interested in buying it?"

Yosef saw the fish and was truly impressed.

"I have never seen such a fish," he said. "I must have it so that I may honor the Shabbos properly."

Even when he heard the very high price, he did not hesitate, but paid it. He then took it to the kitchen, and began to slice it, so as to prepare it for Shabbos. Imagine his amazement when he saw, inside the fish, a magnificent precious stone! He took the stone and sold it, and with the money, he became wealthy and a doer of good for the rest of his life.

(Adapted from the pages of the Talmud by Rabbi Sholom Klass. Copied from TorahTots.com, published by "The Jewish Press." http://www.torahtots.com/jewishpress/20090515a_midrash.htm. Reprinted with permision)

Introduction

Stories from the Maggid: *A Tzaddik's Tears*

By Rabbi Yerachmiel Tilles

About 30 years ago, an American rabbi visiting Miami, Florida gave a lecture on the life and accomplishments of the famed "Chafetz Chaim" (Rabbi Israel Meir HaCohen Kagan, 1838-1933). He described the life of the great sage who lived a humble life as a shopkeeper in in the village of Radin, in Poland, yet was recognized throughout the Jewish world as a great scholar, *tzaddik* (righteous person) and leader.

There was another story the rabbi wanted to tell, but he hesitated, for he only knew part of it. As he stood at the lectern, he thought for a moment and then decided that he would tell it anyway. He rationalized that even an unfinished story about the Chafetz Chaim would have a meaningful message.

He began to relate an incident about a teenage boy in the Chafetz Chaim's yeshiva who was found smoking a cigarette on Shabbat -- the sacred day of rest. The faculty and student body were shocked, and some of the faculty felt that the boy should be expelled. However, when the Chafetz Chaim heard the story, he asked that the boy be brought to his home.

At this point, the rabbi interrupted the narrative and said, "I don't know what the Chafetz Chaim said to the boy. I only know that they were together for a few minutes. I would give anything to know what he said to this student, for I am told that the boy never desecrated the Shabbat again. How wonderful it would be if we could relay that message -- whatever it was -- to others, in order to encourage them in their observance of Shabbat." The rabbi then continued with his lecture.

After his talk, the hall emptied of everyone except for one elderly man, who remained in his seat, alone with his thoughts. From the distance, it seemed he was trembling, as if he was either crying or suffering from chills. The rabbi walked over to the elderly man and asked him, "Is anything wrong?"

The man responded, "Where did you hear that story of the cigarette on Shabbat?" He did not look up and was still shaken. "I really don't know," answered the rabbi. "I heard it a while ago and I don't even remember who told it to me." The man looked up at the rabbi and said softly, "I was that boy." He then asked the rabbi to go outside, and as the two walked together, he told the rabbi the following story:

"This incident occurred in the 1920's when the Chafetz Chaim was in his eighties. I was terrified to have to go into his house and face him. But when I did go into his home, I looked around with disbelief at the poverty in which he lived. It was unimaginable to me that a man of his stature would be satisfied to live in such surroundings.

"Suddenly he was in the room where I was waiting. He was remarkably short. At that time I was a teenager and he only came up to my shoulders. He took my hand and clasped it tenderly in both of his. He brought my hand in his own clasped hands up to his face, and when I looked into his soft face, his eyes were closed for a moment.

"When he opened them, they were filled with tears. He then said to me in a hushed voice full of pain and astonishment, 'Shabbat!' And he started to cry. He was still holding both my hands in his, and while he was crying he repeated with astonishment, 'Shabbat, the holy Shabbat!'

"My heart started pounding and I became more frightened than I had been before. Tears streamed down his face and one of them rolled onto my hand. I thought it would bore a hole right through my skin. When I think of that tear today, I can still feel its heat. I can't describe how awful it felt to know that I had made the great tzaddik weep. But in his rebuke -- which consisted only of those few words -- I felt that he was not angry, but rather sad and fearful. He seemed frightened at the consequences of my actions."

The elderly man then caressed the hand that bore the invisible scar of a precious tear. It had become his permanent reminder to observe the "holy Shabbat" for the rest of his life.

(Copied from Chabad.org. Reprinted with permission. Visit Chabad.org/Shabbat to learn more about Shabbos. http://www.chabad.org/library/article_cdo/aid/ 257834/jewish/A-Tzaddiks-Tear.htm)

Shabbos Night
ליל שבת

This section has been generously sponsored by

❧ The Roth Family ❦

In honour of Cydney Roth's graduation

Candle Lighting - הדלקת נרות

❧ The lighting of Shabbos candles is a Rabbinically ordained Mitzvah. The lights are kindled approximately eighteen minutes before sunset, to welcome Shabbos Kodesh. The Mitzvah serves a dual purpose. The first is for Kavod Shabbos (honouring the Shabbos) by filling the home, and specifically the place of the festive meal, with light. The second purpose is for Shalom Bayit (peace in the home). Traditionally, candlelighting is done by the woman of the household. A man living alone, however, is required to kindle his own lights. The prevalent custom is for two or more candles to be lit. Some have the custom to light an additional candle for each child. Either way, a single candle is sufficient to fulfill the Mitzvah.

Generally, blessings are recited before the performance of a Mitzvah. On Shabbos, however, the candles are lit before saying the blessing. The moment the blessing is said, the candle-lighter officially ushers in Shabbos and accepts all of its restrictions. Thus, to say the blessing and then light the candles would be breaking Shabbos. In order to properly fulfill the dictum of saying a blessing first and then doing the act, one covers one's eyes immediately after lighting, says the blessing, and then uncovers the eyes in order to fully enjoy the light of the Shabbos candles.

Light the candles, stretch out your hands, and move them inwards in a circular motion three times. Cover your eyes and recite the following blessing:

בָּרוּךְ אַתָּה יְיָ אֱלֹהֵינוּ מֶלֶךְ הָעוֹלָם, אֲשֶׁר קִדְּשָׁנוּ בְּמִצְוֹתָיו וְצִוָּנוּ לְהַדְלִיק נֵר שֶׁל שַׁבָּת

Baruch Ata Ado-nai, Elo-heinu Melech Ha'Olam, asher kideshanu be'mitzvotav ve'tzivanu le'hadlik ner shel Shabbat.
Blessed are You, Hashem our G-d, King of the universe, Who has sanctified us with His commandments and has commanded us to kindle the light of Sabbath.

❧ With the candles lit, Shabbos has been officially ushered into the home. It is traditional to wish everyone present a "Shabbat Shalom" or "Gut Shabbos."

Blessing of the Children – ברכת הבנים

> There is a widespread custom for parents to bless their children upon returning from Shul on the eve of Shabbos. The blessing of "May G-d make you like Ephraim and Menashe" is the blessing that Yaakov Avinu imparted to his grandchildren, the two sons of Yosef, before his death (Bereishit 48:20). They were the first Jews to be born and raised in exile, and they grew to be great sources of pride to Yaakov. Despite the fact that they were steeped in Egyptian culture, they maintained their Jewish lifestyle and upheld the values with which they were raised. Similarly, the blessing we confer upon our children is that they, too, will remain true to the values and practices they learned in their homes, despite all foreign influences. What better time is there to give such a blessing than when the home itself is filled with the beauty and splendour of Shabbos Kodesh? <u>Both hands should be laid upon the head of the child when saying the blessing.</u>

For a son -

יְשִׂמְךָ אֱלֹהִים כְּאֶפְרַיִם וְכִמְנַשֶּׁה

Ye'sim'cha Elo-him ke'Ephraim v'chi'Menashe.
May G-d make you like Ephraim and Menashe.

For a daughter -

יְשִׂמֵךְ אֱלֹהִים כְּשָׂרָה, רִבְקָה, רָחֵל, וְלֵאָה

Ye'sim'ech Elo-him ke'Sarah, Rivka, Rachel, ve'Leah.
May G-d make you like Sarah, Rebecca, Rachel, and Leah.

For all children -

יְבָרֶכְךָ יְיָ וְיִשְׁמְרֶךָ. יָאֵר יְיָ פָּנָיו אֵלֶיךָ וִיחֻנֶּךָּ. יִשָּׂא יְיָ פָּנָיו אֵלֶיךָ וְיָשֵׂם לְךָ שָׁלוֹם.

Ye'varech'cha Ado-nai v'yishm'recha. Ya'er Ado-nai panav ei'lecha vi'chuneka. Yisa Ado-nai panav ei'lecha, v'yasem l'cha shalom.
May Hashem bless you and watch over you. May Hashem cause His countenance to shine upon you and be gracious to you. May Hashem raise His countenance toward you and grant you peace.

Shalom Aleichem – שלום עליכם

The Talmud (Shabbat 119b) teaches that two angels escort a person home from Shul on Erev Shabbos: a good one and and an evil one. If a Jew arrives home and finds a kindled lamp, a set table, and a made bed, the good angel says, "May it be Hashem's will that it also be so next Shabbos," and the evil angel is compelled to answer, "Amen!" But if the house is not properly prepared for Shabbos Kodesh, the evil angel says, "May it be Hashem's will that it also be so next Shabbos," and the good angel is compelled to answer, "Amen!" The Kabbalists of the 17th century composed **Shalom Aleichem** based on this passage. Rabbi Mordechai Rhine (in "The Magic of Shabbos") teaches that our intention is not really to welcome the angels, but to welcome Hashem Himself, whom they represent. Ultimately, all our Shabbos preparations -- the set table, the clean house, the kindled lamps -- are in order to welcome Hashem into our homes as we sanctify them with the holiness of Shabbos Kodesh. The Kotzker Rebbe would say, "Where can Hashem be found? Wherever man lets Him in!" When we welcome Hashem into our homes by creating a holy and special environment, we are blessed by His angels to merit Hashem's presence in our homes the next week. <u>Recite each verse three times.</u>

שָׁלוֹם עֲלֵיכֶם מַלְאֲכֵי הַשָּׁרֵת מַלְאֲכֵי עֶלְיוֹן מִמֶּלֶךְ מַלְכֵי הַמְּלָכִים הַקָּדוֹשׁ בָּרוּךְ הוּא.

Shalom Aleichem malachei ha'sharet, malachei elyon, mi'melech malchei ha'm'lachim, hakadosh baruch hu.

Peace upon you, ministering angels, messengers of the Most High, of the the Supreme Kings of kings, the Holy One Blessed is He.

בּוֹאֲכֶם לְשָׁלוֹם מַלְאֲכֵי הַשָּׁלוֹם מַלְאֲכֵי עֶלְיוֹן מִמֶּלֶךְ מַלְכֵי הַמְּלָכִים הַקָּדוֹשׁ בָּרוּךְ הוּא.

Bo'achem l'shalom malachei ha'shalom, malachei elyon, mi'melech malchei ha'm'lachim, hakadosh baruch hu.

Come in peace, angels of peace, messengers of the Most High, of the the Supreme Kings of kings, the Holy One Blessed is He.

Shabbos Night

בָּרְכוּנִי לְשָׁלוֹם מַלְאֲכֵי הַשָּׁלוֹם מַלְאֲכֵי עֶלְיוֹן מִמֶּלֶךְ מַלְכֵי הַמְּלָכִים הַקָּדוֹשׁ בָּרוּךְ הוּא.

Barchuni l'shalom malachei ha'shalom, malachei elyon, mi'melech malchei ha'm'lachim, hakadosh baruch hu.

Bless me for peace, angels of peace, messengers of the Most High, of the the Supreme Kings of kings, the Holy One Blessed is He.

צֵאתְכֶם לְשָׁלוֹם מַלְאֲכֵי הַשָּׁלוֹם מַלְאֲכֵי עֶלְיוֹן מִמֶּלֶךְ מַלְכֵי הַמְּלָכִים הַקָּדוֹשׁ בָּרוּךְ הוּא.

Tzeitchem l'shalom malachei ha'shalom, malachei elyon, mi'melech malchei ha'm'lachim, hakadosh baruch hu.

May your departure be for peace, angels of peace, messengers of the Most High, of the the Supreme Kings of kings, the Holy One Blessed is He.

Midrash Eishet Hayil

By Dr. Anna Urowitz-Freudenstein

The medieval midrash entitled *Midrash Eishat Hayil* is actually a tiny genre of midrashim that are all grouped around the biblical poem from the Book of Mishle that is sung around traditional Shabbat tables on Friday nights. That is, there is no definitive text, but rather a group of texts, mostly in manuscript form, that use these verses from Mishle as their literary structure.

A typical *Midrash Eishat Hayil* uses each line of the poem to introduce a new midrashic idea about a different biblical woman. Even though the "original" Eishet Hayil, or Woman of Valour, is believed to be the mother of King Solomon, this midrash takes advantage of her anonymity in the biblical text to assume that she is "everywoman," or, at least, "every-biblical-woman." Therefore, *Midrash Eishat Hayil* can be seen as a mini-anthology of midrashim about biblical women. Most of these midrashim are already known from earlier texts, and it is probably for this reason that they are recorded in this Midrash in a shortened and sometimes confusing manner.

The biblical women mentioned in *Midrash Eishat Hayil* are: Noah's wife; Sarah; Rebecca; Zipporah; Leah; Rachel; Bitya, daughter of Pharaoh; Yocheved; Miriam; Hannah; Tamar; Yael; the Tzarfatit widow, who sustained Eliyahu; the Shunamitte woman; Tzalfonit, the mother of Samson; Michal; Elisheva; Serach, daughter of Asher; Ovadiah's wife; Ruth; Vashti; and Esther.

Of all of the midrashic ideas in these texts, there are some that are more unusual and intriguing than others. One example of this is the midrash about Samson's mother, connected to the line in Eishet Hayil from Mishle 31:22: "'She maketh for herself coverlets' (Mishle 31:22). This is Tzalfonit, the mother of Samson, who would spin and sell in the market and raise her son; and that is not enough, but rather, she would sit and expound the Torah until she made it clear."

This is an unusual midrash, in that it not only names a woman who is unnamed in the Bible, it also attributed to her two actions that were not considered "normal" by the social standards of her era. The first action involvs skills for her profession were not unusual-- the Eishet Hayil had them, too. However, it was considered unusual-- and perhaps not even proper-- to spin and sell in public. Perhaps that is why the midrash explains that her ultimate goal in these acts was appropriate - they gave her the ability to raise her son properly.

The other unusual action is even more shocking. It is probably based on the main Hebrew letters in her name Tzalfonit, that are shared with the Hebrew root of the word "to make clear." If she is the-one-who-can-make-things-clear, what better a subject for expounding and clearly explaining than the Torah itself, even if these clarifications come from a woman!

For more information, see: http://www.jewishvirtuallibrary.org/jsource/judaica/ejud_0002_0006_0_06079.html.

A version of Midrash Eishet Hayil may be found at the amazing website HebrewBooks.org: http://hebrewbooks.org/pdfpager.aspx?req=21179&st=אשת&pgnum=152&hilite=.

Eishet Chayil - אשת חיל

Eishet Chayil is a twenty-two letter alphabetical acrostic poem written by King Solomon, which concludes the book of Proverbs (Mishlei 31). The poem describes the perfect wife: a woman of valour, energetic and righteous. According to various commentators, the poem is an allegorical reference to different concepts: namely, the Shabbos Queen, the Shechinah (Divine Presence), the Shabbos, the Torah, wisdom, and the soul. The fact that King Solomon used a portrait of the Jewish woman to describe holy and divine themes is in itself a great tribute to her. Jewish thought highly glorifies the Jewish woman on many accounts. According to the Rashbam, the miracles of Purim, Chanukah, and Pesach were brought about by women (see Tosafot on Megillah 4a). Chazal even teach us that the Mashiach and final redemption of the Jewish people will come about in the merit of women (Sotah 11a). It is customary for a man to recite Eishet Chayil every Shabbos as a display of gratitude to and praise for his wife, for all the work she has done for him and their family over the past week.

אֵשֶׁת חַיִל מִי יִמְצָא. וְרָחֹק מִפְּנִינִים מִכְרָהּ:
בָּטַח בָּהּ לֵב בַּעְלָהּ. וְשָׁלָל לֹא יֶחְסָר:

Eishet Chayil mi yimtza, v'rachok mi'pninim michrah.
Batach bah lev ba'alah, vshalal lo yechsar.
An accomplished woman, who can find? Her value is far beyond pearls.
Her husband's heart relies on her and he shall lack no fortune.

גְּמָלַתְהוּ טוֹב וְלֹא רָע. כֹּל יְמֵי חַיֶּיהָ:
דָּרְשָׁה צֶמֶר וּפִשְׁתִּים. וַתַּעַשׂ בְּחֵפֶץ כַּפֶּיהָ:

G'malat'hu tov v'lo ra kol y'mei chayeha.
Darsha tsemer ufishtim, v'ta'as b'chefetz kapeha.
She does him good and not evil, all the days of her life.
She seeks wool and flax, and works with her hands willingly.

הָיְתָה כָּאֳנִיּוֹת סוֹחֵר. מִמֶּרְחָק תָּבִיא לַחְמָהּ:
וַתָּקָם בְּעוֹד לַיְלָה. וַתִּתֵּן טֶרֶף לְבֵיתָהּ וְחֹק לְנַעֲרֹתֶיהָ:

Hay'tah k'oniyot socher, mimerchak tavi lachma.
Va'takam b'od layla. V'titen teref l'beitah v'chok l'na'aroteha.
She is like the merchant ships; she brings her bread from afar.
She arises while it is still night, and gives food to her household and a portion to her

maidservants.

זָמְמָה שָׂדֶה וַתִּקָּחֵהוּ. מִפְּרִי כַפֶּיהָ נָטְעָה כָּרֶם:
חָגְרָה בְעוֹז מָתְנֶיהָ. וַתְּאַמֵּץ זְרוֹעֹתֶיהָ:

Zam'mah sadeh v'tikachehu, mi'pri kapeha nat'ah karem.
Chag'rah b'oz motneha, va't'ametz z'ro'oteha.
She plans for a field, and buys it. With the fruit of her hands she plants a vineyard.
She girds her loins in strength, and makes her arms strong.

טָעֲמָה כִּי טוֹב סַחְרָהּ. לֹא יִכְבֶּה בַלַּיְלָה נֵרָהּ:
יָדֶיהָ שִׁלְּחָה בַכִּישׁוֹר. וְכַפֶּיהָ תָּמְכוּ פָלֶךְ:

Ta'a'ma ki tov sochrah, lo yichbe balayla nerah.
Yadeha shil'cha b'kishor, v'kapeha tam'chu phalech.
She knows that her merchandise is good. Her candle does not go out at night.
She sets her hands to the distaff, and holds the spindle in her hands.

כַּפָּהּ פָּרְשָׂה לֶעָנִי. וְיָדֶיהָ שִׁלְּחָה לָאֶבְיוֹן:
לֹא תִירָא לְבֵיתָהּ מִשָּׁלֶג. כִּי כָל בֵּיתָהּ לָבֻשׁ שָׁנִים:

Kapah par'sah l'ani, v'yadehah shil'cha l'evyon.
Lo tira l'veitah m'shaleg, ki kol beitah l'vush shanim.
She extends her hands to the poor, and reaches out her hand to the needy.
She fears not for her household because of snow, because her whole household is warmly dressed.

מַרְבַדִּים עָשְׂתָה לָּהּ. שֵׁשׁ וְאַרְגָּמָן לְבוּשָׁהּ:
נוֹדָע בַּשְּׁעָרִים בַּעְלָהּ. בְּשִׁבְתּוֹ עִם זִקְנֵי אָרֶץ:

Marvadim as'tah lah, shesh v'argaman l'vushah.
Nodah ba'sh'arim ba'alah, b'shivto im ziknei aretz.
She makes covers for herself; her clothing is fine linen and purple.
Her husband is known at the gates, when he sits among the elders of the land.

סָדִין עָשְׂתָה וַתִּמְכֹּר. וַחֲגוֹר נָתְנָה לַכְּנַעֲנִי:
עֹז וְהָדָר לְבוּשָׁהּ. וַתִּשְׂחַק לְיוֹם אַחֲרוֹן:

Sadin as'tah v'timkor, v'chagor nat'nah la'kna'ani.
Oz v'hadar l'vushah, vatischak l'yom acharon.
She makes a cloak and sells it, and she delivers aprons to the merchant.
Strength and honor are her clothing; she smiles at the future.

פִּיהָ פָּתְחָה בְחָכְמָה. וְתוֹרַת חֶסֶד עַל לְשׁוֹנָהּ:
צוֹפִיָּה הֲלִיכוֹת בֵּיתָהּ. וְלֶחֶם עַצְלוּת לֹא תֹאכֵל:

Piha pat'cha b'chochmah, v'torat chesed al l'shonah.
Tsofiya halichot beita, v'lechem atzlut lo tochel.
She opens her mouth in wisdom, and the lesson of kindness is on her tongue.
She watches over the ways of her household, and does not eat the bread of idleness.

קָמוּ בָנֶיהָ וַיְאַשְּׁרוּהָ. בַּעְלָהּ וַיְהַלְלָהּ:
רַבּוֹת בָּנוֹת עָשׂוּ חָיִל. וְאַתְּ עָלִית עַל כֻּלָּנָה:

Kamu vaneha va'y'ash'ruhah, ba'alah vay'hal'lah.
Rabot banot asu chayil, v'at alit al kulanah.
Her children rise and praise he;, her husband lauds her.
Many women have done worthily, but you surpass them all.

שֶׁקֶר הַחֵן וְהֶבֶל הַיֹּפִי. אִשָּׁה יִרְאַת יְיָ הִיא תִתְהַלָּל:
תְּנוּ לָהּ מִפְּרִי יָדֶיהָ. וִיהַלְלוּהָ בַשְּׁעָרִים מַעֲשֶׂיהָ:

Sheker hachen v'hevel hayofi, ishah yir'at adonai hi tit'halal.
T'nu lah mi'p'ri yadeha, vi'y'hal'luha ba'sh'arim ma'aseha.
Charm is deceptive and beauty is vain, but a woman who fears God shall be praised.
Give her of the fruit of her hands, and let her works praise her in the gates.

Kiddush

By Aaron Goldberg

There is a special ritual done twice every Shabbat that is held dear in the hearts of Jews everywhere. It is called Kiddush. On Friday evening, after coming home from the synagogue, Kiddush is recited for the first time. Said over wine or grape juice, this Kiddush includes the passage from the Torah outlining the end of the sixth day and the seventh day of creation, and is the more important of the two Kiddushes. After shul on Saturday morning, Kiddush is again recited. This time, it includes the passage from the Torah which explains how the Jewish people kept Shabbat.

Why is Kiddush so special? What makes it such a staple for all holidays, and why *must* it be done?

The Torah commands the Jews to remember and keep the Shabbat. "Remembering" is interpreted as doing special things throughout the day to distinguish Shabbat from regular days. Accordingly, reciting Kiddush is construed as a biblical commandment, giving light to its significance.

What does the word Kiddush even mean? As with all words, translators have an extraordinarily tough time attempting to convey all the same meanings of a word from one language to another. Even more so, it is almost impossible to explain the word Kiddush in any language, even Hebrew itself! Thus, this poses as a problem.

The most common usage of the word Kadosh is to connote the term 'holy.' Even in English, such a word is somewhat ambiguous. For something to be holy, it must have an elevated status. Holiness refers to something that is different, but special. In Judaism, when referring to something as holy, or Kadosh, the connotation is even more pronounced. Something is holy when it remains separate from other things. An object that is set aside to be given to the Temple is holy, and a person who devotes his life to Temple service is holy. Additionally, the Torah exhorts the Jews to be "Kedoshim," i.e., to separate themselves from the other nations. The Jewish people must remain distinct, through which they may become 'holy.'

This may be extrapolated much further. In order to achieve a degree of sanctity in life, what must be pursued is holiness. As such, to become holy, one must separate oneself from everyday activities, and infuse one's life with a degree of distinctness. This can be achieved by treating everyday occurrences as special, and realizing that there is value in all actions.

We are brought back to Kiddush. Kiddush is a chance every week to make Shabbat special. By reciting Kiddush, we are stating outright that

Shabbat remains separate from the other six days of the week. Whereas during the week we traverse our mundane lives and nothing more, on Shabbat we wish to create an environment in which every activity is special. To do so, we recite Kiddush, which not only ushers in a new state of mind, but also enables us to enact the changes we wish to make in our lives. Through Kiddush, we state that we wish for our lives to become infused with holiness, and that we hope to exalt all of our actions until we ourselves become sanctified.

Kiddush is a magical thing. It acts, both symbolically and physically, as a means of spiritual elevation, and is the conduit between the everyday and Shabbat. Through this conduit, Jews everywhere are able to bring in Shabbat, with the hope that it will be as special and inspiring as possible. Through Kiddush, Jews everywhere are able, once a week, to make an ordinary day extraordinary.

Shabbos Night Kiddush - קידוש ליל שבת

❧ Before making Kiddush, the table should be set with both Challahs, covered on top and below (a Challah cover on top and a Challah board below). Usually, the Beracha (prayer) on bread is said before the Beracha on wine or grape juice. However, on Shabbos, we say Kiddush over wine or grape juice first, in order to sanctify this holy day. As such, we cover the bread while making kiddush in order not to "embarrass" it. Commentators point out that we are not actually concerned with the feelings of the inanimate Challah. The true lesson relates to the fact that Shabbos represents peace and harmony, and these goals are only achievable if we are sensitive to the feelings of others.

One should use a special cup for Kiddush that holds at least 4 1/2 ounces (135 ml), but if this is not possible, any non-disposable cup able to hold that amount will do. The cup should be filled to the rim to symbolize that our joy should be "full." Any kosher wine or grape juice can be used. The one making Kiddush should keep two things in mind while saying the prayer. First, that he is including all others at the table in his Kiddush and thus discharging them from their obligation. The people present should also have that in mind. Second, he should have in mind that the obligation itself is a Mitzvah (commandment) from the Torah.

There are many different customs as to whether one stands or sits during the recitation of Kiddush. Some stand for both parts of the prayer, like witnesses in a Jewish court; just as witnesses stand when giving testimony, we are witnessing the entrance of the Shabbos. Others sit for both parts, while others stand for the first blessing and sit for the second. After both blessings ("Borei Pri HaGafen" and "Mekadesh HaShabbat"), be sure to answer 'Amen.'

When Kiddush is completed, all those at the table should sit down and refrain from talking. We do not speak between the recitation of a Beracha and its fulfillment. The one who said Kiddush should drink at least two ounces (a "cheekful") in one or two gulps. The rest of the Kiddush wine or grape juice is then distributed to everyone else. This can be done in a number of ways. The person making Kiddush can distribute the liquid from his cup, or, before drinking, he can spill about four ounces (the majority of the cup) into a another cup and drink from it, then spill the remainder from the original cup into smaller cups and pass it around. One can also give everyone an individual glass for wine or grape juice before Kiddush.

When you are ready to begin Kiddush, everyone should be quiet and stand or sit according to your family custom. Lift up the cup in your right hand. Begin with the text below. It is preferable if Kiddush is said in Hebrew, but it is acceptable to say it in any language you understand. (One still fulfills one's obligation if one says it in Hebrew but does not understand the words).

In an undertone - וַיְהִי עֶרֶב וַיְהִי בֹקֶר:

יוֹם הַשִּׁשִּׁי. וַיְכֻלּוּ הַשָּׁמַיִם וְהָאָרֶץ וְכָל צְבָאָם: וַיְכַל אֱלֹהִים בַּיּוֹם הַשְּׁבִיעִי מְלַאכְתּוֹ אֲשֶׁר עָשָׂה. וַיִּשְׁבֹּת בַּיּוֹם הַשְּׁבִיעִי מִכָּל מְלַאכְתּוֹ אֲשֶׁר עָשָׂה: וַיְבָרֶךְ אֱלֹהִים אֶת יוֹם הַשְּׁבִיעִי וַיְקַדֵּשׁ אֹתוֹ. כִּי בוֹ שָׁבַת מִכָּל מְלַאכְתּוֹ אֲשֶׁר בָּרָא אֱלֹהִים לַעֲשׂוֹת:

(*In an undertone* - Va'yehi erev va'yehi boker) Yom Ha'Shishi. Va'yechulu ha'shamayim ve'ha'aretz ve'chol tzeva'am. Va'yechal Elo-him ba'yom ha'shevi'i melachto asher asa, va'yishbot ba'yom ha'shevi'i mikol melachto asher asa. Va'yevarech Elo-him et yom ha'shevi'i va'yekadesh oto, ki vo shavat mikol melachto asher bara Elo-him la'asot.

(There was evening and there was morning:) The sixth day. And the heavens and the earth and all their host were completed. And G-d completed on the seventh day the work that He had performed, and He refrained on the seventh day from all the work which He had performed. And G-d blessed the seventh day and He sanctified it, for thereon He refrained from all His work that G-d created to do.

סַבְרִי מָרָנָן וְרַבָּנָן וְרַבּוֹתַי:
בָּרוּךְ אַתָּה יְיָ אֱלֹהֵינוּ מֶלֶךְ הָעוֹלָם בּוֹרֵא פְּרִי הַגָּפֶן:

(Savri maranan ve'rabanan ve'rabotai)
Baruch Ata Ado-nai Elo-heinu Melech Ha'Olam, Borei p'ri ha'gafen.
(Permit me, distinguished ones, rabbis, and my teachers)
Blessed are You, Hashem our G-d, King of the Universe, Who creates the fuit of the vine.

בָּרוּךְ אַתָּה יְיָ אֱלֹהֵינוּ מֶלֶךְ הָעוֹלָם. אֲשֶׁר קִדְּשָׁנוּ בְּמִצְוֹתָיו וְרָצָה בָּנוּ. וְשַׁבַּת קָדְשׁוֹ בְּאַהֲבָה וּבְרָצוֹן הִנְחִילָנוּ. זִכָּרוֹן לְמַעֲשֵׂה בְרֵאשִׁית. כִּי הוּא יוֹם תְּחִלָּה לְמִקְרָאֵי קֹדֶשׁ זֵכֶר לִיצִיאַת מִצְרָיִם. כִּי בָנוּ בָחַרְתָּ וְאוֹתָנוּ קִדַּשְׁתָּ מִכָּל הָעַמִּים וְשַׁבַּת קָדְשְׁךָ בְּאַהֲבָה וּבְרָצוֹן הִנְחַלְתָּנוּ: בָּרוּךְ אַתָּה יְיָ מְקַדֵּשׁ הַשַּׁבָּת:

Baruch Ata Ado-nai Elo-heinu Melech Ha'Olam, asher kideshanu be'mitzvotav ve'ratzah vanu, ve'Shabbat kodsho be'ahavah ue've'ratzon hinchilanu zikaron le'ma'aseh beresheet. Ki hu yom techilah le'mikraei kodesh, zeicher li'yetziat Mitzrayim. Ki vanu vacharta ve'otanu kidashta mi'kol ha'amim, ve'Shabbat kodshecha be'ahavah u've'ratzon hinchaltanu. **Baruch ata Ado-nai, Mekadesh Ha'Shabbat.**

Blessed are You, Hashem our G-d, King of the Universe, Who sanctified us with His commandments, and favoured us, and with love and favour gave us His holy Sabbath, as a reminder of the Creation. It is the first amongst the holy festivals, commemorating the Exodus from Egypt. For You chose us and sanctified us out of all the nations, and with love and favour You gave us Your Holy Sabbath. **Blessed are You, Hashem, Who sanctifies the Sabbath.**

Lechem Mishnah

By Mrs. Esther Friedman

After the recitation of the Kiddush, every Shabbat and Holiday meal begins with the Hamotzi blessing recited over two loaves of challah bread. The custom of taking two loaves is based on a Talmudic interpretation of the Biblical verses discussing the "manna", the food of the Jews during their 40 years in the desert. Every morning, each individual would walk to the edge of the camp and gather his daily food from the manna that coated the camp's perimeter. Each day, despite how hard an individual tried to take more, he would end up with with exactly one Omer (a large biblical measure) of manna.

The Torah tells us that on Shabbat (and festivals), no manna would fall. Instead, every Friday, each person would gather "Lechem Mishnah"-- a term which refers to a double portion, but, literally means "double bread." To commemorate this weekly occurrence, we, too, crown our Shabbat and festival meals with two loaves.

The Midrash explains that the practice in the desert was to make four loaves from this double portion. One was eaten Friday morning, and the remaining three were left for Shabbat. Of these, one was eaten Friday night, and the other two were left for the two meals of the Shabbat day. The Torah Temimah (Rabbi Baruch HaLevi Epstein) points out that, from this Midrash, we can deduce two details of the custom. First, although two loaves were brought to each meal, only one was eaten-- hence the two remaining loaves for the Shabbat day. Second, it would appear from the Midrash that only one loaf is required for the final meal of Shabbat, Seudah Shelishit, eaten Saturday afternoon-- for by then, they had eaten three of the four loaves they had baked! Common custom today is to take two loaves even for Seudah Shelishit, but this Midrash implies that that is not necessary.

In the Friday night Kiddush, we quote the verse from the creation story about Shabbat. We say that G-d both blesssed the Shabbat and made it holy. Rashi, the famous commentator on the Torah, says that this blessing and holiness actually refers to the manna, because a double portion fell on Friday and nothing fell on Shabbat. In order to understand this somewhat odd reasoning, one must understand that the Hebrew word for blessing, 'Bracha,' is similiar to the word 'Breichah' in Hebrew, which means a pool. Based on the similarity of the words, we understand a blessing to be an increase of G-d's goodness. Kedusha, or holiness, on the other hand, means to separate or set aside. Shabbat in the desert, therefore, was distinguished by the extra that fell, and separated as the day of rest when no manna collection took place. What is strange about this explanation is that all the holiness and blessing of Shabbat seems to be limited to a 40-year period. But if one were to look at that 40-year period as a time of clarity and close connection to G-d in regard to the earning of one's bread, an interesting Shabbat idea unfolds. The blessing of Shabbat and its holiness tells us that G-d provides us with our Shabbat needs for free on Friday, and gives us this special day as a day of rest.

By honouring the Shabbat with lechem mishnah, we are connecting ourselves with the customs of our ancestors as they celebrated the earliest days of Shabbat, and we are reminding ourselves of G-d's help with earning our daily bread.

Ritual Handwashing - נטילת ידים

❧ *Fill the washing cup to the top with water and hold it in your left hand. Pour the water over your right hand until the wrist. Then pour a second time on the same hand. Switch the cup to the right hand and pour twice over the left hand. Before drying your hands, recite the Beracha:*

בָּרוּךְ אַתָּה יְיָ אֱלֹהֵינוּ מֶלֶךְ הָעוֹלָם, אֲשֶׁר קִדְּשָׁנוּ בְּמִצְוֹתָיו וְצִוָּנוּ עַל נְטִילַת יָדָיִם.

Baruch Atah Ado-nai Elo-heinu Melech Ha'Olam, asher kideshanu be'mitzvotav, vi'tzivanu al netilat yada'im.

Blessed are You, Hashem our G-d, King of the Universe, Who has sanctified us with His commandments and has commanded us regarding washing the hands.

Blessing on the Bread - ברכת "המוציא"

❧ *Hold the two Challah loaves in both your hands, lift them up, and recite the Beracha:*

בָּרוּךְ אַתָּה יְיָ אֱלֹהֵינוּ מֶלֶךְ הָעוֹלָם הַמּוֹצִיא לֶחֶם מִן הָאָרֶץ.

Baruch Atah Ado-nai Elo-heinu Melech Ha'Olam, ha'motzi lechem min ha'aretz.

Blessed are You, Hashem our G-d, King of the Universe, Who brings forth bread from the earth.

❧ *Cut the Challahs and dip the bread in salt. The person who made the Beracha should eat first, so as not to pass over a Mitzvah. The bread should then be distributed to everyone at the table.*

Kol Mekadesh Shevii - כל מקדש שביעי

כָּל מְקַדֵּשׁ שְׁבִיעִי כָּרָאוּי לוֹ.
כָּל שׁוֹמֵר שַׁבָּת כַּדָּת מֵחַלְּלוֹ.
שְׂכָרוֹ הַרְבֵּה מְאֹד עַל פִּי פָעֳלוֹ.
אִישׁ עַל מַחֲנֵהוּ וְאִישׁ עַל דִּגְלוֹ:

Kol m'kadesh shvi'i kara'ui lo,
kol shomer shabbat, kadat mechalelo,
s'charo harbeh m'od al pi fo'alo,
ish al machaneihu v'ish al diglo.

Whoever sanctifies the Shabbat properly,
whoever guards the Shabbat from desecration,
his great reward will fit his efforts.
"Every man at his own camp; every man at his own banner."

אוֹהֲבֵי יְיָ הַמְחַכִּים בְּבִנְיַן אֲרִיאֵל.
בְּיוֹם הַשַּׁבָּת שִׂישׂוּ וְשִׂמְחוּ כִּמְקַבְּלֵי מַתַּן נַחֲלִיאֵל.
גַּם שְׂאוּ יְדֵיכֶם קֹדֶשׁ וְאִמְרוּ לָאֵל.
בָּרוּךְ יְיָ אֲשֶׁר נָתַן מְנוּחָה לְעַמּוֹ יִשְׂרָאֵל:

Ohavei Ado-nai ham'chakim b'vinyan Ariel,
b'yom hashabbat sisu v'simchu kimkab'lei matan nachaliel,
gam s'u y'deichem kodesh v'imru la'eil,
"Baruch Ado-nai asher natan m'nucha l'amo Yisrael."

Lovers of G-d who long for the building of Jerusalem
on Shabbat rejoice and be glad, as if receiving the gift of G-d's inheritance.
Raise your hands in holiness and proclaim to G-d:
"Blessed is Hashem Who gave rest to his nation Israel."

דּוֹרְשֵׁי יְיָ זֶרַע אַבְרָהָם אוֹהֲבוֹ.
הַמְאַחֲרִים לָצֵאת מִן הַשַּׁבָּת וּמְמַהֲרִים לָבֹא.
וּשְׂמֵחִים לְשָׁמְרוֹ וּלְעָרֵב עֵרוּבוֹ.
זֶה הַיּוֹם עָשָׂה יְיָ נָגִילָה וְנִשְׂמְחָה בוֹ:

Dorshei Ado-nai zera Avraham ohavo,
Ham'acharim latzeit min haShabbat um'maharim lavo,
Usmeichim l'shomro ul'areiv eiruvo,

Zeh hayom asah Ado-nai nagila v'nismecha vo.

Seekers of G-d, seed of Abraham His beloved,
who delay departing from the Shabbat, and rush to enter,
glad to safeguad it and set its eruv;
"This is the day G-d has made, let us rejoice and be glad with it."

זִכְרוּ תּוֹרַת מֹשֶׁה בְּמִצְוַת שַׁבָּת גְּרוּסָה.
חֲרוּתָה לְיוֹם הַשְּׁבִיעִי כְּכַלָּה בֵּין רֵעוֹתֶיהָ מְשֻׁבָּצָה.
טְהוֹרִים יִירָשׁוּהָ וִיקַדְּשׁוּהָ בְּמַאֲמַר כָּל אֲשֶׁר עָשָׂה.
וַיְכַל אֱלֹהִים בַּיּוֹם הַשְּׁבִיעִי מְלַאכְתּוֹ אֲשֶׁר עָשָׂה:

Zichru Torat Moshe b'mitzvat Shabbat g'rusah,
Charuta l'yom ha'sh'vi'i, k'challah bein rei'oteha m'shubatzah,
T'horim yirashuha vikad'shuha b'ma'amar kol asher asah,
Vaye'chal Elo-him ba'yom ha'sh'vi'i m'lachto asher asah.

Remember Moses' Torah as the Shabbat commandment is explained,
inscribed with teachings for the seventh day, like a bride among her friends.
Pure ones receive it and sanctify it by saying: "All that He has made,"
"G-d completed all His work on the seventh day."

יוֹם קָדוֹשׁ הוּא מִבּוֹאוֹ וְעַד צֵאתוֹ.
כָּל זֶרַע יַעֲקֹב יְכַבְּדוּהוּ כִּדְבַר הַמֶּלֶךְ וְדָתוֹ.
לָנוּחַ בּוֹ וְלִשְׂמוֹחַ בְּתַעֲנוּג אָכוֹל וְשָׁתוֹ.
כָּל עֲדַת יִשְׂרָאֵל יַעֲשׂוּ אוֹתוֹ:

Yom kadosh hu mi'bo'o v'ad tzeito,
Kol zera Ya'akov ye'chab'duhu kidvar hamelech v'dato,
Lanu'ach bo v'lismo'ach b'ta'anug achol v'shato,
Kol adat Yisrael ya'asu oto.

It is a holy day, from beginning to end.
All the descendants of Jacob will honor it according to the King's word and decree.
To rest on it and to be happy with the pleasure of food and drink.
"The entire congregation of Israel will observe it."

מְשֹׁךְ חַסְדְּךָ לְיוֹדְעֶיךָ אֵל קַנָּא וְנוֹקֵם.
נוֹטְרֵי לְיוֹם הַשְּׁבִיעִי זָכוֹר וְשָׁמוֹר לְהָקֵם.
שַׂמְּחֵם בְּבִנְיַן שָׁלֵם בְּאוֹר פָּנֶיךָ תַּבְהִיקֵם.
יִרְוְיֻן מִדֶּשֶׁן בֵּיתֶךָ וְנַחַל עֲדָנֶיךָ תַשְׁקֵם:

M'shoch chasd'cha l'yod'echa Eil kano v'nokeim,
Notrei yom ha'sh'vi'i zachor v'shamor l'hakeim,
Sam'cheim b'vinyan shalem b'or panecha tav'hikem,
Yirv'yun mideshen beitecha v'nachal adanecha tashkeim.

Extend Your kindness to those who know You, jealous and vengeful G-d,
those who eagerly await the seventh day, to uphold 'remember' and 'safeguard'.
Make them happy with the complete rebuilding; in the light of Your face make them radiant.
"Sate them from the abundance of your house, and quench their thirst from the stream of Your delicacies."

עֲזוֹר לַשׁוֹבְתִים בַּשְּׁבִיעִי בֶּחָרִישׁ וּבַקָּצִיר עוֹלָמִים.
פּוֹסְעִים בּוֹ פְּסִיעָה קְטַנָּה. סוֹעֲדִים בּוֹ לְבָרֶךְ שָׁלֹשׁ פְּעָמִים.
צִדְקָתָם תַּצְהִיר כְּאוֹר שִׁבְעַת הַיָּמִים.
יְיָ אֱלֹהֵי יִשְׂרָאֵל הָבָה תָמִים.
יְיָ אֱלֹהֵי יִשְׂרָאֵל תְּשׁוּעַת עוֹלָמִים:

Azor lashovtim ba'sh'vi'i becharish u'vakatzir olamim,
Pos'im bo p'si'ah k'tanah so'adim bo l'vareich shalosh pe'amim,
Tzidkatam tatz'hir k'or shiv'at hayamim,
Ado-nai Elo-hei Yisrael havah tamim,
Ado-nai Elo-hei Yisrael t'shu'at olamim.

Always help those who rest from plowing and harvesting on Shabbat,
who only walk on Shabbat with short steps and eat three meals on it to bless You.
May their righteousness shine brightly, like the light of the seven days.
Hashem, G-d of Israel, show Tammim!
Hashem, G-d of Israel, a salvation for eternity!

Kah Ribon Olam - יה רבון עלם

> Composed by Rabbi Yisrael ben Moshe of Najara, student of the Arizal (16th century, Safed)

Yah ribon alam v'al'maya
ant hu malka melech malchaya.
Ovad g'vur'teich v'timhaya
sh'far kodamach l'hachavaya.
    Yah ribon alam v'al'maya
    ant hu malka melech
    malchaya.

G-d, Sovereign of all the Worlds, You are the Ruler, above all rulers. Your mighty deeds and wonders, it is beautiful to declare before You.

Sh'vachin asadeir tsafra v'ramsha
lach Ela-ha kadisha di v'ra kol nafsha,
irin kadishin uv'nei enasha,
cheivat b'ra, v'ofei sh'maya.
    Yah ribon alam...

I speak your praises both morning and evening, to You, Holy G-d, who created all Life: sacred spirits and human beings, beasts of the field and birds of the sky.

Rav'r'vin ov'deich v'takifin,
machich r'maya v'zakif k'fifin.
Lu yichyeh g'var sh'nin alfin
la yei'ol g'vur'teich b'chush'b'naya.
    Yah ribon alam...

Great and mighty are your deeds, humbling the proud and raising the humble. Even if one were to live a thousand years, he would not suffice to fathom Your might.

יָהּ רִבּוֹן עָלַם וְעָלְמַיָּא.
אַנְתְּ הוּא מַלְכָּא מֶלֶךְ מַלְכַיָּא.
עוֹבַד גְּבוּרְתֵּךְ וְתִמְהַיָּא.
שְׁפַר קָדָמָךְ לְהַחֲוַיָּא:
יָהּ רִבּוֹן עָלַם וְעָלְמַיָּא.
אַנְתְּ הוּא מַלְכָּא מֶלֶךְ
מַלְכַיָּא.

שְׁבָחִין אֲסַדֵּר צַפְרָא וְרַמְשָׁא.
לָךְ אֱלָהָא קַדִּישָׁא דִּי בְרָא כָל נַפְשָׁא.
עִירִין קַדִּישִׁין וּבְנֵי אֱנָשָׁא.
חֵיוַת בָּרָא וְעוֹפֵי שְׁמַיָּא:
יָהּ רִבּוֹן עָלַם...

רַבְרְבִין עוֹבְדָךְ וְתַקִּיפִין.
מָכִיךְ רְמַיָּא וְזַקִּיף כְּפִיפִין.
לוּ יִחְיֶה גְּבַר שְׁנִין אַלְפִין.
לָא יֵעוֹל גְּבוּרְתֵּךְ בְּחוּשְׁבְּנַיָּא:
יָהּ רִבּוֹן עָלַם...

Ela-ha di leih y'kar ur'vuta,
p'rok yat anach mipum ar'y'vata.
V'apeik yat amach migo galuta,
ameich di v'chart mikol umaya.
      Yah ribon alam...
O G-d, to whom glory and greatness belong, save Your flock from the lions' jaws. Bring Your people out of exile, the people You chose from all the nations.

L'mikdasheich tuv ul'kodesh kudshin,
atar di veih yechedun ruchin v'nafshin.
Vizam'run lach shirin v'rachashin,
bi'y'rush'leim karta d'shufraya. Yah ribon alam...
Return to Your Temple and to the Holy of Holies, the place where spirits and souls can rejoice. They will sing to You songs and melodies in Jerusalem, city of beauty.

אֱלָהָא דִי לֵיהּ יְקַר וּרְבוּתָא.
פְּרוֹק יַת עָנָךְ מִפּוּם אַרְיְוָתָא.
וְאַפֵּיק יַת עַמֵּךְ מִגּוֹ גָּלוּתָא.
עַמֵּךְ דִּי בְחַרְתְּ מִכָּל אֻמַּיָּא:
יָהּ רִבּוֹן עָלַם...

לְמִקְדָּשֵׁךְ תּוּב וּלְקֹדֶשׁ קוּדְשִׁין.
אֲתַר דִּי בֵיהּ יֶחֱדוּן רוּחִין וְנַפְשִׁין.
וִיזַמְּרוּן לָךְ שִׁירִין וְרַחֲשִׁין.
בִּירוּשְׁלֵם קַרְתָּא דְשׁוּפְרַיָּא:
יָהּ רִבּוֹן עָלַם...

Stories from the Maggid: *A Personal and Historical Testimony*

By Rabbi Shlomo Riskin

One of the great miracles of the last quarter of the twentieth century was the collapse of the Iron Curtain of the Soviet Union and the nearly one million Russian Jews who emigrated to Israel. There are many who maintain that the first and ultimately lethal blow against the Communist "Evil Empire" was dealt by the Soviet Jewish refuseniks, who refused to bow down to Communist atheism. Strangely enough, it was not until the early sixties that news of the horrific anti-Semitic oppression against Soviet Jews began to be publicised in the free world, and we (at that time I was chairman of the Center for Russian Jews) began to picket the consulate and the UN. Always sensitive to public relations, the Communist government dispatched Rav Levin, the Chief Rabbi of Moscow, to New York in June 1969, armed with a newly published Soviet edition of the Jewish prayer book, called The Siddur of Peace. The Rabbi was to demonstrate with this publication the Soviet dedication to the continuity of the Jewish religion and culture in the Soviet Union.

Rav Levin stayed in Essex House, where he held a private *minyan* (prayer quorum) each morning, which I attended. The "launch" of the new Soviet prayer book publication was to be that Sunday at the Hunter College auditorium. Since the synagogue closest to Essex House was my own fledgling (at the time) Lincoln Square Synagogue, I was introduced as the Rabbi of the neighbourhood, and Rav Levin invited me to breakfast with him that Friday morning.

The Rav had come to New York with two attendants, one of whom (underground rumour had it) was a KGB (Soviet Secret Police) agent sent to "spy" on his activities. Since I was active on behalf of demonstrations for Soviet Jews, I tried to use the breakfast to gain much-needed hard facts about their plight. "Are there synagogues in Russia? Day schools? Zionist organizations?" I queried. The Rav looked uncomfortable, glanced over at his attendant and answered by questions with counter-questions: "Are there synagogues in America? Day schools, Zionist organizations—in America?"

Seeing as I was getting nowhere, I decided to switch tactics. Knowing that Rav Levin had studied as a youth in the renowned Slobodka

Yeshiva, I asked about the curriculum of studies and the various personalities that had made the institution unique. Somewhere in the midst of his lengthy reply, the problematic attendant left the table for the bathroom. Suddenly, Rav Levin began to sing—at first in a whisper. He sang *Kah Ribon*—and when he reached the stanza, "G-d—to Whom our honour and greatness belong, Save Your sheep from the mouth of the lions…," his voice rose to a great crescendo and tears rolled down his cheeks. He sang these same words again and again as if they were a mantra, and his tears never stopped flowing. The spell was interrupted by the indignant voice of the attendant who had just exited from the bathroom, "It is not yet Shabbat, Rav Levin! What are you singing, Rav Levin?!"

The sage turned white, and then red. Clearly embarrassed, he mumbled that "the young Rabbi wanted to know how they sang *zemirot* (Shabbat songs) in Slobodka."

I excused myself from the breakfast table. Clearly the Rav couldn't speak—but he had told it all through the immortal words of *Kah Ribon*.

(From "Around the Family Table: Songs and Prayers for the Jewish Home With Insights and Commentary" by Rabbi Shlomo Riskin, Copyright 2005, Ohr Torah Stone and Urim Publications, Jerusalem, Israel. Reprinted with permission.)

Kah Echsof - יה אכסף

> Composed by the Holy Rebbe Aharon of Karlin

יָהּ אֶכְסֹף נֹעַם שַׁבָּת הַמַּתְאֶמֶת וּמִתְאַחֶדֶת בִּסְגֻלָּתֶךָ.
מְשֹׁךְ נֹעַם יִרְאָתְךָ לְעַם מְבַקְשֵׁי רְצוֹנֶךָ.
קַדְּשֵׁם בִּקְדֻשַּׁת הַשַּׁבָּת הַמִּתְאַחֶדֶת בְּתוֹרָתֶךָ.
פְּתַח לָהֶם נֹעַם וְרָצוֹן לִפְתּוֹחַ שַׁעֲרֵי רְצוֹנֶךָ:

יָהּ הֱוֵה שָׁמוֹר שׁוֹמְרֵי וּמְצַפִּים שַׁבַּת קָדְשֶׁךָ.
כְּאַיָּל תַּעֲרֹג עַל אֲפִיקֵי מָיִם
כֵּן נַפְשָׁם תַּעֲרֹג לְקַבֵּל נֹעַם שַׁבָּת הַמִּתְאַחֶדֶת בְּשֵׁם קָדְשֶׁךָ.
הַצֵּל מְאַחֲרֵי לִפְרשׁ מִן הַשַּׁבָּת לְבִלְתִּי תִּהְיֶה סָגוּר מֵהֶם.
שִׁשָּׁה יָמִים הַמְקַבְּלִים קְדֻשָּׁה מִשַּׁבַּת קָדְשֶׁךָ.
וְטַהֵר לִבָּם בֶּאֱמֶת וּבֶאֱמוּנָה לְעָבְדֶךָ:

וְיִהְיוּ רַחֲמֶיךָ מִתְגּוֹלְלִים עַל עַם קָדְשֶׁךָ.
לְהַשְׁקוֹת צְמֵאֵי חַסְדֶּךָ מִנָּהָר הַיּוֹצֵא מֵעֵדֶן.
לְעַטֵּר אֶת יִשְׂרָאֵל בְּתִפְאֶרֶת הַמְפָאֲרִים אוֹתְךָ עַל יְדֵי שַׁבַּת קָדְשֶׁךָ.
כָּל שִׁשָּׁה יָמִים לְהַנְחִילָם נַחֲלַת יַעֲקֹב בְּחִירֶךָ:

הַשַּׁבָּת נֹעַם הַנְּשָׁמוֹת.
וְהַשְּׁבִיעִי עֹנֶג הָרוּחוֹת.
וְעֵדֶן הַנְּפָשׁוֹת.
לְהִתְעַדֵּן בְּאַהֲבָתְךָ וְיִרְאָתֶךָ.
שַׁבָּת קוֹדֶשׁ נַפְשִׁי חוֹלַת אַהֲבָתֶךָ.
שַׁבָּת קוֹדֶשׁ נַפְשׁוֹת יִשְׂרָאֵל בְּצֵל כְּנָפֶיךָ יֶחֱסָיוּן.
יִרְוְיֻן מִדֶּשֶׁן בֵּיתֶךָ:

Tzur Mishelo - צור משלו

> *An introduction to Bircat HaMazon, following its pattern and beginning with a "Zimun" - invitation to bless.*

Tsur Mishelo Achalnu, Bar'chu Emunai, Sava'anu vehotarnu kidvar Ado-nai.

צוּר מִשֶּׁלּוֹ אָכַלְנוּ בָּרְכוּ אֱמוּנַי,
שָׂבַעְנוּ וְהוֹתַרְנוּ כִּדְבַר יְיָ.

Hazan et olamo roeinu avinu, achalnu et lachmo v'yeino shatinu, al kein nodeh lishmo unhal'lo b'finu, amarnu v'aninu ein kadosh k'Ado-nai.

הַזָּן אֶת עוֹלָמוֹ רוֹעֵנוּ אָבִינוּ,
אָכַלְנוּ אֶת לַחְמוֹ וְיֵינוֹ שָׁתִינוּ,
עַל כֵּן נוֹדֶה לִשְׁמוֹ וּנְהַלְלוֹ בְּפִינוּ,
אָמַרְנוּ וְעָנִינוּ אֵין קָדוֹשׁ כַּיְיָ.

Tsur Mishelo Achalnu, Bar'chu Emunai, Sava'anu vehotarnu kidvar Ado-nai.

צוּר מִשֶּׁלּוֹ אָכַלְנוּ בָּרְכוּ אֱמוּנַי,
שָׂבַעְנוּ וְהוֹתַרְנוּ כִּדְבַר יְיָ.

B'shir v'kol todah n'varech l'Eloheinu, al eretz chemdah tovah shehinchil lavoteinu. Mazon v'tzeidah hisbia l'nafsheinu, chasdo gavar aleinu v'emet Ado-nai.

בְּשִׁיר וְקוֹל תּוֹדָה נְבָרֵךְ לֵאלֹהֵינוּ,
עַל אֶרֶץ חֶמְדָּה טוֹבָה שֶׁהִנְחִיל לַאֲבוֹתֵינוּ,
מָזוֹן וְצֵדָה הִשְׂבִּיעַ לְנַפְשֵׁנוּ,
חַסְדּוֹ גָּבַר עָלֵינוּ וֶאֱמֶת יְיָ.

Tsur Mishelo Achalnu...

צוּר מִשֶּׁלּוֹ אָכַלְנוּ...

Rachem b'chasdecha al am'cha tsurein, al Tzion mishkan k'vodecha z'vul beit tifarteinu. Ben David avdecha yavo v'yig'aleinu, ruach apeinu m'shiach Ado-nai.

רַחֵם בְּחַסְדְּךָ עַל עַמְּךָ צוּרֵנוּ,
עַל צִיּוֹן מִשְׁכַּן כְּבוֹדֶךָ זְבוּל בֵּית תִּפְאַרְתֵּנוּ,
בֶּן דָּוִד עַבְדֶּךָ יָבוֹא וְיִגְאָלֵנוּ,
רוּחַ אַפֵּינוּ מְשִׁיחַ יְיָ.

Tsur Mishelo Achalnu...

צוּר מִשֶּׁלּוֹ אָכַלְנוּ...

Yibaneh hamikdah ir Tzion timaleh, v'sham nashir shir chadash uvirnanah na'aleh. Harachaman hanikdash yibarach v'yitalehal kos yayin maleh k'virkat Ado-nai.

יִבָּנֶה הַמִּקְדָּשׁ, עִיר צִיּוֹן תְּמַלֵּא,
וְשָׁם נָשִׁיר שִׁיר חָדָשׁ וּבִרְנָנָה נַעֲלֶה,
הָרַחֲמָן הַנִּקְדָּשׁ יִתְבָּרַךְ וְיִתְעַלֶּה,
עַל כּוֹס יַיִן מָלֵא כְּבִרְכַּת יְיָ.

Tsur Mishelo Achalnu...

צוּר מִשֶּׁלּוֹ אָכַלְנוּ...

The Rock, from whose food we have eaten, bless Him, my faithful! We have eaten enough and have left over, according to Hashem's word.

The Provider for His universe, our Shepherd, our Father, we have eaten His bread and drunk His wine. Therefore let us thank Him and speak His praise. We have said and have responded, "There is none as holy as Hashem!"

With song and sound of thanks, we will bless our G-d, for the good, desirable land, that He gave as a heritage to our forefathers. With nourishment and sustenance He has satisfied our souls, His kindness has overpowered us, and Hashem is true.

Be merciful in your kindness upon Your people, our Rock, upon Zion, the home of Your Glory, the House of our splendour. The son of David Your servant will come and redeem us, the breath of our life, the Mashiach of Hashem.

The Temple will be rebuilt, the City of Zion will be filled. There we will sing a new song, and ascend with joy. May the Merciful One, the Sanctified One, be blessed and exalted, over a cup filled with wine, according to Hashem's blessing.

Shabbos Day
יום שבת

*This section has been
generously sponsored by*

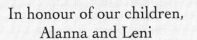

The Weisberg Family

In honour of our children,
Alanna and Leni

Shabbos Day Kiddush - קידוש רבא ליום שבת

☙ The daytime Kiddush was introduced by the Sages as a Rabbinic obligation, and its status is secondary to that of the nighttime Kiddush, which is Biblically mandated (Pesachim 106b). Therefore, it is euphemistically called "Kiddusha Raba," The Great Kiddush. It originally consisted solely of the blessing over wine, and the verses from Scripture were added over the centuries. There are many different customs regarding which passages are said. Some only say the last one, beginning with "Al kein." Either way, all customs sufficiently fulfill the Rabbinic obligation.

Kiddush is made around lunchtime, after the morning services. It is usually said in Shul. One who plans on discharging his Rabbinic obligation to make a daytime Kiddush then should eat some cake or cookies equal in volume to a slice of bread. This fulfills the ordinance of "Kiddush be'makom seudah" - Kiddush said in the place where one is eating a set meal.

Kiddush can also be said at home prior to lunch in order to discharge those who did not hear Kiddush in Shul from their obligation. Similar to the nighttime Kiddush, the cup should hold at least 4 1/2 ounces and wine or grape juice should be used. The person making Kiddush should sit or stand according to his family custom, and the others should sit or stand as the leader does.

Once Kiddush is said, those who were included in the blessing do not need to partake in the wine or grape juice (but may if they want to), as long as a "Seudah," a meal, is eaten. The procedure following Kiddush is the same as for Shabbos night: we wash our hands before eating the Challah and then make the Hamotzi blessing.

Shabbos Day

וְשָׁמְרוּ בְנֵי יִשְׂרָאֵל אֶת הַשַּׁבָּת. לַעֲשׂוֹת אֶת הַשַּׁבָּת לְדֹרֹתָם בְּרִית עוֹלָם: בֵּינִי וּבֵין בְּנֵי יִשְׂרָאֵל אוֹת הִיא לְעֹלָם כִּי שֵׁשֶׁת יָמִים עָשָׂה יְיָ אֶת הַשָּׁמַיִם וְאֶת הָאָרֶץ. וּבַיּוֹם הַשְּׁבִיעִי שָׁבַת וַיִּנָּפַשׁ:

V'sham'ru v'nei Yisrael et haShabbat, la'asot et haShabbat l'dorotam b'rit olam. Beini u'vein b'nei Yisrael ot hi l'olam, ki sheishet yamim asa Ado-nai et ha'shamayim v'et ha'aretz, u'va'yom ha'sh'vi'i shavat va'yinafash.

The Children of Israel shall observe the Sabbath, to make the Sabbath throughout their generations as an everlasting covenant. Between Me and the children of Israel, it is a sign forever that in six days Hashem created the heavens and the earth, and on the seventh He ceased and rested.

זָכוֹר אֶת יוֹם הַשַּׁבָּת לְקַדְּשׁוֹ. שֵׁשֶׁת יָמִים תַּעֲבֹד וְעָשִׂיתָ כָּל מְלַאכְתֶּךָ. וְיוֹם הַשְּׁבִיעִי שַׁבָּת לַייָ אֱלֹהֶיךָ לֹא תַעֲשֶׂה כָל מְלָאכָה אַתָּה וּבִנְךָ וּבִתֶּךָ עַבְדְּךָ וַאֲמָתְךָ וּבְהֶמְתֶּךָ וְגֵרְךָ אֲשֶׁר בִּשְׁעָרֶיךָ כִּי שֵׁשֶׁת יָמִים עָשָׂה יְיָ אֶת הַשָּׁמַיִם וְאֶת הָאָרֶץ אֶת הַיָּם וְאֶת כָּל אֲשֶׁר בָּם וַיָּנַח בַּיּוֹם הַשְּׁבִיעִי:

Zachor et yom haShabbat l'kad'sho. Sheishet yamim ta'avod v'asita kol m'lachtecha. V'yom ha'sh'vi'i Shabbat la'Adon-nai Elo-heicha, lo ta'aseh chol m'lacha ata u'vincha u'vitecha avd'cha va'amat'cha uvhem'techa v'geir'cha asher bish'arecha. Ki sheishet yamim asa Adonai et ha'shamayim v'et ha'aretz, et ha'yam v'et kol asher bam, va'yanach ba'yom ha'sh'vi'i.

Remember the Sabbath day to keep it holy. Six days you may work and perform all your labour, but the seventh day is a Sabbath to Hashem your G-d, you shall perform no labour, neither you, your son, your daughter, your manservant, your maidservant, your beast, nor your stranger who is in your gates. For in six days Hashem made the heaven and the earth, the sea and all that is in them, and He rested on the seventh day.

עַל כֵּן בֵּרַךְ יְיָ אֶת יוֹם הַשַּׁבָּת וַיְקַדְּשֵׁהוּ:

Al kein beirach Ado-nai et yom haShabbat va'ye'kad'sheihu.

Therefore Hashem blessed the Sabbath and made it holy.

סַבְרִי מָרָנָן וְרַבָּנָן וְרַבּוֹתַי:
בָּרוּךְ אַתָּה יְיָ אֱלֹהֵינוּ מֶלֶךְ הָעוֹלָם בּוֹרֵא פְּרִי הַגָּפֶן:

(Savri maranan ve'rabanan ve'rabotai)
Baruch Ata Ado-nai Elo-heinu Melech Ha'Olam, Borei p'ri ha'gafen.

(Permit me, distinguished ones, rabbis, and my teachers)
Blessed are You, Hashem our G-d, King of the Universe, Who creates the fuit of the vine.

Ritual Handwashing – נטילת ידים

▸ *Fill the washing cup to the top with water and hold it in your left hand. Pour the water over your right hand until the wrist. Then pour a second time on the same hand. Switch the cup to the right hand and pour twice over the left hand. Before drying your hands, recite the Beracha:*

בָּרוּךְ אַתָּה יְיָ אֱלֹהֵינוּ מֶלֶךְ הָעוֹלָם, אֲשֶׁר קִדְּשָׁנוּ בְּמִצְוֹתָיו וְצִוָּנוּ עַל נְטִילַת יָדַיִם.

Baruch Atah Ado-nai Elo-heinu Melech Ha'Olam, asher kid'shanu b'mitzvotav, v'tzivanu al netilat yada'im.

Blessed are You, Hashem our G-d, King of the Universe, Who has sanctified us with His commandments and has commanded us regarding washing the hands.

Blessing on the Bread – ברכת "המוציא"

▸ *Hold the two Challah loaves in both your hands, lift them up, and recite the Beracha:*

בָּרוּךְ אַתָּה יְיָ אֱלֹהֵינוּ מֶלֶךְ הָעוֹלָם הַמּוֹצִיא לֶחֶם מִן הָאָרֶץ.

Baruch Atah Ado-nai Elo-heinu Melech Ha'Olam, ha'motzi lechem min ha'aretz.

Blessed are You, Hashem our G-d, King of the Universe, Who brings forth bread from the earth.

▸ *Cut the Challahs and dip the bread in salt. The person who made the Beracha should eat first, so as not to pass over a Mitzvah. The bread should then be distributed to everyone at the table.*

Baruch Kel Elyon – ברוך אל עליון

Composed by Rabbi Baruch ben Shmuel, one of the Tosafists (13th century; Mainz, Germany).

Baruch Eil elyon asher natan m'nucha,	בָּרוּךְ אֵל עֶלְיוֹן אֲשֶׁר נָתַן מְנוּחָה.
L'nafsheinu fidyom misheit va'anacha.	לְנַפְשֵׁנוּ פִּדְיוֹם מִשֵּׁאת וַאֲנָחָה.
V'hu yidrosh l'Tziyon ir hanidacha.	וְהוּא יִדְרוֹשׁ לְצִיּוֹן עִיר הַנִּדָּחָה.
Ad ana tug'yon nefesh ne'enacha?	עַד אָנָה תּוּגְיוֹן נֶפֶשׁ נֶאֱנָחָה:
Hashomer Shabbat, habein im habat, la'Eil yeiratsu k'mincha al machavat.	הַשּׁוֹמֵר שַׁבָּת הַבֵּן עִם הַבַּת לָאֵל יֵרָצוּ כְּמִנְחָה עַל מַחֲבַת:

Rocheiv ba'aravot, melech olamim,
Et amo lishbot izein ban'imim.
B'ma'achalot areivot, b'minei mat'amim,
B'malbushei kavod zevach mishpacha.
Hashomer Shabbat…

רוֹכֵב בָּעֲרָבוֹת מֶלֶךְ עוֹלָמִים.
אֶת עַמּוֹ לִשְׁבּוֹת אִזֵּן בַּנְּעִימִים.
בְּמַאֲכָלֵי עֲרֵבוֹת בְּמִינֵי מַטְעַמִּים.
בְּמַלְבּוּשֵׁי כָבוֹד זֶבַח מִשְׁפָּחָה:
הַשּׁוֹמֵר שַׁבָּת…

V'ashrei kol chocheh l'tashlumei keifel,
Mei'eit kol socheh shochein ba'arafel.
Nachala lo yizkeh bahar uvashafel,
Nachala um'nucha, kashemesh lo zar'cha.
Hashomer Shabbat…

וְאַשְׁרֵי כָּל חוֹכֶה לְתַשְׁלוּמֵי כֶפֶל.
מֵאֵת כָּל סוֹכֶה שׁוֹכֵן בָּעֲרָפֶל.
נַחֲלָה לוֹ יִזְכֶּה בָּהָר וּבַשָּׁפֶל.
נַחֲלָה וּמְנוּחָה כַּשֶּׁמֶשׁ לוֹ זָרְחָה:
הַשּׁוֹמֵר שַׁבָּת…

Kol shomer Shabbat kadat meichal'lo,
Hein hechsheir chibat kodesh goralo.
V'im yatsa chovat hayom ashrei lo,
El Eil adon m'chol'lo mincha hi sh'lucha.
Hashomer Shabbat…

כָּל שׁוֹמֵר שַׁבָּת כַּדָּת מֵחַלְּלוֹ.
הֵן הֶכְשֵׁר חִבַּת קֹדֶשׁ גּוֹרָלוֹ.
וְאִם יָצָא חוֹבַת הַיּוֹם אַשְׁרֵי לוֹ.
אֶל אֵל אָדוֹן מְחוֹלְלוֹ. מִנְחָה הִיא שְׁלוּחָה:
הַשּׁוֹמֵר שַׁבָּת…

Chemdat hayamim k'ra'o Eili tsur,
V'ashrei litmimim im yih'ye natsur.
Keter hilumim al rosham yatsur,
Tsur ha'olamim rucho bam nacha.
Hashomer Shabbat...

חֶמְדַּת הַיָּמִים. קְרָאוֹ אֵלִי צוּר.
וְאַשְׁרֵי לִתְמִימִים. אִם יִהְיֶה נָצוּר.
כֶּתֶר הִלּוּמִים. עַל רֹאשָׁם יָצוּר.
צוּר הָעוֹלָמִים רוּחוֹ בָּם נָחָה:
הַשּׁוֹמֵר שַׁבָּת...

Zachor et yom haShabbat l'kad'sho,
karno ki gav'ha neizer al rosho.
Al kein yitein ha'adam l'nafsho
oneg v'gam simcha, bahem lo l'mosh'cha.
Hashomer Shabbat...

זָכוֹר אֶת יוֹם הַשַּׁבָּת לְקַדְּשׁוֹ
קַרְנוֹ כִּי גָבְהָה נֵזֶר עַל רֹאשׁוֹ.
עַל כֵּן יִתֵּן הָאָדָם לְנַפְשׁוֹ
עוֹנֶג וְגַם שִׂמְחָה בָּהֶם לְמָשְׁחָה:
הַשּׁוֹמֵר שַׁבָּת...

Kodesh hi lachem Shabbat hamalka,
el toch bateichem l'haniach b'racha.
B'chol mosh'voteichem lo ta'asu m'lacha,
b'neichem uv'noteichem, eved v'gam shifcha.
Hashomer Shabbat...

קוֹדֶשׁ הִיא לָכֶם שַׁבָּת הַמַּלְכָּה.
אֶל תּוֹךְ בָּתֵּיכֶם לְהָנִיחַ בְּרָכָה.
בְּכָל מוֹשְׁבוֹתֵיכֶם לֹא תַעֲשׂוּ מְלָאכָה.
בְּנֵיכֶם וּבְנוֹתֵיכֶם עֶבֶד וְגַם שִׁפְחָה:
הַשּׁוֹמֵר שַׁבָּת...

Blessed is the exalted G-d, Who gave rest for our souls, a respite from calamity and woe. He will seek out Zion, the rejected city. How long will You torment a sighing soul? Those who keep the Sabbath, the sons and the daughters, are as pleasing to G-d as a meal-offering on a fire pan.

He Who rides among the willows, Ruler of Worlds, decreed with kindness that G-d's people should rest, with pleasant foods and assorted delicacies, with elegant clothing and a family feast.

Praiseworthy are those who hope for the double reward from He Who sees all, Who dwells in the heavens. G-d has set aside for them an inheritance of hills and valleys, inheritance and rest shining for them like the sun.

Whoever keeps the Sabbath properly from desecrating it, deserves that love of holiness be his lot. And he who fulfills the obligation of the day is praiseworthy. To G-d, the Master Who fashioned him, it is sent as an offering.

"Remember the Sabbath day to make it holy." When its honour is raised, one merits a diadem on his head. For this reason, let each man provide for himself delight and also gladness with which to anoint.

Favourite of the days, my God, my Rock, called it. Happy are the innocent, if they are within it; a diamond crown shall be made on their heads. Rock of worlds, His Spirit rested in them.

Holy is she for you, the Sabbath Queen; [welcome her] into the midst of your homes to deposit blessing. In all your dwellings do not do work, your sons and daughters, the slave and also the maidservant.

Yom Zeh Mechubad – יום זה מכבד

Yom Zeh M'chubad Mikol yamim, ki vo shavat tsur olamim.
Sheishet yamim ta'ase m'lachtecha,
V'yom ha'sh'vi'i l'Elo-hecha,
Shabbat lo ta'ase vo m'lacha
Ki chol asah sheshet yamim.
    Yom Zeh M'chubad Mikol ysamim, ki vo shavat tsur olamim.

Rishon hu l'mikra'ei kodesh,
Yom Shabbaton yom Shabbat kodesh,
Al kein kol ish b'yeino y'kadesh
al shtei lechem yivtz'u t'mimim.
    Yom Zeh M'chubad...

Echol mashmanim shteh mamtakim
ki El yiten l'chol bo d'vekim,
beged lilbosh, lechem chukim
basar v'dagim v'chol mat'amim.
    Yom Zeh M'chubad...

Lo techsar kol bo v'achalta v'savata,
Uverachta et Ado-nai Elo-hecha asher ahavta,
Ki verach'cha mikol ha'amim.
    Yom Zeh M'chubad...

Hashamayim m'sap'rim k'vodo,
V'gam ha'aretz mal'ah chasdo,
R'u ki kol eleh astah yado
Ki hu hatsur po'alo tamim.
    Yom Zeh M'chubad...

יוֹם זֶה מְכֻבָּד מִכָּל יָמִים.
כִּי בוֹ שָׁבַת צוּר עוֹלָמִים:
שֵׁשֶׁת יָמִים תַּעֲשֶׂה מְלַאכְתֶּךָ.
וְיוֹם הַשְּׁבִיעִי לֵאלֹהֶיךָ.
שַׁבָּת לֹא תַעֲשֶׂה בוֹ מְלָאכָה.
כִּי כל עָשָׂה שֵׁשֶׁת יָמִים:
יוֹם זֶה מְכֻבָּד מִכָּל יָמִים. כִּי בוֹ שָׁבַת צוּר עוֹלָמִים:

רִאשׁוֹן הוּא לְמִקְרָאֵי קוֹדֶשׁ.
יוֹם שַׁבָּתוֹן יוֹם שַׁבַּת קוֹדֶשׁ.
עַל כֵּן כָּל אִישׁ בְּיֵינוֹ יְקַדֵּשׁ.
עַל שְׁתֵּי לֶחֶם יִבְצְעוּ תְמִימִים:
יוֹם זֶה מְכֻבָּד...

אֱכוֹל מַשְׁמַנִּים שְׁתֵה מַמְתַּקִּים.
כִּי אֵל יִתֵּן לְכֹל בּוֹ דְבֵקִים.
בֶּגֶד לִלְבּוֹשׁ לֶחֶם חֻקִּים.
בָּשָׂר וְדָגִים וְכָל מַטְעַמִּים:
יוֹם זֶה מְכֻבָּד...

לֹא תֶחְסַר כֹּל בּוֹ וְאָכַלְתָּ וְשָׂבָעְתָּ.
וּבֵרַכְתָּ אֶת יְיָ אֱלֹהֶיךָ אֲשֶׁר אָהַבְתָּ.
כִּי בֵרַכְךָ מִכָּל הָעַמִּים:
יוֹם זֶה מְכֻבָּד...

הַשָּׁמַיִם מְסַפְּרִים כְּבוֹדוֹ.
וְגַם הָאָרֶץ מָלְאָה חַסְדּוֹ.
רְאוּ כִּי כָל אֵלֶּה עָשְׂתָה יָדוֹ.
כִּי הוּא הַצּוּר פָּעֳלוֹ תָמִים:
יוֹם זֶה מְכֻבָּד...

This day is honoured from among all days, for on it rested the Rock of the universe. Six days you may do your work, but the Seventh day belongs to G-d. The Sabbath: do not do on it any work, for everything He completed in six days.

First it is of the holy convocations, a day of rest, the day of the holy Sabbath. For this reason let every man with his wine recite Kiddush, and over two loaves of bread, let them break whole loaves.

Eat rich foods, drink sweet wines, for G-d will give to all who cling to Him clothes to wear and bread of allotment to eat, meat and fish and all delicacies.

You will not lack anything on it; you will eat and be satisfied, and you will bless Hashem your G-d, Whom you love, for He has blessed you beyond all nations.

The heavens declare His glory, and also the earth is full of his kindness. Percieve that all these did His hand make, for He is the Rock Whose work is perfect.

Ki Eshmerah Shabbat – כי אשמרה שבת

Composed by Rabbi Avraham Ibn Ezra (12th century, Spain).

Ki Eshm'rah Shabbat El Yishm'reini, Ot hi l'ol'mei Ad Beino uveini.

כִּי אֶשְׁמְרָה שַׁבָּת אֵל יִשְׁמְרֵנִי. אוֹת הִיא לְעוֹלְמֵי עַד בֵּינוֹ וּבֵינִי

Asur m'tsa chefetz, asot d'rachim,
Gam mil'daber bo divrei ts'rachim,
Divrei s'chora af divrei m'lachim,
Eh'geh b'torat El ut'chak'meini.
    Ot hi l'ol'mei Ad Beino uveini.

אָסוּר מְצֹא חֵפֶץ עֲשׂוֹת דְּרָכִים
גַּם מִלְּדַבֵּר בּוֹ דִּבְרֵי צְרָכִים.
דִּבְרֵי סְחוֹרָה אַף דִּבְרֵי מְלָכִים
אֶהְגֶּה בְּתוֹרַת אֵל וּתְחַכְּמֵנִי:
אוֹת הִיא לְעוֹלְמֵי עַד בֵּינוֹ וּבֵינִי

Bo emtsa tamid nofesh le'nafshi,
Henei le'dor rishon natan kedoshi,
Mofet, be'tet lechem mishneh ba'shishi,
Kacha be'chol shishi yachpil mezoni.
    Ot hi...

בּוֹ אֶמְצָא תָמִיד נֹפֶשׁ לְנַפְשִׁי
הִנֵּה לְדֹר רִאשׁוֹן נָתַן קְדוֹשִׁי.
מוֹפֵת בְּתֵת לֶחֶם מִשְׁנֶה בַּשִּׁשִּׁי
כָּכָה בְּכָל שִׁשִּׁי יַכְפִּיל מְזוֹנִי:
אוֹת הִיא לְעוֹלְמֵי עַד בֵּינוֹ וּבֵינִי

Rasham be'dat ha'El chok el seganav,
Bo la'aroch lechem panim be'fanav,
Al ken lehitanot bo al pi nevonav,
Asur levad mi'yom kipur avoni.
    Ot hi...

רָשַׁם בְּדַת הָאֵל חֹק אֶל סְגָנָיו
בּוֹ לַעֲרֹךְ לֶחֶם פָּנִים בְּפָנָיו.
עַל כֵּן לְהִתְעַנּוֹת בּוֹ עַל פִּי נְבוֹנָיו
אָסוּר, לְבַד מִיּוֹם כִּפּוּר עֲוֹנִי:
אוֹת הִיא לְעוֹלְמֵי עַד בֵּינוֹ וּבֵינִי

Hu yom mechubad, hu yom ta'anugim.
Lechem ve'yayin tov, basar ve'dagim.
Ha'mitab'lim bo achor nesogim
Ki yom semachot hu, ut'samecheni.
    Ot hi...

הוּא יוֹם מְכֻבָּד הוּא יוֹם תַּעֲנוּגִים
לֶחֶם וְיַיִן טוֹב בָּשָׂר וְדָגִים.
הַמִּתְאַבְּלִים בּוֹ אָחוֹר נְסוֹגִים
כִּי יוֹם שְׂמָחוֹת הוּא וּתְשַׂמְּחֵנִי:
אוֹת הִיא לְעוֹלְמֵי עַד בֵּינוֹ וּבֵינִי

Mechel melacha bo, sofo lehachrit,
Al ken achabes bo libi kevorit.
Ve'etpalela el El ar'vit ve'shacharit,
Musaf ve'gam mincha hu ya'aneini.
    Ot hi...

מֵחֵל מְלָאכָה בּוֹ סוֹפוֹ לְהַכְרִית
עַל כֵּן אֲכַבֵּס בּוֹ לִבִּי כְּבוֹרִית.
וְאֶתְפַּלְלָה אֶל אֵל עַרְבִית וְשַׁחֲרִית
מוּסָף וְגַם מִנְחָה הוּא יַעֲנֵנִי:
אוֹת הִיא לְעוֹלְמֵי עַד בֵּינוֹ וּבֵינִי

Because I guard the Sabbath, G-d guards me. It is a sign for eternity between Him and me.

It is forbidden to seek to do regular things;
Discussing only what is necessary,
Not words of business, not even words of politics.
I study G-d's Torah, and it makes me wise.
Because I guard the Sabbath, G-d guards me. It is a sign for eternity between Him and me.

On Shabbat, I always find rest for my soul,
Behold, He gave the first generation holiness.
From the miraculous giving of the double loaves of bread on Friday;
Thus on every Friday He doubles my portion.
Because I guard the Sabbath, G-d guards me. It is a sign for eternity between Him and me.

It is written in G-d's Torah, a portion to His priests
The display bread is laid out for him,
Therefore, to fast on Shabbat, in accordance with His sages,
Is forbidden; only on the day of atonement do I fast.
Because I guard the Sabbath, G-d guards me. It is a sign for eternity between Him and me.

It is a day of honour, it is a day of pleasure,
Good bread and wine, meat and fish.
Those who mourn on Shabbat, cease
Because it is a day of joy, and I am made joyful.
Because I guard the Sabbath, G-d guards me. It is a sign for eternity between Him and me.

He who labours on Shabbat will be destroyed in the end.
Therefore I wash my heart on Shabbat as if with lye,
And I pray to G-d, evening and morning prayers,
The additional prayer and also the afternoon prayer; He answers me.
Because I guard the Sabbath, G-d guards me. It is a sign for eternity between Him and me.

Yom Shabbaton – יום שבתון

> Composed by Rabbi Yehudah HaLevi, one of the most famous Payatanim and author of "Kuzari" (12th century, Spain)

Yom Shabbaton ein lishko'ach, Zichro k'rei'ach hanicho'ach, Yonah matz'ah vo mano'ach V'sham yanuchu ye'gi'ei ko'ach.	יוֹם שַׁבָּתוֹן אֵין לִשְׁכּוֹחַ. זִכְרוֹ כְּרֵיחַ הַנִּיחוֹחַ: יוֹנָה מָצְאָה בּוֹ מָנוֹחַ. וְשָׁם יָנוּחוּ יְגִיעֵי כֹחַ:
Yonah matz'ah vo mano'ach v'sham yanuchu y'giei choach.	
Hayom nichbad livnei emunim Z'hirim l'shomro avot uvanim, Chakuk bishnei luchot avanim, Merov onim v'amitz ko'ach.	הַיּוֹם נִכְבָּד לִבְנֵי אֱמוּנִים. זְהִירִים לְשָׁמְרוֹ אָבוֹת וּבָנִים. חָקוּק בִּשְׁנֵי לוּחוֹת אֲבָנִים. מֵרוֹב אוֹנִים וְאַמִּיץ כֹּחַ.
Yonah matz'ah vo mano'ach…	יוֹנָה מָצְאָה בּוֹ…
Uva'u chulam bivrit yachad, Na'aseh v'nishma amru k'echad, Ufat'chu v'anu Ado-nai echad, Baruch hanotein laya'ef ko'ach.	וּבָאוּ כֻלָּם בִּבְרִית יַחַד. נַעֲשֶׂה וְנִשְׁמַע אָמְרוּ כְּאֶחָד. וּפָתְחוּ וְעָנוּ יְיָ אֶחָד. בָּרוּךְ הַנּוֹתֵן לַיָּעֵף כֹּחַ.
Yonah matz'ah vo mano'ach…	יוֹנָה מָצְאָה בּוֹ…
Diber b'kodsho b'har hamor, Yom hash'vi'i zachor v'shamor, V'chol pikudav yachad ligmor Chazak motna'im v'ametz ko'ach.	דִּבֶּר בְּקָדְשׁוֹ בְּהַר הַמּוֹר. יוֹם הַשְּׁבִיעִי זָכוֹר וְשָׁמוֹר. וְכָל פִּקּוּדָיו יַחַד לִגְמוֹר. חַזֵּק מָתְנַיִם וְאַמֵּץ כֹּחַ.
Yonah matz'ah vo mano'ach…	יוֹנָה מָצְאָה בּוֹ…
Ha'am asher na katzon ta'ah, Yizkor l'fokdo bivrit ushvua, L'val ya'avor bam mikrei ra'ah, Ka'asher nishba'ata al mei No'ach.	הָעָם אֲשֶׁר נָע כַּצֹּאן טָעָה. יִזְכּוֹר לְפָקְדוֹ בִּבְרִית וּשְׁבוּעָה. לְבַל יַעֲבוֹר בָּם מִקְרֵי רָעָה. כַּאֲשֶׁר נִשְׁבַּעְתָּ עַל מֵי נֹחַ.
Yonah matz'ah vo mano'ach…	יוֹנָה מָצְאָה בּוֹ…

The day of rest should not be forgotten; its memory is like a pleasing aroma. The dove found rest that day, and there shall rest those of exhausted strength.

This day is honoured by those who are faithful, who are scrupulous to safegaurd it, parents and children. [It is] engraved in the two Tablets of stone, from the One with abundant potency and vigourous strength.

And all of them joined together in a covenant, "We will do and we will listen," they said as one. They opened and called out, "Hashem is One." Blessed is He who gives strength to the exhausted.

He declared, in His holiness, at the mountain of myrrh: "The Seventh day, remember and safegaurd!" And all His precepts should equally be studied. Strengthen your loins and gather your strength.

The people that wanders, like sheep that have gone astray, may He remember to invoke them for His covenant and oath, that there not pass among them an evil incident, as You swore over the Waters of Noach.

Shabbos Day

Dror Yikra – דרור יקרא

Composed by Donash ben Labrat, grammarian and Paytan (10th century, Baghdad)

D'ror yikra l'ven im bat, v'yintzorchem k'mo vavat, n'im shimchem v'lo yushbat, sh'vu v'nuchu b'yom Shabbat.	דְּרוֹר יִקְרָא לְבֵן עִם בַּת. וְיִנְצָרְכֶם כְּמוֹ בָבַת. נְעִים שִׁמְכֶם וְלֹא יוּשְׁבַּת. שְׁבוּ וְנוּחוּ בְּיוֹם שַׁבָּת.
D'rosh navi v'ulami, v'ot yesha aseh imi, n'ta sorek b'toch karmi, sh'e shav'at b'nei ami.	דְרוֹשׁ נָוִי וְאוּלְמִי וְאוֹת יֶשַׁע עֲשֵׂה עִמִּי נְטַע שׂוֹרֵק בְּתוֹךְ כַּרְמִי שְׁעֵה שַׁוְעַת בְּנֵי עַמִּי.
D'roch purah b'toch Botzrah, v'gam Bavel asher gavrah, n'totz tzarai b'af v'evrah, sh'ma koli b'yom ekra.	דְּרוֹךְ פּוּרָה בְּתוֹךְ בָּצְרָה. וְגַם בָּבֶל אֲשֶׁר גָּבְרָה. נְתוֹץ צָרַי בְּאַף וְעֶבְרָה. שְׁמַע קוֹלִי בְּיוֹם אֶקְרָא.
Elo-him ten b'midbar har, hadas shitah b'rosh tid'har, v'lamaz'hir v'laniz'har, sh'lomim ten k'mei nahar.	אֱלֹהִים תֵּן בַּמִּדְבָּר הַר הֲדַס שִׁטָּה בְּרוֹשׁ תִּדְהָר וְלַמַּזְהִיר וְלַנִּזְהָר. שְׁלוֹמִים תֵּן כְּמֵי נָהָר.
Hadoch kamai, El kanah, b'mog levav uvamginah, v'narchiv peh un'malenah, l'shonenu l'cha rinah.	הֲדוֹךְ קָמַי אֵל קַנָּא בְּמוֹג לֵבָב וּבַמְגִינָה וְנַרְחִיב פֶּה וּנְמַלְאֶנָּה לְשׁוֹנֵנוּ לְךָ רִנָּה.
D'eh chochmah l'nafshecha, v'hi cheter l'roshecha, n'tzor mitzvat k'doshecha, sh'mor Shabbat kodshecha.	דְּעֵה חָכְמָה לְנַפְשֶׁךָ וְהִיא כֶתֶר לְרֹאשֶׁךָ. נְצוֹר מִצְוַת קְדוֹשֶׁיךָ. שְׁמוֹר שַׁבַּת קָדְשֶׁךָ:

He will proclaim freedom for all His sons and daughters
And will keep you as the apple of His eye.
Pleasant is your name and will not be destroyed;
Repose and rest on the Sabbath day.

Seek my sanctuary and my home.
Give me a sign of deliverance.
Plant a vine in my vineyard.
Look to my people, hear their laments.

Tread the wine-press in Bozrah,
And in Babylon, that city of might.
Crush my enemies in anger and fury.
Hear my voice on the day that I cry.

Plant, Oh G-d, in the mountain's wasteland
Fir and acacia, myrtle and elm.
To those who teach and to those who obey
Give peace, like the flow of a river.

Repel my enemies, Oh zealous G-d.
Fill their hearts with fear and despair.
Then we shall open our mouths,
And fill our tongues with Your praise.

Know wisdom for your soul,
And it shall be a diadem for your brow.
Keep the commandment of your Holy One;
Observe the Sabbath, your sacred day.

Seudah Shlishit
סעודה שלישית

Introduction to Seudah Shlishit

By Zachary Zarnett-Klein

As Shabbat draws to a close, we are commanded to eat the third and final meal of the day. Seudah Shlishit, literally translated as "the third meal," is usually not as elaborate as the other two meals of Shabbat, to show our sadness that Shabbat is leaving us. On the same note, it is customary to sing slow songs after the meal, to show our sadness that Shabbat will soon end.

If one is so full from lunch that he feels he cannot enjoy Seudah Shlishit, he is exempt from the meal. The purpose of Seudah Shlishit is Oneg Shabbat, and if one cannot enjoy the meal, he is not doing justice to this commandment. Of course, one should try one's best to ensure that this does not occur; one should attempt not to be too full from lunch to partake in Seudah Shlishit.

Women are also obligated to perform this mitzvah. Why, you may ask? The first reason is that women are commanded equally in the mitzvah of Shabbat as men are. Another reason is that women were equal recipients of the double portion of Manna that was given on Friday for Friday and Shabbat, and they are therefore obligated to partake in Seudah Shlishit as well.

A key part of Seudah Shlishit is to do the mitzvah with a special kind of Kavana, and eat the meal while keeping in mind that, by doing so, one is successfully completing the commandment of eating three meals on Shabbat.

Seudah Shlishit may be eaten starting at the beginning of Minchah time, which is half a "Halachic hour" after noon. The meal may be eaten as late as one wishes, as long as one begins eating within the time that one is allowed to pray Minchah.

It is customary to sing zmirot such as Mizmor L'David and Y'did Nefesh in a slow fashion, since they express the love that Israel shows toward Shabbat and the sadness we experience as it goes away.

Learning Torah is also a key part of the meal, and it is customary for Divrei Torah to be shared during Seudah Shlishit. As Shabbat winds down, the songs and words of Torah are what carry us through the long week ahead. They allow us to remain happy as Shabbat leaves, because we know that it will come back next week.

Seudah Shlishit should not be overlooked. We should endeavour to treat all three Shabbat meals equally, and partake in meaningful and spiritual Seudot Shlishiot.

Ritual Handwashing – נטילת ידים

❧ *Fill the washing cup to the top with water and hold it in your left hand. Pour the water over your right hand until the wrist. Then pour a second time on the same hand. Switch the cup to the right hand and pour twice over the left hand. Before drying your hands, recite the Beracha:*

בָּרוּךְ אַתָּה יְיָ אֱלֹהֵינוּ מֶלֶךְ הָעוֹלָם, אֲשֶׁר קִדְּשָׁנוּ בְּמִצְוֹתָיו וְצִוָּנוּ עַל נְטִילַת יָדַיִם.

Baruch Atah Ado-nai Elo-heinu Melech Ha'Olam, asher kid'shanu b'mitzvotav, v'tzivanu al netilat yada'im.

Blessed are You, Hashem our G-d, King of the Universe, Who has sanctified us with His commandments and has commanded us regarding washing the hands.

Blessing on the Bread – ברכת "המוציא"

❧ *Hold the two Challah loaves in both your hands, lift them up, and recite the Beracha:*

בָּרוּךְ אַתָּה יְיָ אֱלֹהֵינוּ מֶלֶךְ הָעוֹלָם הַמּוֹצִיא לֶחֶם מִן הָאָרֶץ.

Baruch Atah Ado-nai Elo-heinu Melech Ha'Olam, ha'motzi lechem min ha'aretz.

Blessed are You, Hashem our G-d, King of the Universe, Who brings forth bread from the earth.

A tkinu Seudata - אתקינו סעודתא

> The following two Zemirot were composed by the Arizal (Ari HaKadosh), Rabbi Yitzchak Luria.

אַתְקִינוּ סְעוּדָתָא דִמְהֵימְנוּתָא שְׁלֵמָתָא חֶדְוָתָא דְמַלְכָּא קַדִישָׁא: אַתְקִינוּ סְעוּדָתָא דְמַלְכָּא. דָא הִיא סְעוּדָתָא, דִזְעֵיר אַנְפִּין, וְעַתִּיקָא קַדִישָׁא וַחֲקַל תַּפּוּחִין קַדִישִׁין אַתְיָן לְסַעֲדָא בַּהֲדֵיה.

Atkinu se'udata di'm'heim'nutah shleimatah, chedvatah d'malka kadisha. Atkinu se'udata d'malka, da hi se'udata diz'eir anpin. V'atika kadisha va'chakal tapuchin kadishin at'yan l'sa'adah ba'hadeih.

Prepare the feast of perfect faith, the joy of the Holy King. Prepare the feast of the King; this is the feast of the Miniature Presence, and the Ancient Holy One and the Field of Sacred Apples come to feast with it.

Bnei Heichalah - בני היכלא

בְּנֵי הֵיכָלָא דִכְסִיפִין. לְמֶחֱזֵי זִיו דִזְעֵיר אַנְפִּין:
יְהוֹן הָכָא. בְּהַאי תַּכָּא. דְבֵיה מַלְכָּא בְּגִלוּפִין:
צְבוּ לַחֲדָא. בְּהַאי וַעֲדָא. בְּגוֹ עִירִין וְכָל גַדְפִין:
חֲדוּ הַשְׁתָּא. בְּהַאי שַׁעֲתָא. דְבֵיה רַעֲוָא וְלֵית זַעֲפִין:
קְרִיבוּ לִי. חֲזוּ חֵילִי. דְלֵית דִינִין דִתְקִיפִין:
לְבַר נַטְלִין. וְלָא עָאלִין. הַנָךְ כַּלְבִּין דַחֲצִיפִין:
וְהָא אַזְמִין. עַתִּיק יוֹמִין. לְמִצְחָא עֲדֵי יְהוֹן חַלְפִין:
רְעוּ דִילֵה. דְגַלֵי לֵיה. לְבַטָלָא בְּכָל קַלִיפִין:
יְשַׁוֵי לוֹן. בְּנוֹקְבֵיהוֹן. וִיטַמְרוּן בְּגוֹ כֵפִין:
אֲרֵי הַשְׁתָּא. בְּמִנְחָתָא. בְּחֶדְוָתָא דִזְעֵיר אַנְפִּין:

B'nei heichalah, di'chsifin, l'mechezei ziv diz'eir anpin.
Ye'hon hachah, b'hai takah, d'bei malka b'gilufin.
Tz'vu la'chadah, b'hai va'adah, b'go irin v'chol gad'fin.
Chadu hashta, b'hai sha'tah, d'bei ra'avah v'leit za'afin.
Krivu li, chazu cheili, d'leit dinin ditkifin.
L'var natlin, v'lo a'lin, hanach kalbin da'chatzifin.

V'ha azmin, atik yomin, l'mitzchah adei ye'hon chalfin.
R'u dilei, d'galei lei, l'vatalah b'chol ka'lifin.
Ye'shavei lon, b'nokveihon, vi'tamrun b'go cheifin.
Arei hashtah, b'minchata, b'chedvatah diz'eir anpin.

Members of the Sanctuary, who yearn to see the splendour of the Miniature Presence. May they be here at this table, on which the King is inscribed. They desire intensely to join in this assembly, among the angels and all the winged beings. Be exultant now, at this time, in which there is favour, and no anger. Approach Me, see My strength, when there are no strict judgements. Let them camp outside, and not enter, those brazen dogs. Behold, I invite the One of Ancient Days at Minchah, the time when they will fade away. His will, when He reveals it, is to negate all shells. May He place them in their holes and let them hide among the rocks. Because now, at Minchah time, it is the exultation of the Miniature Presence.

Mizmor L'David - מזמור לדוד

Tehilim (Psalms) 23

מִזְמוֹר לְדָוִד. יְיָ רֹעִי לֹא אֶחְסָר: בִּנְאוֹת דֶּשֶׁא יַרְבִּיצֵנִי. עַל מֵי מְנוּחוֹת יְנַהֲלֵנִי: נַפְשִׁי יְשׁוֹבֵב. יַנְחֵנִי בְמַעְגְּלֵי צֶדֶק לְמַעַן שְׁמוֹ: גַּם כִּי אֵלֵךְ בְּגֵיא צַלְמָוֶת לֹא אִירָא רָע. כִּי אַתָּה עִמָּדִי. שִׁבְטְךָ וּמִשְׁעַנְתֶּךָ הֵמָּה יְנַחֲמֻנִי: תַּעֲרֹךְ לְפָנַי שֻׁלְחָן נֶגֶד צֹרְרָי: דִּשַּׁנְתָּ בַשֶּׁמֶן רֹאשִׁי כּוֹסִי רְוָיָה: אַךְ טוֹב וָחֶסֶד יִרְדְּפוּנִי כָּל יְמֵי חַיָּי. וְשַׁבְתִּי בְּבֵית יְיָ לְאֹרֶךְ יָמִים:

Mizmor l'David, Hashem ro'i lo echsar. Bin'ot desheh yarbitzeini, al mei m'nuchot ye'nahaleini. Nafshi ye'shovev yancheini b'ma'g'lei tzedek l'ma'an sh'mo. Gam ki eileich b'gei tzalmavet, lo ira ra ki ata imadi. Shivt'cha u'mishantecha hema ye'nachamuni. Ta'aroch l'fanai shulchan neged tzor'rai, dishanta vashemen roshi, cosi r'vayah. Ach tov va'chesed yird'funi kol ye'mei chayai v'shavti b'veit Hashem l'orech yamim.

A song of David. Hashem is my shepherd; I shall not want. He causes me to lie down in green pastures; He leads me beside still waters. He restores my soul; He leads me in paths of righteousness for His name's sake. Even when I walk in the valley of death's shadow, I will fear no evil, for You are with me. Your rod and Your staff -- they comfort me. You set up a table before me in the presence of my enemies. You anointed my head with oil; my cup overflows. May only goodness and kindness pursue me all the days of my life, and I will dwell in the house of Hashem for length of days.

Yedid Nefesh – ידיד נפש

> Composed by Rabbi Eliezer Azkiri, the great Kabbalist and Paytan (16th century, Eretz Yisrael)

Ye'did nefesh av harachaman,
M'shoch avd'cha el r'tzonecha.
Yarutz avd'cha k'mo ayal,
Yishtachave el mul hadarecha.
Ye'erav lo ye'didutecha,
Minofet tsuf v'chol ta'am.

Hadur na'eh ziv ha'olam,
Nafshi cholat ahavatecha.
Anah El nah r'fah nah lah,
B'harot lah no'am zivecha,
Az tit'chazek v'titrapeh,
V'hay'tah lah shifchat olam.

Vatik yehemu nah rachamecha
V'chusa na al ben ahuvecha.
Ki zeh kamah nichsof nichsafti,
Lir'ot b'tiferet uzecha.
Anah Eili, machmad libi,
Chushah nah v'al titalam.

Higaleh nah uf'ros chavivi alai,
Et sukkat sh'lomecha
Ta'ir eretz mik'vodecha,
Nagilah v'nismechah bach.
Maher ahuv, ki va mo'ed,
v'chaneini kimei olam.

יְדִיד נֶפֶשׁ אָב הָרַחֲמָן.
מְשׁוֹךְ עַבְדְּךָ אֶל רְצוֹנֶךָ.
יָרוּץ עַבְדְּךָ כְּמוֹ אַיָּל.
יִשְׁתַּחֲוֶה אֶל מוּל הֲדָרֶךָ.
יֶעֱרַב לוֹ יְדִידוֹתֶיךָ
מִנוֹפֶת צוּף וְכָל טָעַם:

הָדוּר נָאֶה זִיו הָעוֹלָם.
נַפְשִׁי חוֹלַת אַהֲבָתֶךָ.
אָנָּא אֵל נָא רְפָא נָא לָהּ.
בְּהַרְאוֹת לָהּ נֹעַם זִיוֶךָ.
אָז תִּתְחַזֵּק וְתִתְרַפֵּא.
וְהָיְתָה לָהּ שִׁפְחַת עוֹלָם:

וָתִיק יֶהֱמוּ נָא רַחֲמֶיךָ.
וְחוּסָה נָּא עַל בֵּן אֲהוּבֶךָ.
כִּי זֶה כַּמָּה נִכְסוֹף נִכְסַפְתִּי
לִרְאוֹת בְּתִפְאֶרֶת עֻזֶּךָ.
אָנָא אֵלִי מַחְמַד לִבִּי.
חוּשָׁה נָּא וְאַל תִּתְעַלָּם:

הִגָּלֶה נָא וּפְרוֹס חֲבִיבִי עָלַי
אֶת סֻכַּת שְׁלוֹמֶךָ.
תָּאִיר אֶרֶץ מִכְּבוֹדֶךָ.
נָגִילָה וְנִשְׂמְחָה בָּךְ.
מַהֵר אָהוּב כִּי בָא מוֹעֵד
וְחָנֵּנִי כִּימֵי עוֹלָם:

Seudah Shlishit

Lover of my soul, merciful G-d, bring Your servant close to Your will. Your servant will run like a gazelle, to prostrate before Your glory. For Your companionship is more pleasing than any fine taste or flavour.

Perfect, pleasing, radiance of the world, my soul desires Your love. Please, G-d, heal her now, as You show her the pleasantness of Your light. Now, strengthen and heal her, and she will be for You an eternal servant.

Ancient One, many Your mercies be made manifest, and have compassion on the child of Your lover. For it is so long that I have faithfully waited, to see the glory of Your strength. Please, my G-d, the desire of my heart, hurry and do not hide!

Please, reveal Yourself and spread over me, my beloved, the shelter of Your peace. Light the world with Your glory, so that we may rejoice and be happy in You. Be quick, my lover, for the time has come, and have mercy on me for all time.

The Time In-Between

By Becky Friedman

Judaism sets great store by separation and differentiation. In our Friday night Kiddush, we thanked G-d for "choosing us out of all the other nations," and our prayers are full of references to the Jewish people being separate from the other peoples. And, just as G-d separated us, we keep our holy days separate from the rest of the year, and Shabbos Kodesh separate from the rest of the week. We separate the beginning of Shabbat from Friday by lighting the Shabbos candles; likewise, we separate the end of Shabbat from the new week with fire: the Havdala ceremony.

By now, it is dark; Havdala, just over an hour after the Friday night candle-lighting time, traditionally takes place after the stars appear in the sky. The special Havdala candle, with its multiple intertwined wicks, acts as a torch against the darkness, starkly contrasting the sedate Shabbat candles; we begin Havdala with the bold statement that we trust in G-d and have no fear.

Havdala is, indeed, a queer time, hovering as it does on the edge between the mundane and the holy. Before we begin, it is still Shabbat; once we finish, it will be simply Saturday night. In between, we have those precious few moments of something else, of Havdala-time, a torch flickering against the darkness.

We are sad to be ending Shabbat, but the words of Havdala hardly reflect that. We recite psukim that denote our trust in G-d and verses proclaiming joy for the Jewish people. We may feel bittersweet about bidding farewell to the Shabbat Queen until a week from now, but we are determined to make our happy moods last, at least until after Havdala-time.

Shabbat, as we know, is a day of rest: we could see it as the "good night's sleep" to the rest of the week's "working day". What, then, is Havdala, hovering on the edge between the two? Havdala is the time of waking up. We do not want to wake up from a pleasant dream, but know that we must, to start our day; so, too, we do not wish to wake up from Shabbat, but we perform Havdala anyway, to start our working week.

The Besamim, spices, are our answer to the question of how to wake up from Shabbat. No one wants to be jolted out of sleep with the beeping of an alarm clock. Instead, we are gently wafted into wakefulness with the fragrance of the spices, strong but sweet, until we are ready to face the week with our dreams-- our memories of the Shabbat that is ending-- preserved in our minds.

There are four blessings to the Havdala ceremony. The first three are for the physical things we use in the ceremony, the wine, the spices, and the flame. The fourth and final blessing is of a different, more abstract sort, and this leads straight to the crux of Havdala.

In the fourth blessing, we talk about separation and differentiation: Havdala. We praise G-d for His differentiation between the holy and the mundane, between the light and the darkness, between Yisrael and the other nations, and between Shabbat and the six days of the work week.

Why are these specific examples given? The last one is easy; that is what we are directly dealing with. So, too, with the first; we are separating the holy Shabbat from the mundane week. The third is easily explained, for, as mentioned earlier, the separation of the Jewish nation is a prevailing theme throughout our prayers and literature. What, then, about the remaining differentiation, between the light and the darkness?

Shabbat is a time of spiritual light. We start Shabbat by lighting candles, and-- though they eventually burn out-- spiritually, the candles stay lit throughout Shabbat. But now, it has gone dark, both inside and out; the stars have appeared and the greyness of the work week looms over us. As soon as we conclude this final blessing, we will douse the Havdala candle, plunging the room into darkness until someone can reach the light switch.

Havdala-time is a special time of the week. We no longer have the light of Shabbos shining upon us, but the shadow of the work week does not cover us yet. Havdala-time hovers on the edge between holy and mundane, between light and darkness. It is, itself, neither light nor dark.

Havdala is our chance to bid a formal farewell to the Shabbat Queen. It is a time of opposites and contradiction; feeling bittersweet, we express our uncorrupted joy. It is symbolized by a cup of wine, an ornate spice box.

And a torch, flickering against the darkness.

Havdalah - הבדלה

Shabbos ends when three medium-sized stars are visible plainly in the evening sky. In North America, this is generally one hour and ten minutes after the candle-lighting time. It is imperative, however, to follow the exact times for the end of Shabbos as delineated in Jewish calenders or websites. Once Shabbos has passed, one can recite the following words in order to engage in regular weekday activities: ברוך המבדיל בין קודש לחול - Baruch ha'mavdil bein kodesh le'chol - Blessed is the One Who divides between the sacred and the mundane. Another separation between Shabbos and Chol is found in the Ma'ariv (evening) prayer service after Shabbos, in a special insertion in the Amidah prayer. Both of these prayers formally end Shabbos and allow one to do "work." There remains, however, a requirement to make Havdalah over wine or grape juice.

Havdalah is a Mitzvah from the Torah, derived from the commandment to "Remember the Sabbath," which is also the source of the Mitzvah of Kiddush on Shabbos night. The Rambam explains that "remembering" entails making a verbal differentiation between Shabbos and all other days. The ceremony of Havdalah is a sharp distinction between the great holiness of Shabbos Kodesh and the rest of the week, and one should be conscious of their differences in order to truly appreciate the most awesome day that has just passed.

The ceremony requires a cup of wine or grape juice, a double-wicked candle (or two candles held together), and spices. It consists of five sections: **1)** Verses from Isaiah, Psalms, and the Book of Esther. **2)** The blessing over wine. **3)** The blessing over spices. The Talmud tells us that we each receive an extra soul on Shabbos. As Shabbos leaves, so does that soul. The aroma of the spices are meant to comfort our soul for the loss of its heightened spirituality on Shabbos. **4)** The blessing over the flame. The Talmud (Pesachim 54a) teaches that Hashem gave Adam HaRishon the gift of fire on Motzei Shabbos (Saturday night). For that reason, we say the blessing "Who creates the illuminations of fire." As with all blessings, we must benefit from the thing for which we are thanking Hashem. As such, we hold our fingers up to the flame and inspect the light on our fingernails. **5)** The Havdalah blessing, the verbal distinction between the holiness of Shabbos Kodesh and the rest of the week.

◌‿ *Havdalah* ‿◌

Fill a Kiddush cup with wine or grape juice until the liquid overflows, to symbolize that the blessings of Shabbos should overflow into the coming week. Light the Havdalah candle and have someone other than the person making the blessing hold it. If this is not possible, put the candle in a holder. One should stand or sit according to one's custom. All others should respond "Amen" at the conclusion of each blessing. When you are ready to begin Havdalah, pick up the Kiddush cup in your right hand and begin with the verses below.

הִנֵּה אֵל יְשׁוּעָתִי אֶבְטַח וְלֹא אֶפְחָד: כִּי עָזִּי וְזִמְרָת יָהּ יְיָ. וַיְהִי לִי לִישׁוּעָה: וּשְׁאַבְתֶּם מַיִם בְּשָׂשׂוֹן. מִמַּעַיְנֵי הַיְשׁוּעָה: לַיְיָ הַיְשׁוּעָה. עַל עַמְּךָ בִרְכָתֶךָ סֶּלָה: יְיָ צְבָאוֹת עִמָּנוּ. מִשְׂגָּב לָנוּ אֱלֹהֵי יַעֲקֹב סֶלָה: יְיָ צְבָאוֹת. אַשְׁרֵי אָדָם בֹּטֵחַ בָּךְ: יְיָ הוֹשִׁיעָה. הַמֶּלֶךְ יַעֲנֵנוּ בְיוֹם קָרְאֵנוּ:

Hineh El yeshu'ati evtach ve'lo efchad. Ki ozi ve'zimrat Ya Ado-nai, va'ye'hee li li'shu'ah. U'shavtem mayim b'sason mi'ma'ai'nei ha'ye'shu'ah. La'Ado-nai ha'ye'shu'ah al am'cha vircha'techa selah. Ado-nai tz'va'ot imanu, misgav lanu Elo-hei Ya'akov selah. Ado-nai tz'va'ot ashrei adam botei'ach bach. Ado-nai hoshi'ah ha'melech ya'aneinu b'yom kar'einu.

Behold, G-d is my salvation; I shall trust and not fear. For my might and my praise is G-d, Hashem, and He was for me a salvation. You will draw water in joy from the springs of salvation. To Hashem is salvation, upon your people is Your blessing, Selah. Hashem, Master of Legions, is with us, a stronghold for us is the G-d of Jacob, Selah. Hashem, Master of Legions, praiseworthy is the man who trusts in You. Hashem, save us! The King will answer us on the day that we call.

❧ *The leader reciting Havdalah pauses. All others should say the following verse in unison. The leader repeats:*

לַיְּהוּדִים הָיְתָה אוֹרָה וְשִׂמְחָה וְשָׂשׂוֹן וִיקָר. כֵּן תִּהְיֶה לָּנוּ: כּוֹס יְשׁוּעוֹת אֶשָּׂא. וּבְשֵׁם יְיָ אֶקְרָא:

111

La'ye'hudim hay'ta ora v'simcha v'sason vi'kar. Kein ti'h'yeh lanu. Kos ye'shu'ot esa, u'v'sheim Ado-nai ekra.

The Jews had light, gladness, joy, and honour. So may it be for us! I shall lift up a cup of salvations, and I shall call out in the name of Hashem.

סַבְרִי מָרָנָן וְרַבָּנָן וְרַבּוֹתַי:
בָּרוּךְ אַתָּה יְיָ אֱלֹהֵינוּ מֶלֶךְ הָעוֹלָם. בּוֹרֵא פְּרִי הַגָּפֶן:

(Savri maranan v'rabanan v'rabotai)
Baruch Ata Ado-nai Elo-heinu Melech Ha'Olam, Borei p'ri ha'gafen.

(Permit me, distinguished ones, rabbis, and my teachers)
Blessed are You, Hashem our G-d, King of the Universe, Who creates the fuit of the vine.

> Pass the cup to your left hand and pick up the spices with your right. Recite the following blessing before smelling the spices. When done, pass them around for all to smell.

בָּרוּךְ אַתָּה יְיָ אֱלֹהֵינוּ מֶלֶךְ הָעוֹלָם. בּוֹרֵא מִינֵי בְשָׂמִים:

Baruch Ata Ado-nai Elo-heinu Melech Ha'Olam, Borei min'ai v'samim.

Blessed are You, Hashem our G-d, King of the Universe, Who creates fragrant species.

> With the wine cup in your left hand, recite the blessing over the fire. When done, everyone should extend their hands toward the flame and inspect their fingernails.

בָּרוּךְ אַתָּה יְיָ אֱלֹהֵינוּ מֶלֶךְ הָעוֹלָם. בּוֹרֵא מְאוֹרֵי הָאֵשׁ:

Havdalah

Baruch Ata Ado-nai Elo-heinu Melech Ha'Olam, Borei m'orei ha'eish.

Blessed are You, Hashem our G-d, King of the Universe, Who creates the light of fire.

> *Return the cup to your right hand and conclude:*

בָּרוּךְ אַתָּה יְיָ אֱלֹהֵינוּ מֶלֶךְ הָעוֹלָם. הַמַּבְדִּיל בֵּין קֹדֶשׁ לְחֹל. בֵּין אוֹר לְחֹשֶׁךְ. בֵּין יִשְׂרָאֵל לָעַמִּים. בֵּין יוֹם הַשְּׁבִיעִי לְשֵׁשֶׁת יְמֵי הַמַּעֲשֶׂה: בָּרוּךְ אַתָּה יְיָ. הַמַּבְדִּיל בֵּין קֹדֶשׁ לְחֹל:

Baruch ata Ado-nai Elo-heinu melech ha'olam, ha'mavdil bein kodesh l'chol, bein ohr l'choshech, bein Yisrael la'amim, bein yom ha'shevi'i l'sheishet ye'mei ha'ma'aseh. Baruch ata Ado-nai, ha'mavdil bein kodesh l'chol.

Blessed are You, Hashem, our G-d, King of the universe, Who separates between the sacred and the secular, between light and darkness, between Israel and the nations, between the Seventh day and the six days of work. Blessed are You, Hashem, Who separates between sacred and secular.

> *The leader sits down and drinks the majority of the wine or grape juice. The rest of the liquid is used to extinguish the flame. This demonstrates that the candle was kindled solely for the Mitzvah of Havdalah. After the candle has been extinguished, many have the custom of dipping a finger into the spilled liquid and running the finger across one's forehead, just above the eyes. This custom is rooted in the verse, "The command of Hashem is clear, enlightening the eyes" (Psalms 19:9). Even the leftovers of the Mitzvah of Havdalah can brighten our eyes for the coming week. After Havdalah, many sing "Eliyahu Ha'Navi" or other Zemirot. It is traditional to wish everyone "Shavuah Tov" or "A Gut Voch," meaning "A good week."*

Bircat HaMazon
ברכת המזון

This section has been generously sponsored by

The Hoffman Family

Introduction to Bircat HaMazon

By Gabriel Hoffman

Bircat Hamazon is the prayer said after eating a meal that included bread. The terms 'benching' and 'Grace after Meals' are synonyms for the name of this prayer. Bircat Hamazon is the Hebrew name for the prayer, literally meaning "blessing of the food." Benching is the Yiddish name for blessing, and Grace after Meals is the English way of saying Bircat Hamazon. One is obligated to say this blessing if he ate and was satisfied, as it says in Devarim (Deuteronomy 8:10): "And you will eat and be sated, and you shall bless the Lord, your God, for the good land He has given you."

This prayer is recited after one finishes a meal in which he ate a "kezayit" of bread. Eating a kezayit refers to eating an olive-sized portion. These are the approximate portions:

TYPE OF BREAD:	SIZE OF SLICE:
White bread	one-third of a slice (8 grams)
Rye bread	half a center slice (10 grams)
Bagel	10% of an average size bagel (13 grams)
Matzah	slightly less than half of a standard machine matzah (15 grams)

Bircat Hamazon consists of four brachot. Each bracha thanks Hashem for something different, and they were thought of by different people, at different times. The first bracha is attributed to Moshe, and thanks Hashem for the food that He has given to all creatures, including us. Moshe made this bracha once the manna came down from Heaven.

Yehoshua (Joshua) made the second bracha in two parts. First he thanks Hashem for taking us out of Egypt and for the giving us the Torah. In the second part, he thanks Hashem for the land of Israel. He wrote this part once he had entered the land of Israel.

The third bracha begs Hashem to have mercy on Am Yisrael and asks to rebuild the Beit Hamikdash (Holy Temple) soon. King David wrote that bracha, after he was crowned. The part about the Beit Hamikdash was added after the building of the first one.

In the fourth bracha, we praise Hashem for many aspects of His goodness. Rabban Gamliel wrote that beracha, in Yavneh.

The people mentioned only structured these brachot. The "Anshei Knesset Hagdolah," the same people who wrote the daily prayers, wrote the actual text.

This is not all there is to the prayer. In certain cases, special additions are said. On any day, if three or more men (over the age of 13) have eaten together, a few lines are added before benching. Those lines are called the "Zimmun," and those lines invite other people to bench with them. If there are ten men, then a few words are added to the zimmun, and the name changes to "Zimun B'shem."

On Shabbat, we add a paragraph called *R'tzei*, and on holidays (such as Rosh Chodesh, Passover, Shavuot, Rosh Hashanah, Succoth, Shmini Ateret, and Simchat Torah), we add a paragraph called *Ya'aleh V'Yavo*. On Chanukah and Purim, we add a prayer called *Al Ha'Nissim*. In that prayer, we thank Hashem for the miracles that He made for us in those times.

Blessing After Meals - ברכת המזון

שִׁיר הַמַּעֲלוֹת בְּשׁוּב יְיָ אֶת שִׁיבַת צִיּוֹן הָיִינוּ כְּחֹלְמִים. אָז יִמָּלֵא שְׂחוֹק פִּינוּ וּלְשׁוֹנֵנוּ רִנָּה אָז יֹאמְרוּ בַגּוֹיִם הִגְדִּיל יְיָ לַעֲשׂוֹת עִם אֵלֶּה. הִגְדִּיל יְיָ לַעֲשׂוֹת עִמָּנוּ הָיִינוּ שְׂמֵחִים. שׁוּבָה יְיָ אֶת שְׁבִיתֵנוּ כַּאֲפִיקִים בַּנֶּגֶב. הַזֹּרְעִים בְּדִמְעָה בְּרִנָּה יִקְצֹרוּ. הָלוֹךְ יֵלֵךְ וּבָכֹה נֹשֵׂא מֶשֶׁךְ הַזָּרַע בֹּא יָבוֹא בְרִנָּה נֹשֵׂא אֲלֻמֹּתָיו.

Shir ha'ma'alot, beshuv Ado-nai et shivat Tzion hayinu ke'cholmim. Az yimalei s'chok pinu u'l'shoneinu rinah az yomru va'goyim higdil Ado-nai la'asot im eileh. Higdil Ado-nai la'asot imanu hayinu s'meichim. Shuvah Ado-nai et sh'viteinu ka'afikim ba'negev. Ha'zor'im b'dimah b'rinah yiktzoru. Haloch yeileich u'vachoh nosei meshech ha'zara, bo yavo ve'rinah nosei alumotav.

Song on the steps: When Hashem returned the returnees of Tzion, we were as dreamers. Then laughter fulled our mouths and our tongues were filled with joy; then they said among the nations, "Hashem has done great things with these." Hashem has done great things with us; we were happy. Return, Hashem, our return, like streams in the Negev. Those who planted in tears will reap in joy. He will walk along and weeping, carrying the bundle of seeds; he will come back in joy, carrying his sheaves.

At this point, we wash Mayim Achronim. Spill a little bit of water over your right fingers and then your left. Once everyone is finished, continue below:

If three or more people ate together, they make a Zimun. The Leader (Mezamen) starts:

רַבּוֹתַי, נְבָרֵךְ!
Rabotai nevareich.
Honoured fellows, let's bless.

All respond, followed by the Leader:

יְהִי שֵׁם יְיָ מְבֹרָךְ מֵעַתָּה וְעַד עוֹלָם.

Yehi sheim Ado-nai m'vorach mei'atah ve'ad olam.

Hashem's name shall be blessed now and always.

Leader:

בִּרְשׁוּת מָרָנָן וְרַבָּנָן וְרַבּוֹתַי, נְבָרֵךְ (*If ten men are present* - אֱלֹהֵינוּ) שֶׁאָכַלְנוּ מִשֶּׁלוֹ.

Birehut maranan v'rabanan v'rabotai, n,vareich (If ten men are present - Elo-heinu) she'achalnu mishelo

With the permission of [the master of the house, etc.] the honoured people present, let's bless (our G-d,) He from Whose we have eaten.

All respond:

בָּרוּךְ (אֱלֹהֵינוּ) שֶׁאָכַלְנוּ מִשֶּׁלוֹ וּבְטוּבוֹ חָיִינוּ.

Baruch (Elo-heinu) she'achalnu mishelo uv'tuvo chayinu.

Blessed is (our G-d,) He from Whose we have eaten and in Whose good we have lived.

Leader:

בָּרוּךְ (אֱלֹהֵינוּ) שֶׁאָכַלְנוּ מִשֶּׁלוֹ וּבְטוּבוֹ חָיִינוּ.

Baruch (Elo-heinu) she'achalnu mishelo uve'tuvo chayinu.

Blessed is (our G-d,) He from Whose we have eaten and in Whose good we have lived.

All:

בָּרוּךְ הוּא וּבָרוּךְ שְׁמוֹ.

Baruch Hu u'varuch sh'mo.

Blessed is He and blessed is His name.

בָּרוּךְ אַתָּה יְיָ אֱלֹהֵינוּ מֶלֶךְ הָעוֹלָם הַזָּן אֶת הָעוֹלָם כֻּלּוֹ בְּטוּבוֹ בְּחֵן בְּחֶסֶד וּבְרַחֲמִים, הוּא נֹתֵן לֶחֶם לְכָל-בָּשָׂר כִּי לְעוֹלָם חַסְדּוֹ וּבְטוּבוֹ הַגָּדוֹל תָּמִיד לֹא חָסַר לָנוּ וְאַל יֶחְסַר לָנוּ מָזוֹן לְעוֹלָם וָעֶד בַּעֲבוּר שְׁמוֹ הַגָּדוֹל כִּי הוּא אֵל זָן וּמְפַרְנֵס לַכֹּל וּמֵטִיב לַכֹּל וּמֵכִין מָזוֹן לְכָל-בְּרִיּוֹתָיו אֲשֶׁר בָּרָא בָּרוּךְ אַתָּה יְיָ הַזָּן אֶת הַכֹּל.

Baruch ata Ado-nai, Elo-heinu melech ha'olam, ha'zan et ha'olam kulo b'tuvo b'chein b'chesed uv'rachamim hu notein lechem l'chol basar, ki l'olam chasdo. Uv'tuvo ha'gadol tamid lo chasar lanu v'al yech'sar lanu mazon l'olam va'ed. Ba'avur sh'mo ha'gadol ki hu El zan u'm'farneis la'kol u'meitiv la'kol u'meichin mazon l'chol b'riyotav asher bara. Baruch ata Ado-nai, ha'zan et ha'kol.

Blessed are You, Hashem, our G-d, King of the world, Who nourishes all the world in His goodness, with favour, with kindness, and with mercy; He gives bread to all flesh, for his kindness lasts forever. And in His great goodness, He has never deprived us, and He will never deprive us, nourishment, forever and always, for His great name, for He is G-d Who nourishes and provides for all and is good to all, and prepares nourishment for all His creatures that He created. Blessed are You Hashem, Who nourishes all.

נוֹדֶה לְךָ יְיָ אֱלֹהֵינוּ עַל שֶׁהִנְחַלְתָּ לַאֲבוֹתֵינוּ אֶרֶץ חֶמְדָּה טוֹבָה וּרְחָבָה וְעַל שֶׁהוֹצֵאתָנוּ יְיָ אֱלֹהֵינוּ מֵאֶרֶץ מִצְרַיִם וּפְדִיתָנוּ מִבֵּית עֲבָדִים וְעַל בְּרִיתְךָ שֶׁחָתַמְתָּ בִּבְשָׂרֵנוּ וְעַל תּוֹרָתְךָ שֶׁלִּמַּדְתָּנוּ וְעַל חֻקֶּיךָ שֶׁהוֹדַעְתָּנוּ וְעַל חַיִּים חֵן וָחֶסֶד שֶׁחוֹנַנְתָּנוּ, וְעַל אֲכִילַת מָזוֹן שָׁאַתָּה זָן וּמְפַרְנֵס אוֹתָנוּ תָּמִיד, בְּכָל יוֹם וּבְכָל עֵת וּבְכָל שָׁעָה.

Nodeh l'cha Ado-nai Elo-heinu al she'hinchalta la'avoteinu eretz chemdah tovah u'r'chavah v'al she'hotzeitanu Ado-nai Elo-heinu mei'eretz mitzrayim u'f'ditanu mi'beit avadim, v'al b'rit'cha she'chatamta bi'v'sareinu, v'al Torat'cha she'limad'tanu, v'al chukecha she'hodatanu, v'al chayim chein va'chesed she'chonantanu, v'al achilat mazon sha'ata zan u'm'farneis otanu tamid b'chol yom uv'chol eit uv'chol sha'ah.

she'chonantanu, v'al achilat mazon sha'ata zan u'm'farneis otanu tamid b'chol yom uv'chol eit uv'chol sha'ah.

We will thank You, Hashem, our G-d, for bequeathing to our fathers a choice land, good and wide, and for taking us, Hashem, our G-d, from the land of Egypt, and redeeming us from the house of slaves, and for Your covenant that You signed with our flesh, and for Your Torah that You taught us, and for Your laws that You made known to us, and for lives of favour and kindness that You granted us, and for the consumption of the nourishment with which You nourish and provide us always, every day and every moment and every hour.

On **Chanukah**, recite "Al HaNissim" below:

(וֹ)עַל הַנִּסִּים וְעַל הַפֻּרְקָן וְעַל הַגְּבוּרוֹת וְעַל הַתְּשׁוּעוֹת וְעַל הַמִּלְחָמוֹת שֶׁעָשִׂיתָ לַאֲבוֹתֵינוּ בַּיָּמִים הָהֵם בַּזְּמַן הַזֶּה.

(V')Al ha'nisim v'al ha'purkan v'al ha'g'vurot v'al ha't'shuot v'al ha'milchamot she'asita la'avoteinu ba'yamim ha'heim ba'zman hazeh.

For the miracles, and for the redemption, and for the heroics, and for the salvations, and for the wars, that You did for our fathers, in those days, in this time.

בִּימֵי מַתִּתְיָהוּ בֶּן יוֹחָנָן כֹּהֵן גָּדוֹל חַשְׁמוֹנַאי וּבָנָיו. כְּשֶׁעָמְדָה מַלְכוּת יָוָן הָרְשָׁעָה עַל עַמְּךָ יִשְׂרָאֵל לְהַשְׁכִּיחָם תּוֹרָתֶךָ וּלְהַעֲבִירָם מֵחֻקֵּי רְצוֹנֶךָ: וְאַתָּה בְּרַחֲמֶיךָ הָרַבִּים עָמַדְתָּ לָהֶם בְּעֵת צָרָתָם. רַבְתָּ אֶת רִיבָם. דַּנְתָּ אֶת דִּינָם. נָקַמְתָּ אֶת נִקְמָתָם. מָסַרְתָּ גִּבּוֹרִים בְּיַד חַלָּשִׁים. וְרַבִּים בְּיַד מְעַטִּים. וּטְמֵאִים בְּיַד טְהוֹרִים. וּרְשָׁעִים בְּיַד צַדִּיקִים. וְזֵדִים בְּיַד עוֹסְקֵי תוֹרָתֶךָ. וּלְךָ עָשִׂיתָ שֵׁם גָּדוֹל וְקָדוֹשׁ בְּעוֹלָמֶךָ. וּלְעַמְּךָ יִשְׂרָאֵל עָשִׂיתָ תְּשׁוּעָה גְדוֹלָה וּפֻרְקָן כְּהַיּוֹם הַזֶּה: וְאַחַר כֵּן בָּאוּ בָנֶיךָ לִדְבִיר בֵּיתֶךָ. וּפִנּוּ אֶת הֵיכָלֶךָ. וְטִהֲרוּ אֶת מִקְדָּשֶׁךָ. וְהִדְלִיקוּ נֵרוֹת בְּחַצְרוֹת קָדְשֶׁךָ. וְקָבְעוּ שְׁמוֹנַת יְמֵי חֲנֻכָּה אֵלּוּ. לְהוֹדוֹת וּלְהַלֵּל לְשִׁמְךָ הַגָּדוֹל.

Bimei Matityahu ben Yochanan Kohen Gadol Chashmonai u'vanav - ke'she'amdah malchut yavan ha'rasha'ah al amcha Yisrael le'hosha'ki'cham Toratach u'le'ha'aviram mei'chukei retzonach -

Biy'mei Matit'yahu ben Yochanan Kohen Gadol Chashmona'ai u'vanav - k'she'amdah malchut yavan ha'r'sha'ah al am'cha Yisrael l'hash'ki'cham Toratecha u'l'ha'aviram mei'chukei r'tzonecha - v'atah b'rachamecha ha'rabim amad'ta la'hem b'eit tzaratam ravta et rivam danta et dinam nakamta et nikmatam. Masarta giborim b'yad chalashim v'rabim b'yad me'atim u'tmei'im b'yad t'horim u'r'sha'im e'yad tzadikim v'zeidim b'yad oskei Toratecha. L'cha asita sheim gadol v'kadosh b'olamecha, u'l'am'cha Yisrael asita t'shu'ah g'dolah u'furkan k'ha'yom ha'zeh, v'achar kein ba'u vaneicha li'dvir beitecha u'finu et heichalccha v'tiharu et mikdashecha v'hidliku neirot b'chatzrot kod'shecha v'kav'u sh'monat ye'mei Chanukah eilu l'hodot u'l'halel l'shimcha ha'gadol.

In the days of Matityahu son of Yochanan the High Priest, the Hasmonean, and his sons, the evil kingdom of Yavan stood against Your people Israel, to make them forget Your Torah, and to bring them away from Your chosen laws; and You, in Your infinite mercy, stood with them in their time of trouble. You fought their fight, You judged their judgement, You avenged their revenge, You delivered the strong into the hand of the weak, and the many into the hand of the few, and the impure into the hand of the pure, and the evil into the hand of the righteous, and the wicked into the hand of those who deal with Your Torah. And You made for Yourself a great and holy name in Your world, and for Your people Israel you made a great salvation and redemption that very day. And after that, Your children came to the sanctuary of Your House, and they opened Your Temple, and they purified Your holy place, and they lit the candles in Your holy courtyards and designated these eight days of Chanuka, to thank and praise Your great name.

וְעַל הַכֹּל יְיָ אֱלֹהֵינוּ אֲנַחְנוּ מוֹדִים לָךְ וּמְבָרְכִים אוֹתָךְ, יִתְבָּרַךְ שִׁמְךָ בְּפִי כָּל חַי תָּמִיד לְעוֹלָם וָעֶד, כַּכָּתוּב: "וְאָכַלְתָּ וְשָׂבָעְתָּ, וּבֵרַכְתָּ אֶת יְיָ אֱלֹהֶיךָ עַל הָאָרֶץ הַטּוֹבָה אֲשֶׁר נָתַן לָךְ". בָּרוּךְ אַתָּה יְיָ, עַל הָאָרֶץ וְעַל הַמָּזוֹן.

V'al ha'kol Ado-nai Elo-heinu anachnu modim lach u'm'varchim otach yitbarach shimcha b'fi kol chai tamid l'olam va'ed. Ka'katuv, v'achalta v'savata u'veirachta et Ado-nai Elo-hecha al ha'aretz ha'tovah asher natan lach. Baruch atah Ado-nai, al ha'aretz v'al ha'mazon.

And for everything, Hashem, our G-d, we thank You, and bless You, that Your name be blessed by the mouth of every living thing, forever and always, as it is written, "You shall eat and you shall be sated, and you shall bless Hashem, your G-d, for the good land that He gave you." Blessed are You, Hashem, for the land and for the nourishment.

רַחֶם נָא יְיָ אֱלֹהֵינוּ עַל יִשְׂרָאֵל עַמֶּךָ, וְעַל יְרוּשָׁלַיִם עִירֶךָ, וְעַל צִיּוֹן מִשְׁכַּן כְּבוֹדֶךָ, וְעַל מַלְכוּת בֵּית דָּוִד מְשִׁיחֶךָ, וְעַל הַבַּיִת הַגָּדוֹל וְהַקָּדוֹשׁ שֶׁנִּקְרָא שִׁמְךָ עָלָיו. אֱלֹהֵינוּ, אָבִינוּ, רְעֵנוּ, זוּנֵנוּ, פַּרְנְסֵנוּ וְכַלְכְּלֵנוּ וְהַרְוִיחֵנוּ, וְהַרְוַח לָנוּ יְיָ אֱלֹהֵינוּ מְהֵרָה מִכָּל צָרוֹתֵינוּ. וְנָא אַל תַּצְרִיכֵנוּ יְיָ אֱלֹהֵינוּ, לֹא לִידֵי מַתְּנַת בָּשָׂר וָדָם וְלֹא לִידֵי הַלְוָאָתָם, כִּי אִם לְיָדְךָ הַמְלֵאָה הַפְּתוּחָה הַקְּדוֹשָׁה וְהָרְחָבָה, שֶׁלֹּא נֵבוֹשׁ וְלֹא נִכָּלֵם לְעוֹלָם וָעֶד.

Racheim (na) Ado-nai Elo-heinu al Yisrael amecha v'al Yerushalayim irecha v'al tziyon mishkan k'vodecha v'al malchut beit David m'shichecha v'al ha'bayit ha'gadol v'ha'kadosh she'nikra shimcha alav. Elo-heinu avinu r'einu zuneinu parn'seinu v'chalk'leinu v'harvicheinu v'harvach lanu Ado-nai Elo-heinu m'heirah mi'kol tzaroteinu. V'na al tatzricheinu Ado-nai Elo-heinu lo liy'dei matnat basar va'dam v'lo liy'dei halva'atam, ki im l'yadcha ha'm'lei'ah ha'p'tucha ha'k'doshah v'ha'r'chavah, she'lo neivosh v'lo nikaleim l'olam va'ed.

Have mercy, please, Hashem, our G-d, on Israel Your people, and on Yerushalaim Your city, and on Tzion, the resting place of Your glory, and on the kingdom of the house of David, Your anointed one, and on the great, holy House which is called by Your name. Our G-d, our Father, shepherd us, nourish us, provide for us, and sustain us, and bring us gain, and bring us relief, Hashem, our G-d, rapidly, from all our troubles. And please, do not make us dependent, Hashem, our G-d, not upon the gifts of flesh and blood and not upon their loans. But rather only upon Your full, open, holy, and wide hand, that we will never be embarrassed and will never be abashed, forever and always.

רְצֵה וְהַחֲלִיצֵנוּ יְיָ אֱלֹהֵינוּ בְּמִצְוֹתֶיךָ וּבְמִצְוַת יוֹם הַשְּׁבִיעִי הַשַּׁבָּת הַגָּדוֹל וְהַקָּדוֹשׁ הַזֶּה. כִּי יוֹם זֶה גָּדוֹל וְקָדוֹשׁ הוּא לְפָנֶיךָ לִשְׁבָּת בּוֹ וְלָנוּחַ בּוֹ בְּאַהֲבָה כְּמִצְוַת רְצוֹנֶךָ. וּבִרְצוֹנְךָ הָנִיחַ לָנוּ יְיָ אֱלֹהֵינוּ שֶׁלֹּא תְהֵא צָרָה וְיָגוֹן וַאֲנָחָה בְּיוֹם מְנוּחָתֵנוּ. וְהַרְאֵנוּ יְיָ אֱלֹהֵינוּ בְּנֶחָמַת צִיּוֹן עִירֶךָ וּבְבִנְיַן יְרוּשָׁלַיִם עִיר קָדְשֶׁךָ כִּי אַתָּה הוּא בַּעַל הַיְשׁוּעוֹת וּבַעַל הַנֶּחָמוֹת.

R'tzeih v'hachalitzeinu Ado-nai Elo-heinu b'mitzvotecha uv'mitzvat yom ha'sh'vi'i ha'Shabbat ha'gadol v'ha'kadosh ha'zeh. Ki yom zeh gadol v'kadosh hu l'fanecha lishbot bo v'lanu'ach bo b'ahavah k'mitzvat r'tzonecha. Uvir'tzoncha hani'ach lanu Ado-nai Elo-heinu she'lo t'hei tzarah v'yagon va'anachah b'yom m'nuchateinu. V'hareinu Ado-nai Elo-heinu b'nechamat tziyon irecha uv'vinyan Yerushalayim ir kodshecha ki atah hu ba'al ha'ye'shu'ot u'va'al ha'nechamot.

Desire and invigorate us, Hashem, our G-d, with Your commandments, and with the commandment of the seventh day, this great and holy Shabbat. For this day is great and holy before You, to rest on it and to relax on it in love according to the commandment of Your desire, and by Your desire soothe us, Hashem, our G-d, that there may not be trouble and anguish and sighing on the day of our rest. And show us, Hashem, our G-d, the comfort of Tzion Your city, and the rebuilding of Yerushalaim Your holy city, for You are the Master of salvations and the Master of comforting.

On **Rosh Chodesh** and **Yom Tov**, *we recite the following:*

אֱלֹהֵינוּ וֵאלֹהֵי אֲבוֹתֵינוּ. יַעֲלֶה וְיָבוֹא וְיַגִּיעַ. וְיֵרָאֶה וְיֵרָצֶה וְיִשָּׁמַע. וְיִפָּקֵד וְיִזָּכֵר זִכְרוֹנֵנוּ וּפִקְדוֹנֵנוּ וְזִכְרוֹן אֲבוֹתֵינוּ. וְזִכְרוֹן מָשִׁיחַ בֶּן דָּוִד עַבְדֶּךָ. וְזִכְרוֹן יְרוּשָׁלַיִם עִיר קָדְשֶׁךָ. וְזִכְרוֹן כָּל עַמְּךָ בֵּית יִשְׂרָאֵל. לְפָנֶיךָ. לִפְלֵיטָה לְטוֹבָה. לְחֵן וּלְחֶסֶד וּלְרַחֲמִים. לְחַיִּים וּלְשָׁלוֹם בְּיוֹם:

- On Rosh Chodesh - רֹאשׁ חֹדֶשׁ - On Pesach - חַג הַמַּצּוֹת - On Shavuot -
חַג הַשָּׁבוּעוֹת
- On Sukkot - חַג הַסֻּכּוֹת - On Shemini Etzeret - הַשְּׁמִינִי חַג הָעֲצֶרֶת
- On Rosh HaShanah - הַזִּכָּרוֹן

הַזֶּה, זָכְרֵנוּ ה' אֱלֹהֵינוּ בּוֹ לְטוֹבָה. וּפָקְדֵנוּ בּוֹ לִבְרָכָה. וְהוֹשִׁיעֵנוּ בּוֹ

Bircat HaMazon

לְחַיִּים. וּבִדְבַר יְשׁוּעָה וְרַחֲמִים חוּס וְחָנֵּנוּ וְרַחֵם עָלֵינוּ וְהוֹשִׁיעֵנוּ. כִּי אֵלֶיךָ עֵינֵינוּ. כִּי אֵל מֶלֶךְ חַנּוּן וְרַחוּם אָתָּה.

Elo-heinu ve'Elohai avoteinu, ya'aleh v'yavo v'ya'gi'ah v'yei'ra'eh v'yei'ratzeh v'yi'shamah v'yipakeid v'yizacheir zichroneinu u'fikdoneinu v'zichron avoteinu, v'zichron Mashiach ben David avdecha v'zichron Yerushalayim ir kodshecha v'zichron kol am'cha beit Yisrael l'faneicha li'fleita l'tova l'chein u'l'chesed u'l'rachamim l'chai'im u'l'shalom b'yom (Rosh Chodesh/ Chag Ha'Matzot/ Chag Ha'Shavu'ot/ Chag Ha'Sukkot/ Ha'Sh'mini Chag Ha'Atzeret/ Ha'Zikaron) hazeh, zachreinu Ado-nai Elo-heinu bo l'tova, u'pakdeinu vo li'vracha, v'hoshi'einu vo l'chai'im, bi'd'var ye'shu'ah v'rachamim, chus v'chaneinu v'racheim aleinu, v'hoshi'einu ki eilecha eineinu, ki Eil melech chanun v'rachum atah.

Our G-d and the G-d of our fathers, let our remembrance and appointment, and the remembrance of our fathers, and the rememberance of the anointed son of David Your servant, and the remembrance of Yerushalaim Your holy city, and the remembrance of all the nation of the house of Israel, rise and come and arrive and be seen and be desired and be heard and be appointed and be remembered before you, for survival and for good, for favour and for kindness and for mercy, for life and for peace on this day, [this first of the month] / [this holiday of matzot] / [this holiday of weeks] / [this holiday of succot] / [this eighth additional holiday] / [this day of remembrance]. Remember us, Hashem, our G-d, on it for good. And appoint us on it for a blessing. And save it on us for life. And in the matter of salvation and mercy, have pity and kindness and mercy on us and save us, for our eyes are turned to You, for You are a kind and merciful G-d-King.

וּבְנֵה יְרוּשָׁלַיִם עִיר הַקֹּדֶשׁ בִּמְהֵרָה בְיָמֵינוּ. בָּרוּךְ אַתָּה יְיָ, בּוֹנֶה בְּרַחֲמָיו יְרוּשָׁלַיִם. אָמֵן.

U'v'nei Yerushalayim ir ha'kodesh bi'm'heirah v'yameinu. Baruch atah Ado-nai, boneh b'rachamav Yerushalayim. Amein.

And build Yerushalaim the holy city rapidly in our days. Blessed are You, Hashem, who builds Yerushalaim in His mercy; Amen.

בָּרוּךְ אַתָּה יְיָ אֱלֹהֵינוּ, מֶלֶךְ הָעוֹלָם, הָאֵל אָבִינוּ, מַלְכֵּנוּ, אַדִּירֵנוּ, בּוֹרְאֵנוּ, גּוֹאֲלֵנוּ, יוֹצְרֵנוּ, קְדוֹשֵׁנוּ קְדוֹשׁ יַעֲקֹב, רוֹעֵנוּ רוֹעֵה יִשְׂרָאֵל,

הַמֶּלֶךְ הַטּוֹב וְהַמֵּטִיב לַכֹּל, שֶׁבְּכָל יוֹם וָיוֹם הוּא הֵיטִיב, הוּא מֵיטִיב, הוּא יֵיטִיב לָנוּ, הוּא גְמָלָנוּ, הוּא גוֹמְלֵנוּ, הוּא יִגְמְלֵנוּ לָעַד, לְחֵן וּלְחֶסֶד וּלְרַחֲמִים וּלְרֶוַח הַצָּלָה וְהַצְלָחָה, בְּרָכָה וִישׁוּעָה, נֶחָמָה פַּרְנָסָה וְכַלְכָּלָה וְרַחֲמִים וְחַיִּים וְשָׁלוֹם, וְכָל טוֹב; וּמִכָּל טוּב לְעוֹלָם אַל יְחַסְּרֵנוּ.

Baruch atah Ado-nai, Elo-heinu melech ha'olam, ha'Eil avinu malkeinu adireinu boreinu go'aleinu yotzreinu k'dosheinu k'dosh Ya'akov, ro'einu ro'eih Yisrael ha'melech ha'tov v'ha'meitiv la'kol sheb'chol yom va'yom hu heitiv hu meitiv hu yeitiv lanu. Hu g'malanu hu gomleinu hu yigm'leinu la'ad l'chein u'l'chesed u'l'rachamim u'l'revach hatzalah v'hatzlacha b'racha viy'shu'ah nechama parnasa v'chal'kalah v'rachamim v'chai'im v'shalom v'chol tov, umi'kol tuv l'olam al ye'chas'reinu.

Blessed are You, Hashem, our G-d, king of the world, the G-d our Father, our King, our Noble, our Creator, our Redeemer, our Maker, our Holy One, the Holy One of Ya'akov, our Shepherd, the Shepherd of Israel. The good King, and Who is good to all, that every single day He has been good, He is good, He will be good to us. He treated us, He treats us, He will treat us forever with favour and kindness and mercy, and relief, rescue, and success, blessing and salvation, comfort, provision and sustenance, and mercy, and life, and peace, and everything good; and He will never deprive us of everything good.

הָרַחֲמָן הוּא יִמְלוֹךְ עָלֵינוּ לְעוֹלָם וָעֶד. הָרַחֲמָן הוּא יִתְבָּרַךְ בַּשָּׁמַיִם וּבָאָרֶץ. הָרַחֲמָן הוּא יִשְׁתַּבַּח לְדוֹר דּוֹרִים, וְיִתְפָּאַר בָּנוּ לָעַד וּלְנֵצַח נְצָחִים, וְיִתְהַדַּר בָּנוּ לָעַד וּלְעוֹלְמֵי עוֹלָמִים. הָרַחֲמָן הוּא יְפַרְנְסֵנוּ בְּכָבוֹד. הָרַחֲמָן הוּא יִשְׁבּוֹר עֻלֵּנוּ מֵעַל צַוָּארֵנוּ, וְהוּא יוֹלִיכֵנוּ קוֹמְמִיּוּת לְאַרְצֵנוּ. הָרַחֲמָן הוּא יִשְׁלַח לָנוּ בְּרָכָה מְרֻבָּה בַּבַּיִת הַזֶּה, וְעַל שֻׁלְחָן זֶה שֶׁאָכַלְנוּ עָלָיו. הָרַחֲמָן הוּא יִשְׁלַח לָנוּ אֶת אֵלִיָּהוּ הַנָּבִיא זָכוּר לַטּוֹב, וִיבַשֶּׂר לָנוּ בְּשׂוֹרוֹת טוֹבוֹת יְשׁוּעוֹת וְנֶחָמוֹת.

Ha'rachaman hu yimloch aleinu l'olam va'ed. Ha'rachaman hu yitbarach ba'shamayim uva'aretz. Ha'rachaman hu yishtabach l'dor dorim v'yitpa'ar banu la'ad u'l'neitzach n'tzachim v'yit'hadar banu la'ad ul'olmei olamim. Ha'rachaman hu ye'farn'seinu b'chavod. Ha'rachaman hu yishbor uleinu mei'al tzavareinu v'hu yolicheinu kom'miyut l'artzeinu. Ha'rachaman hu yishlach b'rachah m'rubah ba'bayit ha'zeh v'al shulchan zeh she'achalnu alav. Ha'rachaman hu yishlach lanu et Eiliyahu ha'navi zachur la'tov viy'vaser lanu b'sorot tovot ye'shuot v'nechamot.

The Merciful One, He will rule over us forever and always. The Merciful One, He will be blessed in the skies and on the earth. The Merciful One, He will be praised in every generation, and will be admired amongst us forever and for eternity, and will be glorified amongst us forever and for all times. The Merciful One, He will provide for us with honour. The Merciful One, He will break our yoke from off our necks and He will walk us upright to our land. The Merciful One, He will sent us a multifold blessing in this house and on this table upon which we ate. The Merciful One, He will send us the prophet Eliahu, remembered for good, and He will notify us of good news, salvations and comforts.

הָרַחֲמָן הוּא יְבָרֵךְ אֶת אָבִי מוֹרִי - *One who ate at his parent's table* בַּעַל הַבַּיִת הַזֶּה, וְאֶת אִמִּי מוֹרָתִי בַּעֲלַת הַבַּיִת הַזֶּה, אוֹתָם וְאֶת בֵּיתָם וְאֶת זַרְעָם וְאֶת כָּל אֲשֶׁר לָהֶם

Ha'rachaman hu ye'vareich et avi mori ba'al ha'bayit v'et imi morati ba'alat ha'bayit ha'zeh, otam v'et beitam v'et zaram v'et kol asher lahem.

The Merciful One, He will bless my father, my teacher, the master of this home, and my mother, my teacher, the mistress of this home, them and their home and their offspring and all that they have...

הָרַחֲמָן הוּא יְבָרֵךְ אוֹתִי, - *A married man eating at his own table* וְאֶת אִשְׁתִּי, וְאֶת זַרְעִי, וְאֶת כָּל אֲשֶׁר לִי

Ha'rachaman hu ye'vareich oti v'et ishti v'et zari v'et kol asher li

The Merciful One, He will bless me and my wife and my offspring and all that I have...

הָרַחֲמָן הוּא יְבָרֵךְ אוֹתִי, - *A married woman eating at her own table* וְאֶת בַּעֲלִי, וְאֶת זַרְעִי, וְאֶת כָּל אֲשֶׁר לִי

Ha'rachaman hu ye'vareich oti v'et ba'ali v'et zari v'et kol asher li

The Merciful One, He will bless me and my husband and my offspring and all that I have...

הָרַחֲמָן הוּא יְבָרֵךְ אֶת בַּעַל הַבַּיִת - *A guest at someone else's table* הַזֶּה וְאֶת בַּעֲלַת הַבַּיִת הַזֶּה, אוֹתָם וְאֶת בֵּיתָם וְאֶת זַרְעָם וְאֶת כָּל אֲשֶׁר לָהֶם

Ha'rachaman hu ye'vareich et ba'al ha'bayit ha'zeh v'et ba'alat ha'bayit ha'zeh, otam v'et beitam v'et zaram v'et kol asher lahem

The Merciful One, He will bless the master of this home and the mistress of this home, them and their home and their offspring and everything that they have...

הָרַחֲמָן - *When eating at a communal meal without a specific host* הוּא יְבָרֵךְ אֶת כָּל הַמְסֻבִּים כַּאן

Ha'rachaman hu ye'vareich et kol ha'm'subim kan

The Merciful One, He will bless all who feast here...

אוֹתָנוּ וְאֶת כָּל אֲשֶׁר לָנוּ, כְּמוֹ שֶׁנִּתְבָּרְכוּ אֲבוֹתֵינוּ אַבְרָהָם יִצְחָק וְיַעֲקֹב "בַּכֹּל"-"מִכֹּל"-"כֹּל" – כֵּן יְבָרֵךְ אוֹתָנוּ כֻּלָּנוּ יַחַד בִּבְרָכָה שְׁלֵמָה. וְנֹאמַר: "אָמֵן".

Otanu v'et kol asher lanu, k'mo she'nitbarchu avoteinu Avraham Yitzhak v'Ya'akov ba'kol mi'kol kol, kein ye'vareich otanu kulanu yachad biv'rachah sh'leimah v'nomar amein.

Us and all that we have; as our fathers Avraham, Yitzchak, and Ya'akov were blessed, in everything, from everything, with everything, so, too, He will bless us, all of us together, with a complete blessing; and we will say Amen.

בַּמָּרוֹם יְלַמְּדוּ עֲלֵיהֶם וְעָלֵינוּ זְכוּת שֶׁתְּהֵא לְמִשְׁמֶרֶת שָׁלוֹם. וְנִשָּׂא בְרָכָה מֵאֵת יְיָ, וּצְדָקָה מֵאֱלֹהֵי יִשְׁעֵנוּ, וְנִמְצָא חֵן וְשֵׂכֶל טוֹב בְּעֵינֵי אֱלֹהִים וְאָדָם.

Ba'marom ye'lam'du aleihem v'aleinu z'chut she'tehei l'mishmeret shalom. V'nisa v'rachah mei'eit Ado-nai u'tz'dakah mei'Elo-hei yisheinu. V'nimtza chein v'seichel tov b'einei Elo-him v'adam.

In the heavens they will teach to them and to us merit, that will be watched over for peace, and we will take a blessing from Hashem, and justice from our G-d and Saviour, and we will find favour and good sense in the eyes of G-d and man.

הָרַחֲמָן הוּא יַנְחִילֵנוּ יוֹם שֶׁכֻּלוֹ שַׁבָּת וּמְנוּחָה לְחַיֵּי הָעוֹלָמִים.

Ha'Rachaman hu yanchileinu yom she'kulo Shabbat u'm'nuchah l'chayei ha'olamim.

The Merciful One, He will bequeath us a day that is wholly rest and relaxation for the lives of all times.

On Yom Tom - הָרַחֲמָן הוּא יַנְחִילֵנוּ יוֹם שֶׁכֻּלוֹ טוֹב.

Ha'Rachaman hu yanchileinu yom she'kulo tov.

The Merciful One, He will bequeath us a day that is wholly good.

On Rosh Chodesh - הָרַחֲמָן הוּא יְחַדֵּשׁ עָלֵינוּ אֶת הַחֹדֶשׁ הַזֶּה לְטוֹבָה וְלִבְרָכָה.

Ha'Rachaman hu ye'chadeish aleinu et ha'chodesh ha'zeh l'tovah v'livracha.

The Merciful One, He will renew for us this month, for good and for blessing.

On Rosh HaShanah - הָרַחֲמָן הוּא יְחַדֵּשׁ עָלֵינוּ אֶת הַשָּׁנָה הַזֹּאת לְטוֹבָה וְלִבְרָכָה.

Ha'Rachaman hu ye'chadeish aleinu et ha'shanah ha'zot l'tovah v'livracha.

The Merciful One, He will renew for us this year for good and for blessing.

On Sukkot - הָרַחֲמָן הוּא יָקִים לָנוּ אֶת סֻכַּת דָּוִד הַנּוֹפֶלֶת.

Ha'Rachaman hu yakim lanu et sukat David ha'nofelet.

The Merciful One, He will raise us for us the fallen booth of David.

הָרַחֲמָן הוּא יְזַכֵּנוּ לִימוֹת הַמָּשִׁיחַ וּלְחַיֵּי הָעוֹלָם הַבָּא. מִגְדּוֹל יְשׁוּעוֹת מַלְכּוֹ, וְעֹשֶׂה חֶסֶד לִמְשִׁיחוֹ, לְדָוִד וּלְזַרְעוֹ עַד עוֹלָם. עֹשֶׂה שָׁלוֹם

בִּמְרוֹמָיו, הוּא יַעֲשֶׂה שָׁלוֹם עָלֵינוּ וְעַל כָּל יִשְׂרָאֵל. וְאִמְרוּ: "אָמֵן".

Ha'rachaman hu ye'zakeinu liy'mot ha'mashi'ach ul'chayei ha'olam ha'ba. Migdol ye'shu'ot malko v'oseh chesed li'm'shicho l'David ul'zaro ad olam. Oseh shalom bi'm'romav hu ya'aseh shalom aleinu v'al kol Yisrael v'imru amein.

The Merciful One, He will let us merit the days of the anointed one and the lives of the world to come. The Tower of His king's salvation, and Who does kindness to His anointed one, to David and his children until eternity. He who makes peace in His heavens, He will make peace for us and for all of Israel; and you shall say Amen.

יְראוּ אֶת יְיָ קְדֹשָׁיו, כִּי אֵין מַחְסוֹר לִירֵאָיו. כְּפִירִים רָשׁוּ וְרָעֵבוּ, וְדֹרְשֵׁי יְיָ לֹא יַחְסְרוּ כָל טוֹב. הוֹדוּ לַיְיָ כִּי טוֹב, כִּי לְעוֹלָם חַסְדוֹ. פּוֹתֵחַ אֶת יָדֶךָ, וּמַשְׂבִּיעַ לְכָל חַי רָצוֹן. בָּרוּךְ הַגֶּבֶר אֲשֶׁר יִבְטַח בַּיְיָ, וְהָיָה יְיָ מִבְטַחוֹ. נַעַר הָיִיתִי גַם זָקַנְתִּי, וְלֹא רָאִיתִי צַדִּיק נֶעֱזָב, וְזַרְעוֹ מְבַקֶּשׁ לָחֶם. יְיָ עֹז לְעַמּוֹ יִתֵּן, יְיָ יְבָרֵךְ אֶת עַמּוֹ בַשָּׁלוֹם.

Y'ru et Ado-nai k'doshav ki ein machsor liy'rei'av. K'firim rashu v'ra'eivu v'dorshei Ado-nai lo yachseru chol tov. Hodu l'Ado-nai ki tov ki l'olam chasdo. Potei'ach et yadecha u'masbi'a l'chol chai ratzon. Baruch ha'gever asher yivtach ba'Ado-nai v'hayah Ado-nai mivtacho. Na'ar hayiti gam zakanti v'lo ra'iti tzadik ne'ezav v'zaro m'vakeish lachem. Ado-nai oz l'amo yitein Ado-nai ye'vareich et amo va'shalom.

Revere Hashem, His holy ones, for there is nothing lacking for those who revere Him. Lions grew humble and ravenous, and those who seek Hashem will not lack anything good. Thank Hashem, for He is good, for His kindness is forever. You open Your hands, and sate every living will. Blessed is the man who trusts in Hashem, and Hashem will be trustworthy for him. I was a young man, and I have grown old, too, and I have not seen a righteous person abandoned, and his children requesting bread. Hashem will give strength to His nation, Hashem will bless His nation with peace.

Blessing After Other Foods - ברכות אחרונות

The Three Faceted Blessing - ברכת מעין שלש

This blessing is recited after eating 1) Grain products made from wheat, barley, rye, oats, or spelt OTHER THAN bread or matzah; 2) Grape wine or grape juice; 3) Grapes, figs, pomegranates, olives, or dates. If two or three of the food groups were eaten, connect the insertions with וְעַל in place of עַל. In the second and third insertions, if the fruit is from Eretz Yisrael, replace פְּרִי הַגֶּפֶן with פְּרִי גַפְנָהּ (pri hagafna) and פֵּרוֹת with פֵּרוֹתֶיהָ (peiroteiha).

בָּרוּךְ אַתָּה יְיָ, אֱלֹהֵינוּ מֶלֶךְ הָעוֹלָם,

Baruch ata Ado-nai, Elo-heinu melech ha'olam,
Blessed are You, Hashem, our G-d, King of the universe,

1) AFTER GRAIN PRODUCTS	2) AFTER WINE	3) AFTER FRUITS
עַל הַמִּחְיָה וְעַל הַכַּלְכָּלָה	עַל הַגֶּפֶן וְעַל פְּרִי הַגֶּפֶן	עַל הָעֵץ וְעַל פְּרִי הָעֵץ
Al Ha'michyah v'al ha'kalkalah,	Al ha'gefen v'al pri ha'gefen,	Al ha'eitz v'al pri ha'eitz,
For the nourishment and the sustenance,	*(And) for the vine and for the fruit of the vine,*	*(And) for the tree and for the fruit of the tree,*

וְעַל תְּנוּבַת הַשָּׂדֶה וְעַל אֶרֶץ חֶמְדָּה טוֹבָה וּרְחָבָה שֶׁרָצִיתָ וְהִנְחַלְתָּ לַאֲבוֹתֵינוּ לֶאֱכוֹל מִפִּרְיָהּ וְלִשְׂבּוֹעַ מִטּוּבָהּ. רַחֵם (נָא) יְיָ אֱלֹהֵינוּ עַל יִשְׂרָאֵל עַמֶּךָ וְעַל יְרוּשָׁלַיִם עִירֶךָ וְעַל צִיּוֹן מִשְׁכַּן כְּבוֹדֶךָ, וְעַל מִזְבְּחֶךָ, וְעַל הֵיכָלֶךָ. וּבְנֵה יְרוּשָׁלַיִם עִיר הַקֹּדֶשׁ בִּמְהֵרָה בְיָמֵינוּ. וְהַעֲלֵנוּ לְתוֹכָהּ וְשַׂמְּחֵנוּ בְּבִנְיָנָהּ, וְנֹאכַל מִפִּרְיָהּ וְנִשְׂבַּע מִטּוּבָהּ וּנְבָרֶכְךָ עָלֶיהָ בִּקְדֻשָּׁה וּבְטָהֳרָה.

V'al t'nuvat ha'sadeh v'al eretz chemdah tovah u'rchava she'ratzita v'hinchalta la'avoteinu le'echol mi'pir'yah ve'lisbo'a mi'tuvah. Rachem (na) Ado-nai Elo-heinu al Yisrael amecha v'al Yerushalayim irecha v'al Tzion mishkan k'vodecha, v'al mizb'checha, v'al heichalecha. U'vneih Yerushalayim ir ha'kodesh bimheirah b'yameinu. V'ha'aleinu l'tochah v'samcheinu b'vin'yanah, v'nochal mi'pir'yah ve'nisbo'a mi'tuvah u'n'varech'cha aleiha bi'k'dusha u'vtaharah.

And for the produce of the field; for the land, desirable and good and spacious, that You desired and gave as a heritage to our forefathers, to eat of its fruit and to be satisfied with its goodness. Have mercy (we beg You) Hashem, our G-d, on Israel, Your people; and on Jerusalem, Your city; and on Zion, the resting place of Your glory; and on Your Altar and on Your Temple. Rebuild Jerusalem, the City of holiness, speedily in our days. Bring us up into it and gladden us in its rebuilding; let us eat from its fruit and let us be satisfied with its goodness, and let us bless You upon it in holiness and purity.

וּרְצֵה וְהַחֲלִיצֵנוּ בְּיוֹם הַשַּׁבָּת הַזֶּה.

U'r'tzeih v'hacha'litzeinu b'yom ha'Shabbat ha'zeh.

And may it be pleasing to You to give us rest on this Sabbath day.

On Rosh Chodesh - וְזָכְרֵנוּ (לְטוֹבָה) בְּיוֹם רֹאשׁ חֹדֶשׁ הַזֶּה.

V'zachreinu (l'tova) b'yom Rosh Chodesh ha'zeh.
And remember us (for goodness) on the day of this New Month.

On Pesach - וְשַׂמְּחֵנוּ בְּיוֹם חַג הַמַּצּוֹת הַזֶּה.

V'sam'cheinu b'yom Chag Ha'Matzot ha'zeh.
And gladden us on the day of this Festival of Matzot.

On Shavuot - וְשַׂמְּחֵנוּ בְּיוֹם חַג הַשָּׁבֻעוֹת הַזֶּה.

V'sam'cheinu b'yom Chag Ha'Shavu'ot ha'zeh.
And gladden us on the day of this Festival of Shavuot.

On Rosh HaShanah - וְזָכְרֵנוּ (לְטוֹבָה) בְּיוֹם הַזִּכָּרוֹן הַזֶּה.

V'zachreinu (l'tova) b'yom Ha'Zikaron ha'zeh.
And remember us (for goodness) on this Day of Remembrance

Bircat HaMazon

On Sukkot - וְשַׂמְּחֵנוּ בְּיוֹם חַג הַסֻּכּוֹת הַזֶּה.

V'sam'cheinu b'yom Chag Ha'Sukkot ha'zeh.
And gladden us on the day of this Festival of Sukkot.

On Shemini Etzeret/Simchat Torah - וְשַׂמְּחֵנוּ בְּיוֹם הַשְּׁמִינִי חַג הָעֲצֶרֶת הַזֶּה.

V'sam'cheinu b'yom ha'sh'mini Chag Ha'Atzeret ha'zeh.
And gladden us on the day of this Festival of Shemini Etzeret.

כִּי אַתָּה יְיָ טוֹב וּמֵטִיב לַכֹּל וְנוֹדֶה לְךָ עַל הָאָרֶץ וְעַל...

Ki ata Ado-nai tov u'meitiv la'kol v'nodeh l'cha al ha'aretz v'al...

For You, Hashem, are good and do good to all, and we thank You for the Land and for...

1) AFTER GRAIN PRODUCTS	2) AFTER WINE	3) AFTER FRUITS
הַמִּחְיָה (וְעַל הַכַּלְכָּלָה)	(וְעַל) פְּרִי הַגֶּפֶן	(וְעַל) הַפֵּרוֹת.
Ha'michyah (v'al ha'kalkalah).	(v'al) p'ri ha'gefen.	(v'al) ha'peirot,
For the nourishment (and for the sustenance)	*(And) for the fruit of the vine.*	*(And) for the fruit.*

בָּרוּךְ אַתָּה יְיָ, עַל הָאָרֶץ וְעַל...

Baruch ata Ado-nai al ha'aretz v'al...

Blessed are You, Hashem, for the land and...

1) AFTER GRAIN PRODUCTS	2) AFTER WINE	3) AFTER FRUITS
הַמִּחְיָה (וְעַל הַכַּלְכָּלָה)	(וְעַל) פְּרִי הַגֶּפֶן	(וְעַל) הַפֵּרוֹת
Ha'michyah (v'al ha'kalkalah).	(v'al) pri ha'gefen.	(v'al) ha'peirot,
For the nourishment (and for the sustenance)	(And) for the fruit of the vine.	(And) for the fruit.

❧ Borei Nefashot - בורא נפשות

This blessing is recited after eating any food to which neither Bircat HaMazon nor the Three-Faceted Blessing applies, such as other fruits, vegetables, or non-wine/grape beverages.

בָּרוּךְ אַתָּה יְיָ אֱלֹהֵינוּ מֶלֶךְ הָעוֹלָם בּוֹרֵא נְפָשׁוֹת רַבּוֹת וְחֶסְרוֹנָן עַל כָּל מַה שֶׁבָּרָא לְהַחֲיוֹת בָּהֶם נֶפֶשׁ כָּל חָי. בָּרוּךְ חֵי הָעוֹלָמִים:

Baruch ata Ado-nai, Elo-heinu melech ha'olam, borei n'fashot rabot v'chesronan al kol ma she'bara l'hacha'yot ba'hem nefesh kol chai. Baruch chei ha'olamim.

Blessed are You, Hashem, our G-d, King of the universe, Who creates numerous living things with their deficiencies; for all that He has created with which to sustain the life of every being. Blessed is He, the Life-giver of the worlds.

Songs
שירים

This section has been generously sponsored by

The Weissberg Family

In honour of all the great teachers at TanenbaumCHAT

Songs for Shabbos Kodesh
שירים לשבת קודש

Acheinu - אחינו

אַחֵינוּ כָּל בֵּית יִשְׂרָאֵל, הַנְּתוּנִים בְּצָרָה וּבַשִּׁבְיָה, הָעוֹמְדִים בֵּין בַּיָּם וּבֵין בַּיַּבָּשָׁה, הַמָּקוֹם יְרַחֵם עֲלֵיהֶם, וְיוֹצִיאֵם מִצָּרָה לִרְוָחָה, וּמֵאֲפֵלָה לְאוֹרָה, וּמִשִּׁעְבּוּד לִגְאֻלָּה, הַשְׁתָּא בַּעֲגָלָא וּבִזְמַן קָרִיב.

Acheinu kol beit Yisrael, han'tunim b'tzara u'vashivya, ha'omdim bein bayam u'vein bayabasha, HaMakom ye'rachem aleihem, v'yotzi'eim mitzara lirvacha, u'mei'afeila l'ora, u'mishibud li'g'ulah, hashta ba'agalah u'vizman kariv.

Our brothers, the whole house of Israel, who are in distress and captivity, who wander over sea and over land -- may G-d have mercy on them, and bring them from distress to comfort, from darkness to light, from slavery to redemption, now, swiftly and soon.

Ana Be'Choach - אנא בכח

אָנָּא בְּכֹחַ גְּדֻלַּת יְמִינְךָ תַּתִּיר צְרוּרָה. קַבֵּל רִנַּת עַמְּךָ, שַׂגְּבֵנוּ טַהֲרֵנוּ נוֹרָא.

Ana b'cho'ach g'dulat ye'mincha tatir tz'rurah kabel rinat am'cha, sagveinu, tahareinu, norah.

Please, with the might of Your right, untie the bundle.
Accept Your people's song; heighten us, purify us, Mighty One.

Ani Ma'amin - אני מאמין

אֲנִי מַאֲמִין בֶּאֱמוּנָה שְׁלֵמָה בְּבִיאַת הַמָּשִׁיחַ, וְאַף עַל פִּי שֶׁיִּתְמַהְמֵהַּ, עִם כָּל זֶה אֲחַכֶּה לוֹ בְּכָל יוֹם שֶׁיָּבוֹא.

Ani ma'amin b'emunah shleimah b'viat HaMashiach, v'af al pi she'yitmame'hah, im kol zeh achakeh lo b'chol yom she'yavo.

I believe with complete faith in the coming of the Messiah, and even though he may linger, despite this I will wait for him each day, that he may come.

Baruch HaGever - ברוך הגבר

בָּרוּךְ הַגֶּבֶר אֲשֶׁר יִבְטַח בַּה׳, וְהָיָה ה׳ מִבְטַחוֹ.

Baruch ha'gever asher yivtach ba'Hashem v'hayah Hashem mivtacho.

Blessed is the man who trusts in Hashem, for Hashem will be his trust.

Beshem Hashem - בשם ה׳

בְּשֵׁם ה׳ אֱלֹקֵי יִשְׂרָאֵל, מִימִינִי מִיכָאֵל, וּמִשְּׂמֹאלִי גַּבְרִיאֵל, וּמִלְּפָנַי אוּרִיאֵל, וּמֵאֲחוֹרַי רְפָאֵל, וְעַל רֹאשִׁי שְׁכִינַת אֵ-ל.

Be'sheim Hashem Elokei Yisrael, mimini Micha'el u'mismoli Gavri'el, U'milfanai Uri'el u'me'acho'ai Refa'el, v'eal roshi shechinat Kel.

In the name of Hashem, G-d of Yisrael, on my right is Michael, and on my left is Gavriel, and in front of me is Uriel, and behind me is Refael, and above my head is the Presence of G-d.

David Melech Yisrael - דוד מלך ישראל

דָּוִד מֶלֶךְ יִשְׂרָאֵל חַי וְקַיָּם.

David melech Yisrael chai v'kayam.

David King of Israel lives and exists.

Esa Enai - אשא עיני

אֶשָּׂא עֵינַי, אֶל הֶהָרִים מֵאַיִן, יָבֹא עֶזְרִי. עֶזְרִי, מֵעִם ה׳ עֹשֵׂה, שָׁמַיִם וָאָרֶץ. אַל-יִתֵּן לַמּוֹט רַגְלֶךָ אַל יָנוּם שֹׁמְרֶךָ. הִנֵּה לֹא-יָנוּם, וְלֹא יִישָׁן שׁוֹמֵר, יִשְׂרָאֵל.

Esa einai el he'harim, mei'ayin yavo ezri. Ezri mei'im Hashem, ose shamayim va'aretz. Al yiten lamot raglecha, al yanum shom'recha. Hinei lo yanum v'lo yishan shomer Yisrael.

I will lift up my eyes to the mountains; from where shall my help arrive? My help comes from Hashem, who made heaven and earth. He will not suffer your foot to be moved; He Who keeps you will not slumber. Behold, He Who keeps Yisrael neither slumbers nor sleeps.

HaMalach HaGo'el - המלאך הגואל

הַמַּלְאָךְ הַגֹּאֵל אֹתִי מִכָּל־רָע, יְבָרֵךְ אֶת־הַנְּעָרִים, וְיִקָּרֵא בָהֶם שְׁמִי, וְשֵׁם אֲבֹתַי אַבְרָהָם וְיִצְחָק, וְיִדְגּוּ לָרֹב בְּקֶרֶב הָאָרֶץ.

Hamalach hago'el oti mikol ra ye'varech et han'arim viy'kareh bahem sh'mi v'shem avotai Avraham v'Yizchak v'yidgu larov b'kerev ha'aretz.

May the angel who has delivered me from all harm bless these lads. May they carry on my name and the names of my fathers, Abraham and Isaac, and may they grow into a multitude on earth.

HaRachaman - הרחמן

הָרַחֲמָן הוּא יִשְׁלַח לָנוּ אֶת אֵלִיָּהוּ הַנָּבִיא זָכוּר לַטּוֹב, וִיבַשֵּׂר לָנוּ בְּשׂוֹרוֹת טוֹבוֹת יְשׁוּעוֹת וְנֶחָמוֹת.

Ha'rachaman hu yishlach lanu et Eiliyahu ha'navi zachur la'tov viy'vaser lanu b'sorot tovot ye'shuot v'nechamot.

May the Merciful One send us Elijah the Prophet, may he be remembered for good, and may he bring us good tidings, salvation, and consolation.

Hineh Ma Tov - הנה מה טוב

הִנֵּה מַה טּוֹב וּמַה נָּעִים שֶׁבֶת אַחִים גַּם יָחַד.

Hineh ma tov u'ma na'im shevet achim gam yachad.

How good and pleasant is it when brothers sit together.

Songs

Im Eshkacheich - אם אשכחך

אִם אֶשְׁכָּחֵךְ יְרוּשָׁלָיִם, תִּשְׁכַּח יְמִינִי. תִּדְבַּק לְשׁוֹנִי לְחִכִּי אִם לֹא אֶזְכְּרֵכִי,אִם לֹא אַעֲלֶה אֶת יְרוּשָׁלַיִם עַל רֹאשׁ שִׂמְחָתִי.

Im eshkachech Yerushalayim tishkach ye'mini. Tidbak l'shoni l'chiki im lo ezk'reichi, im lo a'aleh et Yerushalayim al rosh simchati.

If I forget you, O Jerusalem, let my right hand wither; let my tongue stick to my palate if I cease to think of you, if I do not elevate Jerusalem above my greatest happiness.

Ivdu Et Hashem - עבדו את ה'

עִבְדוּ אֶת ה' בְּשִׂמְחָה בֹּאוּ לְפָנָיו בִּרְנָנָה.

Ivdu et Hashem b'simcha bo'u l'fanav birnanah.

Serve Hashem with gladness, come before Him with joyous song.

Ki Va Moed - כי בא מועד

אַתָּה תָקוּם תְּרַחֵם צִיּוֹן כִּי-עֵת לְחֶנְנָהּ כִּי-בָא מוֹעֵד:

Ata takum t'racheim Tzion ki eit l'chan'nah ki va mo'ed.

Rise up, comfort Zion, because it is time to be gracious to her, because her time has come!

Kol Ha'Olam Kulo - כל העולם כלו

כָּל הָעוֹלָם כֻּלּוֹ גֶּשֶׁר צַר מְאוֹד וְהָעִיקָר לֹא לְפַחֵד כְּלָל.

Kol ha'olam kulo gesher tzar m'od v'ha'ikar lo l'fached klal.

The whole world is a very narrow bridge, but the important thing is not to fear at all.

LeShanah HaBa'ah - לשנה הבאה

לְשָׁנָה הַבָּאָה בִּירוּשָׁלַיִם הַבְּנוּיָה.

L'shana ha'ba'ah bi'Yerushalayim hab'nuyah.

Next year in the rebuilt Jerusalem.

Mi Ha'Ish - מי האיש

מִי-הָאִישׁ, הֶחָפֵץ חַיִּים; אֹהֵב יָמִים, לִרְאוֹת טוֹב. נְצֹר לְשׁוֹנְךָ מֵרָע; וּשְׂפָתֶיךָ, מִדַּבֵּר מִרְמָה. סוּר מֵרָע, וַעֲשֵׂה-טוֹב; בַּקֵּשׁ שָׁלוֹם וְרָדְפֵהוּ.

Mi ha'ish ha'chafetz chai'im ohev yamim lirot tov. N'tzor l'shoncha mei'ra u's'fatecha midabeir mirma. Sur mei'ra va'asei tov bakesh shalom v'rodfeihu.

Who desires life, loving each day to see good? Guard your tongue from evil and your lips from speaking deceit. Turn from evil and do good, seek peace and pursue it.

Mikolot Mayim - מקולות מים

מִקֹּלוֹת מַיִם רַבִּים אַדִּירִים מִשְׁבְּרֵי יָם, אַדִּיר בַּמָּרוֹם ה'.

Mikolot Mayim Rabim, adirim mishb'rei yam, Adir ba'marom Hashem.

Above the voices of many waters, the mighty breakers of the sea, Hashem on high is mighty.

Mitzvah Gedolah - מצוה גדולה

מִצְוָה גְדוֹלָה לִהְיוֹת בְּשִׂמְחָה תָּמִיד.

Mitzvah g'dolah l'hiyot b'simcha tamid.

It is a great mitzvah to be happy always.

Od Yishama - עוד ישמע

עוֹד יִשָּׁמַע בְּעָרֵי יְהוּדָה וּבְחוּצוֹת יְרוּשָׁלַיִם קוֹל שָׂשׂוֹן וְקוֹל שִׂמְחָה קוֹל חָתָן וְקוֹל כַּלָּה.

Od yishama b'arei Yehudah u'v'chutzot Yerushalayim, kol sason v'kol simcha, kol chatan v'kol kalah.

It will yet be heard in the cities of Judah and in the streets of Jerusalem, the voice of joy and the voice of happiness, the voice of a groom and the voice of a bride.

Oseh Shalom - עושה שלום

עֹשֶׂה שָׁלוֹם בִּמְרוֹמָיו, הוּא יַעֲשֶׂה שָׁלוֹם עָלֵינוּ וְעַל כָּל יִשְׂרָאֵל. וְאִמְרוּ: אָמֵן.

Oseh shalom bimromav, hu ya'aseh shalom aleinu v'al kol Yisrael v'imru amen.

He who makes peace in High Places, He will make peace for us and for all of Israel, and let us say, Amen.

Pia Patcha - פיה פתחה

פִּיהָ פָּתְחָה בְחָכְמָה, וְתוֹרַת חֶסֶד עַל לְשׁוֹנָהּ. צוֹפִיָּה הֲלִיכוֹת בֵּיתָהּ, וְלֶחֶם עַצְלוּת לֹא תֹאכֵל. קָמוּ בָנֶיהָ וַיְאַשְּׁרוּהָ, בַּעְלָהּ וַיְהַלְלָהּ. רַבּוֹת בָּנוֹת עָשׂוּ חָיִל, וְאַתְּ עָלִית עַל כֻּלָּנָה.

Piy'ha pat'cha b'chochma v'torat chesed al l'shonah, tzofiyah halichot beitah v'lechem atzlut lo tocheil. Kamu vaneiha vay'ash'ruha, ba'alah vay'hal'lah, rabot banot asu chayil v'at alit al kulanah.

Her mouth opens in wisdom, and a Torah of lovingkindness is upon her lips. She looks after the affairs of her household, and will not eat the bread of laziness. May her children rise up and bless her; her husband praises her: "Many women have been valiant, and you surpassed them all."

Shema - שמע

שְׁמַע, יִשְׂרָאֵל: ה' אֱלֹהֵינוּ, ה' אֶחָד.

Sh'ma Yisrael Hashem Elokeinu Hashem echad.

Hear, Yisrael, Hashem is our G-d, Hashem is One.

Tov LeHodot - טוב להודות

טוֹב לְהֹדוֹת לַה', וּלְזַמֵּר לְשִׁמְךָ עֶלְיוֹן. לְהַגִּיד בַּבֹּקֶר חַסְדֶּךָ, וֶאֱמוּנָתְךָ בַּלֵּילוֹת

Tov l'hodot la'Hashem, u'l'zamer l'shimcha elyon. L'hagid baboker chasdecha v'emunat'cha ba'leilot.

It is good to give thanks to [You,] G-d, and to sing to Your name on high - to tell in the morning of Your kindness, and in the evening of Your faithfulness.

Yibaneh HaMikdash - יבנה המקדש

יִבָּנֶה הַמִּקְדָּשׁ, עִיר צִיּוֹן תְּמַלֵּא, וְשָׁם נָשִׁיר שִׁיר חָדָשׁ וּבִרְנָנָה נַעֲלֶה.

Yibaneh HaMikdash, ir Tzion timaleh, v'sham nashir shir chadash, u'virnana na'aleh.

Rebuild the Temple, and the city of Zion will be filled; and there we will sing a new song, and be uplifted with rejoicing.

Divrei Torah
דברי תורה

This section has been generously sponsored by

The Goodman Family

Dedicated L'iluy Nishmas Chaim ben Dov Z"l, their beloved father and grandfather Harry (Chaim) Farber

בראשית ברא אלקים את השמים ואת הארץ והארץ היתה תהו ובהו

Bereishit
בְּרֵאשִׁית

This Sefer of Chumash has been generously sponsored by

The Silver Family

Dedicated L'iluy Nishmas Aidel bas David, Chana
Feigel bas Yitzchak, and Shmuel Nachum ben Yosef

The Shofar's SHABBOS COMPANION

Bereishit • בראשית

This Parsha has been generously sponsored by the Vernon family in honour of their children

I am Nothing
By Matthew Goodman

A pasuk in Parshat Bereishit states, "And Hashem made two luminaries: The great luminary (haMaor haGadol) to rule in the day, and the minor luminary (haMaor haKatan) to rule at night, and the stars" (Bereishit 1:16). Rashi quotes Chazal and explains that originally the sun and moon were created equal. However, the moon came to Hashem with the complaint that two Kings can not possibly share one single crown. Hashem then commanded the moon to minimize itself, and then there was a profound difference between the sun and the moon. As a result, according to Chazal, the sun is much larger than the moon.

What is most distinct about these two "Great Luminaries" is that the sun generates its own light, while the moon is only a reflection of light of the sun.

Rav Yosef Soloveitchik, quoted by Rav Yissocher Frand, suggests that this pasuk in Bereishit provides us with the Torah's definition of the words "Gadol" and "Katan."

The sun is called a Gadol because it is able to generate its own light. The moon is called Katan because it does not generate its own light. We express this very idea in a prayer at every Brit Milah. "This is the Katan, he will become a Gadol" - *Zeh HaKatan Gadol Yehei*. When a child is raised, he reflects the light generated by those who brought him into the world and raised him. But the blessing is that the child should take this light and generate his own power of illumination.

The source in which Rashi quotes Chazal is in Massechet Chulin 60b, which expresses an idea that can be seen as very contradictory. *Said Hashem (to the moon): The righteous shall be called by your name. Yaakov the Katan. Shmuel the Katan. David the Katan.* According to the Rav's explanation, Yaakov, Shmuel HaNavi, and David HaMelech, by being Katan, only ever expressed "reflected" light and not their own. And not only does this verse refer to just them, but also all of the righteous, by which we could conclude that even Moshe Rabbeinu was a Katan.

When the Gemara refers to these great leaders of Klal Israel as Katan, it really means that the righteous who carry the world on their shoulders are those who who see themselves as nothing. Those who see themselves as merely a reflection of others. Moshe, the man who was chosen to receive the Torah, told Hashem that he was not good enough. King Saul hid when he was chosen as Israel's first king. And King David, at the height of his glory, would sing songs about his worthlessness.

What is amazing about this is that Moshe, in the end of Parshat V'Zot HaBrachah, is referred to as a Moreh Gadol, but according to Chazal, shall always been known as a Katan. Why? Because every single Gadol HaDor, from Moshe Rabbeinu to Rabban Gamliel to the Rambam and the Chofetz Chaim, became a gadol, became great, by essentially being nothing. By having such a deep humbleness. Their own light is really the light of a Katan. A reflection of those who brought them up and made them a Gadol. A reflection of their parents, of their teachers, of their students, and of all of Klal Israel, making them fitting to be our leaders.

Parshat Bereishit, the Parsha of beginnings, teaches us that those who are truly great become so by being nothing.

To See The Darkness
By Becky Friedman

Reading Bereishit, I was momentarily perplexed by a particular pasuk (in reference to the sun, moon, and stars): "And to rule by day and by night and to differentiate between the light and the darkness; and G-d saw that it was good" (1:18).

What confused me was the contrast of this pasuk with pasuk 4 in the same perek: "And G-d saw the light, that it was good; and G-d differentiated between the light and the darkness."

How could the sun, moon, and stars be differentiating between light and darkness on Day Four when light and darkness had already been separated on Day One? Furthermore, how could the sun, moon, and stars– sources of light– be separating light and darkness? Where does darkness come into the picture?

All these questions were the work of a moment; an instant later, I had an epiphany, answering my questions and shedding light, if you'll excuse the pun, on many related and seemingly unrelated matters.

On the first day, G-d had separated light from darkness– absolute light and absolute darkness. But on the fourth day– the day before He created living creatures– He made the heavenly bodies, to temper the absolutes. The sun ("the great light-source") reigns by day, while the moon ("the small light-source") reigns by night. How is it that separating sun and moon separates light and darkness? The sun gives a great light, by which we can easily see and conduct our daily activities. Moonlight, on the other hand is dim (being only, as we now know, a reflection of the sunlight), and barely enables us, at times, to make out silhouettes and shadows.

But if it weren't for the dim light of the moon and stars (and excluding the possibility of secondary lighting, such as candles, electricity, bioluminescence, etc.), we would be left in utter, absolute darkness– a darkness so dark that the term "dark" becomes meaningless; we might as well have our eyes closed. In fact, without the moon and stars, it would be so dark that *we would not know that it was dark at all.*

Just as it has been said that we need bad in the world in order to appreciate the good, we need light in order to see the darkness.

As we embark on a new year -- a new cycle of the Torah-- it is worthwhile to remember that no matter how miserable a situation, our very awareness of misery is proof of the presence of "light"; it is only when we do not even know of our own suffering that life is truly bleak.

Divrei Torah on **Bereishit**

Noach • נֹחַ

This Parsha has been generously sponsored by the Nathanson family in honour of Logan and Dylan Nathanson, with love

Actions Speak Louder Than Words
By Elianne Neuman

"These are the offspring (toldot) of Noah—Noah was a righteous man, perfect in his generations; Noah walked with G-d."

Noah is a disputed character in Tanach. Some commentators praise Noah, saying that he was righteous even though he lived in a generation of evildoers and was surrounded by the wicked. Others take the approach that, had he lived in another generation, he wouldn't have been considered to be righteous.

Rashi comments on the verse "Noah walked with G-d" that Noah needed support from G-d while Abraham was able to be righteous on his own. Sforno takes the opposite approach: Noah walked in G-d's ways. This means that Noah behaved well toward others and tried to get the corrupt individuals around him to change their ways.

Obviously, there is much confusion: was Noah truly righteous, or was he just an exception to the abominable behaviour of his time?

Let's go back to the first verse to try to answer this question. The word *toldot* can have many meanings: generations, descendants, products, and history. Ramban and Onkelos both agree that in this case, the word *toldot* means offspring. Rashi says that by mentioning Noah's offspring, the Torah is praising him, for it is written in Proverbs 10:7: "The mention of a righteous person is for a blessing." Rashi also explains that the verse mentions Noah's righteous behaviour because the 'offspring' of the righteous are their good deeds. Noah's righteousness is contested, even though he is praised for his actions.

But when we think about incontestably righteous people in Tanach, we immediately think of their commendable actions. Abraham was willing to sacrifice Yitzchak in the name of G-d. Moshe advocated for Bnei

Yisrael when they sinned. Jonathan defied his father Saul in order to save the life of his friend, David.

Noah sinned, but he also performed many good deeds. He wasn't influenced by his neighbours, and he continued to be righteous. He was the person in his generation who merited to be saved from a massive flood. He built the ark as G-d wished. He took care of the animals on the ark, which couldn't have been an easy job. He loved and feared G-d, following the ways of the Torah.

The Torah doesn't need to mention the extent of Noah's righteousness because his actions speak for themselves. <u>Was</u> Noah as righteous as Abraham? That's hard for us to judge. But he did have a bevy of merits based on his good deeds.

We should look at Noah as a role model for ourselves. He was able to stand up and stand out. He was willing to serve G-d when others around him behaved inappropriately. And he did as G-d wished. In short, his actions spoke louder than any words that could've been written concerning him.

Responding to Failure
By Matthew Goodman

How do you react when you don't succeed? When things don't go your way, what's the next step you take? In Parshat Noach, we learn a lesson in responding to failure.

Humans became corrupted and evil, and immorality filled the earth. Hashem told Noach that He was going to wipe out all human beings, and Noach and his family alone would survive on an ark of gopher wood. Noach spent 120 years building the ark and anticipating the destruction of the world. Not once, however, did he make any attempt to save his generation. The Zohar tells us that Noach did not pray for the salvation of the world. He did not ask Hashem for mercy. All he asked of Hashem was, "What will you do with me?" The Tzaddik of the generation, the greatest man on the face of the earth at the time, did not try to save the millions of people who were about to be massacred by a flood. He cared solely about his own survival.

When the rains began to descend and Noach closed the ark with his family and the animals inside, the Midrash (Sefer Haazinu 47) tells us that chaos broke loose. Thousands of people began trying to break into the ark. Noach heard terrible screaming and yelling. The entire world was crying out. When their voices were finally drowned out by the water, Noach then prayed for mercy. But it was too late. The flood had already made its impact. The Tzaddik of the generation failed to save humanity.

When the flood ended and the ark opened, Noach did something highly perplexing. He became "a master of the soil (Ish Adama), and he planted a vineyard" (Bereishit 9:20). Rashi explains that it would have been far more sensible for Noach to have planted trees that produced food. Then he would be able to nourish the last remnants of life on earth. Rav Simcha Wasserman tells us that Noach should have upheld his mission aboard the ark: to sustain, care, and feed for the animals and his family in order to ensure the continuity of life! Thus, after the flood, Noach should have continued to work on sustaining the world by planting food! According to Rashi, Noach abandoned his mission and purpose, and engaged in "chulin," the mundane. The Tzaddik did what was easy and simple. He became mundane.

How did the Ish Tzaddik, who merited to survive the flood, end up losing his ambition and drive to do good? Why did he resort to becoming dull?

According to Abarbanel, Noach suffered from deep guilt and torrent. He was so upset at life because he did not succeed in saving his generation. He was so angry at the flood that he pledged never to drink or see water again. He would only drink wine. Noach wanted to numb himself to the tormenting pain of failure and consequently preoccupied himself with the mundane.

Noach's outlook after his lack of his success was staunchly negative. He lost his drive, ambition, and will to act righteously.

The great Avraham Avinu also did not succeed. Hashem confided in him that He planned on wiping out the cities of Sdom and Ammorah. Unlike Noach, Avraham began to beg and plead for mercy. He cared so much about fellow human beings that he would simply not stand by and watch the destruction of whole populations. However, Avraham Avinu did not succeed. Hashem destroyed the cities. Rashi then comments that in response, Avraham moved to the Negev. Since the cities were destroyed, wayfarers would have no reason to travel near the Dead Sea area. Therefore, Avraham picked up his belongings and looked for new opportunities for hospitality.

Avraham Avinu's outlook after his lack of success was inspiringly positive. He maintained his drive and ambition, and sought new ways to continue to act righteously. He continued his mission to act in the most humane, holy, good way possible.

Life is filled with opportunities to succeed and to fail, to win and to lose. How do we respond to failure? When we don't succeed, how do we react? We could certainly act like Noach, run ourselves into a corner and wallow in guilt. Then, without a doubt, we will have lost. Or we can respond like Avrahan Avinu, and use the failure to grow and continue striving to accomplish whatever mission we have here on earth. We can maintain a positive outlook and seek new means of achievement.

Let's say you fail a test at school. You could very easily get angry and upset. You could rip up your test, blame your teacher, and refuse to attempt to improve. Or you could use your failure as a step to greater successes. You could investigate what you did wrong, work on improving your mistakes, and study harder next time. If that is how we react when we don't succeed, then, without a doubt, we haven't really failed at all. In fact, we will have won.

Failure is the Only Option
By Becky Friedman

Parshat Noach seems to exist to reinforce the notion of the supremacy of G-d.

The builders of the Tower of Bavel stated as their objective that they would build themselves a city and a tower to prevent themselves from being "scattered across the land." In direct response to this action, G-d confuses their languages and scatters them across the land.

This seems, at first glance, perplexing. Is failure, indeed, the only option for these people? Through no fault of their own-- indeed, despite their efforts to the contrary-- they achieved the exact result which they had hoped to avoid! The haftarah, however, which seems the polar opposite of its corresponding parsha, with its soothing, comforting language in contrast to the parsha's harsh, condemning tones, may be able to give us some answers.

The haftarah opens by telling someone-- presumably the people of Israel-- that they will, indeed, spread out far and wide. In this case, though, it is unequivocally a good thing. Just as the builders of the Tower of Bavel hoped not to be scattered but were thwarted by G-d, so-- in a reversal of sorts-- the people of Israel, just when they had all but given up, are told by G-d that they shall be more numerous than before.

What does this teach us? It would seem more than a little strange were I to say it teaches us never to try anything. Rather, it tells us that anything we attempt should only be attempted with the acknowledgement that its success or failure rests in G-d's hands. Only then will G-d deliver to us success.

The builders spared not a thought for G-d-- indeed, they made a point of making use of their own resources in building, and placed all their faith in man. Because they did not place their trust in G-d, they were doomed to failure from the start.

The people of Israel, on the other hand, have their good news delivered by a prophet-- and already, if they believe his word, they are tacitly accepting the higher power of G-d. Furthermore, every promise of redemption and greatness given in the haftarah comes in the same breath as a reminder that it is G-d who does this for us, because of His special relationship with the Jewish people. The people of Israel are assured of success because they know that this good fortune comes directly from G-d.

May we all have a year full of G-d-given blessings; may we remember G-d in all we do, that G-d remember us.

Lech Lecha • לך לך

This Parsha has been generously sponsored by the Goldman family in honour of all the excellent teachers at TanenbaumCHAT

Mission Possible

By Matthew Goodman

A teacher asked her students what they wanted to become when they grew up. She received a chorus of responses: "A doctor," "An astronaut," "A fireman," "A football player." Tommy, however, quietly sat at his desk and gave no response. "Tommy, the teacher said to him, "what do you want to be when you grow up?" "Possible," Tommy replied. "Possible?" Asked the teacher? "Yes. My Mom always tells me that I'm impossible. So when I grow up, I want to be possible."

In Parshat Lech Lecha, we learn about our ability to make the impossible possible.

Hashem "took [Avraham] outside, and He said, 'Look up at the heavens and count the stars, if you are able to count them.' And He said to him, 'So will be your descendants.'" (Bereishit 15:5). Rav Meir Shapiro, Rosh Yeshiva of Chochmei Lublin, asks what out reaction would if someone told us to go outside and count the stars. He answers that we would simply ignore the request! The task is so impossible to complete! Why would you even bother attempting to start it? But what did Avraham Avinu do? He went out and started to count the stars. He attempted to do the impossible, and upon doing so, Hashem told him, "This is how your descendants will be!"

Rav Meir Shapiro explains: "When it looks impossible, when it looks beyond the reach of human beings, nevertheless to try; nevertheless to give it one's best" - that is the characteristic of Klal Yisrael. Jews, the descendants of Avraham, are blessed with the innate ability to persevere and overcome tasks that may seem to be outside the sphere of possibility.

The key to success is to try, and when we, like Avraham, begin to count the stars, we can accomplish what seemed to be impossible. What holds us back, however, is our own personal conviction that "I can't do it!"

Most of the time, that "I can't do it" really means something completely different.

Rabbi Levi Yitzchak of Berditchev was working on himself. He was trying to overcome a struggle of a very high spiritual level, but he became resigned that it simply was not possible to change.

Immediately afterward, the Rabbi stepped out into the street and saw an argument between a wagon driver and a store owner. The store owner wanted the wagon driver to unload the goods into his store, and the driver kept on insisting, "I can't! I can't!" The store owner barked back, "It's not that you can't! It's that you don't want to!" The fight continued and the volume and intensity increased. "I can't!" "You can! You just don't want to!" Finally, the store owner quietly reached into his pocket, took out a few bills and said, "What if I offered you 50 zlotys? Then would you be able to?" The wagon driver soberly answered, "I'll give it a try."

Rabbi Levi Yitzchak marveled that the wagon driver was indeed capable of doing the job. He was never unable to do it, he merely did not want to, and thus told himself, "I can't!" The Rabbi also understood that if he, too, could convince himself of how much he wanted to overcome his own struggle, what he had called impossible could become very possible.

Avraham's actions teach us that if a Jew feels strongly enough that "I can," and begins to attempt to achieve the seemingly impossible, then no struggle will ever really be unfeasible. This is a powerful lesson in how we go about accomplishing and overcoming anything that is placed in front of us. For instance, one might find it extremely difficult to succeed in a particular class, or fix a certain personality trait, or even start a volunteer project or school committee. How many times have you said, "This calculus homework is impossible!" or "It's impossible to make me a better person! It won't work!"

If Avraham Avinu was able to do the naturally impossible by simply trying, then his blessed descendants certainly should be able to do what is only seemingly futile. Most of the time we are not trying to defy the laws of nature. What we are really doing is moving from a state of "I can" to "I can't," from "I won't try" to "I'll give it a shot."

The next time Hashem gives us the opportunity to look up and the count the stars, we should have the strength, with the help of G-d, to give it a try. For a descendant of Avraham Avinu, any mission is possible.

Ill-Gotten Gains

By Becky Friedman

Parshat Lech-Lecha teaches us some valuable-- no pun intended-- lessons about the place ethics holds in monetary matters.

After Avraham's victory in the war of the four kings and the five kings, the king of Sdom proposes that he keep the people involved as slaves, and, in exchange, Avraham could keep all the loot. Not only does our exalted forefather refuse this arrangement, he does so in no uncertain terms. He tells the king of Sdom that he would not take even a single shoelace from the king.

Avraham's given reason was that he did not want the king of Sdom claiming credit for Avraham's wealth. The most obvious interpretation for his reasoning is that it would simply be false: Avraham was already exceedingly wealthy before this incident, so he didn't want the king of Sdom to have an excuse to lie about it.

The next valid explanation is deference to G-d. Avraham, knowing that it is G-d who gave him his prodigious wealth, wants to protect against anyone claiming credit and effectively cutting G-d out of the picture. This answer has particular resonance, as it ties in with exhortations in the book of Dvarim not to forget that it was G-d, and not men, who gave us all the good things in our lives.

Furthermore, Avraham is rejecting the king of Sdom as an individual. "You shall not say 'I have enriched Avram,'" Avraham (then Avram) tells the king of Sdom. In the next parsha, we learn that the people of Sdom were evil and deserved extermination; already, Avraham, a good person, wants nothing to do with him. This is also, by extension, a rejection of the system of slavery implicit in the king of Sdom's proposal. While slavery was a social norm in those days-- and yes, Avraham himself had slaves-- he was not prepared to directly profit from selling slaves, particularly not to such a despicable owner as the king of Sdom.

I hope we can all emulate Avraham Avinu, no matter how tempting an offer we are faced with, in refusing to receive even a shoelace of ill-gotten gains.

Divrei Torah on **Bereishit**

Avraham's Legacy
By Zachary Zarnett-Klein

This week's Haftarah comes from the book of Yeshayahu, and discusses Avraham Avinu, who is the main focus of this week's Parshah, Lech Lecha.

"Who inspired the one from the east, at whose every footstep righteousness attended?" is but the first reference to Avraham Avinu. Parshat Lech Lecha begins with the famous words from Hashem to Avraham, "Lech Lecha MeArtzecha UMimoladetcha UMiBeit Avicha el Haaretz Asher Areka," translated as "Go forth from your land, from your homeland, and from the land of your fathers, to the land that I shall show you." The first verse of the Haftarah confirms that G-d remembers Abraham, the pioneer of the Jewish people, and the righteousness he exemplified from the first thing that G-d commanded him. This shows that despite Israel thinking that "G-d's ways are hidden to us," He has not abandoned him by any means.

Next: "Who delivered nations to him, and subdued kings before him? Who made his enemies like dust before his sword, like straw blown before his bow? He pursued him and emerged unhurt on a path where his feet had never gone." This refers to Avraham's rescue of the captives and booty which the four kings had taken from the five kings in war, related in Bereishit chapter 14. With this reference, Yeshayahu teaches the people that just as Hashem subdued Avraham's enemies before him with ease, and did not let harm come upon Avraham, so, too, is Hashem safeguarding Bnei Yisrael, even at a time when G-d's protection is in doubt.

"The islands saw and feared... Each man would help his fellow [worship idols]." The "islands" refer to the nations who saw G-d's might and His unprecedented coalition with any human being that was exhibited with Avraham. They all turned towards their artisans and craftspeople to make idols grander and more lavish than before. This verse reassures Bnei Yisrael that the seemingly mighty and powerful "G-ds" of the nations were only made to try to match the greatness of Hashem and His loyalty to the Israelites, exhibited from Avraham's days and continuously thereafter.

The Haftarah ends with the inspiring words, "Fear not, O worm of Jacob, O men of Israel, for I help you-- the word of Hashem, your Redeemer." The fact that the verse reads "for I help you" and not "for I will help you" shows that G-d is with Israel through every generation--

from the time of the Torah, to the prophets, to the modern day. He continues to safeguard and protect us as He did Avraham, and does not wait a second to act.

As well, Yeshayahu refers to HaShem as "your Redeemer." This word indicates that if we ever find ourselves in a difficult situation, G-d will redeem us, just as He redeemed Avraham from his idol-worshipping roots, from his ordeal with the king of Egypt, from the famine, and from the war against the mighty kings. Redemption is a recurring theme in the Parshah, and throughout the entire book of Isaiah. Today, we await the time when Hashem will help us become, from lowly worms, a formidable force, defeating our enemies, and living peacefully in Israel with the redemption of the Mashiach.

Fair-Weather Husband
By Yaron Milwid

In this week's Parsha, there is the well-known story of how, in order to save his own skin, Abraham told Pharaoh that Sarah was his sister and not his wife. There are two questions that are raised by this story that I can see: how could he endanger another person's life in order to save his own life, and how could G-d get angry with Pharaoh if Pharaoh did not know that Sarah was Abraham's wife. There are many answers for the first question; however, I only like two of them; these are the explanations offered by the Tiferes Yehonason, and by the Be'er Mayim Chayim. For the second question, Rashi offers an explanation that makes the situation make more sense.

The Tiferes Yehonason explains the first question by saying that the patriarchs were not bound by Jewish Law when they were not in the land of Israel. He goes on to explain that according to Noahite Law, a man is divorced from his wife by disassociating himself from her; this means that Abraham was actually doing Sarah a favor in saying that she was not his wife. Now if she was forced to sleep with Pharaoh, or one of his ministers, it would not be a sin and she would not need to be killed. This means that the question of whether or not he was endangering Sarah to save his own life was not a factor, because he was doing the very opposite and saving her life.

The Be'er Mayim Chayim explains the question by saying that Abraham did not say that he was not Sarah's husband, but that Sarah's husband did not accompany *them*. He did not say that he was not her husband, and thus he was not lying in order to save his own life, but deceiving because he did not deem it expedient to tell the Egyptians that he was married to her. This is not as good an answer as that of the Tiferes Yehonason because it does not answer the question, but it is better than the other explanations because it explains that he did not lie, whereas the others give an excuse for Abraham's actions.

Rashi's explanation of the second question is that it was not G-d who got angry with Pharaoh, but rather Sarah prayed to G-d to punish Pharaoh. This interpretation sheds a lot of light upon the question, because one can easily see how Sarah would feel violated. If Sarah feels violated by the way she is being treated, she will pray to G-d, and if she is such a great Tzadeket, G-d will answer her prayer. If G-d was just answering her prayer, we have a reason for why a G-d who is supposed to be so impartial would just go and send a plague for something that a person did unknowingly.

Human Deception
By Dylan Shaul

There are numerous examples in the Torah of stories following similar narrative formulae. In this week's parsha, we read of the first of three repetitions of a narrative formula. A patriarch journeys to a foreign land, lies to the monarch of the land, and calls his wife his sister. The monarch tries to marry her, but repents when he learns the truth.

Why have such repetitions? Let us look at each of these stories, and from them we may be able to derive their meaning.

In the first story, Abram and Sarai travel to Egypt. Abram deceives Pharaoh; Pharaoh attempts to take Sarai, and G-d is angered. G-d sends terrible plagues on Egypt, and eventually Pharaoh clues in. Pharaoh appeals to Abram, and the whole thing comes out. Abram and Sarai go back to Canaan.

In the second story, Abraham and Sarah-- their names having been changed in the interim-- journey to Gerar, and Abraham deceives Abimelech. Abimelech takes Sarah into his house, but does not touch her.

G-d appears to Abimelech in a dream and reveals Abraham's deception. Abimelech repents, and is thankful that G-d prevented him from breaking the sanctity of Abraham's marriage.

In the last story, Isaac and Rebecca journey to Gerar, and Isaac deceives Abimelech. Abimelech again wishes to take Rebecca, but stops himself when he sees Isaac and Rebecca "playing". In this story, G-d is absent.

This story can be seen as a foreshadowing of a future deception, which Isaac's son, Jacob, will perpetrate against him. In that case, as in Abimelech's deception, G-d will not be there to reveal it. If the third story foreshadows the future, perhaps the other stories are also foreshadowing.

Let us apply this to the second story. In it, G-d stays Abimelech's hand before he can sin. Shortly after this, G-d stays Abraham's hand, moments before Abraham was to sacrifice Isaac on Mount Moriah. The second story is also foreshadowing.

The first story is decidedly different, as Abimelech is not present, and the story takes place in Egypt, not Gerar. Here we see a foreshadowing of the Israelites' descent into Egypt, and the plagues sent onto its inhabitants as a result.

Why is there so much deception in the Torah? The Snake deceives Eve, Abraham deceives Pharaoh, Abraham deceives Abimelech, Isaac deceives Abimelech, Jacob deceives Isaac, Jacob's children deceive him, Joseph deceives his brothers-- the whole book of Genesis is filled with deception! Although human may be able to deceive human, and indeed does, nothing can be concealed from G-d. In the end, every human is judged by his own worth, and G-d cannot be deceived.

Divrei Torah on **Bereishit**

Vayeira • וירא

This Parsha has been generously sponsored by Brenda Medjuck in honour of her mother, Helen Simpson

A Test of Faith
By Becky Friedman

It's easy to find the contradictions in Parshat Vayera troubling. Avraham argued with Hashem repeatedly to save a city full of terrible people-- people who had only one good man among them-- a city of strangers. But later, when he is commanded to sacrifice his son, his only son, whom he loves, he obeys without a word. Is this the same man?

First, there's the separation of these two incidents. Avraham, a pious, self-effacing man, may have felt more comfortable arguing for the lives of strangers-- when no one can call him biased in the matter-- than arguing for his own son's life, when he clearly has a prejudice.

Moreover, a city in general terms might include people previously looked over-- perhaps G-d neglected the righteous people by classing them in with the sinners in their gates? But when one person in singled out, G-d's meaning cannot be doubted and therefore His purpose cannot be averted.

But that isn't enough-- the difference between the two scenarios is perhaps explained away, but the discomfort we experience when we read about Avraham's complaisance in sacrificing his son is not so easily dispelled.

Akeidat Yitzchak was explicitly described as a test. Maybe Avraham knew that it was a test-- and he just did the best he could.

But not every test is black-and-white-- not every test has only one right answer. Some tests are more subjective. There are many ways to answer the questions, several different right answers, and the correctness of an answer may even vary from person to person. Some tests, too, have no right or wrong answers; the questions simply aim to discern the personality of the person answering-- more important than the answer is the reason behind it.

What then, was the "right" answer for this test? Or, if there is no such thing, what were Avraham's reasons for his actions? The most unsavoury response would be to point out that human sacrifice was common in Avraham's day, and he couldn't have been surprised by G-d's request-- that inasmuch as none of his neighbours were any better, Avraham was in the right to obey G-d blindly in this.

Did he obey *blindly*? Unquestioningly, yes, but blindly? I hope not. It's troubling that he didn't argue-- but maybe we're not giving Avraham Avinu enough credit. Maybe, after all, Avraham knew it was a test. Maybe he obeyed, not blindly, but in the hopes of "calling G-d's bluff" as indeed he arguably did, when the sacrifice was called off just in the nick of time. Or, then again, maybe not. Maybe he did expect to kill his son, and did it with a sorrowful heart but the expectation of achieving something greater, fulfilling G-d's will.

But was this the only answer? Was Avraham's willingness to sacrifice his son, his only son, whom he loves, one hundred percent necessary in ensuring his legacy? I think not.

Had Avraham refused, he may have found himself on shaky ground with G-d, it's true. And Avraham, as the founder of his new religion, was far less prone to arguing with G-d-- let alone defying Him outright-- than was Moses, a more typical role model of the don't-kill-people-needlessly variety.

But had Avraham called G-d on it, had he said not only that he refused to kill his son but that he didn't truly believe that to be G-d's will-- had he, in short, cut out the angel's middle man and jumped straight to the part where G-d told him not to shed the lad's blood-- what then?

No one can know. We can't change the past, and we can't fathom the mind of G-d. But judging from the story, and from other stories in the Bible-- including Moses, the famous proponent of not-killing-people-needlessly-- I can hazard a guess. And that guess is that it would undoubtedly have been acceptable to G-d. Things may have been different, it's true. After all, a personality test often has several different possible results. Perhaps Yitzchak would not have favoured his elder son; perhaps we would not blow the shofar on Rosh Hashana. But Avraham would surely have been accepted as he was, and tasked with the legacy of the Jewish People.

None of us can know what would have happened; none of us can say what we would do in his place. But just like Akeidat Yitzchak, all of life is a test. And what do we do? We don't have all the answers. We never do; none of us can know. So when we're faced with a test of personality, a test of values, a test of faith-- what do we do? What do we do, if there's no one right answer? We just do the best we can.

The Ultimate Test
By Teddy Kravetsky

In this week's parsha, many stories take place-- from the city of Sodom being destroyed to the tenth test that G-d gave to Avraham. In this parsha, Avraham has to deal with many hardships, starting with the destruction of Sodom.

As we all know, Sodom was destroyed because of all the wicked people in the land. However, Avraham stood up for the people and tried to stop G-d from destroying it. He first asked G-d to spare the city if he could find fifty righteous people in it, as, he explained to G-d, it would be unjust to let them suffer for the rest of the city's sins. He eventually worked his way down to finding just ten people in the city, which still proved impossible. In the end, only Avraham's nephew Lot and his family escaped before the city's destruction.

But why was Avraham even remotely concerned with Sodom, a city full of wicked people? Well, the answer to this comes from a very famous twentieth-century rabbi named Rabbi Moshe Feinstein. He explains that, unlike other people, Avraham felt no animosity towards evildoers; he only wanted them to change and become better, more righteous people. If there were ten righteous people in the city, they could influence others to change their bad ways.

The compassion and determination that we see from Avraham shows us that we must be the same. In many situations, it would be a lot easier for us to just stand around and watch the evil that's about to happen, but from Avraham's actions we learn that we must take action and do what we can to the best of our abilities to stop it. It's not enough in Judaism to just stand by and not partake in the sins that are going on; we must do our best to stop them before they happen.

Another lesson that we can learn in this week's parsha comes from the tenth test that G-d gave to Avraham. The test was to sacrifice Sara's only child, Yizchak. Avraham very unwillingly went to the place that G-d told him to go to and, just before he was about to sacrifice Yizchak, an angel told him to stop and to sacrifice a ram that was stuck in the bushes instead.

This test was extremely hard for Avraham to carry out, as he almost had to sacrifice his own son! However, this also teaches us another important lesson. It teaches us to work through the tests and challenges put in our way, as that's what life is all about.

We must rise to the occasion and exceed even our own expectations for what's possible. And if we work hard enough, maybe-- just maybe-- we'll come through successfully.

Gratitude Saved the City
By Matthew Goodman

Parshat Vayeira is recognized for its abundant examples of Avraham Avinu's great kindness. It teaches us a great deal regarding Ahavat Chesed and Mentschlechkeit. It also, however, contains a very powerful message regarding receiving kindness from other people.

After the three angels visited Avraham Avinu, and Hashem told Avraham that He was going to destroy Sdom and Amorah, two of the angels visited Lot and his family in Sdom. They warned him of the impending destruction of the city, and Lot prayed to Hashem to spare the nearby city of Tzoar so that he and his family could flee to it for safety, to which Hashem consented.

Rav Yechezkel Levenstein, Mashgiach (spiritual adviser) of the Ponevezh Yeshiva, finds this to be highly perplexing. How is it that Avraham Avinu's prayer was unable to save Sdom and Amorah while Lot's was able to save Tzoar? He answers with a midrash (Bereishit Rabbah). Lot had provided food and lodging to the angel whose job it was to destroy Tzoar. As such, the angel owed him a debt of Hakarat HaTov (gratitude/recongnizing kindness), and repaid his debt by saving an entire city.

Rav Daniel, Rosh Yeshiva of Kelm, notes that HaKarat HaTov is also found in this week's Haftorah. Elisha the Navi blessed the Shunamite woman with a son and later brought him back to life through prayer. The woman had provided him with lodging every time he stayed in the area, and his HaKarat HaTov for her Hachnasat Orchim (hospitality) created the obligation to perform miracles on her behalf.

How great, then, is HaKarat HaTov, if it obliged the angel to save a city and Elisha HaNavi to perform a miracle? How great is the debt we owe to those who show us kindness?

Divrei Torah on **Bereishit**

These two incidents teach us a great deal about receiving kindness from others. If another person goes out of their way to do something for us, whether we asked for it or not, we become indebted to them. They have given precious time and effort for our sake, and have shown care for our physical and/or spiritual well being. Therefore, we certainly owe a great deal to anyone who displays even a minute amount of Ahavat Chesed. Accordingly, we see that for the mitzvah of Hachnasat Orchim, Elisha HaNavi and the angel were OBLIGATED to repay the kindness in terrific ways!

We learn from their actions that when someone does an act of kindness for us and they in turn ask for our own help, it is our obligation to reciprocate. We should certainly display our vast gratitude and appreciation when we actually receive their kindness, but true HaKarat HaTov, a true display of our sincere appreciation, comes when we in turn give our own Ahavat Chesed. This is resonant for any act of kindness. The following story illustrates this well:

One time, the Chofetz Chaim went to the bathhouse. There was no one in the building except for him and the bathhouse caretaker. As the Chofetz Chaim was washing, he began to feel weaker and weaker. Suddenly, he fell to the floor. The great tzaddik had fainted and no one was in the room to help him. A short while later, the caretaker came in and saw the Chofetz Chaim lying on the floor. He had great difficulty in waking him up, but eventually succeeded, and the tzaddik was lifted up from the floor.

For the rest of his life, the Chofetz Chaim felt immensely grateful for the actions of the caretaker, and continuously displayed to him his gratitude. When the caretaker came to shul, the Chofetz Chaim sat by his side. On Yom Tov, the Chofetz Chaim always had a L'Chaim with him. He even gave him a bracha that he should outlive him. True enough, the caretaker lived a long life and passed away a few months after the Chofetz Chaim.

The great Chofetz Chaim consistently displayed sincere HaKarat HaTov for the caretaker's kind actions. He understood the value of Chesed and how indebted he was for receiving it.

There are many people in our lives who deserve so much for what they have given to us. Our parents. Our teachers. Our friends. Our Rabbis. Hashem. For every bit of chesed they do, they deserve sincere thanks and words of gratitude. We need to show them how much we appreciate all the time, energy, and thought that they give us. And when they come to us and ask, in turn, for our help and our kindness, we need to run to their aid and go above and beyond their request, acting to the fullest extent of our potential. Just like the angel and Elisha HaNavi, we need to show genuine and heartfelt HaKarat HaTov for everything that comes to us. We should all, with the help of Hashem, be able to aptly recognize and give back all the beautiful kindness that we are blessed to receive in this world.

The Value of Hospitality
By Zachary Zarnett-Klein

The Haftarah for Parshat Vayeira is taken from Melachim Bet, Chapter 4, Verses 1-37. A major phenomenon included in the Parashah is Sarah giving birth, at the age of ninety, to her son Yitzchak. The Haftarah discusses a story of the prophet Elisha, Eliyahu's disciple. He was visiting the city of Shunem, and staying at the home of an elderly couple, who always hosted him when he visited the city. On this particular visit, Elisha learned that this couple was childless.

In the beginning of the Parashah, we see one of the most well-known examples of *Hachnasast Orchim,* making guests feel welcome and comfortable. When three angels disguised as men come to visit Avraham a mere three days after his Brit Milah, he not only greets them, but "he ran unto them and bowed down to the ground before them." He continues by inviting them to have a full meal, all while Avraham is in considerable pain from his circumcision at the age of one hundred. As a result, Avraham is rewarded and the angels tell him that because of his kindness because he walked in the ways of G-d, he will be granted a son at that time next year, and he shall name him Yitzchak.

Similarly, the old couple in the Haftarah show such remarkable Hachnasat Orchim by providing for Elisha not only a place to stay, but a room of his own which they built for him from their own means. Elisha informs them that because of their hospitality, G-d will bless them with a son the next year.

Another important quality exemplified in this week's Parashah is *Bikur Cholim,* visiting and assisting the sick. The angels, who come to visit Avraham on the third and most painful day after having a Brit Milah, are a perfect example of the importance of *Bikur Cholim.*

In the Haftarah, when Elisha returns after the baby was born to the couple, he is told that the child is dead. The woman is very upset, afraid that all those years of barrenness and the excitement of being promised a child have all been in vain. Elisha goes "above and beyond" in what some say is the highest act of *Bikur Cholim* ever performed. Elisha immediately makes his way up to the chamber where the child is lying dead. He performs a miracle by bringing the child back to life.

These miracles are the essential components of the Parashah and Haftarah, and teach us that the qualities of *Hachnasat Orchim* and *Bikur Cholim* are critical to our survival and well-being. This is the reason why we continue to invite guests to our home and make people feel welcome in every situation. May we all continue to be blessed with good health and the freedom to reach out to others by hosting them as our guests!

The Banishments of Hagar
By Idan Bergman

In Parashat Vayeira, Sarah Imeinu banishes Hagar, her Egyptian maid, and her son, Yishmael, from her and Avraham Avinu's home forever. A similar case took place in last week's parasha, Parashat Lech Lecha, in which Sarah-- then Sarai-- deals harshly with the pregnant Hagar, resulting in Hagar fleeing from the home.

The two similar instances raise the question of how could Sarah the righteous have done such a seemingly unjust thing, and for what reasons?

Beginning with the case in Lech Lecha, Sarai still had not yet borne a child for herself and Avraham. Thus, to continue Avraham's vital legacy, Sarai had no choice but to allow Hagar to lie with Avraham. However, when it is evident that Hagar has conceived a child, the Torah writes that Sarai was "lowered in her esteem" (16:4), literally meaning that she [Sarai] had become "lighter in [Hagar's] eyes." Rashi comments here that Hagar, after becoming pregnant, began to tease her mistress, saying that Sarai was not the righteous woman she claimed and seemed to be, because she had never borne a child, while Hagar soon would after lying with Avraham Avinu but once. Understandably, Sarai was angered by Hagar's insolent and competitive remarks. In retaliation, Sarai blamed Avraham for Hagar's outrageous remarks. Rashi clarifies here that Sarai blamed him for only praying for a child of Avraham, and not for a child of Avraham and Sarai. Rashi also adds that when he heard Hagar's teasing of Sarai, Avraham was silent.

Now, on the surface it may seem that Sarai is primarily blaming Avraham more because of her jealousy and anger than anything else, but another way of interpreting Sarai is that she is deeply saddened and upset that a stranger will carry Avraham Avinu's legacy instead of her. And even if Sarai is falsely accusing her righteous husband of favouring Hagar, one must also remember that blaming someone very close to you is sometimes done to receive consolation from that very same person. Your parent is usually the wrong person to blame for getting a bad mark on a test, but the reason you do this may only be to let off some steam and receive moral support and encouragement.

Now, looking at Parashat Vayeira, Sarah bluntly asks Avraham to banish Hagar and her son, Yishmael. One could assume that Sarah just has it in for her slave, but it is not Hagar she blames, but her son, Yishmael. Sarai claims to Avraham that Yishmael "mocks" (29:9). Rabeinu Shlomo Efraim from Lunshitz explain that Ishmael did not only "mock," but he conducted the prohibition of *Gilui Arayot*, incest. Rabeinu Shlomo Efraim adds that the Egyptians took incest lightly, as did Hagar. Rashi agrees with this explanation and also adds that not only did Yishmael conduct *Giului Arayot*, he also performed *Avodah Zarah*, idol worship, and *Shfichut Damim*, murder. Yishmael also disputed with Yitzhak over their inheritance and would shoot arrows at him with the intention of killing him, all the while claiming that he was merely jesting. As such, it seems justifiable that Sarah banished Yishmael and his mother only for the sake of Yitzhak's future.

Yet the next pasuk reads, "So [Sarah] said to Avraham, 'Drive out this slavewoman and her son, for the son of that slavewoman shall not inherit with my son, with Isaac'" (29:10). Why does Sarah, when first telling Avraham of the problem, only mention the inheritance and not Yishmael's wrongdoings? This could actually be interpreted that when saying that Yishmael should not receive the inheritance, Sarah also meant that he is *not worthy* of the inheritance, as opposed to Yitzhak.

I hope that these thoughts clarify Sarah's seemingly questionable conduct and shed further light on Sarah Imeinu.

Divrei Torah on **Bereishit**

Chayei Sarah • חַיֵּי שָׂרָה

This Parsha has been generously sponsored by the Roskies-Neuman family in honour of Elianne Neuman and The Shofar staff

Our Terminal Condition
By Matthew Goodman

Mr. Cohen was pacing nervously in the waiting room of a hospital maternity ward. Inside, his wife was giving birth to their first child. Suddenly, the door swung open and the doctor appeared. "Mr. Cohen," he begins, "I have good news and bad news. The good news is that the birth went smoothly. The bad news is that your son has a condition, which, in time, will be terminal." Mr. Cohen, in shock, exclaimed, "This is terrible! What can we do?" "I'm afraid nothing can be done," replied the doctor. "A cure has not been found and scientists have long since abandoned hope of ever finding one." "Oh no...." grieved Mr. Cohen, "What is the condition called?" "Life," answered the doctor. "Life." (Told by Rav Shraga Simmons)

Life is short and the time that we have on earth is limited. I know that I can barely comprehend this concept. For most of us, life hasn't really started yet, and we have, please G-d, so much to look forward to. This idea, however, can have a profound impact on what we make of everything that comes to us. This week's Parsha teaches us a profound lesson in this regard.

The Parsha begins with the words, "Sarah's lifetime was one hundred years, twenty years, and seven years" (Bereishit 23:1). The Midrash (Midrash Rabba 58:3) records that Rebi Akiva was once sitting and teaching Torah. He noticed that his students were dozing off. He wanted to wake them up, so he asked, "Why was Esther seen fit to rule over 127 provinces?" He answered, "Let Esther, who was the descendant of Sarah - who lived for 127 years - rule over 127 provinces."

Why did Rebi Akiva use these words to wake up his sleeping students? Rav Yitzchak Mayer Alter in Chidushei HaRim explains that Rebi Akiva wanted to impress on his students the value of time. Sarah Imeinu lived her whole life with righteousness and modesty. The Midrash says that she was innocent and faithful every second of her life. Thus, for every year Sarah Imeinu lived, her descendant Esther, who mirrored Sarah's midot (characteristics), merited rule over a whole province. Every month, then, may have merited a city. Every week, a village. Every day, a town. Rebi Akiva was stressing to his students that time well spent, as in the case of Sarah Immeinu and Esther, brings great reward. Reversely, wasting time comes at a great price. You can lose precious seconds that could have been utilized for great things but were instead thrown away.

HaRav Moshe Feinstein was once delivering a Shmuz to his students on Chanukah about the importance of not wasting time. He pointed out, "In America, there is a saying that one can 'kill time.'" Suddenly, without warning, he leaned forward and smacked the table in front of him. He stared at his students and shouted "Es iz takeh retzichoh!" - *This is really murder!*

Think of how much time we "kill" in a day on top of all the time we spend engaged in routine. A lot of precious time in every single day can go by without us even noticing. Rav Simmons points out that in the modern American lifestyle, the average adult spends 250 hours a year commuting, 200 hours a year standing in line, and 18 000 hours working in an average 40 year career. Think of how much time we spend commuting to school every year! A lot of time can go down the drain without being used to its fullest extent. Specifically, time is wasted when we as a soul are standing still. When we are staring at the television. When we are mindlessly surfing the internet. Or even when we are alone, and not taking the time to simply think and reflect. When we are not growing, we are wasting time.

Chidushei HaRim further stresses the importance of time by quoting Hillel, who said, "If not now, when?" (Pirkei Avot 1:14). He interprets this statement to mean that at every point in time, in every second, there is an opportunity and purpose that is unique to that moment. It could be any innate action, from eating to sleeping to studying. But every second that you are involved in that action, there is a potential for growth. If it is not done now, when can it be done? It can't. If we don't take advantage of now, then that moment is lost forever.

We can give our lives so much meaning by using every moment in the right way. That means that we need to reap the opportunity to grow in every action; we need to make every second purposeful and a tool for our growth. Make those minutes in class count. Bask in the time you spend with your family. Don't talk Lashon HaRa (gossip) and nonsense with your friends. Try your best to engage in meaningful and connected conversation. And if you really need the time to just stop and "be," then by all means stop and "be," but use the time to connect to yourself. It also means that we can't fill our free time with "time killers" and allow ourselves to simply stand still. There is so much you can get out of studying for your Tanach test and absorbing the beauty and wisdom of Torah. You can find very little of that if you put the Tanach to the side and turn on the television.

We all have a terminal condition called life. Thank G-d every second of our existence is filled with opportunity to reach higher and make life meaningful. That is a precious gift. Why waste it?

Life and Death
By Teddy Kravetsky

In this week's parsha, Avraham and Sara, the father and mother of Judaism, both die. Sara died at age 127 and Avraham at 175. Both were devoted to G-d, and because of this, they died sinless.

After such a tragedy occurred, it is only natural to feel a certain amount of sadness that these two great people finally passed away. However, we should also feel a certain level of happiness, as now the religion of Judaism has passed its first generation and moved on to Yizchak and his new wife. It may have been the end of a life, but it was also the birth of Judaism. Like a flower blooms, Judaism was born.

The death of such great figures also leaves us with many lessons to be learned. The first is that we should live life to the maximum, and enjoy every minute of it. After all, it is said that Avraham and Sara did not waste a day of their lives. This doesn't mean that we should constantly party and take trips around the world in order to get materialistic pleasure, but rather that we should try to enjoy life in such a way that we get a good balance of both spiritual and material pleasure. As well, G-d put us on this earth to serve Him, and although this may seem like a hard task at some times, we still can enjoy the world within the realm of Judaism.

Another lesson we can learn is that death isn't the end; it is also the beginning of the soul's journey up to heaven, where it sits in front of G-d and os judged. This in itself is an entire other life that the soul of each person can experience.

Finally, yet another lesson that can be learned is that each person is put on this earth for a reason. When we fulfill the mission that G-d sent us to do, we can embrace the fact that death is just another way of saying "Mission accomplished."

So the next time you have to deal with one of these awful experiences, take the time to look over the person's life. See what that person accomplished while living; think about what that soul will accomplish after death; and remember that from death, a new beginning is inevitable.

But It's Not My Problem!

By Elianne Neuman

Eliezer, Abraham's servant, was given a challenge to find the ideal wife for his master's son, Yitzchak: he planned to ask a maiden for some water, and the girl who was to be Yitzchak's wife would not only give him water but give water to his camels, too.

Rebecca passed this test with flying colours, by giving both Eliezer and his camels water.

Sforno comments that Eliezer was looking for a woman who would not only fulfill his request, but would go above and beyond it. Thus by only asking for water for himself, Eliezer gave Rebbeca the opportunity to water his camels without a request to do so.

Not only did Rebecca show a willingness to do more than was required of her, she did it in a very modest way. The verse tells us that when Rebecca gave Eliezer water from her jug, she told him to "Drink, my lord," and there was no mention that she would water his camels. It was only <u>after</u> Eliezer finished drinking that Rebecca hurried off as she informed him that she was going to bring water for his camels. Rav Feinstein explained Rebecca's reluctance to mention giving water to Eliezer's camels on the basis that it was Rebecca's second nature to look after another's needs and watering his camels was a given for her. Therefore, she advises Eliezer of her actions in passing, as a mere afterthought.

Rebecca's generosity is all the more remarkable because, while it may be difficult to turn down a direct request for help, it is all too easy to overlook the needs of another when you aren't even asked to help.

Eliezer only asked Rebecca for some water for himself. Rebecca could have satisfied this direct request and avoided taking responsibility for the camels. She could have said that she had done all that she was required to do and that, if the camels were to be watered, then someone else standing at the well ought to assume the responsibility.

But Rebecca didn't stand on principle. Instead, she quietly went and gave Eliezer's camels water, too.

It's not uncommon to shy away from taking on responsibility because we may feel that we aren't obligated to do something. When we find a lost item in the hallway, or when we see someone who is carrying a large box and is struggling to open a door, many of us will fall victim to the old adage "It's not my problem." Indeed, why should one help, if other people are just as capable of doing so?

Many things in this world may not directly be "our problems," yet if we leave them for someone else to take care of, they may not get attended to. If everyone took the attitude "It's not my problem," the world would, surely, be a much less friendly pace.

Rebecca's actions are exemplary. She teaches us that doing more than what is required of us, doing it quietly, and doing it without looking for praise, ought to be second nature. How much better the world would be if we all followed Rebecca's example.

The Man Behind the Man
By Yaron Milwid

This week's parsha focuses on Eliezer. There is much ambiguity about Eliezer's identity. His debut in the parsha is as Abraham's senior servant. Eliezer then becomes a "man" but he refers to Abraham as his master. Despite this reference to Abraham as his master, the Torah insists on calling him a "man." The commentaries say that this is because when Eliezer praised Hashem, he became a servant of Hashem and not Abraham. The interesting thing is that throughout the whole conversation with Rebecca's family, he always refers to himself as Abraham's servant, and never once as Isaac's servant; yet when Rebecca asks him who the man she sees is and he says "my master," she understands that he means Isaac. How does she know that he means Isaac?

I think that it is possible to understand this strange knowledge by interpreting "*eved*" not as servant, but as slave. Using this translation, Eliezer is one of Abraham's possessions. When Abraham sends Eliezer to look for a wife for Isaac, it says "Then the servant took ten of his master's camels and set out with all the bounty of his master in his hand." According to Rashi, Abraham gave Eliezer a deed stating that he had given everything he owned to Isaac as a gift. It is possible that this deed could have been worded in such a manner that it only came into effect if Eliezer managed to bring home a wife for Isaac. If Eliezer is understood to be one of Abraham's belongings, when Eliezer brings Rebecca home, he is transferred to being Isaac's slave. Now, presumably when Eliezer was attempting to get Rebecca's family to agree to let her come back with him he would have shown them the document. As such, when Eliezer said that the man was his master, Rebecca would have known that according to the stipulations of the deed, that meant that the man was Isaac.

What can this possibly teach us? It is possible to learn from this that when we gain a new position, we should be careful not to lie about it. We can also learn from this that when we refer to people we should not use familiar terms, but rather we should refer to them by their proper titles, and pay them the proper respect.

However, I do not believe that it is meant to teach us any of these things, because it is not reasonable to expect such behaviour from the average person. Rather, I think that it is just meant to tell us that Abraham is no longer the person who is meant to bring G-d's message to the world. With Isaac's inheritance of Eliezer and the rest of Abraham's property, he also inherited Abraham's mission in life.

What's In a Name?

By Zachary Zarnett-Klein

Why is this Parshah called Chayei Sarah?

This Shabbat, we read about the deaths of two prominent men who helped shape the face of Jewish identity and history. We read in the Torah portion about the death of Avraham and in the Haftarah about the death of King David. It is quite odd that there are so many parallels between the deaths of both Avraham and David, seeing as that they lived in to totally different eras; furthermore, while Avraham was a man focused on enhancing the bond of humankind through enriching our Midot, David spent most of his life fending off people, as opposed to gathering them, since he was involved in many wars with Israel's adversaries.

Nevertheless, along with their many differences, there is also a striking similarity, integrated with a further important difference. In regards to Avraham becoming advanced in years, Scripture states, "V'Avaraham Zaken Ba BaYamim V'Hashem Berach Et Avraham BaKol." This translates to, "And Avraham was old, advanced in years, and G-d Blessed Avraham with everything." In contrast, in regards to David, Scripture states, "V'Hamelech David Zaken Ba Ba'Yamim Va'Yechasuhu Ba'Bgadim V'Lo Yicham Lo," which means, "And King David was old, advanced in years, and he was covered in garments and still was not warm." As we can see, although these two verses start on the same note-- these two leaders are becoming "old, advanced in years"-- the endings to both of these verses leave us with a totally opposite feeling. Whereas we learn that Avraham was comforted by all that with which G-d had blessed him when he reached the time of his seniority, David was extremely uncomfortable, not being able to become warm no matter what he tried.

Whatever the differences of their situations, these two men both reacted to becoming "old" in the same manner-- by searching for a woman. When Avraham became advanced in years, he searched for a wife for his son Yitzchak, and David searched for a woman who could possibly help keep him warm. Avraham charges his servant Eliezer to return to Avraham's homeland and seek a wife for Yitzckak. Eliezer does so and returns wih Rivka, who becomes Yitzvhak's wife. David's servants search throughout Israel to seek for him the perfect woman who will keep him warm in his final stages of life, and find Avishag HaShunammit.

You may be asking yourself, what in the world is going on? What do women have to do with impending death, and why do these two strong men seem bent on finding the perfect one? It's quite simple, really! Both Avaraham and David are men whose relationships with their wives are so eminent as to be highlighted by Scripture. Both of these men had faithful wives whom they loved dearly and who loved them dearly. Avraham, along with Sarah, built the Jewish people and established a nation based on caring for one another and good Midot. In turn, Avraham wants to assure that just as Sarah provided him with a lifelong love, his son, too, would be able to experience this and continue the development of the Jewish people. As well, we learn in Scripture that David felt so dearly towards his late wives Michal, Avigail, and Achinoam, who each helped support him throughout the many battles he fought, that he thought that with a woman he could possibly reexperience that warmth that he used to experience with his wives, and she could serve as a support system to him in his final days. This being said, it is only fitting that the Parshah be called "Chayei Sarah", because it is her legacy as a dedicated wife and role model which shaped the image of the perfect wife, and lives on forever as the meaning of the words "Eshet Chayil".

Toldot • תולדות

This Parsha has been generously sponsored by the Rosenstein family in honour of Aaron Rosenstein

Mercy and Justice
By Dylan Shaul

Abraham and Isaac's old age, the latter of which appears in this week's parsha, are described in contrasting ways: The Torah says, "Abraham was old, advanced in days" (Genesis 24:1). It says of Isaac "that when Isaac was old, and his eyes were dim [...]" (Genesis 27:1). It says elsewhere, "G-d called the light Day, and the darkness He called Night" (Genesis 1:5). Abraham in his old age was filled with days; he was filled with divine light. Isaac in his old age was blind; he lived a life of darkness. However, light and darkness are not synonymous with good and evil; G-d created both Day and Night. We pray on Passover for "the day that is neither day nor night," the time of the Messiah. Both Day and Night can be positive things.

This week's parsha deals with the birth of and subsequent conflict between the twin sons of Isaac: Jacob and Esau. Isaac favoured Esau, and Isaac's wife Rebecca favoured Jacob. Why did Isaac favour Esau? The Zohar sees the creation and interplay of Light and Darkness in Genesis as a reflection of the forces of Hesed and Gevurah, Mercy and Justice. G-d's name Hashem reflects Mercy, while G-d's name Elokim reflects Justice. Both are important parts of G-d's existence, and so both are important traits in humanity. Indeed, from the Seder's reference to the Messianic Age, it is clear that a balance of Mercy and Justice is desirable.

Justice is desirable.

Esau is described as a "cunning hunter" and Jacob is described as "a simple man, a dweller in tents" (Genesis 25: 27). When G-d created Adam and Eve and placed them in the Garden of Eden, He commanded, "Of every tree of the Garden you may eat" (Genesis 2:16). There is no mention of hunting animals in the Garden of Eden. Only later, after the Flood, does G-d compromise with humanity's nature and allow them to eat meat:

"The fear of you and the dread of you shall be on every living thing [...] every moving thing that lives shall be food for you" (Genesis 9:2-3). Esau, being a person of Justice, follows the letter of G-d's law; if G-d allows him to eat animals, he will, despite any merciful inclinations he might have. Jacob acts in a very different way. Isaac favoured Esau, because Esau's acts of Justice most resembled his own way of thinking. The prophet Isaiah said of the children of Jacob that "nations shall walk in your light" (Isaiah 60:3), and that they are "a light unto the nations" (Isaiah 42:6).

As we have established above, light is the marker of Mercy. The children of Israel were chosen by G-d to be examples of Mercy to the nations of the world. This is what is meant by "the dew of Heaven" (Genesis 27:28) in Isaac's blessing of Jacob. Dew appears at the beginning of the day, and is a sign of Mercy. The Dew of Heaven is divine Mercy, and it is this value that Jacob personifies. The children of Esau were chosen to be examples of Justice to the nations of the world. The children of Esau are the arm by which divine retribution is carried out. When Israel transgressed against G-d, he would send the children of Esau to punish them. The children of Israel refer to Abraham as Avinu, our father. This is because we identify with his Mercy more than with Isaac's Justice. Despite this, a balance of Mercy and Justice is needed, just as there must be Day and Night. Light and Darkness, Mercy and Justice, Sabbath and Days of Work, Day and Night, Jacob and Esau: these opposites serve each other, and both must exist for the world to function.

Like Father Like Son

By Yaron Milwid

Every young child wants to be just like his parents. Is that a good thing or a bad thing? The idea of a person wanting to be like his daddy is found in this week's Parsha, but the idea of a child carving its own way in life is also found in this week's Parsha. In this week's Parsha, we see many times that Eisav wants to be like his father, but we also see that the great Yitzchak does not want to be like his legendary father, Abraham. In the first Pasuk of our Parsha, it says twice that Yitzchak was the son of Abraham. Some of the commentators ask why this is; wouldn't once have been enough? The answer is that Yitzchak was so different from Abraham that the skeptics did not believe that Yitzchak was his son. This goes to show that not trying to be like one's father is not the end of the world. As the Parsha goes on, it continues to show this idea by portraying Eisav as wanting not only to please his father, but also to be like his father.

An example of Eisav trying to be like his father but going about it in completely the wrong way is how he married at the age of forty, which the commentaries say was because his father Yitzchak married at the age of forty. They also say that up until that time, Eisav had just taken the wives of other men and raped them. Another part of this example is the fact that when the Tanach talks here about the names of Eisav's wives, it uses pseudonyms. The name it uses for the first wife changes both her name and her father's name. The rabbis say that Eisav changed her name to say that she had turned away from idol-worship. They also say that he changed her father's name because the Torah says that her father was not a good person-- thus Eisav changed his name. What does this have to do with Eisav trying to be like his father, besides the fact that he married the daughter of an evil man? He changed her father's name to Be'eri in order to emulate his father because this means "my well". We have just seen that Yitzchak had a well, and thus Eisav was digging a metaphorical well for himself.

This is an extreme case of irony because Eisav is trying to emulate his father Yitzchak, who is trying not to be like his father. How was Yitzchak different from his father? He feared G-d whereas his father loved G-d, and thus Eisav is not doing as his father did, because he is worshipping idols. This brings us to another interesting occurrence: Eisav, who was trying to make his father so happy, caused his father pain because his and his wives' idol worship tormented Yitzchak and Rivkah. But how do we know that he was trying to make his father happy? According to Rashi, he would ask his father how to take a tenth of wheat and salt because alone they are not worth a lot, but with other things they are worth a lot. Because of this question, Yitzchak was convinced that Eisav was a great Tzadik.

To Thine Own Self Be True
By Matthew Goodman

The society in which we live likes to create molds, and we frequently feel the need to fit into them. We have to follow the new trend. We have to be interested in certain things. We have to act in a particular manner. We have to be who society wants us to be. What ever happened to who we really are? Every single human being has fantastic potential to achieve great things and make positive changes in this world. We can leave our mark for the better. We can also leave our mark for the worse. Rav Shalom Noach Berzovsky, in Netivot Shalom, says that we are each created with a special mission in the world. In order to discover that mission, we need to figure out who we truly are and use that knowledge for the good. The week's Parsha, Toladot, teaches us about figuring out just that.

Eisav, the older twin of Yaakov, is referred to as 'red' twice in this Parsha. The first time describes Eisav's birth, when the Torah states, "The first one came out red, entirely like a hairy mantle" (Bereishit 25:25). The second time is in reference to when Eisav traded his birthright to Yaakov for a pot of lentil soup. The pasuk says, "And Eisav said to Yaakov, 'Pour into me, now, some of that very red stuff, for I am exhausted.' Therefore he was named Edom [red]" (25:30). Why is it that Eisav received the nickname Edom after purchasing the soup, and not after actually emerging from the womb red? Why does a seemingly innocuous incident with "red stuff" fifteen years after his birth result in the nickname Edom?

The Midrash (Midrash Rabba 63:8) quotes R' Abba bar Kahana who said that the significance of Eisav emerging from the womb red is that it shows him to be a spiller of blood. Not an actual spiller of blood, but it makes it clear that he could have been. The Midrash then goes on to say that Shmuel HaNavi was worried that David HaMelech also had a similar trait, based on the pasuk "he was *Admoni*" (Shmuel 16:12) but Hashem reassured him that David had "fair eyes," meaning that he only killed with the consent and will of the Sanhedrin, who were the eyes of the nation. Eisav, on the other hand, killed based on his own volition. We see from the Midrash that both Eisav and David had the traits of a blood spiller, but each channeled their dispositions towards different causes. David for the sake of Klal Yisrael and Eisav for his own sake.

On a similar note, the Gemara (Shabbat 156a) explains that those born at the astrological "hour" of Mars have innate dispositions to spill blood. As such, says Rav Ashi, they can channel their dispositions towards a number of possible professions. Among them, a bloodletter (medical profession of the time involving leaching blood from the body), a criminal, a Shochet (ritual slaughterer), or a Mohel (one trained in circumcision).

When Eisav was born red, it was an indication of his dominant personality trait: he liked blood. So much so that it was as if he was a spiller of blood. Baby Eisav, however, certainly had no blood on his hands, and therefore there was no reason to call him Edom. It was only fifteen years later, when Eisav acted so rash and boorish as to sell his birthright for soup, did he get the name Edom.

Eisav had a choice. He could have used his personality to do mitzvot, and become the greatest Mohel or Shochet the Jewish people ever saw. Or he could have used his personality to become the most infamous bandit or murderer to ever live. He choose the latter, and, indeed, his descendants became one of the greatest murderers of history -- the Roman Empire. David HaMelech, on the other hand, used his disposition to become the most famous King of the Jewish people. The Gemara above admits that there is nothing you can do to change a personality. That is who Eisav fundamentally was: a spiller of blood. How you act on it is the ultimate decider of who you are and what you can achieve.

Rav Chaim Vital, a kabbalist from Tzfat in the 15th century, writes that each person is created with dominant natural dispositions and by identifying your particular disposition, or "element," you can discover where you can achieve your own unique greatness. For example, there are people who are fiery and ambitious. Their personal flames reach up and out to consume and conquer. They can use this personality trait to accomplish, create, and lead, but they can also use it to become arrogant, angry, and controlling.

Eisav teaches us an interesting lesson about being the best we can be. We are all intrinsically unique and special. Unlike character traits, which can be altered and improved, we all inherently have some particular personality traits and dispositions. We have different likes and interests, different goals and ambitions, different ways of dealing with people, and different ways of expressing ourselves. Those differences make us beautiful. They make us special. We can use those traits to achieve a lot, and the more we know about who we really are, the more we can tailor ourselves towards achieving our potential. We just have to use those traits for the good.

The Gemara (Ta'anit 21b) tells a story about a man named Dr. Abba, who, interestingly enough, was a bloodletter. Perhaps we could assume that he also had a disposition towards blood. Every day a voice would descend from the Heavenly Yeshiva and call out to Abba, "Shalom aleicha!" "Peace unto you!" Abaye also received such greetings, but only on Erev Shabbos. Abaye felt distressed by this, and wondered why he, too, did not merit to receive these greetings just as frequently. Perhaps he lacked some virtue that Abba possessed. The Heavens answered Abaye by telling him that he simply cannot do what Abba does, because he is Abaye and not Abba. What exactly were the special deeds of Abba that made him merit heavenly greetings? The Gemara lists that he had separate rooms for men and women; a special garment for women so that he would not have to look at them immodestly; an anonymous system of payment so that those who could not afford to pay could still be treated; and a policy that Torah scholars did not have to pay at all.

Dr. Abba was not a Rabbi nor a scholar nor a famous tzaddik, but he was unique. He took his professional situation, bloodletting, and turned it into something beautiful. A beacon of modesty and kindness. Says Rav Shlomo Freifeld, he created something unique to his situation. He put all his efforts into making the most of the person he was. Thus he merited heavenly greetings.

The best way to be the best you is, first and foremost, to know who you are. Modern society can sometimes pressure us to be people we are not, and in doing so we do ourselves a great disservice. The second step, then, is to stray from the path of Eisav and use who you are to do the most good possible. If you are a bright student, think of how much good you can do if you help others with their work. If you are a good conversationalist, you can make a person very happy while performing the mitzvah of Bikur Cholim, visiting the sick. With the help of Hashem we should all have the insight to understand ourselves, our strengths, and our weakness, and achieve our own special, unique potential. As Shakespeare said in Hamlet, "This above all: To thine own self be true."

Rivka's Deceit
By Zachary Zarnett-Klein

Whenever I read through Parshat Toldot, I view Rivka as committing a tremendous sin. She aids Yaakov in receiving the blessing distinctly set out for Esav, an act that should not go unpunished.

In fact, she goes to great length to help Yaakov. She cooks for Yaakov the food that Yitzchak requested. She also clothes Yaakov in Esav's clothes and put the skins of the animal she had slaughtered on his neck. All Yaakov had to do was get two kid goats, sit back, and be blessed.

For quite some time now, I have been mistakenly thinking that Rivka committs this seemingly sinful act out of favouritism. As it says in the Torah, "VRivka Ohevet et Yaakov"- "And Rivka loved Yaakov."

However, looking deeper into the text, it appears otherwise. Rivka is not acting sinfully and trying to undermine her blind husband. Rather, she is simply carrying out the decree from Hashem. When Rivka was pregnant with Esav and Yaakov, Hashem told her, "Two nations are in your womb, and two regimes from your insides shall be separated; the might shall pass from one regime to the other, and **the elder shall serve the younger**." Rivka was told that there were two rival nations growing in her, who will be the fathers of two great nations, and that the younger one shall prove to be superior over the older one.

Looking at the "sin" in this light, it now appears that Rivka is not committing inquity, but rather she is taking upon herself to carry out G-d's word. Rivka takes an active approach in following the word of Hashem. She refuses simply stand by and allow events to play out.

We can see Rivka as a hallmark for taking an active role in one's community, setting an example to all Jews to takes it upon themselves to do what is right and follow the commandments. Not only does this story *not* display deceit, it displays the utmost loyalty and devotion to Hashem's mitzvot.

Divrei Torah on **Bereishit**

Vayeitzei • ויצא

> *This Parsha has been generously sponsored by the Mevorach family in honour of all the Mevorach kids, Orry, Dana, and Keren*

Yaakov's Loving Rebuke
By Matthew Goodman

Many of our fellow Jews do not always walk on a straight path in life. Sometimes they make mistakes. Sometimes they do things which they should not be doing. Most of us can recall a situation in which a friend did something which he knew was wrong. Some of those times, I am sure, we can even remember a situation in which we told that friend outright that he was doing something wrong, and rebuked him for his actions. The Torah tells us that it is in fact a mitzvah to rebuke our fellow Jew if we know that he is doing something wrong. It states, "You shall not hate your brother in your heart. You shall surely rebuke your fellow, but you shall not bear a sin on his account" (Vayikra 19:17). This mitzvah incurs a particularly difficult question. Most people have a certain amount of pride that makes it very difficult for them to listen to someone tell them that they did something wrong. As such, how does one get a fellow Jew to listen to and accept his rebuke?

This week's Parsha, Vayeitzei, provides us with an interesting case study in rebuking your fellow. Yaakov Avinu, at the bequest of his mother Rivka, leaves Canaan for Haran to find a wife from his mother's family and escape the wrath of his brother Eisav. When he finally reaches Padan Aram, home of Lavan, Rivka's brother, he sees a well in the field and flocks of sheep lying beside it. The herders of Haran would gather at the well and water the sheep. Yaakov comes up to them and says, "My brothers, where are you from?" They answer, "Haran." He asks if they know Lavan, and then inquires as to how is uncle is doing. After all these pleasantries, he tells them, "The day is yet long; it is not the time to take in the livestock. Water the sheep and go on grazing" (Vayikra 19:4-7). What chutzpah! Yaakov just met these men next a well and suddenly he is rebuking them on their herdsmen-ship and telling them what to do with their sheep! How did Yaakov Avinu get away with this?

The Ponevezher Rav explains that Yaakov was able to rebuke the herdsmen and have them listen to him because of one word: "Achai," My brothers. Yaakov's use of the word "Achai" demonstrated that from the onset of his conversation, he was displaying a level of deep connection with the herdsmen by considering them his brothers. He had Ahava, love, for them. Thus, when Yaakov rebuked them for bringing out the livestock too early, he did not receive a negative response from the herdsmen. They did not get angry at his words, nor did they accuse him of being chutzpadik. Rather, they felt that Yaakov cared about them and was looking out for them like a brother. Yaakov did not get away with the rebuke because he called the strangers "Achai." He rebuked them because to him they were his brothers, and he had a responsibility to look out for their welfare. The herdsmen felt this deep compassion emanate from Yaakov, and understood immediately that his actions were loving rather than hostile.

Chazal express the difficulty of proper rebuke. Rebi Elazar ben Azaryah said that he would be amazed if he found anyone in his generation who knew how to properly rebuke (Arachin 16b). If he said that about the generation that produced many of Jewish history's greatest Rabbis, how much more so is it true regarding our own generation! Despite the difficulty, however, it is obvious that the mitzvah is given a tremendous amount of weight and importance, to the extent that the Talmud even obliges a student to rebuke his own Rebbi (Bava Metzia 31a).

Our Rabbis teach us that the most effective way to give proper rebuke and overcome the difficulty of successfully criticizing your friend is through love. The mandatory prerequisite for rebuke is a feeling of compassion and care for the other person, which should in fact be the reason why you are rebuking your friend in the first place. The Kitzur Shuchan Aruch says that one should delineate that the reason why he is correcting his friend's actions is because he cares deeply about him. The Lubavitcher Rebbe explains that "when one Jew rebukes another, a precondition must be Ahavat Yisrael, and the test is if the recipient of the rebuke feels that he is being rebuked out of love."

Passing this test can, at times, be exceptionally hard, especially depending on whom you are rebuking in particular. Our Rabbis and Gedolim, however, have set us good examples. Rav Frand relates the following story about the Ponevezher Rav:

The Rav had made a trip to America to fundraise for the Ponevezher Yeshiva in Eretz Yisrael, and managed to arrange an appointment with a multi-millionaire. The man was only able to meet the Rav for a short amount of time. The Rav made sure that his driver picked him up early for their appointment, but they lost their way and were stuck in a traffic jam. They finally reached the office building with barely two minutes to spare. The parking lot, however, was completely full save for one spot. When the driver saw the sign next to it, his heart sank. "Reserved for the President," it read. "Go ahead," said the Rav, "Pull into that spot." The driver briefly protested but eventually obliged, and the Rav and the driver made their way to meet the multi-millionaire.

He arrived at the meeting on time and briskly began to make his pitch, describing the state and achievements of his remarkable Yeshiva. Several minutes into his proposal, an aide burst into the room, turned towards his boss, and exclaimed, "Did you know that this Rabbi parked in your spot? The spot that is reserved for you!" The driver became very embarrassed and anticipated that the multi-millionaire would kick them out of his office immediately. The Rav, on the other hand, looked at the potential donor and spoke calmly. "Reserved? What does reserved mean? Nothing is reserved for anyone in this world. All that we have is a gift from Hashem. If Hashem grants someone wealth, it is a gift. He should use whatever he needs and give the rest away to good causes." The Rav reiterated rebukingly, "I'm sorry sir, but nothing we have is reserved for us."

The multi-millionaire smiled warmly and wrote out a generous check. The Rav leaned across the table and gave the man his trademark kiss on the check, a symbol of his immense love for fellow Jews. The multi-millionaire accepted the rebuke because he felt that deep compassion and knew that the Rav's message was far from hostile. He was looking out for him.

If we truly love our friends and fellow Jews, we need to know that a natural byproduct of that love is rebuke. For that reason, love is a necessary precondition for proper admonition. Yaakov Avinu rebuked the herdsmen because he treated them as his brothers, and the herdsmen accepted it because they felt that warmth. The Ponevezher Rav rebuked a millionaire over a reserved parking spot and similarly, he, too, accepted it, because he, too, felt the warmth of a terrific and earnest Ahavat Yisrael.

We, too, are put into situations in which we need to display that type of love. A calm, compassionate, loving, caring message of gentle reproach is one of the ultimate displays of Ahavat Yisrael, and can instill great attitude changes in our friends. We can all make mistakes very easily, and sometimes they can be a little bigger than anticipated. We all need our friends, family, and fellow Jews to point us in the right direction and help us to be the best we can be. Such a journey is too hard to do alone. It certainly becomes much easier when we are reminded that there are people who want us to be the best neshama possible and will help us get there with a little bit of rebuke.

Heavenward

By Dylan Shaul

The story of Vayetze begins with an enigmatic description of a dream that Jacob has on his journey from Canaan to Haran. While sleeping, he envisions a ladder stretching skyward from Earth, with angels ascending and descending it. G-d, standing atop the ladder, promises Jacob the land of Canaan as his inheritance. Besides being a unique symbol throughout the Genesis narrative, the description of the ladder utilizes words that only appear a few other times in the Torah. The full text of the description reads "And he dreamt, and behold, a ladder stood on earth, and its top reached heavenward, and angels of G-d were ascending and descending it." The is the only occurrence of the word for 'ladder' in the Torah, as well as the only time this verse's word for 'stand' is used. 'Ascending' is used on only one other occasion and 'descending' is unique to the entire Tanakh.

The most compelling distinctive word in this passage is 'heavenward,' which appears a total of six times throughout the Torah. There is an inner connectivity between these six appearances of the word "hashemayma" which might reveal an important lesson about the place of Heaven as the abode of G-d and the angels in our understanding of divinity and in our understanding of the Torah itself.

The first emergence of the term comes with G-d's promise to Abram that his descendants will be as numerous as the stars. G-d instructs Abram to look 'heavenward' and try to number the stars. G-d knew the feat to be impossible, and therefore His request was rather a command to Abram to witness the majesty and power of G-d, whose power created the vast expanse of the Universe. Looking heavenward was to look upon G-d's providence in the Universe, which rules throughout the vastness of empty space. How small must Abram now seem: "What is man, that You make so much of him, that You should set your heart on him?" To gaze heavenward in the way of Abram is to acknowledge humanity's insignificance within the cosmos.

The second time 'heavenward' is used is in this week's parsha, during Jacob's dream. The top of the ladder reached 'heavenward' and at its top stood G-d. G-d, who sends and recalls His angels to work wonders on Earth, enthroned in Heaven, king of the world: this is the image conjured up in this passage. When G-d speaks to Jacob, promising him the land that will one day bear his name, He speaks with the authority of Heaven. A voice that comes from heaven is a voice to be listened to, at least insofar as the patriarchs are concerned, but we will come to see how the view is lacking, and in fact is unsubstantiated by scripture itself. Suffice it to say that when Jacob awakes, he says, "How awe-inspiring is this place," this place where he witnessed G-d speak from heaven. This feeling of awe is distinct from but unified with that of Abram. Abram looked up and saw emptiness, but knew G-d to be there. Jacob looked up and saw G-d Himself, or rather, he looked up, and G-d showed Himself. In both, G-d reveals Himself from the sky.

The third and fourth uses of 'heavenward' come from the story of the Ten Plagues. The third is used as part of G-d's instructions for the plague of boils, and the fourth is used when Moses and Aaron carry out the task. G-d instructs Moses and Aaron to take handfuls of soot from a furnace and to throw it 'heavenward' in the presence of Pharoah. This seems to be a rather futile task: several other plagues have already happened with no provocation, and there seems to be little reason why Moses and Aaron would have to perform this miracle in front of Pharoah. While earlier plagues, such as the Nile turning to blood, would have been inexplicable to the Pharoah's ancient court, a particularly intense outbreak of skin disease would not have been the greatest wonder the Egyptian king had ever seen. For this reason, G-d tells his prophets to throw the soot 'heavenward,' so that Pharoah will know that the plague is not of earthly origin, but rather comes from heaven; that is to say, from G-d. Pharoah gazes heavenward in much the same way as Abram and Jacob, and in much the same way, he comes to understand the awesome power of Heaven.

The fifth appearance of the terms summarily reflects on the prior four experiences, and makes a harsh warning of them. Moses warns the Israelites, "And when you look up to the sky and see the sun, the moon and the stars, all the heavenly array, do not be enticed into bowing down to them and worshiping things the Lord your G-d has apportioned to all the nations under heaven." Moses warns the Israelites not to see in the heavens what the nations see-- a multitude of competing divine beings, each having power over a different celestial body-- but rather to see what Abram, Jacob, and Pharoah saw: that the majesty and power of the heavens proclaim the name of the one, living G-d. It is interesting to note that the people to whom Moses is speaking were the generation after that of the Exodus; they would not have been witnesses to G-d appearing at Sinai, though they would have undoubtedly heard stories of G-d descending from heaven to

187

Earth from their parents. They would have heard the story that the Torah was given out of the mouth of Heaven, to Moses, who brought it to the people.

All the more powerful and stupefying is the last use of the word 'heavenward' in the Torah, which seems to contradict all prior usage, and our understanding of the nature of the law. I present it here in its entirety:

"For this commandment, which I command to you today, is not a wonder to you, nor is it far away. It is not in heaven, that you should say, 'Who will go heavenward for us, and bring it to us, and make us hear it, that we may do it?' Neither is it beyond the sea, that you should say, 'Who will go over the sea for us, and bring it to us, and make us hear it, that we may do it?' But the word is very close to you, in your mouth, and in your heart, for you to do. See, I have set before you this day life and good, and death and evil."

These are nearly the last words that Moses speaks to the Israelites right before they enter into the land that G-d had promised them. However, the picture of the law that Moses gives to his people seems inconsistent with other accounts. Is the law not absolute, the word of G-d as spoken from Heaven, to be brought down from Heaven, exactly as Moses said it was not? Did Moses not 'go heavenward for us'? Moses presents the people with a choice between life and death; however, the choice of life seems to be following the word that is in their own hearts. Though G-d seems to be in heaven, His word is not; it is living, inside everyone. Even this first assumption is less than true. Seems, madam? Nay, it is not. "The heavens, even the highest heavens, cannot contain you"-- so says Solomon about G-d. It is an equal representation of G-d's will for us, His word. Even the highest heavens cannot contain it. Only G-d's true abode, the infinity of the Universe and beyond, can contain Him-- that is to say, only He can contain Himself. Only the Word's true abode, the infinity of the human heart and soul, can contain it; that is to say, only we, who are G-d's Word, can contain our own infinity.

Divrei Torah on **Bereishit**

Vayishlach • וַיִּשְׁלַח

This Parsha has been generously sponsored by the Shear family in honour of Sarah Shear

Torah Teachings
By Ari Satok

This week's parasha, Parashat Vayishlach, is full of uniquely relevant messages and teachings for our lives today. The parasha starts by describing Jacob, preparing himself for his reunion with Esau. On a purely emotional level, this storyline can be viewed as a heartfelt reconciliation of two brothers, who for years had been bitterly divided. On a deeper level, though, it can be viewed as a testament to the fact that it is never too late to make a change. Jacob and Esau had not seen each other for thirty-four years. One of our fundamental flaws as human beings is that we often let time dull our desire to inspire change. Oftentimes, we decide that because a problem has been going on for a long time, it is not only impractical but impossible to change it. Jacob and Esau's reunion after thirty-four years demonstrates that this idea is a fallacy, and that we as human beings should never allow time to diminish our desire to fix and work on our problems.

Another beautiful message that can be attained from this parasha is articulated by Sforno in his interpretation of Jacob's fight with the angel. Jacob fights with an angel and "Jacob's hip socket was dislocated as he wrestled with him." Sforno offers a beautiful parallel to this fight. Jacob was temporarily injured in the struggle, but in time he prevailed and went on to great things. Likewise, we, the Jewish people, often suffer losses in our struggle to maintain Jewish peoplehood and continuity. However, just like Jacob, although we do suffer setbacks and endure struggles, in time we go on to achieve greater and more important things. What's truly important is to not lose hope and to not let these minor struggles erode our faith and belief in a greater cause.

Another integral theme of this parasha manifests itself during Jacob's meeting with Esau. Jacob offers Esau a gift, and tries to convince Esau to accept it saying, "Please accept my gift which was brought to you, inasmuch as G-d has been gracious to me and inasmuch as I have everything." Jacob's words "I have everything" are indicative of his righteous and selfless attitudes in regards to materialism. Human beings are often seduced into believing that it is important to have more of everything material. Jacob, though, does not need more of everything material to be satisfied. It says in the Mishnah, "Who is rich? He who is satisfied with his lot." Jacob epitomizes this very description. We must learn from Jacob to not only be accepting of our lot, but to be satisfied and thankful for what we have, rather than disappointed about what we don't have.

Yaakov's Struggles
By Zachary Zarnett-Klein

It is very clear from the Parashah that Yaakov's life is far from simple. In this Parashah, we are told that he encounters his brother, his daughter Dinah is taken captive by the Hivites, and his beloved wife Rachel dies.

Yaakov goes from one trial to the next as he leaves his vicious ordeal with Lavan and is immediately told that his brother Esav is approaching him with 400 armed men by his side. Fearful, Yaakov decides to divide his camp into two parts-- himself and the rest of his family. In this act of heroism, he makes sure that only he will be harmed by Esav, for even if he arrives at the rest of the family's camp, Yaakov is his sole target.

Despite the fact that he sent Esav many gifts before the visit, Esav still tries to harm Yaakov. When they finally reunite, it is written in the text that Esav kissed Yaakov, and the word "Vayishakehu" has dots above all the letters. Some Rabbis say that this is to allude that Esav's kisses were insincere. Another Chacham says that instead of kissing Yaakov, Esav tried to bite his neck; however, Hashem caused Yaakov's neck to turn to marble, and therefore he remained unharmed.

Before this visit, a mysterious angel came to duel with Yaakov. This is regarded by many sages as the penultimate battle between good and evil. It is thought that the epitomy of all evil, the Satan himself, came to duke it out with Yaakov. It is therefore noted as the eternal struggle between man's desire to perfect himself and the evil inclination's determination to destroy him.

This same struggle is witnessed when Dinah, Yaakov's daughter is kidnapped by Shechem, the Hivites and ultimately raped. This struggle with immorality and how to defeat it haunts Yaakov especially in this encounter. However, Yaakov also sees the ability of each human being to change for the better and gives the people the town a chance to redeem themselves by circumcising all the males. This ability to see the good in people and the silver lining even in the darkest of situations is what helps Yaakov get through the immense hardships he is faced with throughout his life.

Finally, the death of Rachel, Yaakov's most beloved wife. Yaakov made an oath to Lavan when he was searching Yaakov's camp for his belongings, that whoever is concealing anything which belongs to Lavan, shall surely die. Rachel was hiding idols belonging to her father Lavan, and because of this, she dies at this time. Yaakov decides to bury her in Bet Lechem. This is a very interesting decision, and her burial spot is very important in other parts of Tanach. In the book of Shmuel Aleph, Shaul passes Kvurat Rachel, the burial spot of Rachel, after he is anointed king, to be greeted by two men. Yaakov also foresaw that on the way to the Babylonian exile, Bnei Yisrael would pass by Kvurat Rachel, as it is written in Yirmiyahu: "Rachel weeps for her children." To this day, Kvurat Rachel is frequented by those who seek spiritual guidance.

In conclusion, Yaakov continually overcame adversity throughout his life and used his struggles not only to further himself, but to make sure his descendants would be better off.

Yaakov and Yisrael

By Matthew Goodman

The mood was tense in the Shul shortly before Kol Nidre on Yom Kippur. There were palpably strong feelings of remorse over past deeds and the solemnity of the day weighed heavily upon the congregation. Suddenly, the Rabbi, no longer able to contain himself, rushed up to the ark and cried out, "I'm a nobody! I'm a nobody!" and returned to his seat, a bit relieved. Shortly after, the Shamash followed suit; he also approached the ark and began to cry, "I'm a nobody! I'm a nobody!" Soon, the whole community was lined up in front of the ark to cry out their own confessions of absolute humility. Meanwhile, a beggar wandered into the Shul and took a seat in the back. Bewildered by the all the commotion, he assumed that this must be the Shul's custom and also brought himself to the front of the ark. At that point, the Rabbi turned to the Shamash and said, "Who does that man think he is, calling himself a nobody?"

Humility is treated with the utmost reverence in Jewish thought. We learn: "Rav Levitas of Yavneh taught that one should be exceedingly humble of spirit, for the end of man is worms (Pirkei Avot 4:4)." Great ethicists, such as Aristotle and Kant, placed immense importance and value to the trait of humility. Most of us do, too, and we realize the greatness of a modest person.

For many of us, however, it is exceedingly difficult to obtain humility. One of the reasons why is simply the value system of the society around us. A second reason, and a more workable problem, is the fact that many of us do not exactly know what humility means. It can be confused with meekness, self-loathing, and low self-esteem, which are surely traits for which one should not be encouraged to strive; they are antitheses of the Jewish concept of self value. In fact, humility is perfectly complemented alongside a high level of self-esteem and self-worth, as we learn in this week's parsha, Vayishlach.

After Yaakov famously wrestled with the angel and won, the angel changed his name to Yisrael, meaning, "you have commanding power with G-d and with men, and you have prevailed" (Bereishit 32:29). Later, Hashem speaks to Yaakov and reiterates this name change, stating, "Your name is Yaakov: You shall not be called Yaakov anymore, but Yisrael shall be your name" (Bereishit 35:10). If Yaakov's name was changed to Yisrael, then why does Hashem see fit to first say, "Your name is Yaakov"? The pasuk would make much more sense if that first line was omitted.

The Gemara in Brachot 13a teaches that Yaakov's two names can be used interchangeably. Chazal explain that Avraham's name was changed permanently from the former Avram. Avraham's name is connected to "Av Hamon Goyim," a father to many nations, his "mission" of sorts after his name change; his previous name, meaning "Av leAram," the father to Aram, was not appropriate anymore. In fact, one who calls Avraham by his former name incurs a punishment. This was not so with Yaakov. One would not be transgressing a commandment to refer to him by his former name as opposed to Yisrael, since Yaakov is still referred to by his original name even after the fight with the angel. This insinuates that unlike Avram, the name Yaakov was still applicable and appropriate. Why is this so?

The Spinka Rebbe, Rav Yosef Mayer Wise, in Imrei Yosef, explains that there is a differentiation between the names Yaakov and Yisrael. Yisrael connotes a sense of superiority, as it conveys Yaakov's victory over the angel. Yaakov, however, derives from the word "Akeiv," meaning heel, a symbol of humility. When Hashem said, "your name is Yaakov," He was essentially warning Yaakov about the dangers of superiority. Greatness and success can easily lead to arrogance and haughtiness. Hashem in no way was denying Yaakov the ability to become great, fathering the Jewish people, but was relaying to him the importance of being a Yaakov while being a Yisrael. Yaakov must never forget to retain humility, as embodied by the intrinsic meaning of his name.

The Spinka Rebbe teaches us an important lesson regarding the meaning of true humility. The ultimate litmus test of a truly humble person is how he perceives and contends with his successes and accomplishments. Rav Noach Weinberg Zt"l explains that there are two ways in which a person can react to accomplishment. He can take pride or he can take pleasure. Pride means: "I did it. I am better than other people because I achieved this with my own abilities and my skills." Pleasure means: "Thank Hashem I was given this opportunity to enjoy and to accomplish. I am not better than anyone else, merely fortunate and blessed to have the chance and ability." Notice the difference?

Arrogance is taking pride in our achievements, and Chazal see arrogance as the ultimate antithesis of the Torah because it denies Hashem. Chazal state that one who is arrogant is like one who commits idolatry, and Hashem will not dwell with him in this world (Sotah 4b-5a). A conceited person takes up so much room that there is none left for the presence of Hashem. He worships his own qualities and talents, irrespective of the fact that it was Hashem who endowed them to him in the first place.

Humility is taking pleasure in our achievements. Hashem grants us, from birth, aptitudes and skills which are uniquely our own and perfectly conditioned to help us achieve our personal mission here on earth. We did not earn these traits, nor do we, in effect, really deserve them. They are gifts, and we should cherish them as such. Our achievements are the results of what Hashem has given us, and the best way we can show gratitude is to take pleasure in the facts that we are blessed and that Hashem gave us the opportunity to succeed.

Humility does not mean low self-esteem or self-value. It is the greatest display of self-esteem and self-value. You realize how much worth you have and appreciate all that Hashem has given you to accomplish your personal mission. Rabbi Dr. Twerski explains that a humble person with high self-esteem knows that he can succeed and knows that he has potential, realizes where all those accomplishments come from, and also realizes how much more he has to do. It certainly does not mean that you cannot acknowledge what you have done, as long as you do not seek pride and honour from others.

Rav Elchonon Wasserman was asked if his teacher, the Chofetz Chaim, who was extremely humble, was aware of his own greatness. "Yes," relied Rav Wasserman. "Although the Chofetz Chaim was imbued with great humility, he frequently acknowledged the contribution he had made to the spiritual welfare of the entire generation."

Getting a high mark, receiving an award, doing a mitzvah, visiting the sick, organizing a tzedakah project, and performing chesed are all different types of accomplishments. It is our duty, as Jews, in every situation of success, to quietly and individually take pleasure, not pride. It is not the easiest thing to do by any means, and we naturally have an inclination to seek pride and honour from others. It gives us a feeling of elation, but it is woefully superficial and fails to recognize the source of all accomplishments. The elation of understanding where everything comes from and the feeling that everything with which you are endowed is specially for you to make the world a better place, is a tremendous pleasure. When you are a Yisrael, do not make the mistake of forgetting that you are also a Yaakov.

Divrei Torah on **Bereishit**

Vayeishev • וַיֵּשֶׁב

This Parsha has been generously sponsored by the Glasenberg family in honour of Yonatan Eliyahu Glasenberg

Reminders of Home
By Elianne Neuman

Chanukah commemorates a Jewish revolt which took place over 2,000 years ago —a revolt prompted by opposition to Greek oppression, as well as by a determination to resist assimilation.

Upon becoming the King of Greece, Antiochus Epiphanies embarked on a campaign: to pressure the Jewish people to abandon their religion and to embrace Grecian culture as their own. This worked to a limited extent. Frustrated by Jewish resistance, Antiochus looted the *Beit Hamikdash*, engaged in a murderous campaign against the Jewish people ,and essentially outlawed the practice of Judaism.

Understandably, many Jews were outraged by Antiochus' attack on their institutions and religion. A zealous group of Jews banded together and started the Maccabean revolt. After a hard-fought campaign, the Maccabees, a relatively small force who fought fearlessly against the tremendous Greek armies, were able to rededicate the *Beit Hamikdash* and secure the freedom of the Jewish people.

While there are many miracles of Chanukah, in my opinion, the Maccabee's struggle to regain the *Beit Hamikdash*, the epicentre of *Eretz Yisrael*, the Jewish homeland, and the centre of Jewish sovereignty, is the most wonderful miracle of all.

By recapturing the *Beit Hamikdash*, the Maccabees restored both Jewish self-determination and a sense of national purpose, thereby enabling Judaism to flourish and the Jewish nation to prosper once again. And by standing up to oppression, the Maccabees provided us with a prime example of Jewish survival throughout the ages.

Although we have been without the *Beit Hamikdash* for close to 2,000 years, we adapted to its absence by building alternative, sustainable institutions which are conducive to ensuring Jewish continuity. Our homes, our synagogues, and our *Torah* have become the epicentres of Jewish life, because they provide us with spiritual and physical sustenance and they enable Judaism to blossom.

By acknowledging the extraordinary measures taken by the Maccabees to become the masters of their spiritual home, the *Beit Hamikdash*, and their physical home, the land of Israel, Chanukah challenges us to reflect on our commitment to ensure that the synagogues and the homes we build maximize our ability to embrace *Torah* and to maintain our Jewish identity.

In so doing, Chanukah challenges us to re-evaluate the environment which we have created for ourselves, because it ultimately affects our values, our personalities, and our abilities to perform *mitzvot*. On Chanukah, we should ask ourselves what sacrifices we would be prepared to make in order to preserve our religion and our identity. And on Chanukah, we should strive to create warm, welcoming surroundings which allow us to feel connected to *Torah* and *Am Yisrael*.

The Spirit of the Thing
By Zachary Zarnett-Klein

This Shabbat, we read a special Haftarah portion in honour of Chanukah, which is from the book of Zecharyah. There are a variety of ways in which this Haftarah relates to the holiday of Chanukah. The eradication of evil, the spiritual greatness of the Israelites, and, of course, the sanctity and importance of the Beit HaMikdash and the Golden Menorah are the pertinent themes in this Haftarah and are of extreme relevance to the holiday of Chanukah. The Haftarah begins with talking about "the end of days", as G-d expresses his true love for Israel, saying that his promises to Israel will be fulfilled and that this will be recognized by the Goyim as they observe in awe. HaShem tells Israel that he will destroy all of their adversaries and that he will dwell in their midst in the land of Israel. This is the epitomy of Chanukah: proving to all of our enemies that HaShem, though complex in his ways, is the relentless saviour of the people of Israel.

The Hafatarah continues to speak about Yehoshua the Kohen Gadol. As Radak points out, the Satan accuses him of not being worthy to serve as Kohen Gadol since many of his children had married non-Jews during the Babylonian exile. However, HaShem disregards these claims, since he would not have allowed Yehosuha to be fortunate enough to return to Yerushalayim if he had had no purpose in this. This section of the Haftarah highlights Hashem's Midah of "Kel Rachum"- merciful G-d, who gives people second chances-- and there is no better example of this than G-d miracuously helping Bnei Yisrael win the war against the Yevanim and giving them enough oil for the Menorah to remain lit for eight days.

Finally, the Menorah plays an integral role in this Haftarah portion. Zecharya's famous prophecy of the Menorah with the two olive branches on either side proves an essential part in its relation to Chanukah; after all, it is literally the "Festival of Dedication", and the lighting of the Menorah is symbolic of the dedication of the temple. And what are the olive branches'connection to Chanukah? Olive oil-- Shemen Zayit-- was the type of oil used to light the Menorah by the Kohen at the times of both the first and second temples, and we thus have a tradition to light our Chanukiyot on Chanukah with olive oil.

Most critically, what is the importance of the Pasuk: "Lo B'Chayil V'Lo B'Koach Ki Im B'Ruchi..."? True, G-d's words, "Not through army nor through strength, but through my spirit," are inspirational, but isn't the whole story of Chanukah foceussed on the victory of a *war*? Were the Jews not forced to physically defend their homeland from the Greek invasion? What is this "spirit" all about? To solve this dilemma, one must look at the next Pasuk: "Mi Ata Har Gadol Liphnei Zerubavel L'Mishor," translating to "Who are you, O great mountain? Before Zerubavel [the leader of Judah upon the return from the Babylonian Exile[you will be humbled." This Pasuk depicts the true essence of Chanukah: "HaMeatim Nitzchu et HaRabim," those who appear weak, through hope despite trials and bravery in the face of danger, will succeed in their endeavours. While the Macabees were but a small group of men, with virtually no weapons and no knowledge of war, they believed wholeheartedly that G-d would allow them to defeat the Greeks, and thus the Macabees were able to show absolutely no fear. Just like Zerubavel was but one person in front of a huge mountain of hardship and opponents whom he would have to conquer, the Macabees found themselves as this small group of amateurs who appeared weak to the rest of the world, and yet, through their "spirit", they were able to defeat their enemies with the help of the Almighty, and to look at this "Har Gadol", the Yevanim, as not standing a chance against the faith and the Lord on their side.

Finally, it is our duty to absorb the lessons of Chanukah and apply them to our modern-day world, that we may have the courage as a nation to denounce all of our current enemies and know that although we may be but a small nation compared to this "Har Gadol", we know that "Lo B'Chayil V'Lo B'Koach Ki Im B'Ruchi," that through our courageous spirits, we will be able to ward off all evil. May this be G-d`s will as we celebrate Chanukah and the all year round.

Sukkot
By Becky Friedman

I know what you're thinking, if you just read the title. Succot? What has that got to do with Chanuka? Succot was months ago! But bear with me for a moment: there may be more in common between the two holidays than you think.

As you know, we light the chanukiah in accordance with Beit Hillel, adding another candle each day. But Beit Shammai's opinion-- the one we ended up not using-- suggests *starting* with eight candles and removing one each day. Even though we don't follow this practice, there must be a reason behind it. But why would he have such a crazy idea? After all, according to Hillel, "we rise in holiness, not diminish"! The answer can be given in one word: Succot.

By now I'm at risk of losing my audience, so I'd better cut to the chase. Why is Chanuka called Chanuka? Because of "Chanukat Hamizbeach"-- the Rededication of the Temple. And Succot was the time of the original "Chanukat Hamizbeach"-- the Dedication of the First Temple in the time of Shlomo. Not only that, but in the book of Ezra, it is mentioned that the people celebrated Succot at the time of the Dedication of the Second Temple. Those who made Chanuka a holiday wanted very much to evoke comparisons to Succot.

As was mentioned before, Shammai wanted to remove one candle each day, in order to emulate the Succot sacrifices, in which one bull less is sacrificed each day. Although this practice wasn't adopted, there are several other striking similarities.

Why is Chanuka eight days long, the only holiday with that number of days? Why not seven? After all, the miracle of the oil was only a miracle for the latter seven days that it burned, and not for the first, when it was expected to burn-- and seven is a common number of days for a Jewish holiday. Or why not one day? Why drag it out? Why eight days? Succot.

Succot (in Israel) is seven days, but that becomes eight if we include Shemini Atzeret, the added eighth day of celebration following Succot.

By December, it's too cold to even think about living outside in a Succah, but as you light your chanukiah-- adding candles, rather than subtracting bulls-- it might be worth your while to reflect on Succot anyways-- that was the intention.

Jewish holidays aren't random; they are deeply interconnected. The Shalosh Regalim and Yamim Noraim come from the Torah, but what about the others? They are there, too. Chanuka is hinted at by the segments in the Torah discussing both Succot and the dedication of the Temple, just as Purim is hinted at by Yom HaKiPURIM. I myself have complained that Chanuka gets undeserved stage time just because of its proximity to the major Christian holiday of Christmas, while the Shloshet Regalim are our 'real' holidays, but in fact, Chanuka is as legitimate a holiday, as divinely ordained a holiday, as-- as Succot!

History in the Making
By Matthew Goodman

The human soul is capable of achieving great things through small actions, which, in turn, have the ability to change history. Doing the right thing at a particular instance can affect the future in ways that we cannot possibly comprehend. Unfortunately, we all have the occasional tendency to forget the power of our actions and we behave in ways that are not necessarily bad, but are awfully mundane. This week's Parsha, Vayeishev, teaches us a tremendous lesson regarding the extent of a single good action.

After Yosef related his dream to his brothers, they became very jealous of him and decided to kill him. When Reuven heard what they planned to do, he rescued his brother from their hands and said, "We will not strike him mortally!" (Bereishit 37:21). The Midrash (Vayikra Rabba 34:9) explains that if Reuven would have known that his actions would effectually be inscribed in Hashem's eternal Torah, he would not have simply stopped the brothers from killing Yosef and allowed them to put him in a pit instead. Rather, he would have lifted Yosef up onto his shoulders and carried him home to his father. Rav Yitzchak learns from this that when a person performs a mitzvah, he should do so with a full and happy heart. The deed should be done with an understanding of the effect of one's actions, and not mundanely.

Rav Aharon Kotler (Mishnat Rav Aharon) says that had Reuven realized the extent of the results of his actions, he would have been more careful with his conduct. We, who have little understanding of the influences of our own actions, have to remove our worries and weariness and recognize the merit of every Mitzvah and the positive outcomes that it incur.

Yosef, on the other hand, was careful to act in a proper and Torah-like manner in at all times. When Yosef was arrested and imprisoned, two members of Pharoah's court eventually joined him: the baker and the butler. Rav Frand imagines the situation as if two members of the King's Royal Cabinet were sitting in prison with a good-for-nothing criminal -- a Hebrew slave. The Torah tells us that baker and butler both had distressing dreams on the same night. In the morning, Yosef saw that they were disturbed and asked them, "Why are your faces sad today?"

Because of those four kind words, the baker and the butler related their dreams to Yosef. He interpreted them, and they came true. Sometime after, the butler remembered Yosef and the help he gave in the prison and brought him to Pharaoh to interpret the dreams of the great King of Egypt. Yosef became second in command, managing the storehouses of the entire kingdom and providing food to the whole world, including his own family.

Rabbi Dov Weinberger (Shemen HaTov, quoted by Rav Frand) explains that history was made because Yosef had the decency to see that two people looked terribly upset and ask them how they were doing. Those few kind words made a huge difference.

Sometimes we do not have the mindset to be constantly aware of others, intuitive of what is going on around us, and sincere in our performance of Mitzvot. We can get lazy or preoccupied and our actions can lack fullness and meaning. Yosef and Reuven teach us that if we could possibly foresee what our actions could do, we would always act in a way befitting of a good Jew. We would go all the way in everything we did to ensure that our good deeds have as much of an impact as possible. Rav Yerucham Levovitz (Daat Torah, Shemot p.198) explains that our actions can transform future generations. Our forefathers, Avraham, Yitzchak, and Yaakov, dedicated their entire lives to setting a proper example for Klal Yisrael. Their impact on future generations was their lifelong focus, because they realized how much they could do.

75 years ago, Rav Shimon Schwab spent a Shabbat at the home of the Chofetz Chaim. The Chofetz Chaim asked him, "Are you a Kohen?" Rav Schwab replied that he was not. The Chofetz Chaim asked him, "Why not?" Rav Schwab, somewhat confused, replied, "Because my father was not a Kohen." "And why was he not a Kohen?" asked the Chofetz Chaim. "Because his father was not a Kohen!" answered Rav Schwab, even more confused. The Chofetz Chaim looked at the young man and told him, "I am a Kohen. Three thousand years ago, when Moshe Rabbeinu, after the sin of golden calf, proclaimed 'Whoever is to Hashem follow me,' my great-great-great grandfather, along with the whole tribe of Levi, flocked to his side. Your ancestor did not. In reward for their dedication, the entire tribe of Levi was made into Hashem's emissaries. Their future generations were privileged to serve in the Beit HaMikdash and will be privileged to serve in the future Beit HaMikdash. Any action of any person can incalculably influence generations to come."

No one can expect us to be absolutely perfect and never slip once in our entire lives. We occasionally do forget the power of our actions. If we can remember, however, every so often, that our good deeds are eternal and can really change the world, then we truly can make a difference in our own lives. We can change the way we perform Mitzvot. The next time you do any sort of good deed, try to think of what type of example you want to set for the next generation. What do you want to show them? How do you want history to remember you? Once you set the standard for yourself, act accordingly. Perhaps we could all start with something small. Perhaps the next time we see someone looking a bit down, we could approach him and show sincere concern for his well-being. Yosef's "How are you?" changed history. Ours can, too.

Life Altering Decisions
By Teddy Kravetsky

This week's parsha is parshat Vayeshev, which starts off with the dreams of Joseph and goes on to explain how he ended up in jail in Egypt. Some very fundamental points of Judaism are brought out from this story.

The ideas on which I'm focusing were derived from when Joseph was thrown into a pit by his brothers due to their jealousy. From this small section of the story of Joseph, two important lessons can be learned.

The first involves the jealousy that Joseph's brothers had for him. They were at one point considering killing Joseph because of it, and would have, if Reuven hadn't stopped them. Why, you may ask, did they go as far as trying to kill their own brother from something as small as an emotion?

The answer is a step-by-step process which can turn an emotion into something so much larger that it becomes an uncontrollable urge. First, an idea is brought into a person's thoughts due to recent events in his life; seconds that idea impacts the way he feels about the issue raised. If that issue is jealousy, it can stay with that person, bottled up inside, for a long time. This emotion can then become a serious problem as, when mixed with anger, bad things can and will result, all due to a little thought that came into one's mind weeks, months, or even years ago. This small and simple emotion then has the ability to ruin a life.

This is one of the reasons why it is so vitally important not to get caught up with what others have and not to be jealous of them. It's also important to speak to the person of whom you are jealous and try to resolve the issue at hand; otherwise, realize that no one's life is perfect and that each of us has his own set of problems. Either of these options is better than bottling up your anger and jealousy inside.

This leads me to my second point, dealing with voicing one's opinion. In the story of Joseph, the only reason why he isn't killed is because Reuven tells his brothers not to do it and instead to just leave him in a pit. This may seem small and insignificant; however, it brings out another important lesson of Judaism and life in general. It shows us that everyone has a voice and that we should all should use it to our advantage and make clear what we want to be heard.

In the story of Joseph, Reuven, just by using his mouth, was able to save his brother's life and stop a horrible death from occurring. Although most of us, thank G-d, don't have to make decisions like these, we can use our voices to express ideas that are important to us.

In today's society, many controversial issues in school, at home, and in society surround us, and by voicing our opinions, it becomes apparent that even the smallest voices can make a difference. This is why it's so important to speak up as, if you don't have a say in what's going on, then the ideas inside won't make a difference in the world. Who knows-- maybe one of those ideas would have lead to a life-saving decision! And is that really worth not speaking a few words? Think about it.

Divrei Torah on **Bereishit**

Maase Avot Siman L'vanim
By Michali Glasenberg

The Navi Amos, in the opening pasuk of the Haftorah, says: "Thus said Hashem: for three transgressions of Yisrael I have looked away, but for the four I will not pardon them: for selling a righteous man for money and a poor man for shoes."

In Parshat Lech Lecha, the Ramban introduces a concept that shapes his commentary to Sefer Bereishit. "Maase avot siman levanim"-- "the deeds of our forefathers are a sign to their children." The main event in Parshat Vayeishev is the sale of Yosef by his brothers; this event haunts us as it follows us through Jewish history and the Jewish calendar. The Navi Amos makes this clear to us in the Haftorah.

At two of the most auspicious moments in the Jewish calendar, the sale of Yosef comes to the forefront. The first is subtle, a hint; the second is more dramatic in nature.

The first thing we do at the seder after Kiddush, which is part sippur yetziat mitzraim and part of kedushat hayom, is Karpas: we dip a vegetable in salt water. What does Karpas signify and what does it mean? Rashi, in this Parsha, says on the words 'Ketonet Pasim,' Yosef's coat of fine wool: "Kemo karpas utechelet"-- karpas and fine wool. Karpas at the seder is a reenactment of dipping the coat in blood by the brothers. Mechirat Yosef is act one, scene one of events that took Bnei Yisrael to mitzrayim and the subsequent story of Yetziat mitzrayim. We don't mention it explicitly at the seder for it is a night of celebration, but the Baal Hagaddah brings us the subtle reminder.

On Yom Kippur, in Mussaf, we re-enact the avodah service of the Kohen gadol. Rav Soloveitchik insisted that the aron remain open and for the chazzan to say it out loud, with the congregation saying it with him. We bow when the people bowed in the Azara, and we are transported to a different world of the bais hamikdash. However, soon the joy of reciting the avodah is transformed to mourning, as Yom Kippur is transformed to Tisha Beav. We reach the most wrenching moment as we recite Eileh Ezkerah, the story of the ten sages murdered by the Romans. These events were caused by the sale of Yosef. Yom Kippur is also about atonement for Mechirat Yosef.

There are many more connections between the two. The Rambam, in Morei Nevuchim, explains that the goat that was sent over the cliff on Yom Kipuur was a reminder of Mechirat Yosef and the brothers dipping his coat in the blood of a goat. The Meshech Chochma tells us that red wool that was tied on the horns of this goat had the weight of 2 selaim, and the gemarah in Shabbat says that the weight of Yosef's coat was 2 selaim. The Meshech chochma also tells us that one of the reasons the Kohen gadol went into the kadosh kedoshim on Yom Kippur to ask for atonement was that it was the one place in the bais hamikdash that belonged to the tribe of Binyamin; Binyamin was the only brother who did not participate in the sale of Yosef.

The Rambam also explains that all korbanot relating to communual sins were korbanot of se'erim, he-goats. All communual sins are rooted in the event of Mechirat Yosef.

In the Meshech Chochma, Rav Meir Simcha MiDvinsk writes that there are 2 sins that pursue us throughout history: the sale of Yosef and the sin of the egel hazahav, the golden calf. We say in the mussaf prayer of Yom Kippur: "Ki Ata Salchan Leyisrael uMacahlan Leshivtei Yeshurun Bechol Dor Vador."-- "You are the Forgiver of Israel and the Pardoner of the tribes of Yeshurun in every generation." The first part refers to the chait haegel and the latter to the sin of the shevatim, Mechirat Yosef.

Why has this act impacted us so much through the ages? According to the Ramban, Yosef is included in Avot-- his death is described in Sefer Bereishit-- but he is 'Banim' too; his death is repeated in Sefer Shemot, the book of Bnei Yisrael. He is the bridge that connects the Avot to the Banim-- the Bnei Yisrael. However, 'Maase avot siman lebanim' does not seem reason enough for these events to haunt us through history.

Perhaps the reason is that Mechirat Yosef was the action of the Tzibbur of Clal Yisrael. The brothers were the first minyan of Jews. Rav Soloveitchik describes these events as the beginning of Jewish History. Halacha tells us that we should daven with a tzibbur a minyan, and even when we pray at home, we should do so at the same time as the minyan in the Beit Haknesset. We are always connected to the tzibbur. The Rav wrote in one of his essays that when a Jew davens with a minyan, that minyan and its prayers are connected to all minyanim present and past. These actions were taken by the first tzibbur and will always be with us.

Perhaps that is why there is the concept of Mashiach Ben Yosef: only when we correct this wrong can we move on to the ultimate goal.

Divrei Torah on **Bereishit**

Mikeitz • מקץ

> *This Parsha has been generously sponsored by the Cash family in honour of their children and grandchildren*

The Revelation of Joseph
By Elianne Neuman

In this Parsha, all of Joseph's brothers, except Binyamin, had come to Egypt to get food for the family. They appeared before Joseph, but they didn't recognize him, and he didn't reveal himself to them. Rather, he requested that they return again and bring Binyamin with them.

Why did Joseph not reveal himself to his brothers? Why did he specifically request that they must return to Egypt with the youngest brother, Binyamin?

There are two traditional answers to this question.

First, according to the Midrash, Joseph refused to reveal himself to his brothers and requested that Binyamin must come to Egypt in order to fulfill the prophecy of in the previous Parsha: that all eleven brothers would bow down to Joseph.

Second, according to Rabbi Hirsch, Joseph specifically requested that Binyamin travel to Egypt because he wanted to test his brothers' reaction to his subsequent enslavement of Binyamin. Joseph wanted to see if his siblings had changed after they sold him into slavery. He wondered if his brothers had truly repented and gotten over their jealousy of Rachel's children, himself and Binyamin, and would refuse to see Binyamin enslaved.

Thus Joseph only revealed himself once his brothers had passed his test. When Joseph heard Yehuda beg him not to punish Binyamin, he started to cry, for he saw that his brothers had gotten over their animosity and had overcome their jealousy.

I would like to offer an additional explanation as to why Joseph was reluctant to reveal himself to his brothers.

When Joseph's brothers arrived in Egypt, the Torah clearly mentions that they didn't recognize him. Time had passed. Joseph had changed. He had become viceroy. He had two children. He was wealthy and successful.

Joseph was conscious of the fact that his appearance and his life had changed because he was now living in Egypt. This is clearly stated in the Torah, when Joseph names his second son Ephraim because "G-d has made me fruitful in the land of my suffering." Abarbanel elaborates that even though Joseph was an esteemed viceroy, he had a negative perception of Egypt and wanted to return to Jacob and his family.

And now that his brothers had appeared before him and didn't recognize him, Joseph was conflicted. The fact that his own family didn't know who he was fact made Joseph realize that maybe he had changed for the worse, that maybe Egypt had separated him from his family and faith.

And so Joseph asked to see Binyamin, the only sibling with whom he shared a mother. Perhaps he hoped that Binyamin would recognize him after all these years, and his fears that he had become a different person would be allayed.

But Binyamin arrived and didn't know that the viceroy was his brother. And so Joseph wept, not only because he felt a deep connection to his brother, but also because he had changed so much that his own sibling couldn't recognize him. The Torah says, "Joseph rushed because his compassion for his brother had been stirred and he wanted to weep; so he went into the room and wept there."

Why, then, did Joseph put his cup into Binyamin's sack? Because he wanted the brothers to return one more time. He wanted to give them one last opportunity to recognize him. He wanted one last chance to assure himself that he was still, fundamentally, the same person.

Of course, the brothers were stopped and taken back to the palace to explain the disappearance of the cup. And then something miraculous happened: Yehuda begged Joseph not to punish Binyamin. Yehuda had shown Joseph that the brothers had repented and were no longer jealous of Rachel's children. Yehuda revealed to Joseph that the brothers had changed drastically.

Once Joseph recognized that his siblings had changed, he came to terms with himself. Joseph couldn't deny that his brothers failed to recognize him because he had become a different person. But Yehuda's actions relayed to Joseph that significant change isn't necessarily a negative thing. The brothers had changed for the better. Perhaps Joseph's new lifestyle wasn't something to be ashamed of, either.

Thus Joseph came to realize that his experience in Egypt was actually a positive one, for even though he had become viceroy, he had still maintained his family's traditions. It is only when he had complete assurance in himself and his connection to his family that he revealed himself to his brothers.

The True Meaning of Chanukah
By Matthew Goodman

For many hundreds of years, Klal Yisrael endured a harsh and painful Galut from Eretz Yisrael. A people oppressed and slaughtered, it was only by Divine will that we prevailed through so much terror. Numerous attempts were made to forcibly change our ancestors' beliefs and convert them to other religions. They, however, were willing to put everything on the line to preserve their Judaism and the Torah that had sustained them since they had received it on Har Sinai. Tens of thousands of Jews gave up their lives to stay Jewish. They were martyrs who sanctified the name of Hashem in this world by remaining true and loyal to their convictions, and overcoming the obstacles to living their lives according to the Torah.

Chanukah is chronologically the last Chag before the destruction of the Second Temple and the beginning of the Galut of Klal Yisrael. Alongside its miracles, it commemorates the martyrdom of thousands of Jews who could not bear to accept the decrees of their Greek opressors. The book of Antiochus tells of unbelievable Kiddush Hashem. It relates that over one thousand men, women, and children hid in a cave to keep Shabbos. They were caught by the Greeks, who offered to spare their lives if they joined them, but the Jews would not give in. The Greeks responded by burning wood at the mouth of the cave and suffocating all of its inhabitants.

Today, thank G-d, Jews no longer have to deal with the same oppression that our ancestors did a mere one hundred years ago. In North America, we are free to live our lives according to the Torah without physical opposition. What does a holiday about martyrdom have to do with our lives today? What message can Chanukah teach us modern Jews, who have never had to compromise on our physical well-being in order to fulfill a mitzvah? The answer can be found in the story of Yosef, detailed in this week's Parsha.

The Shaloh, HaRav Yeshaya HaLavei Horowitz, comments that the Parshiot of Vayeishev, Vayigash, and Miketz, all of which include the story of Yosef and his brothers, are always read immediately before, during, or immediately after Chanukah. Since every festival and fast instituted by Chazal has a special connection to the Torah Parsha in whose weeks they fall, there is a connection between these Parshiot and the upcoming holiday. Says the Shaloh, the story of Yosef was destined to be repeated with the royal Hashmonai family during the time of the Greeks. We certainly do not see any Greeks in the story of Yosef, nor do we find anything about the Beit HaMikdash, a menorah, or a battle. The Parshiot do not even mention martyrdom, which seems to be a major theme of the holiday. So where, then, does the story of Yosef parallel Chanukah?

In last week's Parsha, Vayeishev, we learn that Potiphar's wife constantly tried to seduce Yosef. On one particularly day, she managed to corner him and again tried to seduce him. Yosef fought off her advances and the Torah says, "Vayema'ain" - and he refused (Bereishit 39:8). The trope above the word "Vayema'ain" is a little zigzag line called a Shalshelet (meaning "chain"), which is read by singing a scale up and then down, up and down, and up and down. The Shalshelet is only used three other times in the entire Torah. Once when angels warned Lot of the destruction of Sodom and "he lingered (Vayitmameha)" (Bereishit 19:16). Another time when Avraham's servant, Eliezer, was entrusted to find a wife for Yitzchak, and he "talked (Vayomer)" to Hashem (Bereishit 24:12). The final occurrence was when Moshe took the "Eil Hamelu'im," ram of consecration, to finally consecrate Aharon and his sons as Kohanim, and he "slaughtered" it (Vayikra 8:23).

Each of these instances were moments of great dilemma, and the Shalshelet is located on the pivotal verb that decided the individuals response to that problem. Each verb was a moment of introspection and soul searching, as well as doubt. For that reason, the trope is sung by moving from one end of a scale to another three times. Do I do this or this? Do I choose to do this action or this action? Do I give in or do I fight?

Did Yosef immediately refuse the advances of Potiphar's wife? No! He had to fight against his urge to give in. He had to fight to make the right decision. His mind was moving back and forth, back and forth, like the Shalshelet. In the end, after struggling with himself, he defeated his evil inclination and he ran outside. For that act of piety, Yosef is referred to by

Chazal as HaTzaddik, a name granted uniquely to him and no other forefather.

Yosef was the only individual out of all of the forefathers in Bereishit who spent the majority of his life in Galut, outside of Eretz Yisrael. The Lubavitcher Rebbe explains that in Galut, Yosef was derived of his "home" -- an environment that preserved faith and nourished growth. He was thrust into a world that utterly rejected the values and teachings of Avraham, Yitzchak, and Yaakov. A world that did not know of Hashem. There he had to struggle to maintain his identity and Jewishness. The Rebbe points out that Galut compels a person to turn to the inner reaches of his soul and extract from there reserves of commitment and determination never tapped into during more tranquil times. Galut introduces a person to new concepts and circumstances which he could never have experienced at "home," many of them contrary to the values with which he was raised. A person who resists these challenges and stays true to himself redeems "the spark of holiness" within him and lights up the world.

This is exactly what Yosef did when he refused the advances of Potiphar's wife. He was thrown into a situation that was the utter antithesis of his own values, and despite the seduction, he stayed true to himself and truly lit up the world. In this week's Parsha, Mikeitz, Yosef names his first son Menashe, which means "forgetting" (Bereishit 41:51), referring to his struggle against forgetting the ways of his forefathers amidst an environment of great struggle.

Chanukah could not be a more perfect parallel to the story of Yosef. Like Yosef, Klal Yisrael was oppressed by a foreign culture that ran contrary to the Torah. The Greek decrees made by King Antiochus attempted to rid all Klal Yisrael of their values and convert them to Hellenism. We fought back and displayed a commitment to our faith and a determination to maintain it that would set the tone for the two thousand years of Galut that would soon follow. Jews resisted, with their lives, to follow the Torah. Like Yosef, Klal Yisrael endured the back and forth of the Shalshelet and chose to do the right thing, despite how hard it was.

After understanding the story of Yosef, does Chanukah still seem like an irrelevant holiday? The struggle of the Hashmonaim was a physical struggle, and we certainly do not face a physical struggle to be Jewish nowadays. The story of Yosef, however, was an inner struggle, and the modern world incurs more internal struggle to be Jewish than our ancestors could have ever imagined. There is so much that a person has to fight off. Our world worships celebrities, encourages blind pursuit of honour and wealth, and demands an infatuation with the material. Television, media, internet, and culture make demands of us that usually do not see eye to eye with the Torah values that have sustained the Jewish people for so long.

The Sefat Emet on the Torah has a very interesting comment regarding the "Makom Hadlakat HaNeirot" - the place where one lights the Chanukah candles. According to Halacha, the candles should preferably be lit in front of one's home in order to publicize the miracle of the holiday. Due to danger of advertising one's Jewish identity in Galut, it soon became the prevalent custom to light the Chanukiah indoors. The Chanukah lights, explains the Sefat Emet, represents the light of the Torah. Years ago, the inside of Jewish homes were saturated with Jewish values, and placing the Chanukiah outside the doorpost represented the keeping away of foreign influences. Nowadays, however, our very homes have fallen prey to those foreign values which are so against our Torah. Today it is necessary to bring the light of Torah and the light of the Chanukiah back into our homes. The struggle was a physical, outside battle. Now it is an inner battle that we must all face.

We are young Jewish people, and we need to find within ourselves the determination and commitment to stay Jewish in spiritual Galut. We do not have to fight for our lives, but we have to fight for our souls. We need to find meaning, purpose, and holiness in everything that goes on in every day. We need to rebel against a culture of self-satisfaction and focus on the things that make us truly happy. We need to stop taking things for granted. Dressing modestly, praying, eating kosher, and covering one's head in awe of Hashem are not values supported by the world that we live in, but that certainly does not mean that we should give them up simply because it is challenging to do them.

Chanukah teaches us that we cannot just give in to something that is difficult or tough to do. Like the Lubavitcher Rebbe explained, it is in such situations that we can demonstrate the most determination and see the most growth as result. For thousands of years, Klal Yisrael has been fighting to do the right thing, and their strength passes on from generation to generation, imbuing us with that same commitment and courage. The Chanukah lights that softly flicker in our homes every evening for eight days are gentle reminders of the light that we can bring to the world by trying our very best to act Jewish, no matter what.

Divrei Torah on **Bereishit**

Ends vs. Means
By Becky Friedman

The haftarah for Parshat Miketz deals with King Shlomo. Although we don't read this haftarah this week, passing over it in favour of the haftarah for Shabbat Chanukah, it is a surprisingly apropos passage for the holiday.

The haftarah tells the quintessential story of Shlomo's wisdom and justice. Two women come to him with a baby, each claiming that the baby is hers; only when Shlomo bluffs them with the suggestion of cutting the baby in half does the truth come out. The liar, having lost her own child, is content for her neighbour to be equally miserable; the real mother relinquishes her claim in order to keep the baby alive. With that, Shlomo restores the baby to its proper mother, and the people rejoice in his wisdom.

This happened in the very early days of Shlomo's reign, when all seemed idyllic. Later, he grew arrogant, intermarrying and committing idolatry. Shlomo's sins caused the kingdom to be split into the kingdoms of Yisrael and Yehuda, ultimately destroying Jewish life in Israel.

What does this remind us of? The Maccabees fought valiantly to prevent Antiochus from destroying Judaism; idealistic in their victory, they rededicated the temple, instated the holiday of Chanukah, and set up a Jewish monarchy, the Hasmonean dynasty. But just a few short generations later, the Hasmoneans had grown corrupt and power-grubbing; their infighting and intermarriage led eventually to the Destruction of the Second Temple and, again, an exile of all or nearly all Jews from the vicinity of Israel.

History has a way of repeating itself.

In the story of Shlomo's wisdom, the baby represents the Jewish faith, and each mother is a different aspect of the Jewish people. The real mother is us when we're at our strongest, when we know what's important to us and are willing to fight for it. The real mother is Shlomo in his early days; she is the Maccabees when they were in their prime. The lying woman is us when we've grown complacent, when we lose sight of what is right, pursuing instead what is convenient. The lying woman is the Shlomo who built idols; she is the decadent Hasmoneans.

Throughout history, we've had to contend with these warring aspects of our nature. With our backs against the wall, do we sacrifice what we must, in order to preserve that which is most important, our Judaism? Or do we trade in the idealistic for the idyllic, throw out the baby with the bathwater, and become what once we fought to avoid?

They say, or argue, that the ends justifies the means. But what do we do in the face of claims that the means justify the ends? Do good deeds in the past justify bad decisions in the present? The stories of Chanukah and Shlomo seem to imply that this is the case: Shlomo is remembered as a great king, despite the instrumental role he played in the downfall of the kingdom of Israel; the Maccabees are revered as heroes, their holiday celebrated yearly, despite the part their descendants played in ending yet another era of Jewish life in Israel.

But to draw these simple conclusions, to declare that the end result matters not so long as it was arrived at by a road paved with good intentions, is to throw the baby out with the bathwater. The means do not *justify* the end, but they do *mitigate* it. We admire Shlomo's wisdom, but not his idolatry; we celebrate, with Chanukah, the Maccabees' victory, but not their decline.

In fact, the celebration of Chanukah, like the story of the two mothers and the baby, should serve to remind us, in no uncertain terms, *not* to fall victim to that fallacy. We celebrate the triumph of faith over oppression, of hope over hubris, of light in a dark place. We celebrate the mothers who would give up their child to save that child's life; we celebrate the people who would sacrifice their peace in order to protect their way of life.

We celebrate, and we have, in our celebration, a warning not to fall victim to the siren song of the primrose path: a warning that if we do not emulate these heroes we revere-- if we instead turn to the darker face of the Jewish people-- if we do what is easy rather than what is right-- we will meet the fate that our heroes fought so hard to avoid. We see, in these stories, that even the heroes themselves are not immune to temptation; as Nechemia pointed out, if even the great King Shlomo fell victim to temptation and sin, all the more that we lesser people must strive to avoid it.

So what do we do? We celebrate. We celebrate Chanukah, with the warning in our ears and in our hearts not to throw the baby out with the bathwater and go the way of the Hasmoneans, but rather to make the sacrifices necessary to preserve our faith, preserve our religion, following in the footsteps of their Maccabee forebears.

This Chanukah, may we all be Maccabees, not Hasmoneans; may we continue to make the right decisions to preserve our faith-- and may our ends need no justification from our means, the former being as pure as the latter.

Arise Like a Lion
By Dylan Shaul

The Shulchan Aruch begins by saying, "Arise like a lion to serve your Creator in the morning." Rabbi Yosef Caro, in his opus that attempted to contain the totality of Jewish law, chose this precept-- waking up in the morning with vigor, strength, and the desire to do good-- to be the very first, perhaps the most essential of all.

The story of Joseph is the story of dreams, and in this week's parsha we read the story of two frightening dreams experienced by Pharaoh. In the first, seven fat, healthy cows emerge from a river, only to be eaten by seven sickly, gaunt cows. In the second dream, seven good ears of corn emerge, but are swallowed up by seven thin ears. The parsha begins by recounting the first dream; after it is over, it is written, "and Pharaoh awoke." Immediately following his waking, Pharaoh goes right back to sleep: "And he slept and dreamed a second time."

Pharaoh has here failed to fulfill his duty to his Creator. Though he was confronted with a prophetic message of clear pertinence, he ignores it, and instead lets his consciousness drift back into oblivion. G-d must rouse Pharaoh into action again. This time, Pharaoh does not even awake after his dream. It is only the next morning, that "his spirit was troubled," and he decides to look for some advice about the meaning of his visions. This is not, however, the way in which the patriarchs respond to their own dreams.

Earlier in the book of Genesis, Joseph has a dream in which he and his brothers were gathering sheaves of wheat in the field. His stood upright, while his brothers' bowed to it. After experiencing this dream, Joseph immediately told his brothers about it. After he had recounted the dream, Joseph had another, in which eleven stars, the sun, and the moon bowed to him. Once that dream was finished, he promptly related it to his family, though they were rightly angered with its perceived meaning.

It might have been that Pharaoh sensed the meaning of his own dream-- how else could he have known that Joseph offered the correct interpretation?-- but initially refused to heed it for fear of the political ramifications of making such a startlingly pessimistic statement about his kingdom's future. Pharaoh, who was supposed to be an intercessory between the G-ds and mankind, should have been able to prevent famine; that was what his subjects expected of him. Only after the second dream, in which the situation's direness was made absolutely clear to him, did Pharaoh get up to serve his Creator.

But what a pathetic job he did at that! Instead of immediately announcing the terrible news, he called in all sorts of magicians and sorcerers to interpret the dream, trying to delay its being made public. Only after Joseph offered a reasonable solution to the problem was Pharaoh willing to concede his powerlessness in the face of G-d.

As an example of a lion rising in the morning, we can look as well to Jacob, and his dream of the angels ascending and descending a ladder stretching to Heaven. In it, G-d promises Jacob and his descendants inheritance of the land of Canaan. Jacob rapidly arose from his dream, and declared the site at which he slept to be holy, "the gate to Heaven." He then erected a pillar symbolic of his vision, and anointed it with oil, naming the site the "House of G-d." Moved by a spiritual stirring, Jacob springs into action. Moved by the renewed miracle of our continued existence, we must spring into action every day. "The lion has roared: who will not fear? G-d has spoken; who can but prophesy?"

It's Never Too Late

By Teddy Kravetsky

In this week's parsha, the story of Joseph continues, as he goes from being a prisoner with no future to the viceroy of Egypt. But how did this occur; what caused Pharaoh to release Joseph from prison after he had been there for so many years?

He was released because the butler, who had been released two years earlier, had finally remembered Joseph and mentioned to Pharaoh that he might be able to interpret the dreams he was having.

From this another question arises: why did it take the butler two years to remember Joseph? There are many answers to this question; however, the one I found most fascinating was said by Rabbi Moshe Feinstein. He explains that Joseph should have realized that G-d was involved in making

Joseph able to understand the dreams, but, because he didn't, Joseph spent another two years in prison.

But what does all of this suggest in terms of what a modern-day Jew can take from it? It suggests that it's never too late to make a change in your life. Although Joseph didn't recognize G-d, G-d still released Joseph from prison; it just took longer. This tells us that when things seem rough and the going gets tough, it's never too late to change certain aspects in your life.

When people say that it's too late to follow their dreams or to start a new career, it's because they aren't trying hard enough. Perseverance is key in making a change, and in order to do this, one must first realize that a change is possible, and that, once it's made, life can start to seem a whole lot different. Sure, it took Joseph a long time to get to the powerful position he got to, but after going through some pretty rough times, he persevered through it, and came out on top.

This brings me to another point about time. We only get one shot at life, and one of the ways to make sure that it's not wasted is by using the time you have. Time is a crucial part of everyone's life, and the fact of the matter is that no one has enough of it. Every day, all of us are faced with the same challenges of getting up on time, getting in an assignment on time, going to bed on time-- and the list goes on and on. The only way to make sure that you don't waste something as precious as time is by using it wisely, in whatever way will benefit you best. This, mixed with the idea that it's never too late, can make for an unforgettable life-journey that could take you to places you never dreamed of going.

So remember that when you hit a rough patch in your life, just keep working through it, stay motivated, and, above all, remember that your future is up to you.

The Shofar's SHABBOS COMPANION

Vayigash • ויגש

This Parsha has been generously sponsored by the Klompas Family

Little White Lie
By Becky Friedman

Vayigash is a parsha that always upsets me. It begins with Yehuda approaching Yoseph to plead for Benjamin, and... *lying*? That's right: he tells a blatant, outright lie that anyone who read the previous parsha can spot easily.

If you recall, in Miketz, Yoseph accuses his brothers of being spies when they come to Egypt. To argue their case, they insist on their innocence and add that they are all the sons of one father, with another younger brother back home. When they return home, they accurately report the sequence of events to their father (although Yehuda does add some fabrications when he *repeats* it to his father, convincing him to send Binyamin along).

Now, in Vayigash, Yehuda approaches Yoseph and has the audacity to claim to Yoseph's face that it was all Yoseph's fault-- he claims that Yoseph just happened to *ask* them if they had "a father or a brother," and they answered, innocently, that they had an elderly father and a young brother. It's not a big lie, and it's easy enough to notice, considering Yoseph was there when things happened contrary to Yehuda's narrative. But Yehuda's little white lie is jarring, upsetting; if he's trying to appeal to Yoseph's better nature, he should display some more of his own.

The odd thing is that, as Yehuda continues his narrative, he shows a marked aversion to lying. When he gets to the part about the death of Yoseph, which he knows was similarly a huge lie, he says, "[Yakov] *said* 'he must have been eaten, and I have not seen him until now'" (my italics). Rather than say that Yoseph was eaten, which Yehuda knows never happened, he said that *Yakov* said that Yoseph was eaten, which is perfectly accurate.

This second matter is most easily resolved. We understand that Yehuda, naturally, wanted not only to gloss over the matter of how he had dealt with Yoseph, but also to conscientiously be honest about it, because of the guilt he felt about the lead role he had played in selling his brother. Yehuda is ashamed of the act, so he does not mention it; he is also ashamed of lying to his father about what he had done, so, to remedy this, he avoids a lie on his second retelling.

And yet, despite the remorse that Yehuda feels for what he had done some twenty-two years ago, he still cannot shake his bad habits of deception and shifting the blame. When he sold Yoseph, he lied about what he had done, and blamed a wild animal for the boy's demise in order to avoid culpability. Now, in trying to save Binyamin, he lies about the sequence of events which led to Binyamin's presence being requested, trying to make it seem Yoseph's fault rather than his own.

Yehuda's saving grace is that he knows this attempt is futile. He admits at the end of his monologue that he has taken responsibility for Binyamin-- that if he does not bring Binyamin safely home, "*[he]* will have sinned to [his] father for all days." Yehuda may still be trying, immaturely, to shift the blame, but what differentiates the Yehuda who saves Binyamin from the Yehuda who sold Yoseph is that he will accept responsibility for what he has done, even as he denies that he has done it.

After Yehuda's speech, Yoseph bursts into tears and then reveals himself to his brothers, announcing his forgiveness for them. But if he felt so emotionally wrought, why did he wait? Why did he not interrupt Yehuda when he had heard enough, eager to tell them who he was? But until Yehuda finished speaking, Yoseph *had not* heard enough.

Yehuda began with a lie, a little white lie, and one can imagine Yoseph hearing this gravely, seeing that his brothers had not changed from the fratricidal, duplicitous men who had sold him into slavery. Then, however, Yehuda continued with a reference to that very act, which displayed his double remorse. This, in Yoseph's mind, evened the score. Yehuda was now one-for-one, and stood at exactly where he was before he had begun speaking: not good enough. But finally, Yehuda admitted responsibility for his actions, and it was then that he tipped the balance in his favour, showing that he was a changed man.

Only after hearing this final acceptance of responsibility did Yoseph deem his brothers worthy of his reveal. Still, how does he introduce himself? "I am Yoseph, your brother whom you sold to Egypt." Did they not know that they sold him to Egypt? Does he think that they knew several Yosephs and needed this description in order to figure out who he was? Why does he not introduce himself with a simple "I am Yoseph" or "I am your brother Yoseph"?

Yoseph knows that his brothers are remorseful, and that they are now good men. Still, he is troubled by Yehuda's willingness to evade the truth when it is unpleasant-- his unwillingness to tell stories in which he comes out looking bad. Therefore, Yoseph reminds them that he is Yoseph "whom [they] sold to Egypt." Not because they didn't know that-- but to remind them that they must take responsibility for their actions, even if that means admitting to something unsavoury.

It's easy to admire Yehuda's bravery in defending Binyamin, and to forget that he was first in line to sell Yoseph as a slave. It's easy to remember Yehuda's honest, heartfelt speech to Yoseph, and forget that he started with a lie.

None of us are perfect, and sometimes we do something wrong that we come to deeply regret. It is very possible to be forgiven despite all this, if we show ourselves to be truly remorseful. But Yoseph's introduction reminds us that all the forgiveness in the world can't rewrite the past, and all the shame in the world doesn't excuse a lie.

Yehuda opened with a lie, but finished in earnest, and it was this earnestness that merited Yoseph's reveal at all. But the reconciliation could have come much sooner if he had been honest from the start. It's never smart to tell a lie-- not even a little white lie.

Forgive and Forget
By Matthew Goodman

The feeling of having being wronged is obviously terribly unpleasant. Unfortunately, we are exceptionally prone to being wronged multiple times in our lives. Sometimes they can be little things, and sometimes a dear friend can make a very big mistake. There are times when it is really difficult to be able to overlook the pain and distress someone has caused you, and you could harbour ambivalent or even vengeful thoughts towards that person. Over the past few Parshiot, Yosef HaTzaddik had a wrong done to him that most of us could probably not imagine understanding in our entire lives. His brothers sold him into slavery and staged his death, ripping him away from his father Yaakov and exiling him to a foreign, strange, and dangerous land. How would you treat your siblings if they did this to you? What would you say to them the next time you see them? Would you be able to forgive?

One would, perhaps, think that due to all the hardships Yosef endured, he would have at least tried to inflict some humiliation or fear on his brothers. When he revealed himself to them, he could have harshly rebuked them or displayed his anger towards them. Yosef was separated from his father for 22 years! How could he not reprimand them for all the indignity they had done him?

That was not how Yosef reacted, though. Far from it. The Torah tells us that when Yosef said, "I am Yosef," his brothers could not answer him. The Midrash (Tanchuma Vayigash 5) explains that the brothers were filled with shame and embarrassment at their wrongdoings. When Yosef saw this, he immediately says, "But now, do not be sad, and let it not trouble you that you sold me here, for it was to preserve life your that G-d sent me before you" (Bereishit 45:5). Yosef was telling his brothers, "Do not worry about what you did to me. I can see that you are ashamed and upset, and I forgive you wholeheartedly. Everything you did was for the good."

Rav Yerucham Levovitz, in Da'at Torah, says that people understand that there is an entire Shulchan Aruch (Code of Jewish Law) that dictates all the ways a person cannot wrong another human being. There are rules and regulations that mandate that one cannot cause physical, financial, or emotional harm to another. Many people do not realize, however, that there is also a whole Shulchan Aruch that dictates how someone should react to being harmed. If Reuven wronged Shimon and them approached him to apologize, Shimon cannot take the opportunity to berate Reuven for his actions. Reuven's actions may have been utterly unfair and unjust, but that does not give Shimon an excuse to act the same way. If Shimon did indeed forgo proper Torah behaviour and insult his friend, he, too, would have to seek forgiveness!

The correct way to act is like Yosef. We have to sincerely forgive the other person and truly feel that we will not hold the sin in our hearts. It is a sin not to, as the Torah tells us: "You shall not hate your brother in your heart...You shall not take revenge and you shall not bear a grudge" (Vayikra 19:17-19). Furthermore, Rambam, in Hilchot Deot (7:7) states that a person has to "wipe the wrong from his heart entirely, without remembering it at all." We have to clearly delineate to our friend and to ourselves that we will hold nothing against him at all, despite the severity of the harm done.

But that is just the first step. Yosef did not just make it clear that he forgave his brothers. He also took an initiative to express his willingness to make up with them. Before they even had a chance to say sorry, Yosef began to repair his relationship with them. Rav Chaim Zaitchik in Maayanai HaChaim (vol. 3 pg. 262) says that when someone shows sincere regret and asks for forgiveness, one has to go out of one's way to do positive things for him that express love and concern. The Ralbag (Shaar HaShalom no. 7) also says that one should try one's best to return to the state of love and friendship that had previously existed.

It is incumbent upon anyone who wants to personally grow to be very careful in making sure that he acts this way whenever he is wronged. By rushing to forgive sincerely and repair the damages, inculcating a sense of appreciation for the apology and willingness to make up, a person can innately become more loving and forgiving. There are many opportunities to put this into practice. Friends and family can sometimes upset us by causing harm or acting inappropriately. Each time we are hurt and are asked for forgiveness should be seen as a unique test of our loving-kindness. Those are special opportunities to demonstrate to Hashem that we will not hold a grudge. We will not seek revenge. We will not hold our friend's sins in our hearts. Like Yosef, we will forgive sincerely and genuinely, ensuring that we maintain Ahavat Yisrael at all times.

Judah and Joseph
By Zachary Zarnett-Klein

This week's Haftarah comes from Yechezkel Chapter 37, Verses 15-28. The Parashah begins with Judah pouring his soul out to Joseph and telling Joseph of all of the hardships that had happened to him and the entire family of Jacob since selling their brother. Joseph then reveals to his brothers that he is their brother Joseph, whom they sold. After this revelation, the entire family of Jacob comes down to Egypt where they are finally all reunited with Joseph and his family.

The Haftarah has a parallel plot. G-d commands Yechezkel to take two pieces of wood and write about the house of Judah, and take a second piece of wood and write about the house of Joseph. By this point, Judah and Joseph had been separated for quite a while.

After Solomon married many non-Jewish wives, G-d decided to split up the empire and give 10 tribes for the house of Joseph to rule over, while Judah would remain in charge of the tribes of Judah and Benjamin. While over the two kingdoms' existence they did aid each other at some points, most of the time they were following two separate paths, and many spats between them had even amounted into wars.

After the kingdom of Joseph was exiled by Sancheriv, the King of Ashur, the people of the kingdom of Judah lost their already weak connection with their fellow Jews. Yechezkel prophesized from Bavel, where Judah was exiled, and throughout his prophecies, he expresses the disconnect of Judah to the land of Israel; being exiled themselves, the kingdom of Judah lost all hope for any communication with the kingdom of Israel.

The two separate pieces of wood represent this terrible disconnect which had occurred as a result of years of distress between Judah and Joseph. At the time of the Babylonian exile, there was a general sentiment that the two entities would never reunite again.

The Haftarah continues with G-d telling Yechezkel that He will fuse the two pieces of wood together, and they will again become one strong, united kingdom in Messianic times. This prophecy was accepted with excitement among the exiled people of Judah, because if G-d had not forgotten the kingdom of Joseph, who had been exiled 140 years before them, then he surely has not forgotten the kingdom of Judah.

G-d promises that in the future, Judah and Joseph will be brought back to Israel and G-d will purify them from all their sins which they have committed. They will together live in harmony and rebuild the Beit HaMikdash, praying to G-d and returning to the ancient rituals.

The Haftarah concludes with an oath from G-d that once He brings the Jews back to the Land of Israel, He will never again exile them from their homeland, and their future generations will forever dwell in the land. Let us remember this promise given to us by G-d through the prophet Yechezkel, and let it help us to keep everything in perspective, for one day, we will return to the Land of Israel along with the rest of the Jews, and blissful harmony shall be restored for all time.

Vayechi • ויחי

Gam Zu LeTova

By Matthew Goodman

Tragedies and suffering are natural occurrences in the world that Hashem created for us. We all experience different types of pain and problems, whether they be major or minor. Many times we fail to comprehend how Hashem could allow such terrible things to happen to us. How could a loving, caring G-d afflict His creations with so many problems and dilemmas? These are issues that are tough to deal with and severely impact our overall happiness and gladness. There are numerous philosophical and theological approaches that attempt to answer the question of why suffering exists in the world. The study of Theodicy attempts to answer how a just G-d can allow bad things to happen to good people. These approaches, however, oftentimes fail to establish a practical and proper life perspective to this problem. They ask why, but many of us want to know how. How do we realistically cope with suffering?

An answer can be found in the Parshiot of Miketz and Vayechi. In last week's Parsha, Miketz, when Yosef's brothers return from their first trip to Egypt and report back to their father, the Torah details Yaakov's reaction. He replied, "You have bereaved me! Yosef is gone! Shimon is gone! And now, you want to take Binyamin, too! All these troubles have come upon me" (Bereishit 42:36). The Midrash comments that as Yaakov was bewailing all the tragedies that had befallen him, Hashem was sitting in heaven above and laughing at all of Yaakov Avinu's *kvetching*. Yosef is gone? He is the viceroy of Egypt, second in command to Pharaoh! Shimon is gone? He was only imprisoned as long as the brothers were in Egypt. The moment they left, Yosef released him and gave him food and drink (Rashi on 42:24; Bereishit Rabba 91:8). Binyamin will be lost, too? Nothing will happen to him, just like nothing happened to Yosef or Shimon. What Yaakov thought to be disaster after disaster, tragedy after tragedy, was really not so. In truth, nothing bad had happened at all!

In this week's Parsha, Vayechi, Yosef HaTzaddik, after having experienced all the results of the suffering inflicted upon him by his brothers, responds quite differently than his father. After the death of

Yaakov, his brothers, worried that Yosef would now take revenge on them, fell before there brother and said, "Behold, we are your slaves." But Yosef said to them, "Do not be afraid, for am I instead of Hashem? Indeed, you intended evil against me, but Hashem designed it for the good, in order to bring about what is at present to keep a great populace alive."

Rav Herschel Schachter (Rosh Yeshiva of Yeshiva University) writes that oftentimes it is possible to look back at certain things and realize that they were not quite what we figured them to be. What initially appeared as a terrible tragedy can, years later, be understood as part of something truly good and wonderful. Yosef immediately grasped this concept after witnessing all the good that had happened to him and to others due to his brother's actions. Exile from his home and imprisonment was ultimately displaced with great success and prosperity. He honestly relayed to his brothers that everything that happened was part of Hashem's overarching plan and eventually enabled Him to feed those who suffered from famine. It is fantastic that Yosef thought this way, but this was after having seen the results of a long and complex process that started 22 years earlier. It would have been even more fantastic if Yaakov Avinu, sitting at home in Canaan, would have realized the same thing before seeing the outcome of his sufferings.

Yosef's approach can be duly dubbed the "everything happens for the best" way of life. What could have initially appeared to be something bad is actually something good. The Talmud gives two examples of exemplary figures and prime role models who fully internalized this point and lived their lives according to this doctrine. The first was a man named Nachum Ish Gamzu. The Gemara (Taanit 21a) tells us that Nachum, from the town of Gimzo, was called Ish Gam Zu because every time something happened to him, even something seemingly bad, he would say, "Gam zu letovah!" This, too, is for the best!

Another man who had the same approach to life was the great Rebbi Akiva. The Shulchan Aruch states: "A person should acquire the habit of constantly repeating Rebbi Akiva's statement: Whatever the Merciful One does is for the good" (Orach Chaim 230:5). The statement comes from the Gemara in Brachot (60b) which, while discussing the attitude one should have in confronting life's difficulties, tells a fascinating story involving Rebbi Akiva:

Rebbi Akiva was once traveling along the road. When he reached a certain city, he requested lodgings, but no one provided him with any. Although Rebbi Akiva was forced to spend the night sleeping in a field, he did not lament his fate. Instead, he said, "Whatever the Merciful One does is for the best." During the night, a wind came and blew out his lamp, a cat came and ate his rooster, and a lion came and ate his donkey. After suffering all these losses, once more, Rebbi Akiva articulated, "Whatever the Merciful One does is for the best." That very night, an army came and captured the city. Had the lamp been lit, or had the donkey brayed or the rooster crowed, the soldiers would have certainly heard the noise and captured him. Rebbi Akiva turned towards those who had accompanied him, and said, "Did I not tell you? Whatever the Holy One, Blessed Be He, does is all for the good!"

Imagine what our lives would be like if we were able to properly internalize that everything that happens, every difficulty and tragedy, is actually for the best. How could we possibly feel upset or unhappy if we realize that every occurrence is really for the ultimate good? Every conversation, action, and task would make us elated if we truly understood this fact. This Torah perspective, exemplified by Nachum Ish Gamzu and Rebbi Akiva, and likewise displayed by Yosef, is a powerful tool to change our daily attitude. If used correctly, it can help us keep a smile on our face even when things seem awfully challenging. How do we come to this realization, though? And how can we ingrain this into our very attitudes?

The concept of Gam Zu LeTova is basically a subset of the Mitzvah of Bitachon (Trust) in Hashem. One of the fundamental principles of Bitachon is the idea that Hashem is constantly moving the entire world toward an end goal. Slowly, slowly, Hashem changes the world so that it eventually reaches a state of ultimate good and perfection. As such, Rebbitzen Tzippora Heller explains that part of Bitachon is believing that there is an end to the great story in which we are currently involved, and if we knew what the end result would be, we would have no doubt that what is happening to us now is actually good. The Sefat Emet says that we are like deaf people at a concert. We can see the conductor gesticulating wildly, but we have no clue what his movements really mean. Just as deaf people people lack the ability to hear the music and understand what the conductor is really doing, so, too, we lack the ability to perceive the infinite interplay of souls and the working of the Divine plan that occurs behind the curtains of everyday life.

If one understands that not all meets the eye, and every event in our lives is really part of a very big story that will end in ultimate goodness, then nothing can be taken at face value. It would be unfair to perceive suffering as innately bad when, really, everything that happens happens for the best. Everything that happens slowly moves the world towards a state of perfection.

The best way to channel this idea into our attitude is the same way that we achieve any type of growth or success. We have to practice. Just as one has to work out his muscles in order to build them, one has to work out his Bitachon in order to improve it. It is critical, then, for one who seriously wants to change his approach to life to consistently tell himself, "Gam zu letova." Whenever something difficult comes our way, we have to follow the advice of the Shulchan Aruch and articulate Rebbi Akiva's statement: "Whatever the Merciful One does is for the good." Constant repetition of this statement is the most effective way to ingrain its message in our heads and hearts. Only deep commitment to pursue this ideal will effectively enable us to utilize the Torah's amazing tool to living a happy life.

The Mishna in Brachot (54a) teaches that a person is obligated to bless Hashem for the good just as he blesses Him for the bad. In the same way that we thank and praise Hashem for all the good things that come our way, we are obligated to thank and praise Hashem for all the yisurim, pain, and suffering.

A Talmid once found this Mishna to be extremely difficult to understand. How could a person possibly be expected to treat good and bad with true equanimity? How can we thank Hashem for suffering in the same way that we thank Him for prosperity? He took his question to Maggid of Mezeritch, a student of the Ba'al Shem Tov, founder of the Chassidic Movement. He responded to him: "Go ask my student, Reb Zusha. He will have an answer for you." The questioner sought out Reb Zusha and came to his home. He was immediately received warmly and invited inside. He found Reb Zusha to be a cheerful and happy man, constantly expressing his gratitude to Hashem for all He had given him. Yet, Reb Zusha was pauper. There was little to eat in his home and his family was beset with afflictions and illnesses.

The questioner asked him, "Reb Zusha, the Maggid told me to come to you with my question. I need to know how a person can possibly be obligated to bless the good just as he blesses the bad!" Reb Zusha thoroughly considered the matter and replied, "Why did our Rebbe send you to me? I'm very sorry but I have no answer to that question. You need to find a person who experienced good and bad and blessed both equally. He will tell you how to do it. I, on the other hand, have never experienced anything bad in my entire life."

By considering everything that comes our way as being for the best, we, too, can, with the help of Hashem, start to think like Reb Zusha, who, while experiencing suffering, pain, and tragedy, never truly had anything bad ever happen to him.

The Punishment

By Elianne Neuman

In this Parsha, Jacob, father of the twelve tribes and patriarch of the Jewish people, passes away. Before he dies, he gathers his children and blesses them-- but Jacob doesn't bless two of his children, Shimon and Levi. Rather, he relates his disdain for their actions. He says, "Shimon and Levi are comrades; their weaponry is a stolen craft. Into their conspiracy may my soul not enter! Within their congregation do not join... Accursed is their rage for it is intense, and their wrath, for it is harsh; I will separate them within Jacob and I will disperse them in Israel."

There are a number of questions that can be asked concerning Jacob's outburst. 1. Why does he use the word 'comrades' to describe the relationship of Shimon and Levi? And why does he say that their actions are a 'conspiracy'? 2. Why does Jacob punish his sons by denying them a blessing and promising to separate and disperse them? Why does he give them no land and sentence them to be spread out amongst the nation?

I believe that there is an answer that can satisfy these questions.

Jacob is angry with Shimon and Levi for what they had done to Shechem, but he is more upset that they had partnered together. He knows that Shimon and Levi had done evil things, but he also recognizes that they had worsened their sins by conspiring together. Jacob feels that Shimon and Levi should have had the self-control to recognize that they both are troublemakers and should have stayed far away from each other. The two brothers should have realized that they share similar weaknesses, and in order to resist temptation, they should have hesitated to form a partnership as comrades.

Jacob's criticism of Shimon and Levi highlights a core Jewish value: because every person has both a good and an evil inclination, it is imperative to stay away from those who do evil, so that you are not influenced to do evil, too. This sentiment can be found in a verse that we say in our morning prayers: "May it be the will before you, G-d, that you rescue me today and every day from those who are brazen-faced and from brazen-facedness, from a person who is evil, from a companion who is evil, from a neighbour who is evil, from a mishap that is evil, and from a spiritual impediment which is destructive."

Jacob's punishment of Shimon and Levi is appropriate because their dispersal will ensure that they will not be able to influence one another. They will not be able to be comrades, nor will they be able to form conspiracies.

In my opinion, Jacob's punishment has two objectives. It asks Shimon and Levi to stay away from each other, but it also requests something from the nation of Israel: to not be influenced by Shimon and Levi. Rather, they should rebuke them and lead them on a path of goodness.

Rebuking your neighbour is also a Jewish sentiment. We learn in Parshat Kedoshim that "you should reprove your fellow and not bear a sin because of him." Although we should recognize that, as human beings, we have evil inclinations, it is still incumbent upon us to be socially responsible for those around us. By dispersing Shimon and Levi, Jacob is asking us to recognize that, as members of a community, it is imperative that we look out for our neighbours and make sure that they don't go down the wrong path.

When Our Thoughts and Actions Wander
By Rabbi Jeffrey Turtel

Parashat Vayechi begins and ends with two odd requests to be buried in Eretz Yisrael. The first plea comes from Ya'akov, who compels Yosef to swear that he will ensure Ya'akov's immediate burial in the Holy Land. The second request ends Sefer Bereishit, and describes Yosef's desire to have his bones carried to Eretz Yisrael when the soon-to-be Am Yisrael would return to the land.

While the burial of a Diaspora dweller in Eretz Yisrael is an interesting Halachic topic, the philosophical concerns are more pressing. Why would one who had never made the journey to be *Oleh LaAretz* (to move to Eretz Yisrael) want to have his dead body buried in its soil? In fact, there seems to be a disagreement amongst the Tannaim as to whether such a command is appropriate. Midrash Rabba 96 views such a burial as a fulfillment of "I shall walk before Hashem in the land of the living"; conversely, Rabbi Elazar (Sanhedrin 111) opposes the idea, questioning "In your lives you did not go up; shall you, then, in death come and contaminate My land?"

The Abarbanel suggests that these two Ma'amarei Chazal are speaking to two different groups of people. There are many people who live their lives in pursuit of perfection. These individuals strive to be ethical and moral beings who study and follow the philosophy and dictates of the Torah. Such people are welcome to be buried in Eretz Yisrael. They enhance its *K'dusha* (holiness), and "walk before Hashem."

The second group spend their lives in vanity, focus on their own needs, and pay no attention to the more important things in life. Torah values play a limited role in their day-to-day conduct. These people are considered by Chazal to be 'dead', even in life. Yet the Abarbanel explains that there is a segment of this second group who "command that they be buried in a Tallit and Tefillin, while in their lives, they work wool and linen together (shatnez)." This means that even though, in living, Torah ideas were the farthest from their minds, some still desire to be remembered as G-d-fearing individuals. It is such attitudes that "contaminate My land."

Where do we fall? How much do we think about our legacy? How much of our lives are guided by our ideals? Do our actions and our thoughts work in unison? How many of us fall into the group who desires to be good, who desires to get straight As – but in practice fails to implement what we preach?

Eretz Yisrael represents Judaism in its ideal form. Ya'akov and Yosef both announced that their hearts are in the Holy Land, even if, in life, they were forced to spend some time travelling. They spent their entire lives living that idea – they were in the first group. In which group are you?

ואלה שמות בני ישראל הבאים מצרימה את יעקב איש וביתו באו

Shemot
שמות

Shemot • שמות

Even Evil Has Standards
By Becky Friedman

In Parshat Shmot, we see two changes of rule in Egypt. First the Pharoah dies, and a new one rises, who did not know Yosef. Not knowing Yosef, he then proceeds to subject Bnei Yisrael to oppressive slave labour and commands the midwives, and later all his people, to murder all the Jewish boys.

One might think that this fellow is as bad as it gets-- he does seem pretty evil. Nevertheless, his successor is far worse. Some time later, while Moshe is raising his family in Midian, that king dies and a new one presumably rises-- at which point Bnei Yisrael cry out from their suffering to Hashem; it is *this* king who is subject to the ten plagues. So what's going on here? What's the difference between these two kings?

The first king does not know Yosef. "Vayakam melech chadash al Mitzraim asher lo yada et Yosef." "And there arose a new king over Egypt who did not know Yosef." Yes, he did bad things, but he was given the opportunity to repeal those decisions-- when the midwives refused to kill the boys, he could have just given up and repented. He didn't. But while he persisted in behaving badly, he was still clearly decent enough that Moshe was raised in his household-- he still merited that.

His successor, on the other hand, does not know G-d. When Moshe and Aharon confront him for the first time, he tells them, "Lo yadati et Hashem v'gam et Yisrael lo ashaleach." "I have not known Hashem, and Yisrael, too, I will not send." This Pharoah is not given opportunities to repent like his predecessor; rather, Hashem tells Moshe from the outset that Pharoah will not consent to send the people.

The first Pharoah did not know Yosef; he had no personal connection to the Jewish people, and as such treated them badly. He did, however, still understand that G-d was above all, and he behaved accordingly. The second Pharoah did not even know G-d, and acted wantonly, believing his actions would have not consequences; therefore, he became G-d's puppet, his heart hardened by G-d to prevent his repentance and his eventual consent to release the people preordained by G-d in the final pasuk of the perek. This serves to teach us that even someone so evil as the Pharoah who first enslaved the Jewish people merits something for recognizing G-d-- for recognizing that more important than *anything* is belief in and reverence for G-d.

May all our enemies be as foolhardy as the second Pharoah, whose rejection of G-d led directly to his downfall.

The Gadol of a Shepherd
By Matthew Goodman

"The boy grew up (VaYigdal HaYeled)" (Shemot 2:10)

"And it happened in those days that Moshe grew up (VaYigdal Moshe) and went out to his brethren and saw their burdens" (2:11)

The Ramban asks what the two expressions of "VaYigdal" are referring to. He suggests that the first refers to Moshe's physical growth, and the second refers to spiritual growth. First Moshe became an adult. Then he became an "Adam Gadol" - a great man. But the pasuk does not just say that Moshe grew up and became a Gadol. It says that Moshe became a Gadol and saw the burdens of his brethren. Furthermore, after the pasuk, Moshe kills an Egyptian who is ruthlessly beating a Jewish slave.

Essentially, the definition of Moshe's "Gadlut" is the fact that he could go out of his way and carry the burden of other people.

Midrash Rabbah states that Hashem tests the righteous with sheep. He tested King David with sheep and found him to be a good shepherd. David would bring the smallest sheep out first, so that they could graze upon the tender grass. Then he would allow the old sheep to feed from the ordinary grass; and the young sheep to eat the tougher grass. Hashem said, "He who knows how to look after sheep, bestowing upon each the care it deserves, shall come and tend my people.

The Midrash states that Moshe was also tested by sheep. When Moshe was tending the flock of Yitro, a little kid escaped from him. He ran after it until it reached a shady place and found a pool of water to drink from. Moshe said, "I did not know that you ran away because of thirst; you must be weary." So he he placed the kid on his shoulder and walked back.

Hashem said, "Because you were merciful in leading the flock of a mortal, you shall tend My flock, the people of Israel."

A sheep, no matter how old, is always going to be very dependent on its herder for survival, and the herder will always have to know how to deal with their burdens and problems. A person, no matter how old, will always have a share of burdens to deal with and pain to overcome. It is usually helpful to have a "herder" who can empathize and commiserate. A Gadol who knows, who goes out of his way to carry the burden of other people. A Moshe Rabbeinu.

Divrei Torah on **Shemot**

Vaeira • וארא

Fulfilling Our Own Potential
By Elianne Neuman

We are told in this week's Parsha, "And Aharon took Elisheva, daughter of Aminadav, sister of Nachshon."

Why does the Torah mention the identity of Aaron's wife, her father, and her brother?

Ramban explains that there are three instances in which the Torah mentions the identity of the mother in order to honour the children:

The Torah mentions Yocheved, the mother of Moshe and Aharon, in order to honour them by telling us that she was a daughter of Levi, a righteous man. It is also an allusion that a miracle occurred to her—she had her children at an older age. Yocheved merits special attention because, as the Midrash tells us, she was also the midwife who defied Pharaoh's orders to kill all Jewish male babies, and was commended for her righteous actions which insured the future of the Jewish people.

The Torah mentions Elisheva, the wife of Aharon and the mother of the priesthood, in order to tell us that she came from the tribe of Yehuda (the tribe of royalty). Elisheva also merits our attention because she was the sister of Nachshon, who, as the Midrash tells us, went into the Yam Suf before anyone else did, and walked until the water had reached his head -- before Hashem split the sea. This was a fantastic show of faith in G-d, and he was greatly rewarded for this great mitzvah.

The Torah mentions Pinchas' mother as "from the daughters of Putiel." Ramban asks: What is the point of mentioning the family of a person whose identity is not disclosed in the Torah? Our sages say that the name Putiel indicates that Pinchas was from the family of Yosef, who overcame his evil inclinations when surrounded by idolatrous neighbours in Egypt. Pinchas was also a descendant of Yitro, who fattened calves for the worship of idolatry, but turned his life around and served G-d.

Thus, we learn that the name Putiel was mentioned in order to give praise to Yosef and Yitro, who merited, because of their righteous behaviours, the priesthood for their descendants.

In reflecting on this practise of identifying the mother to honour the children, Ramban makes a very interesting point which I believe is incredibly relevant.

In all three instances, Yocheved, Elisheva and bat Putiel's children were all great tzaddikim who came from a tremendous lineage of righteousness. They, feeling overwhelmed by the accomplishments of their ancestors, could have buckled under the pressure to be like their forefathers and could have become reshaim instead, figuring that there was no way that they could live up to the deeds of their predecessors. Instead of bowing to this temptation, they continued on the path of the just and became righteous in their own merits, setting examples for future generations to follow.

We should also be inspired by the legacy of those who preceded us. While we may never achieve the status of Moshe, Aharon, or Pinchas, we are, nonetheless, capable of achieving the greatness which is our unique potential.

The message of this pasuk is that we should use the examples of our ancestors as a springboard, as a way to encourage us to maximize what we are capable of. By doing so, we will not only fulfill our special mission, but we will also help create positive role models for future generations to emulate.

You Can't Handle the Truth!

By Matthew Goodman

"When Pharaoh speaks to you, saying, 'Provide a wonder for yourselves,' you say say to Aharon, 'Take your staff and cast it down before Pharaoh -- it will become a snake!'" (Shemot 7:9)

Why does Pharaoh say "Provide a wonder for yourselves" and not "Provide me with a wonder?"

R' Shalom Rokeach z"l, the first Belzer Rebbe, exlains that Pharaoh did not care about seeing a sign. He already made it clear that he had no belief in Hashem: "Who is Hashem that I should heed His voice?...I do not know Hashem" (5:2). "The fool does not desire understanding" (Mishlei 18:2).

Pharaoh's real intention was to impugn on the faith of Moshe and Aharon. "You are telling me," Pharaoh implies, "that Hashem told you to take the Jewish people out of Egypt? Prove it! Have Hashem give YOU a sign. Make Hashem prove to YOU that he said this." Rashi explains that the term "mofet," sign, in this context, is a sign that would make it known that Hashem is the one who is sending Moshe and Aharon to free the Jewish people.

Pharaoh wanted to say that they must have had doubts. They have to doubt that Hashem is sending them!

Obviously Moshe and Aharon had no doubt of the truth of their mission. However, Pharaoh is, in a way, correct. Many of us experience doubts in our emunah. Sometimes we feel like there are profound contradictions to everything we believe in. Sometimes we even feel like the basis for our faith has been shattered.

R' Rokeach asks why Hashem had to create us with these feelings. Why could He not have made us filled with emunah and bitachon? R' Rokeach answers that those experiences are meant to help us grow. When a person has religious or spiritual doubts, he searches for an answer. Either he goes to a tzaddik and asks, or he searched in our holy literature -- in any case, he tries to find an answer.

The essence of every Jew wants to find the truth in every situation. It is normal to say, "I need proof. I need a wonder for myself." That is what leads to a real dynamic and amazing relationship with Judaism and Hashem, as opposed to a stagnant, mechanical one. Pharaoh, on the other hand, had no care whatsoever for the truth. He had no intention of searching for it either, and it would take a slap on the face from Hashem for him to realize His existence. When Jews search for the truth, they have to be able to realize it, too.

Bo • בא

This Parsha has been generously sponsored by the Gardner family in honour of their children

Emerging From Opression
By Zachary Zarnett-Klein

In this week's Haftarah, found in the book of Jeremiah, the Jews once again encounter Egypt; however, this time, we see Egypt as a victim. The Haftarah describes the Egyptians' defeat by the Babylonians, in their quest for world leadership. As Egypt is defeated, Israel is put in a dire situation, having pledged allegiance to the Egyptians, being now faced with the opposing nation as victor.

G-d assures Israel that while they will be punished for their idol-worship, the punishment will take place over a large span of time, and the entire nation will not be eradicated.

Although this Haftarah may sound completely different from the Exodus from Egypt discussed in this week's Torah portion, many parallels can be drawn between them. First, in both books, locusts plague the Egyptians.

The plague of locusts not only darkens the sky and covers the land, but by the end, Egypt is left with no produce or grain, which is somewhat ironic: Yosef helped Egypt prepare for the famine, but now, since they turned on the Jews, they are once again facing food problems, and this time, they have no one to whom they can turn.

In the Haftarah, the Babylonians are compared to locusts because of their great numbers, and they prove to be as damaging, if not more so, to the Egyptians. Although Egypt is the oppressor in the Torah portion and the victim in the Haftarah, Israel is depicted in both as a nation whose remnant will survive through all struggles.

Arguably, in fact, we should thank Egypt, because if they had not oppressed us, we would not have gained appreciation for our merciful G-d, and the entire house of Israel may have be destroyed by now, as was Ancient Egypt. Although Israel has been oppressed by many nations, our nation has emerged stronger each time, with a renewed sense of patriotism and devotion to our people and to G-d. The Jewish people continue to flourish as a strong and proud nation.

Prioritizing Mercy
By Yaron Milwid

In this week's Parsha, we see Becky's 'ultra-evil Pharaoh' from last week proving to be human. We all know how up until now, Egypt has been afflicted with many plagues. Finally, just before the plague of locusts, Pharaoh and his ministers decide to listen to Moshe and send the Jews to sacrifice to Hashem. The only condition is that the children, women, and livestock stay in Egypt. The words that Pharaoh uses to tell Moshe this condition are as follows: "So be Hashem with you as I will send you forth with your children! Look-- the evil intent is opposite your faces. Not so; let the men go now and you shall serve Hashem, for that is what you seek!" According to Rabbi Zalman Sorotzkin, there are two ways to understand this sentence. The first is that the constellation called "Evil" is rising, and the second is that Moshe plans deceit.

If you understand the quote the first way, you give this evil Pharaoh positive attributes, enough in my opinion for G-d to return his free will. Understanding the quote this way means that you think that Pharaoh feels that the Jews are going into danger because the constellation heralds death and bloodshed. Pharaoh is telling the Jews that they are going into danger, so they should not go, but if they truly want to, they should leave their women and children. While I take this in good faith and attribute to Pharaoh feelings of mercy for the children and women, Rabbi Zalman Sorotzkin only attributes to Pharaoh mercy on the men. According to Rabbi Zalman Sorotzkin, it is more likely that Pharaoh wanted to bathe in the blood of the children, and marry the women off to Egyptians. Why does Rabbi Zalman Sorotzkin feel that the Egyptians had pity on the men but not the women and children? There could be many reasons for this, but I can only think of one reason. Perhaps Pharaoh had pity on all of the Israelites but it was not his predominant emotion.

Rabbi Zalman Sorotzkin sees Pharaoh as thinking first of himself, then about his country, and finally about everything else, including the Jews. Rabbi Zalman Sorotzkin understands that Pharaoh thought, will it really be a loss to me if the Jewish men die? What about Egypt? Did I not want them to die? Pharaoh, having decided that the extermination of Jewish men was not a problem, could think about them. Only now did he realize the difference between his systematic extermination and this sudden and bloody extermination, and how much more painful this one was. Thus, he felt pity that they escaped a relatively painless death, only to suffer an extremely painful one. He then thought about the women. He realized that he did not require the women, but that Egypt could use the women. Therefore, the idea of their pain did not enter his mind, because he did not let it. Had he not decided that they could benefit Egypt, he would have felt pity for them, too. Finally he thought of the children, and realized that they could benefit him, and so he did not think of Egypt or the children. Thus we solve the difficulty with Rabbi Zalman Sorotzkin's commentary. The second way of looking at the quote is obvious, and is just that the Moshe was trying to pull the wool over his eyes, and so he was keeping the women, children, and animals hostage.

A Special Gift
By Elianne Neuman

In this Parsha, the Torah describes the ninth plague that befell the Egyptians:

Hashem said to Moshe, "Stretch forth your hand toward the heavens and there will be darkness upon the land of Egypt, and the darkness will be tangible. Moshe stretched forth his hand towards the heavens and there was a thick darkness throughout the land of Egypt for a three-day period. No man could see his brother nor could anyone rise from his place for a three-day period, bur for all of Israel, there was light in their dwellings."

There are two traditional explanations as to why this plague punished the Egyptians with darkness.

First, G-d recognized that there were many Jews who had assimilated and behaved inappropriately. He felt were not worthy of being freed and should die. But G-d didn't want the Egyptians to see the death of the Jews and claim that the plagues also affected the Jews, so he created a blanket of darkness.

The second reason for darkness was so that the Jews could look through the homes of the Egyptians and find valuables that they would later be able to take with them as compensation for all their years of slave labour.

I would like to offer an alternative reason as to why darkness was an appropriate plague for the Egyptians.

By being stuck for three days in darkness, and not being able to move, talk, or see anything, the Egyptians were offered time to reflect and repent. G-d had given them a gift: three days to contemplate their lives and their society.

But after the three days, it was clear that the Egyptians had not changed. In fact, after this plague, Pharaoh's response to Moshe was more vehement that it had ever been: "Go from me! Beware—do not see my face any more, for on the day you see my face you shall die!"

I would like to venture to say that Pharaoh's response was so extreme; it relates to us that he had, in fact, used the three days to reflect on his life and knew that he had treated the Jews badly. When he saw Moshe, he was embarrassed by how he had acted. But unable to act positively his newfound integrity, Pharaoh could only deal with his thoughts by acting repulsively toward Moshe. He wasn't able to actualize what he had felt during those days of introspection.

And so, Pharaoh and the Egyptians had, once again, failed to recognize the full potential of the gift that G-d had given them.

If we were given the opportunity to have three full days to sit in complete and total darkness, just to relax and to meditate about our lives, I hope that we would all jump at the opportunity to be truly introspective and would emerge from those days as changed individuals.

Luckily for us, G-d has given us a special opportunity every week where we can be introspective: Shabbat. Hopefully, this Shabbat, as we take time off from our busy lives to spend time with our family and friends, we will also take a moment to think about our week and to introspect. Unlike the Egyptians, we shouldn't pass up this gift which G-d has given us.

Miracles

By Matthew Goodman

The early history of the Jewish people is replete with stunningly miraculous occurrences. Avraham and Sarah gave birth to Yitzchak at a tremendously advanced age, despite the fact that Sarah was naturally unable to conceive anymore. This and last week's Parshiot detail the most well-known miracles in the entire Torah: those that occurred during the Exodus of Egypt. Hashem terrorized the Egyptians with ten plagues, each one caused by blatant divine intervention in the natural order of the universe. Klal Yisrael left Egypt guided by a divine cloud by day and a pillar of fire by night. The sea split before the nation and our ancestors walked on dry land, while their pursuers drowned. Mun from the sky nourished them every day. The Menorah in the Mishkan was fashioned miraculously out of fire. The Torah tells us, "During the forty years that I led you through the desert, your clothes did not wear out, nor did the sandals on your feet" (Devarim 29:5). Similarly, "For forty years You sustained them in the desert; they lacked nothing" (Nechemiah 9:21).

The Hebrew word for miracle is "nes." The Bnei Yissachar, HaRav Zvi Elimelech of Dinov (1783-1841, Poland) points out that "nes" also connotes the sail of a boat. A sail enables a boat to move along a set path according to the strength and direction of the wind. A miracle is an outward display of Hashem's control over the world, where His providence, like the sail of a boat, guides us in the right path. When one looks at a sail, billowing with the wind, it is clear that there is a force controlling the direction of the the boat. Similarly, when one experiences a miracle, it is clear that there is a force controlling the direction of their life. (The term in Jewish thought for this concept is "Hashgacha Pratit," literally, divine supervision of the individual.)

If miracles are an outward display of Hashem's personal involvement in our individual and national existence, do we see that involvement today? Is Hashem as intricately involved in our lives as He was with our forefathers, at the time of the Exodus, the wanderings in the desert, and the lives of Judges, Kings, and Prophets? Do we see miracles today? Obviously, not to the same level of grandeur as those great and early periods of our long history. We certainly do not see explicit interference with the natural order of the universe, but there are other Divine workings that go on behind the cosmic veil.

There is an interesting argument regarding Yocheved, Moshe Rabbeinu's mother, discussed in Parshat Vayigash, that teaches an exemplary lesson about miracles. As Yaakov Avinu descends to Egypt, the Torah lists his descendants, all of whom joined him in the move. The pasuk states, "These are the sons of Leah whom she bore to Yaakov... numbered thirty-three" (Bereishit 46:14). Rashi notices that the Torah only lists thirty-two descendants, as opposed to the full thirty-three. He explains that the last descendant was Yocheved, the mother of Moshe, who was conceived in

Canaan but born in Egypt. Ibn Ezra disagrees with Rashi's answer to the problem. If Yocheved had indeed been born at that time, she would have been 130 years old when she gave birth to Moshe Rabbeinu. If the Torah publicizes the fact that Sarah Immeinu gave birth at 90, then certainly it should publicize that Yocheved gave birth at 130! Since no such statement is made, Ibn Ezra holds that Rashi's explanation is flawed, and offers his own. The thirty-third person was actually an allusion to Yaakov himself, and he was mentioned among Leah's family since hers was the largest branch.

Ramban disagrees with Ibn Ezra. He explains that even if Yoceheved had been born later, the birth of Moshe would have still been a great miracle. Levi, her father, was 43 when he descended with his family to Egypt, and Moshe was born 130 years later. Therefore, even if Yocheved was born, for instance, 57 years later, her father would have been 100 when he gave birth to her, and she 83 when she gave birth to Moshe. If Rashi is wrong, then there could have potentially been not one miracle but two great miracles, both of which, according to the Ibn Ezra, should be mentioned in the Torah.

Ramban goes on to confront Ibn Ezra's question, "Why isn't Yocheved's miraculous birth of Moshe Rabbeinu publicized in the text?" Ramban distinguishes between two types of miracles. The first is the one that we are quite familiar with, and rears its head consistently in the Torah, pertinently so in the parshiot of Va'eira, Bo, and Beshalach. They are open miracles: clear divine intervention in the natural order of the world. Sarah Immeinu's birth was an open miracle, for she had long since passed menopause (18:11) and was naturally unable to give birth. The second type are miracles by which we are constantly surrounded and is assuredly consistent in each one of our lives, but to whose existence, at times, we can be oddly ignorant or blind. They are hidden miracles, which work succinctly according to what appears to be natural, and do not blatantly contravene the workings of the natural world as do open miracles. But they are miracles nonetheless, and stem from the will of Hashem. Yocheved's birth was a hidden miracle, for she, unlike Sarah, had a functioning womb. Her menopause was delayed until the the proper time for her to give birth to the redeemer of Klal Yisrael.

Ramban writes that the Torah only mentions miracles that were open or mentioned in prophecy. Regarding hidden miracles, "Why should Scripture mention them? All the fundamental principles of the Torah involve hidden miracles and the people of the Torah has in all of their matters only miracles, and not nature and custom." In another commentary, he similarly points out, "A person has no portion in the Torah of Moshe unless he believes that all our matters and circumstances are miracles" (Ramban on Shemot 13:16). All of Klal Yisrael's doings and experiences are not subjugated to the natural order. What appears to us as a natural occurrence is a carefully concealed divine manifestation, caused by the divine interplay that runs the world. This is highly reminiscent of Chazal's statement that "Ein mazal l'Yisrael" - There is no concept of natural fate when it comes to the Jewish people (Shabbat 156b).

This answer is amazing. According to the Ramban, even today, Hashem is constantly active in our lives. He acts quietly enough that His miracles are not astoundingly explicit, but astounding nonetheless. A similar vein of thought is presented by the Talmud (Taanit 25a):

Rav Chanina ben Dosa was known for his extreme financial straits and the blatant miracles which followed him. One Erev Shabbat, he noticed that his daughter was very upset. He asked her, "My daughter, why are you sad?" She replied, "The oil jar was mixed with the vinegar jar and I accidently lit the Shabbat lights with vinegar!" Rav Chanina replied, "My daughter, why should this trouble you? He Who commands oil to burn will also command the vinegar to burn." Just as Rav Chanina said, the vinegar burned and remaind lit the whole of Shabbat.

Rav Chanina did not say to his daughter, "Want to see something amazing? Look at this miracle!" To him, vinegar burning was no more spectacular than oil burning, even though it is not the nature of vinegar to burn. They are both, in fact, miracles. Rav Eliyahu Dessler, the Ponovezher Mashgiach, in Michtav M'Eliyahu, notes that there is, in fact, no inherent difference between nature and what we call miraculous. We simply use the former word for the miracles to which we are accustomed, and the latter one for those which we have not before experienced. All there is, in the end, is Hashem's will. Ralph Waldo Emerson (1803-1882), the American lecturer, essayist, and poet wrote: "If the stars should appear one night in a thousand years, how would men believe and adore..."

On individual, environmental, and national levels, Hashem's miracles are constantly abound in our world. For that reason, when Chazal formulated the blessings of the Amidah, they wrote in Modim: "Al nisecha shebechol yom imanu" - we thank Hashem for Your miracles that are with us every day. Take, for instance, the birth of a child, an occurrence highly regarded as life's greatest miracle -- the miracle of life itself. So many things can go wrong in the awe-inspiringly complex process from egg to fetus to baby. A healthy child is a miraculous blessing beyond fathomable compare. There are countless books that relate stories about families and individuals who experienced the most bizarre set of coincidences and lucky happenings that can be described as nothing less than a miracle. "Small Miracles of the Holocaust" by Yitta Halberstam and Judith Leventhal is a great example, and so is Rav Yechiel Spero's "Touched by a Story" series. But these accounts are not just found in books. Many of us can relate events that surpass logical understanding. There is no greater account of miraculous happenings than the very history of the Jewish people in Galut (exile) and their survival for two thousand years. The miracles that we see today occurring in the State of Israel are awe-inspiring and have amazed the world.

One can and should duly ask the question, "Why do we not see open miracles in our day?" The Steipler Gaon, HaRav Yaakov Yisrael Kanievsky (1899-1985), in his book Chayei Olam, explains that miracles were the order of the day at the foundation of our people because they needed to learn the important lesson of their tremendous connection to Hashem. That generation needed miracles, and their profound influence spread to later generations, who heard of these great wonders from their ancestors. Open miracles, however, diminish the free will of man. And, having experienced blatant displays of Divine intervention, Hashem's expectations and level of accountability for that generation was duly raised, a phenomenon that could not exist in succeeding generations. Today, Hashem works very differently. Hashem's most obvious character trait is that He is hidden (in Jewish thought, this is referred to as "Hester Panim"). He works quietly, discreetly maneuvering the world and implementing His Divine Will. Slowly, slowly, Hashem moves the world to perfection and guides our lives in the right direction.

We mentioned that the word "nes" connotes a miracle and a sail, but it also means "test." This dichotomy teaches us that one of the functions of miracles is to serve as a test in which Hashem appraises our ability to notice His eternal presence. We do not have miracles equivalent in grandeur to those that occurred at the time of the Exodus. We have miracles that are hidden, and it is incumbent upon all of us to keep our eyes open for them and realize the tremendous Divine supervision that accompanies us always. When we assess our lives through such lenses, we can ascertain clarity in our very existence and learn to appreciate the blessings and gifts that Hashem graciously bestows upon us. Everything is a miracle, and everything is amazing and stupendous. How much more beauty is there in the world when everything is not coincidence, but purposeful phenomena created by Hashem Himself?

Beshalach • בשלח

This Parsha has been generously sponsored by the Garber family

Our Nation's Mood-Swings
By Becky Friedman

Parshat Beshalach reads like the story of a nation with bi-polar affective disorder. In one parsha, Bnei Yisrael continually flip back and forth from a ragtag group of whiny slaves to the dignified people who are G-d's chosen nation.

They begin promisingly, honouring their ancestral promise to take Joseph's remains with them when they leave Egypt. And, indeed, they can't be blamed for their panic when they see their former masters chasing after them, caught between the army and the sea. They amply make up for their temporary lack of faith with the beautiful Song of the Sea. But this parsha has a remarkable amount of complaints. Interspersed with the events above, we have not one but *two* instances-- two in one parsha!-- of Bnei Yisrael whining about water. Not to mention their catch-all complaint about the variety of food.

This is the people that G-d chose? *This* is the people He rescued from Egypt-- a crowd of malcontents who can't walk ten steps without saying "I'm thirsty"? It does seem a little strange. Every time something doesn't go perfectly for them, they start to throw wild accusations at Moshe, claiming that he sneaked them out of "wonderful" Egypt in order to murder them all himself. They say *this* to Moshe? They say *this* to the man who returned for them at great personal risk, and publicly performed miracles that could only have come from G-d, in order to redeem them from generations of slavery? It's more than ingratitude-- it's insane!

But yes. This is the people that G-d chose, this is the people that Moshe led-- and *this* is the people who spontaneously composed the Song of the Sea in their wonderment and thanks to G-d for miraculously saving them. *This* is the peope who kept a promise hundreds of years in the making, despite the inconvenience of carting an embalmed corpse around with them in the desert. *This* is the people who turned their heads to G-d and prevailed against the more prepared forces of Amalek.

Divrei Torah on **Shemot**

Yes, it seems strange. Perhaps, at first, a little unbelievable-- that a people who had witnessed firsthand the will of G-d could be so fickle with their faith. But that is an aspect of human nature, and one we must learn to embrace. It is an aspect of man that cannot be imitated, cannot be feigned: just when he has sunk to the greatest of depths, he goes against all expectations and rises to the greatest of heights.

Why did G-d choose this whiny, perpetually unsatisfied people? Why did G-d choose this people who needed their faith to be constantly reaffirmed? Why did G-d choose this people who seem at times unwilling to lift a finger to help themselves?

Why? Because they're worth it. After all the petty complaints, after all the rudeness to Moshe, this is still the people who sang the Song of the Sea. This is still the people who defeated Amalek. We endure the bad because the good that comes with it is so much more impressive.

Perhaps it's not that Beshalach contains a series of contradictions so much as that it depicts a continual struggle. After all, the "good" wins out, at least in Parshat Beshalach. It begins with the good but it does not end with the bad: it ends with our triumph against Amalek, and G-d's promise to wage eternal war on these our enemies. Just like our Biblical ancestors, we experience that struggle in our daily lives. On any given day, there will be a person acting horribly base and a person being fantastically kind, and often they're the same person.

We are human, and none of us can change our natures. But may we all strive, like Parshat Beshalach, for the good to outweigh the bad; may we all strive, through our good qualities, to be "worth" enduring our faults.

Jump out of bed, sleepyhead!
By Matthew Goodman

I personally find routine to be somewhat difficult to bear. Oftentimes, it mercilessly controls my life. I wake up, get dressed, go into the car, drive to school, learn, drive back, do homework, learn some more, and eventually go to sleep. The next morning, the same routine directs me again. As an observant Jew, the level of rote is increased tremendously. Interspersed throughout this short period of 24 hours are rituals, prayers, and actions that are expected to be repeated every day. I'm sure many of you can relate -- routine is simply a basic part of life itself. This is certainly the order of the day for our own parents, whose routine is focused on caring for other living beings and maintaining a home! This can incur a serious challenge. It is exceptionally difficult to remain constantly excited and inspired in life when most of it is obliged to be routine. What is so exhilarating about brushing one's teeth or driving in a car? How can praying three times each day retain its wonder? What freshness is there when every day requires similar rote? What can inspire us to get out of bed every single morning?

This week's Parsha, Beshalach, gives us a fascinating insight into human psychology that helps us answer this problem. After Klal Yisrael cross the Red Sea and ultimately escape their Egyptian opressors, they travel to the desert of Sin. The Torah tells us that, on the fifteenth day of the second month, just a month and a half after their departure from Egypt, "the entire community of the children of Israel complained against Moshe and against Aaron" (Shemot 16:2). They cried out, "If only we had died by the hand of Hashem in the land of Egypt... for you have brought us out into this desert, to starve this entire congregation to death!" (16:3). In response, Hashem gave the Jewish people Mun. "Behold," Hashem said to Moshe, "I will rain down for you food from heaven; let the people come out and pick each day's portion on its day..." (16:4).

Many times, even the simplest question can yield tremendous lessons. The most obvious question on this pasuk is why did Hashem cause the Mun to fall every day as opposed to once a week, once a month, or even once a year?

The Ktav Sofer, Rav Avraham Shmuel Binyomin Sofer (1815-1871), Rosh Yeshiva of the Pressburg Yeshiva, answers with a parable. A person who receives a large sum of money once a year will certainly be elated on the day that the gift is given to him. In seemingly limitless thanks to his beneficiary, he will be moved to do whatever he can to please this person. As time goes by, however, although he still knows that the money was given to him by someone who loves him, the joy will wear off. Since the Jews received Mun on a daily basis, this present was always fresh and exciting, causing the people to feel a constant state of elation over all the goodness and care that Hashem provided for them. Hashem wanted them to live with the joy of receiving a new gift. Rav Shlomo Wolbe Zt"l (1914-2005) in Maamarei Yemei HaRatzon (p 23) points out that people need a constant sense of newness in order to inspire what they are doing. One who lacks newness will grow uninterested and have a hard time performing what, to him, has become senseless routine.

It seems logical that creating a feeling of newness is essential to living a more inspirational, meaningful, and exciting life, even if it is, indeed, filled with the same activities. This is what Aaron the Kohen Gadol made of his own routine. The Torah, in Parshat Behaalotecha, tells us how Aaron would light the Menorah in the Mishkan (Tabernacle) every single day. The pasuk reads, "Aaron did so; he lit the lamps toward the face of the Menorah, as Hashem had commanded Moshe" (Bamidbar 8:3). The commentators explain that this pasuk praises Aaron for his constant dedication to fulfilling this Mitzvah. Rav Yehudah Aryeh Leib Alter (1847-1905) in Sefat Emet points out that what made Aaron really praiseworthy was the fact that he lit the Menorah every day with a sense of fresh enthusiasm. The Mitzvah always seemed to him like new, as if it was the first time that he was lighting the Menorah.

How can we, like Aaron, invigorate ourselves with a sense of newness every single day, transforming routine into meaning? How can we make life more exciting?

Perhaps one profound insight can inspire us to do just that. Every morning, upon arising, we say, "I give thanks before You... for You have returned my soul into me with compassion. Great is your faithfulness!" "Great is your faithfulness" is the continuation of the verse, "They are new every morning" (Eichah 3:23). Chazal teach us (Eicha Rabba) that Hashem takes our souls when we go to sleep and gives them back to us when we wake up. Rav Alexandry says that if you entrust an object to a person of flesh and blood, when it is returned, the object looks old and worn out. When we entrust our souls to Hashem, however, He gives them back to us fresh and new!

The Chatam Sofer, Rav Moshe Schreiber (1762-1839), explains that we do not really give our souls to Hashem. Rather, He lends them to us and takes them back. We, beings of flesh and blood, return the souls in a state of sullied impurity, but every morning Hashem gives them back to us refreshed, purified, and renewed.

This is a truly amazing concept. Every morning, when we wake up, our souls are like new. Perhaps this is why we can go to sleep feeling angry or upset, and wake up completely content. How many of us actually do wake up angry at what happened the night before? Our souls are renewed, and everything that can tarnish them has been stripped away. Every day, we have the potential to become a new person. A better person. When doing a Mitzvah that is routine, such as praying, this concept can drastically improve its performance. My prayers on Monday are completely different from my prayers on Tuesday. They are a whole world apart. Tuesday was a different, new day, with new potential and new challenges to inhibit growth. When something less meaningful has to be done on a regular basis, such as the secular routine that manages our schedule, this concept can serve as a sense of strength and inspiration. Yes, we have to go through all the routine, and it is simply part of life. But if that is joined with a tremendous sense of newness, our attitude can change. If every day is seen as special and fresh, that Chizuk (strengthening/encouragement), can help us get through anything.

Shulchan Aruch tells us (1:1): "Rise like a lion [every morning] to serve your creator!" A brand new day is certainly a good reason to jump out of bed and should inspire us to live meaningful, exciting, happy lives.

Acknowledging G-d
By Dylan Shaul

At the beginning of this week's parsha, we are given a rare glimpse into the logic behind G-d's decisions regarding His dealings with the Israelites. Instead of allowing His people to take the most direct route from Egypt to the Promised Land, G-d instead traces for them a roundabout path that includes miraculously crossing through Red Sea.

G-d reasons that, should the Israelites encounter war with the Philistines, who live between Egypt and the land of Israel, they might endeavour to return to the house of bondage. Taking the circuitous route would not only avoid armed conflict, but would allow the Israelites to shed the slave mentality that they had accumulated, thanks to several centuries of unmerciful hard labor.

However, G-d's planned pacifism does not last long; at the end of the parsha, Amalek springs an ambush and begins a battle which Moses and his people cannot avoid. Though the Israelites emerge victorious, the psychological effects of victory are costly. In the 25th chapter of the book of Deuteronomy, we read Moses' account of Amalek's attack: "Remember what Amalek did to you as you came out of Egypt [...] when you were faint and weary, and he feared not G-d."

Some sages read Moses' final words as *"you* feared not G-d": an allusion to the Israelites. The sages imply that, at the battle of Amalek, the people lost their faith in G-d. Perhaps it was not the sin of the Golden Calf, but the battle with Amalek, that warranted the Israelites' forty-year wandering through the wilderness. Better yet, perhaps the battle with Amalek was the precursor to the sin of the Golden Calf. G-d had already anticipated the result of war so early in the Israelites freedom: it would engender in them a feeling of self-sufficiency.

We read this week that as long as Moses' hands were raised, the Israelites fought victoriously against Amalek. Moses, growing tired in his old age, ended up sitting on a rock, with Aaron and Hur each holding up one of his arms. Thus it was not an independent act on behalf of the people, but an act of G-d, that allowed Amalek to be defeated.

However, Exodus 17:13 reads: "And Joshua overcame Amalek..." This seems to be in contradiction with the previous account. It was by G-d's actions, through Moses, that Amalek was defeated, not Joshua's. However, the Israelites perceived themselves and their general as being responsible for their victory. It was this lack of acknowledgment of the divine source of everything that would lead, at least subconsciously, to their betrayal of their G-d at the foot of His holy mountain.

It was the same hubris involved in the battle in the desert as was involved in the construction of the most egregious idol: the hubris that the work of man's hands in and of itself deserves praise. It would take forty years for the Israelites to realize that their salvation was to come from G-d alone.

The last sentence of the Song of Sea, which Israel sang in joy after being rescued from the Egyptian horde, is "and G-d *will* be king forever and ever." Rabbi Yossi the Galilean wrote, "Had Israel said 'G-d *is* king forever and ever,' no foreign nation would ever have ruled them." Because the Israelites failed to acknowledge G-d's immediate presence in reality, but only ascribed His reign to some future era, perhaps Messianic, we continue to suffer at the hands of foreign nations.

There were once two cities, one above ground and the other below. Every week, the city above would set aside a portion of their food, which at the week's end they would lower down a hole leading to the city below. The latter city, which was unable to produce its own food, relied on the generosity of the former in order to survive, though there was rarely any communication between the two. Many generations passed, and the two cities had not spoken to each other for centuries. A child from the city below asked his father, "Who sends the weekly portion of food down to us?" The father responded, "No one. That's just the way it is." Let us not commit the father's, and the Israelites', mistake. Such mistakes may allow us to defeat Amalek, but they will not lead us to the Promised Land.

Having a Positive Outlook
By Mindy Chapman

In this weeks Parsha, Beshalach, Hashem took Israel out of Egypt with a mighty hand and an outstretched arm. He split the sea so that Israel could pass through on dry land, and then drowned their oppressors in it. He preformed miracle after miracle and fulfilled all the promises He made. After going through the Sea of Reeds safely, Bnei Yisrael sang a song praising Hashem, and, afterwards, all of the women, with their tambourines, began to sing and dance praises to Hashem.

The Israelite women in this week's parsha teach us a valuable lesson about having an optimistic outlook on life. Why just the women, when all of the Israelites sang the song of the sea? Because, even during the hardest time in their 400 years of slavery to Egypt, when Pharaoh was making many unfair decrees to spite Moshe, the women did not lose their faith. Instead of dreading their current situation and the harsh treatment they were receiving, the Israelite women thought: "Let us prepare for when Hashem will save us and take us to the promised land."

How do we know this? Those tambourines the women suddenly had in the desert had to have come from somewhere, and, according to Rashi, they came from this "we must prepare for the miracles Hashem will bring us" insight that these righteous women had.

How, though, do we apply this to our lives? It is very difficult to keep up that kind of attitude and say "I'll get through all this work" when you're neck-deep in assignments, or to think "we can resolve this" when you are in the middle of a big fight with your best friend. When faced with a situation like that, remember the Israelite women who were given an opportunity to praise Hashem in a way nobody else was able to-- while having a fun time dancing and shaking tambourines-- because they had that positive outlook when they were feeling intense pain for all they had lost, such as their sons who were cast into the Nile, and pain from all the hardship they'd endured.

Maybe doing all that homework will help you get top honours in your grade, and maybe that friendship that seemed unsalvageable but was saved will lead to a future partnership between you two that can cure a disease! Learn from the women of Bnei Yisrael and remember all you can achieve with a positive outlook. Shabbat Shalom.

Divrei Torah on **Shemot**

En Route
By Zachary Zarnett-Klein

After the Israelites left Egypt, they were overwhelmed by the new work that had just begun. They had to transition to a new lifestyle of G-d being their master, and learning that He has their best interests at heart was a difficult thing for the Israelites to do as they journeyed to the Land of Israel.

Parashat Beshalach starts off by discussing the route which Bnei Yisrael took to reach the Promised Land. The Torah records their path as "the way of the Wilderness to the Sea of Reeds," because G-d was fearful that if the Israelites were confronted by war from the Philistines, they would immediately want to return to the land of Egypt.

This is very odd. The Torah tells us that the Israelites left Egypt armed, and if G-d wanted to get the Israelites into the Land of Israel as soon as possible, He could have easily done that. However, G-d's true intent was to make sure that the Israelites were totally committed to Him and would not want to return to Egypt, no matter what hardship they were faced with, and He therefore wanted to take a longer route, to test this. Another opinion says that G-d wanted to get the Israelites as far away from Egypt as possible, so it would harder for them to decide that they wanted to return, and therefore He chose to bring them into Israel through the eastern border as opposed to the western border.

The first place that the Israelites encamp at in this week's Parashah is Etam. This is a very important place, because it is here that the pillar of cloud and the pillar of fire that accompanied the Israelites on their sojourns are first mentioned.

The Parashah then shifts to Pharaoh and his army chasing Israel, followed by the splitting of the Red Sea and the Song of the Sea. The Israelites were very afraid when they saw the Egyptians chasing them; however, G-d calmed their fears by having Moshe assure the Israelites that not only would G-d protect them, but He would also permanently eliminate Egypt as a threat for them. G-d instructed Moshe to tell the Israelites that the time for fear was over, and that they must prove their faith and dedication by plunging into the sea.

An interesting point in this ordeal is that the Torah recounts that the Israelites saw the Egyptians dead on the seashore, and not one of them survived. Why was this so important for the Torah to note? G-d wanted to prove to the Israelites that this time, He had rid them of the Egyptians forever, and they would not have to worry about any future confrontation. From this act, the Israelites could see that G-d was truly fighting for them.

After the great allegiance to G-d that Israel proved by singing the Song of the Sea, they reached a low when they complained about the bitter water they were faced with when they arrived at Marah. G-d told Moshe to throw a tree into the water, and the water became drinkable.

What was the purpose of G-d putting the Israelites through this hardship, especially right after He had split the sea for them? G-d wanted to show Israel that, while the suffering He brought upon Egypt was to destroy them, this was not His intention for Israel. When G-d brings suffering upon Israel, His intention is never to destroy them, but rather to purge them of sin and influence them to repent.

"There were twelve springs of water and seventy date-palms; they encamped there by the water." When the Israelites journeyed to Elim after Marah, the Torah notes that they were provided with all that they needed, and that they had more than enough water.

The giving of the manna is also a huge part of this week's Parashah. When the Israelites reach the Wilderness of Sin, they once again complain to G-d, this time for the lack of food. They even go so far as to say that they were better off in Egypt. Therefore, G-d decided to feed them with the holy manna, to prove that there was no boundary to G-d's might, that not even a desert could cause G-d to be unable to provide the necessities for the Israelites.

The Israelites' final destination in this Parashah is Rephidim, where two very notable events occur. "Why have you taken us out of Egypt to kill myself, my sons, and my cattle in a drought?" was the famous complaint at Masah U'Merivah. For a second time, Israel challenges G-d's ability to provide them with water, even after G-d has established that He is their ultimate provider. G-d commanded Moshe to strike a rock before all the Israelites, and water flowed out for them to drink. Here, G-d taught the Israelites that, when faced with deprivation, they were to turn to Him, and not to Moshe.

Finally, when Amalek came to battle with the Israelites, G-d, strangely, commands Moshe to keep his hands raised the entire time, so that the Israelites would win. Why was such an odd action necessary, and what could this possibly teach the Israelites?

Moses hands' pointing upward was meant as a symbol for the Israelites: that, as long as they look heavenward and fully devote themselves to G-d, they would succeed; however, if they swayed, started complaining and losing faith, they would fall.

We can look at the entire experience of the Israelites in the desert as one which is primarily rooted in the notion of continued learning, growing, and using one's mistakes to become a stronger person. In this case, the "person" is the Israelites, growing up from leaving Egypt and hardly knowing G-d at all to becoming increasingly loyal to G-d and reaching an auspicious level of holiness by the time they defeat Amalek, almost ready to receive the Torah.

May we all be blessed with the opportunity and ability to evolve and develop into better Jews and better people, both for our sake and for the sake of the entire Jewish people. Shabbat Shalom!

Yitro • יתרו

This Parsha has been generously sponsored by the Friedman family, in honour of Becky Friedman, the Zeligson family, in honour of Taya and Eden, & the Ross family, in honour of Natan Ross

Catch Me When I Fall
By Becky Friedman

"You will surely fall, you and this people with you; it is too heavy for you, this burden, and you cannot bear it alone" (Shmot, 18:18).

Moses' father-in-law Yitro is a leader among his own people, a priest of Midian. Therefore, when he gives advice to Moses, as one great leader to another, he is worth listening to, worth following.

When Yitro sees how the people come to Moses for judgement, from morning to evening, he sees, as someone more impartial, with less of a stake in the success of this young nation, that something is wrong.

Yitro teaches his former protegé an important lesson, one which every leader– indeed, not just leaders, but every one of us– must learn, sooner rather than later. No person is omnipotent, nor should he try to be; it is madness to try to bear the weight of an entire nation alone. The art of delegation is one of the keys to success.

Yitro's advice makes sense: find good men who fear G-d and hate bribes, and set them up as delegates, representatives of yourself. Teach them how to make wise decisions, and let them judge the people in the minor matters. Set up a hierarchy, with men overseeing on the levels of ten people, fifty, one hundred, and one thousand. They need only come to you for the greatest of problems, the ones that they cannot solve themselves.

Unlike other instances of potentially unwanted suggestions, G-d notably does not step in to guide Moshe and tell him whether or not the advice is worth following. Moshe takes the advice on his own, setting up judges-- but it is evident that G-d approves.

Yitro is one of the very few people who has a parsha named after him, and a non-Jew at that. Not just any parsha, either-- the parsha named after Yitro is the one that includes the much-lauded Ten Commandments. His advice must have been good, to have so prestigious a parsha named for him.

And indeed it is good. G-d does not make direct mention of Yitro's advice-- but it is only after Moshe listens to it, and sets up men to act as extensions of himself, that G-d gives the Commandments.

Before Ma'amad Har Sinai, G-d instructs Moshe to tell the people to get ready for the event-- but He does not tell Moshe the same thing. Why not? Because He doesn't need to-- Moshe's preparation already happened, by way of setting up the judges in accordance with Yitro's suggestion. Having accepted that he cannot bear the burden of the people alone, and taken the precautions necessary to avoid the people's downfall, Moshe is ready to receive the commandments that these men will help him to enforce.

Similarly, the next parsha up is Mishpatim, the start of a series of parshiot which are comprised almost entirely of laws. It is Yitro's advice that makes this possible; the laws cannot be given until there is a structure in place to deal with the laws. Without a firm foundation, the laws would crumble and fall, like a house of cards built on air.

Yitro teaches us a twofold lesson. Directly, he teaches us the importance of the art of delegation, without which Moshe and Bnei Yisrael would have surely fallen, without which we could never have received our beloved commandments.

Implicitly, we learn from the story of Yitro the more general merit of taking advice. Moshe is no longer an under-shepherd working for his father-in-law; he is now the leader of his own nation. But rather than leaving it for G-d to decide, Moshe swallows his pride and accepts the advice from the more experienced Yitro. He shows us that it's nothing to be ashamed of to rely on others, already taking the first step in following Yitro's advice.

We must learn to trust our friends and acquaintances, enough to make them "officers of thousands" or "officers of tens," and enough to know when it's best to take their advice. We must learn, like Moshe, to swallow our pride in order to make the right decisions for the greater good.

Unless you can trust those around to catch you, you will surely fall.

Kedusha 101

By Matthew Goodman

Nearly three months after the Jewish people left Egypt en masse in a miraculous Exodus, they arrived in the desert of Sinai and encamped opposite a mountain. There, the single greatest event in Jewish history took place. Amidst thunder and lightning, from the depths of a thick cloud upon the mountain, and accompanied by the blast of a shofar, Hashem spoke to three million Jews and gave them the Torah.

Three days before this marvelous occasion, "Moshe ascended to G-d, and Hashem called to him from the mountain, saying, 'So shall you say to the house of Yaakov and tell the sons of Israel... you shall be to Me a kingdom of ministers and a holy nation'" (Shemot 19:3,6).

Kedusha (holiness) is an awfully elusive concept. It may conjure up the image of an old, quiet, and gentle Rabbi, adorned with a grey beard and immersed in study. You may associate it with the Beit HaMikdash that once stood in Jerusalem and its inner most chamber, the Holy of Holies. Or you may even think of Shabbat, whose holiness is endowed by Hashem himself. Despite our ability to realize that something is holy, or at least call it so, do we really know what holiness means? Moreover, do we know how to achieve it?

It might be helpful to first understand what Kedusha is not. Rabbi Sholom Noach Berezovsky (1911-2000), the Slonimer Rebbe, in Netivot Shalom, points out that Kedusha is the opposite of Tuma (impurity). Tuma is a Halachic term that refers to a spiritual impurity that can be imparted on people, food, or objects. The highest degree of Tumah is called "Tumat Met," the impurity of a dead body, caused when a person dies and the soul leaves behind the physical being. The reason why Tumat Met is so virulent teaches us a great deal regarding the underlying meaning of true spiritual impurity.

The Torah tells us that "Hashem G-d formed man of the soil from the earth, and blew into his nostrils the soul of life; and man became a living soul" (Bereishit 2:7). The holy Zohar (3:123b) teaches that when Hashem breathed into the nostrils of man, He "breathed from within Himself" and imparted within us a soul that is a "chelek Eloka mima'al," a piece of Hashem. So long as our neshama (soul) is safeguarded in our body, there is a powerful connection between our "chelek Eloka" and our physical being that allows us to elevate life here on Earth. These are lofty concepts, but the fundamental essence of the matter is that the living human embodies connection between the material and spiritual. When the neshama leaves the body and the connection breaks, the disconnection is called Tuma. Deriving from the same root as "Atimut," blockage, Tuma is when the physical disconnects from the spiritual.

Kedusha is the opposite of Tuma. Kedusha is the opposite of disconnection. Rabbi Lawrence Kelemen points out a Rashi on the first verse in the book of Vayikra. Rashi reveals that Hashem spoke to non-Jewish prophets such as Balaam in "Lashon tuma," impure language, but He spoke to Moshe using "Lashon chiba," affectionate language. Since Rashi here utilizes affection as the opposite of Tuma and Kedusha is also the opposite of Tuma, it is only sensible to infer that real holiness is affection, closeness, intimacy, and connection. Rabbi Kelemen also quotes the Ramchal, Rabbi Moshe Chaim Luzzato, who, in his work "Mesilat Yesharim," Path of the Upright, wrote that Kedusha is a state in which two things become completely and utterly united to a point that all else is irrelevant. As King David wrote in Psalms, "My soul clings to You" (Tehilim 63:9).

The Pshat (simple understanding), however, seems to indicate something a little different. Kedusha in the Torah consistently refers to separation. When Hashem tells the Jewish people that they should be "a holy nation," he couples it with the statement, "you shall be to Me a treasure out of all peoples" (Shemot 19:5), distinguishing Jews from the other nations. When Hashem tells us, "You shall be holy for I, Hashem your G-d, am holy," Rashi points us that holiness really means distancing oneself from sexual immorality. Furthermore, when we make Kiddush and Havdalah on Shabbat, we separate the holy day of Shabbat from the rest of the week. What's going on here? Where's the connection?

Indeed, Kedusha really is a form of separation. And it is also a form of immense connection. How is this so? The Ramchal, at the beginning of his chapter on Kedusha, poetically introduces the topic as follows: "Holiness is twofold. Its beginning is labour and its end reward; its beginning, exertion, and its end, a gift. It begins with one's sanctifying himself and ends with his being sanctified." The Ramchal beautifully explains here that one needs to work hard to achieve Kedusha. He needs to put in effort and strive to reach its lofty heights. When he reaches the summit, he can properly bask in all the magnificence that is Kedusha. That process is done in two parts, and we have already discerned both of them. First one must separate himself from the Tuma-- everything that embodies blockage and disconnection. That is labour; as the Ramchal says, "exertion in this respect consists of one's separation and removal from corporeality." The second part is the reward and gift of achieving immense connection to the point that one is "clinging always, at all periods and times, to his G-d."

Think about the last time that you had a deep and meaningful conversation with another person. In what type of environment did it take place? Was there a lot of noise? Were there a lot of other people talking about different things? Were you in a rush to get somewhere? Many of these distractions make it exceptionally difficult to maintain a closeness with another being simply because they are inherently distractions. Think about the last time that you prayed with sincerity and wholeheartedness. Were you thinking about other things? Were you worried that someone was trying to reach your phone and you couldn't pick up? Consider what you were focused on and what environment, mentally and physically, you created for yourself. What allows you to achieve Kedusha?

I think the truth of the matter is that our most profoundly intimate moments with humans and Hashem lack distractions. We remove everything around us that blocks the connection between the two entities. That does not mean in any way that we remove ourselves completely from the world. It certainly does not mean that we should deny ourselves the pleasures of a physical existence. What it does mean is that when the physical world acts as a distraction and blockage from achieving connection, we have to separate ourselves from it. Truthfully, we should have no greater desire in our lives than to do just that and achieve Kedusha. Chazal tells us (Brachot 17a) that the world to come has no eating or drinking. Tzaddikim (righteous people) sit and take pleasure in the Divine Presence. There can be no greater joy than reaching that level of closeness! In all honesty, what would you rather have in life? Meaningful and deep relationships with people and Hashem, or the fleeting pleasure of eating a slice of chocolate cake?

There are many ways that we can practically achieve this in our lives. We can, for one, choose to spend less time watching television and more time talking with our friends. We can put down our work and halt our busy schedules to make time for others, especially family, perhaps even having a set time to sit down together and enjoy a meal. We can turn our cellphones off while praying, ensuring that we have proper alone time with Hashem. And we can even close everything off and spend some much-needed alone time with ourselves, connecting not just with Hashem and not just with other souls, but our own soul as well. Kedusha also requires a commitment to and understanding of one's priorities. What, indeed, is more important?

Sending a text message in the middle of a proper conversation with someone else, or fully enjoying that other person's presence, and waiting to answer the text later?

Holiness is a fundamental aspect of Judaism. Asks the Slonimer Rebbe, why is it not counted as one of the 613 Mitzvot? He answers that holiness is not just a commandment. It is the essence of everything we do in Judaism. Being holy is synonymous with being Jewish. Being connected and close to everything around us is synonymous with being Jewish. Clinging to Hashem and having a deep and powerful relationship with Him is being Jewish. There is nothing more special in the world than creating closeness and connection, filling our lives with the blessings of Kedusha.

(Please note: many of the ideas in this Dvar Torah come from a shiur by Rabbi Lawrence Kelemen, a Rav at Neve Yerushalayim and popular lecturer, which can be found on aishaudio.com or alternatively in an abridged article called "Elusive Holiness" on aish.com)

The Missing Piece
By Zachary Zarnett-Klein

This week's Parshah is Parshat Yitro, and the Haftarah comes from the Book of Isaiah. What could possibly connect the two? The time periods are totally different, the people, the plot-- what are their messages? How do they complement one another?

In this week's Parshah, we read about the righteous Jethro, Moshe's father-in-law who supposedly converted to Judaism, and the famous advice he gave Moshe: to appoint judges to assist him in his job. The second part of our Parshah is mostly the Ten Commandments, some of the most widely recognized commandments given to the Jewish people.

When we observe the Haftarah, it leaves us wondering what is the correlation between the two. The Haftarah is also divided into two parts. The first is G-d's revelation to Isaiah, and the second is the war fought by Judah against Israel and Aram.

The number two appears many times in the Parshah and Haftarah. There are two sons of Moshe in the Parshah. Similarly, in the Haftarah, Isaiah witnesses angels "with two [wings] to cover their faces, with two their legs, and with two to fly." If one were to be asked to list what items in the Tanakh are mentioned in relation to the number two, the list would likely be relatively short. However, if one were to list all of the items which are mentioned in relation to the number three, the list would be much longer. *[While there are technically more instances of the number two, the number three generally holds more significance and therefore springs quicker to mind.--Ed.]* So why do neither of these examples contain the 'magic' three? Three is strength. Three is bravery. Three is triumph. And in these instances, these three qualities are not apparent.

When Moshe's sons are listed at the beginning of the Parshah, there is a very important son missing. In Isaiah's vision, G-d is apparent and the angels are in sight, but a crucial element is still missing, without which the prophecy cannot be fulfilled. This missing element is Bnei Yisrael! Parshat Yitro was named after this great man because he took attention off himself and Moshe's family, who had been living with him in Midyan while Moshe was in Egypt, and instead insisted that Moshe focus on the people of Israel, and appoint for them judges who could assist them should any difficulties arise. This advice was surely helpful and beneficial to the people throughout their experience in the desert.

Isaiah sees G-d and sees the angels, but still he feels a sense of doom because Bnei Yisrael have not been mentioned. Although this prophecy discusses destruction and terror, he is assured that this destruction is temporary, "like an elm and oak which, when shedding their leaves, still have vitality in them." Isaiah is assured that the people will still maintain a unique sense of holiness and sanctity despite the terrible oppression which is foretold-- "so will the holy seed be the vitality of the land." Bnei Yisrael will maintain their connection to the Land of Israel, and will never be completely uprooted.

The main lesson of this week's Parshah and Haftarah is that G-d and Israel share an eternal bond, that will continue to strengthen us despite the immense challenges presented to Bnei Yisrael in each generation; as it is written, "For greatness in dominion and boundless peace on the throne of David and on his kingdom, to establish it and sustain it through justice and righteousness, from now to eternity; the zealousness of G-d, Master of Legions will accomplish this!"

Divrei Torah on **Shemot**

Honouring Your Parents
By Elianne Neuman

The Ten Commandments were inscribed on two tablets. The mitzvot on the first tablet, the first five commandments, all relate to our relationship with G-d. The mitzvot on the second tablet, the last five commandments, all relate to our relationships with other people.

Why then, does the mitzvah of honouring our parents appear on the first table? Shouldn't it appear on the second tablet, since honouring one's parents is a mitzvah that involves one's relationships with other people?

There are numerous answers to this question; however, I am only going to highlight a couple that struck me as intriguing.

1. Kiddushin 30b-31a states that there are three partners in the creation of a child: G-d, the mother, and the father. By honouring our parents, we are also in a sense, are honouring the third partner in our creation: G-d. Therefore, the mitzvah of honouring one's parents is written on the first tablet, because by honouring our parents, we are also improving our relationship with G-d.

2. By rejecting parental authority, it is a sign that one rejects authority in general-- meaning that one also rejects the authority of G-d. By accepting the authority of his parents, a person shows G-d that he is also capable of accepting Hashem's authority, and therefore, this mitzvah improves his relationship with G-d.

3. For a child, it much easier to grasp the concept of honouring his parents. His parents give him food, shelter, clothing, opportunities, love and caring. But children can't see G-d, nor are they able to grasp the concept of understanding the hand of G-d in everyday life. Honouring parents is a tool to help children understand the importance of honouring something that isn't before their eyes— G-d. Therefore, this mitzvah is written in the first set of commandments because it ultimately helps us build a relationship with G-d.

It is sometimes hard to honour one's parents, just like it is hard to honour G-d, because He isn't someone or something that we can see.

But relationships are something that require practise, and something that we must build overtime. Just as it isn't easy to respect our parents, building a meaningful relationship with G-d is also difficult. But we know that it can be achieved.

By instructing us to honour our parents, the Torah is also reminding us to strengthen our relationships with others: our siblings, our friends, our teachers, and, ultimately, G-d. Doing so will never be simple, but the precious bonds that we make with those around us will last forever.

Mishpatim • משפטים

Sensitivity Training
By Matthew Goodman

The Torah revels in sensitivity. It requires us to show compassion to all living things, including the weak and the downtrodden, and to have sympathy for those who are less fortunate. It expects us to be hospitable to strangers and the poor and to show kindness to all. The Torah can really create a highly sensitive, caring individual-- what we would call a "mentch." A mentch, however, does not act kindly because the Torah simply tells us that we have to be kind. He understands the deeper truths of the Torah's requirements. He understands how to *be* kind, and not just act it. Such training can be found in this week's Parsha. Mishpatim is one of the longest Parshiot in the entire Torah, and details more than 50 different Mitzvot. Among them are numerous injunctions against oppressing those in particularly pressing situations, such as widows, orphans, and slaves. All of these laws are intended to make us deeply considerate of other people. None of them, however, explicitly say why we should not oppress them. It could be that the reason is obvious; basic Torah values dictate that oppression is simply wrong. One specific law, however, does give a reason, and with it, teaches us a tremendous lesson.

The Torah tells us, "Do not oppress a stranger (Ger); you know the feelings of a stranger, for you were strangers in the land of Egypt" (Shemot 23:9). Rashi explains that the Jewish people know how hard it is for strangers when they are oppressed. We were also strangers, and we suffered immense persecution in Egyptian bondage. Since we know what it feels like, we should not oppress the stranger.

This pasuk is very odd and requires some explanation. Previously, the Torah prohibited similar displays of oppression of other people without giving a reason. Suddenly, in regard to strangers, it does. Furthermore, the reason it gives is not that oppressing the stranger is wrong, but that we know how it feels so we should not do it to others!

A slight change to our understanding of the pasuk reveals a lesson in sensitivity. The Torah does not give a reason why we should not oppress people. Indeed, that is an evident Jewish value that is expressed through other means. For instance, the Torah tells us, "Love your neighbour as yourself" (Vayikra 19:18). Rather, here we learn one of the practical ways to love one's neighbour as oneself. The Torah instructs us to be aware of how other people feel in order to not mistakenly hurt them. Don't oppress the stranger! Be aware of how he feels! You know what it's like to suffer as one, for you were strangers in the land of Egypt. If you want to show sensitivity and love to another person, put yourself in his shoes and consider how you would feel in a similar situation.

The Torah is setting out a two-step process to achieving sensitivity. The first step is to notice others and their feelings. Chazal tells us that the real Egyptian bondage began when Yaakov Avinu died and "the eyes and hearts of Yisrael were plugged up" (Rashi on Bereishit 47:28). They could neither see nor feel for other people, for they were too enclosed in themselves. Conversely, the redemption of the Jewish people began when "Moshe grew up and saw their suffering" (Shemot 2:11) and became aware of other people, and noticed their feelings. The second step is to act accordingly. Hillel teaches that the entire Torah can be summed up in the words: Do not do unto others what is hateful to yourself. If you do not like the feeling of an oppressed stranger, do not make someone else feel like an oppressed stranger!

The following story from Rabbi Naftali Reich (of Ohr Somayach) explains this idea beautifully:

A wise old Rabbi was trudging through the snow-filled streets of a little village. He came to the house of a very rich man, knocked on the door, and waited patiently. A servant opened the door, and, seeing the old Rabbi, immediately invited him in. The Rabbi, however, shook his head. He refused to enter the home, and asked to see the rich man.

A moment later, the rich man came hurrying to the door. "Rabbi! Why are you standing outside?" he asked. "It's so cold out there! Please, please come in where it is warmer." "Thank you so much," said the Rabbi, "but I much prefer to stay out here. Can we talk?" "Why certainly," said the rich man. He shivered and pulled his jacket closer around him.

"Well, you see," said the Rabbi, "It's like this. There are a number of poor families in this village who don't have any money—" "I'm sorry for interrupting, Rabbi," interjected the rich man, "You know that I always contribute to the poor and hungry, but why can't we talk about this inside? Why do we have to stand out here in the cold?" "Because these people need firewood," the Rabbi explained, "and I'm collecting firewood for poor families." "So why can't we talk inside?" implored the rich man. "Because," began the Rabbi, "I want you to feel what they are feeling. Even if only for a few minutes. Imagine how they must be shivering in their drafty homes, without the heat of a

furnace to warm them! The more you give me, the more families will be spared this dreadful cold."

Our daily interactions with other people require a great deal of sensitivity. In order to deal with people in a kind, compassionate, and loving manner, it is absolutely imperative to understand how they feel. We need to carefully consider all of our words and actions and their ramifications. Will doing this hurt Reuven? Will saying this to Shimon make him embarrassed? One of the best ways to measure the effects of actions is to simply consider: how would I feel if the same thing was said or done to me? How did I feel the last time something similar was said or done to me? With this level of sensitivity, we can help build a world filled with the blessing of Shalom and Ahavat-Chesed (lovingkindness).

Broken Record
By Becky Friedman

Parshat Mishpatim is composed almost entirely of laws, one after the other, with no apparent rhyme or reason to their order. That said, some special consideration might be accorded to the first, coming, as it does, before all others.

The first law, then: the first law of Parshat Mishpatim is that a Jewish slave (eved ivri) must go free after seven years of service. We don't have the concept of eved ivri in today's society, but back when it existed, this must have been a pretty important rule. After all, it came first in the parsha.

Which is why it's with some surprise that we learn at the beginning of the Haftara-- which takes place in the time of Yirmiyahu, shortly before the huge Babylonian exile-- that this law hadn't been followed in a very long time; significantly longer than seven years.

In the prakim leading up to this story, G-d's been giving Yirmiyahu prophecies of a reprieve, of good things coming, and it's soon easy enough to see why. This important law, long abandoned, has just seen an increase of attention from King Tzidkia. Tzidkia insists that everyone go back to this law, releasing all their slaves.

Well, great! Things are looking up! The Jews are going back to their Halachic roots, the slaves finally get to be free, and G-d's had Yirmiyahu prophesying all sorts of good things.

. . . And then Tzidkia and his bright pals turn right around and recapture all their freed slaves.

At this point, I'm thinking, does this sound familiar? *How stupid can they be*? A couple Parshas ago, after the huge Exodus from Egypt, Pharaoh and his pals turned back around and tried to recapture all the Jews, regretting their release of their slaves. Didn't go too well for them, did it? So the only thing I can wonder about Tzidkia at this juncture is, *what was he thinking*?

G-d's apparently on the same page. Yirmiyahu announces pointedly that G-d commanded Bnei Yisrael, *right after they left slavery in Egypt*, to release their slaves after seven years. Now, Yirmiyahu's cutting them some slack here by not insulting their intelligence to the point of spelling it all out, but there are a few obvious conclusions from what he's saying. Number one, the Exodus from Egypt is the classic 'remember G-d' line; this should remind them that they *really* want to listen to this 'G-d' fellow. Number two, *your ancestors were slaves in Egypt.* You know what it's like! How on earth could you subject that to someone else, after all *your ancestors* had been through? And Number three: you know what *else* happened right after your ancestors left Egypt? The Egyptians tried to get them back! It didn't go too well for the Egyptians then, either.

So it looks like Tzidkia hasn't got an original thought in his head. He's just mimicking that bad old Pharaoh, like a broken record playing out the same scratchy tune over and over again. Great job ruining the salvation, Tzidkia! Because of his brilliant move, G-d rescinds the promises of comfort and good things. Because he went *back* on his release of the slaves, things are just about to get a whole lot worse. Well, we all knew that history repeats itself.

None of us, I hope, is as horrendously blind to history as Tzidkia was. Still, it's easy to second-guess ourselves, to undo a good decision at the last minute, to forget that things have already played out this way, and badly, before.

May we all learn from his example; may we learn to trust our good instincts, rather than putting the broken record or the scratched CD back in the machine for another cycle.

Divrei Torah on **Shemot**

The Bigger Picture
By Zachary Zarnett-Klein

The Haftarah for Parashat Mishpatim comes from the book of Yirmeyahu. As we know, the Parashah deals with many laws and ordinances which Bnei Yisrael must now keep, having accepted the Torah upon themselves. Among these new rules is the rule of being kind to one's slaves, and allowing them to have the chance to leave their work and become free every seven years.

Similarly, the Haftarah deals with King Zedekiah commanding Bnei Yisrael to keep this law so that G-d may be appeased. By this time, Nevuchadnezzar was surrounding Jerusalem, and in a last-ditch effort to save his kingdom and the Jewish nation, King Zedekiah decides that they must start keeping the laws of Hashem. King Zedekiah reminds the Jews that G-d has commanded them to let their slaves free during the seventh year. Initially, the Jews are gung-ho about this idea, and willingly let their slaves go free.

Interestingly enough, the traditional way for sealing a covenant is used in this instance when King Zedekiah makes a covenant with the Jews. In Breishit, chapter 15, G-d makes a covenant with Avraham, then Avram, called "Brit Bein HaBtarim." *Btarim* literally means "parts." King Zedekiah cuts a calf in half and makes the Jews walk between the halves in order to accept upon themselves this covenant.

In the Parashah, Moshe makes a covenant with Bnei Yisrael in which he divides the blood of the offering into two parts. The first part he throws on the altar and the second part is called "the blood of the covenant," which he throws on Bnei Yisrael. It is here that they say the famous words, "Naaseh VNishmah," "We will do and we will hearken."

Unfortunately, it is this same haste that gets the Israelites into trouble in the Haftarah. They are so quick to think of the benefits and rewards they will receive if they follow G-d's commandments that they lose focus of the true purpose of the Mishpatim-- the service of G-d for its own sake.

The Jews immediately let their slaves go free after King Zedekiah advises them to; however, when the going gets tough and the Jews realize that their slaves are gone, they quickly regret their decision and take their slaves back.

In doing this, they effectively forget their saying that they "will hearken," not keeping up their commitment to the commandments. One may, therefore, look at these two words and say that "Naaseh" means that one will take it upon himself and "Nishma" represents ongoing commitment and follow-through, no matter what challenges are faced and despite any temptations that may come up.

The Jews in the Haftarah lose sight of the bigger picture of service of G-d for its own sake, and are agitated when the threat of conquer by the Babylonians is not instantaneously removed. Luckily, G-d is merciful, saying at the end of the Haftarah, "If my covenant with the night and with the day would not be; had I not set up the laws of heaven and earth, so, too, would I reject the seed of Yaakov... for I will return their captivity, and I will show them mercy."

May we never lose sight of what is truly important in life, and may we never forget that the little things are truly what count in G-d's eyes and in the grander scheme of things. If we desire, we have the power to improve ourselves and to help others return from their captivity, and as long as we keep trying to become better Jews and people in general, G-d will continue supporting us and mercifully accept us back, never forgetting us.

It's In Your Best Interest
By Mindy Chapman

This week's parsha, Mishpatim, starts off by listing the many rules that Bnei Yisrael are required to follow. Some of these laws are straightforward, such as "You shall not wrong a stranger or oppress him, for you were strangers in the land of Egypt." Other laws are very strict and have severe punishments, for example: "He who insults his father or mother shall be put to death." Some of these laws are also very confusing if thought about superficially, and Bnei Yisrael surely had difficulty understanding all of them. Even so, as soon as Moshe finished relaying all of the commandments to them, Bnei Yisrael said, in unison, "All the things that the Lord has commanded we will do!"

The fact that the Israelites responded without hesitation and with such enthusiasm astounds me. Today it is difficult enough to follow the most straightforward rules that parents set for their children, from "Eat your vegetables" to "Lights out at 9:30," yet here, Bnei Yisrael are accepting all of these brand new laws, vowing to carry them out with vigour, when just a few parshiot ago they complained about every bump in the road! We can learn a lot from the fantastic attitude our ancestors had about following the laws made for them by Hashem, whom they trusted wholeheartedly to have their best interests at mind. Bnei Yisrael, at this time, are learning how to be a free nation, with the guidance of Hashem's laws.

Similarly, as High School students, we are exploring our freedom, which is limited by the carefully placed rules of our parents. We know that our parents are trying to protect us when they tell us we can go out with our friends, but to be back by 9:30. Instead of complaining about your early curfew, when you know your parents are just in implementing it, say, "Of course," and be home at the set time.

On a more difficult level, if there is a rule that is less obviously for your own good, such as, "No TV or computer until after dinner- even if all your homework is finished," you should consent to follow the rule with the same level of enthusiasm as before, because, as long as there is no way you can be hurt by it, there is likely a very good reason for its enforcement. By modeling yourselves after the Israelites in regards to following rules in your life, you are opening up a world with less arguments with your parents as well as a world of enjoying the newfound freedom and privileges that you have gained over time. You are also gaining a solid understanding of the boundaries that there are in life, so when it's your turn to set those "in your best interest" rules for yourself and your family, you will have a very good idea of what rules you should be making.

Terumah • תרומה

This Parsha has been generously sponsored by the Grammer family in honour of their children, Jonathan, Jake, and Simon

Valuing All Aspects of Your Life
By Teddy Kravetsky

This week's parsha is parshat Terumah, which deals with the many aspects of the Mishkan (tabernacle) and how to build each component. Each piece of the Mishkan is carefully and flawlessly made according to the specifications laid out by the Torah. But why are there so many specific little details? After all, it's only a temporary temple until Bnei Yisroel reach Israel.

Well, to answer this, let's first look at one component of the Mishkan, the two angels that were put on top of the Ark. What do the angels represent, and why are they there? The angels are there to represent how Bnei Yiroel were behaving. If they were facing each other, then the Jews were behaving properly, and if they were facing away from each other, the nation was having problems.

But the angels' detail represents much more than this. Sforno gives us insight into what it all means. He explains that the wings of the angels were pointed up to represent how we should try to strive forward to do G-d's will. As well, the heads of the angels were facing downward and toward each other to represent that the Torah is the only true source of wisdom and that man must use this wisdom to interact properly with other people.

As we see here, each detail on the angels represents another lesson that can be learned. However, how does this help to answer the original question-- why put so much detail into something temporary? Well, the answer is that it teaches us that we must put a lot of effort into all aspects of our daily lives, and that by ignoring any part of our lives, we are ignoring part of who we are, letting perfectly good talent go to waste. That's why so much effort was put into each part of the Mishkan, to teach us that we must put effort into everything we do, no matter how stupid or pointless we may think it is.

Life isn't about waiting for the storm to pass by; it's learning to dance in the rain. So whenever you're given the opportunity to do something out of the ordinary or to improve on part of your life that you've been putting off, jump on it, and don't let the moment to take action pass you by. Good Shabbos!

The Philosophy of Giving
By Matthew Goodman

Giving to someone else can easily be one of the most amazing experiences, and we all, for the most part, understand how extremely important it is to give to others. In fact, it is a fundamentally Jewish concept that we should give to those in need. For instance, the Torah exhorts us to give Ma'aser Ani, a tenth of our produce grown in the third and sixth years of the Shmita (seven-year Sabbatical cycle) designated for the poor, and a Ma'aser Rishon, a tenth of our produce grown each year designated for the Leviim, who were not given a share of land in Eretz Yisrael. Nowadays, there is an obligation called Ma'aser Kesafim, a requirement to give a tenth of one's income to charity, which was a custom initiated by the Avot (see Bereishit 14:20; Rashi on Bereishit 23:12; Bereishit 28:22). Similarly, we are expected to perform acts of Gemilut Chasadim, which, as opposed to just giving monetarily, involves giving through physical work and actions of kindness to others.

What happens, however, when giving is not so easy? Sure, it is wonderful to give charity when you are wealthy, but what if you are desperately pressed for money? What if something you are expected to give is exceptionally valuable or dear to you? Or what if it is just hard for you to give in general?

In this week's Parsha, Hashem commands Klal Yisrael to build a Mishkan (Tabernacle) so that Hashem may "dwell in their midst" (Shemot 25:8). In order to go through with the construction of this enormous project, Klal Yisrael are expected to give contributions of different precious resources, such as gold, silver, copper, wools, skins, wood, oils, and spices, among other things. When Hashem commands the people to give these Terumot (offerings), the language He uses is peculiar. He does not actually ask them to give.

The Torah tells us: "Hashem spoke to Moshe saying: 'Speak to the children of Yisrael, and have them take for Me an offering (v'yikchu li teruma); from every person whose heart inspires him to generosity, you shall take My offering'" (25:2). Many commentators are puzzled by the language, as the pasuk should read "Viyitnu Li Terumah" -- give for Me an offering. Why are we commanded to "take" Terumah as opposed to "give" Terumah?

Rav Moshe Feinstein Z"tl, the great leader of Torah Jewry in the 20th century, explains that the Torah is teaching us a fundamental lesson regarding charity. Many times, when we are required to give Tzedakah, our Yetzer HaRa, evil inclination, naturally makes us wish that we did not have to give. Hashem wanted to teach Klal Yisrael that their desire to give should be similar to their desire to take. Our desire to give to someone should be as strong as our desire to receive.

The Kli Yakar, Rabbi Shlomo Ephraim ben Aaron Luntschitz (1550-1619), quoted by HaRav Mayer Twersky, takes this idea one step further with a beautiful explanation of the pasuk. In the realm of Torah and Mitzvot, one who gives actually receives far more in return. For instance, a teacher of Torah gives his time, wisdom, and knowledge to his students, and, in turn, receives a great deal from them. Rebi Yehudah HaNasi (Makkot 10a) states: "I have learned much from my Rebbeim and even more from my colleagues, but I learned the most from my students." Similarly, the Vilna Gaon comments that the word for "they shall give," venatnu, is a palindrome in Hebrew. When spelled backwards, the word reads the same thing. Thus giving ultimately reverses itself, and the one who gives receives as well.

In our Parsha, the Torah illustrates this teaching by stating that Klal Yisrael should "take" Terumah. While at face value they are simply giving contributions to the Mishkan, in reality, they are taking, as well. Anyone who has ever given something can appreciate this point. What we receive through our actions amounts to something far greater than what we have given away. For one, there is the tremendous feeling of satisfaction and warmth that we get when we help someone else or do a Mitzvah. Furthermore, when giving to an individual, there is the Hakarat HaTov (gratitude) that we receive from that person. That could amount to anything from a touching display of appreciation, to having that very person help you when the tables turn and you yourself need help. Finally, there is always the Divine reward for the performance of Mitzvot in Olam HaBa (the World to Come). Like the Midrash (Midrash Rabba Vayikra 34) states, "More than the benefactor benefits the pauper, the pauper benefits the benefactor."

If we can properly and sincerely internalize this critical lesson, we can drastically improve the nature of our giving. Many times we feel that it is difficult to give. Sometimes it is because we have little to give in the first place. Other times we are sensitive about giving up something precious or valuable. We have to understand that, in reality, we receive a tremendous amount in return. Klal Yisrael were commanded to donate some pretty precious and valuable objects straight from their own pockets. Hashem told them, "Do not think that you are giving me Terumah, for you are actually taking Terumah."

Rav Mordechai Kamenetzky tells the following story:

Max and Irving went fishing on an overcast afternoon. About two hours into their expedition, the clouds began to darken and a fierce storm developed. Their small rowboat tossed and tossed with the waves and finally flipped over into the lake. Max, a strong swimmer, called out to Irving in an attempt to save him, but it was to no avail. Irving did not respond to any plea, and unfortunately drowned. Max swam to shore to break the terrible news to Irving's wife.

"What happened?" she cried, "Tell me the whole story!" Max recounted the entire episode in detail. "But what did you do to try and save my Irving?" she asked. Max explained, "I kept screaming to your husband, 'Irving, give me your hand! Give me your hand!' But Irving just gave me a blank stare and drifted away."

"You fool!" shouted the wife. "You said the wrong thing! You should have said, 'Take my hand!' Irving never gave anything to anybody."

If we can realize that our giving is also taking, there is simply no reason to deny ourselves the fantastic pleasure of "taking Terumah."

Giving Your Best to G-d
By Teddy Kravetsky

This week's parsha talks about all the different components that the Mishkan will have. As we see from the commentaries, these components must meet specific expectations that G-d gave them. Why have such high expectations for something that is only temporary, and why have so much of it be made from gold, silver, and specific wood? To answer these questions, I had to think for quite some time, but I came up with this:

Although the Mishkan was temporary and only around for a short time, why should it be held back from perfection or made quickly and without care? Because the Mishkan was meant to be a holy place where the Jews went for many reasons, to neglect it would be like neglecting G-d. That would be a sin; therefore, much care was put into building it and keeping it.

How can we apply this to our daily lives? After all, aren't we supposed to be able to relate to everything put in the Tanach? Isn't it all supposed to be relevant to today? Well, one way this is relevant today is because we are taught that we should give our best to G-d and the building of the Mishkan was a way of symbolizing the Jews' love and care for G-d. If we are to be the best Jews we can, we must also give our best to G-d; whether buying teffilin or buying a lulav an etrog, we should take initiative and go the extra step to buy the more expensive one. This shows our love for G-d, as we have gone that extra step and shown that we care and believe in G-d just as much as the people who built the Mishkan did.

Another reason for the Mishkan to be built to such specific requirements is because it shows that no matter how short something is around, it has the same importance and significance as if it was built for a long time, as we have put just as much care into making it.

Good Shabbos, and remember: giving your best to G-d is a great way to show you care.

Divrei Torah on **Shemot**

Tetzaveh • תְּצַוֶּה

Paying Attention to Details
By Ben Welkovics

This week's parsha almost exclusively deals with the Kohen HaGadol. Each article of clothing that the Kohen HaGadol is required to wear is described in great detail, ranging from the material used to the exact dimensions. Furthermore, after we are informed about the minute details about the wardrobe, we are told how to inaugurate the Kohen HaGadol in a lengthy 46-pasuk chapter. Why do we make such a big deal of this? Perhaps the Torah needs a lesson in brevity?

Over the course of the past two weeks, we have all been glued to our television screens watching our Olympic heroes compete against athletes from all over the world. Their performances have been truly amazing, and have inspired many young and hopeful athletes all across the globe. However, what we don't see is the intense and often grueling preparation undertaken by these athletes. We don't see the long hours of practice and scrutiny behind perfecting the performance of each athlete. All we see is the finished product, and we are "wowed" by it.

In today's world, we are blessed with the most high-speed and up-to-date technology. We can send an email in a matter of milliseconds and can access the Internet from almost any hand-held device. Although this all seems wonderful-- and for the most part, it is-- society has developed an expectation of immediacy from the quick pace of everyday life. People seem to want immediate success, but often don't have the patience or attention to detail which is required. We all want to be good at things, and are often disappointed when we fall short. In fact, there are many times where we give up on ourselves without putting in the proper effort.

In this week's parsha, we are presented with a wake-up call. I believe that one of the reasons the Torah goes into immense detail describing the Kohen HaGadol is in order to show us the importance of minutiae. The Kohen HaGadol was a major representative and leader of the Jewish people in front of G-d, and he had to be dressed perfectly. In fact, not only was a perfect physical presentation essential, but the Kohen HaGadol also had to have the appropriate traits for the job, such as wisdom, humility, and kindness. He could easily be categorized as the "Olympian" of the Jewish people. Similar to the Olympians today, the Kohen HaGadol was as close to perfect as one could get.

Although most of us will not be competing in an Olympic game during the course of our lifetimes and will not have to put in the intense training required, we will all face challenges along life's journey. Success may not come as quickly as we would like, and we may feel like giving up. However, if there is anything that can be learned from this parsha, it is the importance of detail. Sometimes the difference between success and failure is one small and seemingly insignificant change to the way we act or present ourselves. It could be making a small alteration in the way we study, or it could be as simple as getting an extra hour of sleep in order to have enough energy and attention the next day. Whatever the case may be, it is important that we all pay attention to some of the minutiae in life, because that minutiae often has a major impact.

Fleeing from the Spotlight
By Matthew Goodman

Today's Hebrew date is the 7th of Adar, Moshe Rabbeinu's birthday and Yarzheit (see Megillah 13b). One would expect that the Parsha which falls near to this date would in some way reflect this occasion, perhaps praising Moshe Rabbeinu, or detailing an event that displays his greatness. However, at face value, it seems that none of this is done in this week's Parsha, Tetzaveh. In fact, Tetzaveh is the only Parsha (excluding those in the book of Bereishit) that completely leaves out Moshe's name. He is not mentioned even once.

Chazal explain that this omission was really at Moshe's own request. Next week's Parsha, Ki Tisa, tells of the Sin of the Golden Calf and Hashem's threat to destroy His nation. Moshe pleads with Hashem to spare and forgive Klal Yisrael and says, "And now, if You would but forgive their sin! But if not, erase me now from Your book that You have written" (Shemot 32:32). A curse made by a righteous person always comes true, and even though Klal Yisrael was indeed forgiven, Moshe was partially omitted from the book that Hashem wrote.

Rav Ovadia Yosef, the former Sephardi Chief Rabbi of Israel and one of the foremost Poskim living today, quoted by Rav Yissochar Frand, asks the obvious question. Of all Parshiot in the Torah, why did Moshe's curse affect Parshat Tetzaveh? He answers that it was actually Moshe's own choice. The statement, "Erase me from Your book (sifrecha)" can be divided to read, "Erase me from your sefer chaf" - 20th book, and Tetzaveh is the 20th parsha in the Torah. Simply explaining that it was Moshe's will, however, does not entirely answer our question. Why did Moshe choose this Parsha? What significance does it have?

Parshat Tetzaveh details Hashem's instructions for the seven-day initiation of Aharon and his four sons into the priesthood. Aharon was to serve as the Kohen Gadol, while his sons, and their descendants after them, were to serve as Kohanim. Chazal tell us that Moshe was actually meant to have been chosen as the Kohen Gadol in addition to his position of leader of Klal Yisrael. However, since Moshe originally refused to be sent to Egypt when Hashem spoke to him from the burning bush, the official position was stripped from him. The Midrash (Vayikra Rabba 11:6) tells us that Moshe ministered in the office of Kohen Gadol for the first seven days of the consecration of the Mishkan. On the eighth day, Hashem told him, "It belongs not to you but to your brother Aharon."

Rav Mordechai Kamenetzky explains that Moshe's request to be left out of this week's Parsha is a display of tremendous humility. Many people cannot resist to harp on the fact that "I got him that position," or "it was all because of me." Moshe could have likewise placed himself as the one who brought Aharon into the priesthood. Moshe could have said, "If it was not for me, Aharon would never be where he is today!" Instead, he remained silent. In a Parsha dedicated entirely to Moshe's efforts to direct and guide the process of establishing the priesthood, his name is completely left out. Moshe essentially stepped out of the spotlight and allowed it to shine brightly on his brother.

Rav Kamenetzky tells the following story that emphasizes this point:

Rav Yitzchak Blaser (1837-1907) was once seated at a gathering of the foremost Rabbinic sages of his generation in St. Petersburg. Among the great Rabbis present was the Beit HaLevi, Rav Yosef Dov HaLevi Soleveitchik of Brisk (1820-1892), a world-renown Talmudic genius. He posed a Talmudic question that his young son, Reb Chaim, had asked. A flurry of discussion ensued, and each Rabbi attempted to offer his own explanation. Soon, the room was filled with answers, questions, and rebuttals. During the entire conversation, Rav Blaser, who was known to be a tremendous Talmudic genius, sat silently. He offered no answer, no rebuttal, and no sign of approval or disapproval at his colleagues' answers. He did not say a word.

When Rav Soloveitchik offered his son's solution, Rav Blaser still sat quietly. It seemed that Rav Blaser did not comprehend the depth of the insightful discourse! Bewildered, Rav Soloveitchik began to doubt how truly remarkable Rav Blaser was. Was he truly the remarkable scholar everyone made him out to be?

Later that evening, Rav Soloveitchik was in the main Shul and found the book "Pri Yitzchak," the Talmudic insights authored by Rav Blaser himself. While leafing through the large volume, he discovered the afternoon's entire discourse in print. His son's question, the offered and refuted responses, and the conclusion were all part of an essay that Rav Blaser had published many years earlier. He knew exactly what was going on during the discourse. In fact, he knew all the potential arguments and the final answer.

"Now I realize," thought Rav Soloveitchik, "that Rav Blaser is as much as a genius in humility as he is in Talmudic law!"

If the great Rabbi had given his final answer during the discourse, he would have been highly praised! But if he had told them that he already dealt with the entire topic in his book, the conversation would have been dissolved and the Rabbis would have lost the heart to fight a battle that had already been won. In his tremendous humility, he refrained from speaking and fled from the potential honour that would have been bestowed upon him had the conference realized that he had single-handedly solved the entire Talmudic question. He did not want the credit for his already-formulated ideas to displace the credit due to the other Rabbis.

Rav Blaser did not want the spotlight on himself. Yet, his humility ultimately resulted in him being held in even higher esteem by Rav Soloveitchik. This is exactly what happened to Moshe Rabbeinu.

We read in Tehillim, "Moshe and Aharon were among His Kohanim" (99:6). The Radak, Rav David Kimchi (1160-1235) explains that Moshe and Aharon were High Priests. Similarly, the Talmud also suggests that Moshe was a Kohen Gadol (Zevachim 101b-102a). We read earlier, however, that this position was stripped from him after he refused, multiple times, to go to Egypt! How did he suddenly regain this status?

The Kli Yakar (Shemot 28:1), Rabbi Shlomo Ephraim ben Aaron Luntschitz (1550-1619), tells us that Moshe was catapulted to the position of Kohen Gadol when he prayed for Klal Yisrael and his brother after the Sin of the Golden Calf. I think we can take this idea one step further. Aharon had led the nation to construct an idol, and erred terribly. Despite his mistake, Moshe prayed for both him and the people, and one of the first things he said was, "And now, if You would but forgive their sin! But if not, erase me now from Your book that You have written" (Shemot 32:32). If Hashem had not forgiven Klal Yisrael, Aharon's honour would have been completely destroyed. As such, Moshe entreated, "Take me out of the

Parsha that deals with Aharon and the priesthood! Give him the honour! Let him be praised!" That act gave Moshe the status of Kohen Gadol. His flight from honour brought him honour. Like the Talmud teaches, one who pursues honour will have it flee from him, while one who flees from honour will have it pursue him (Eruvin 13b).

There are countless times in our lives when we are given the golden opportunity to step out of the spotlight. Many times we fail to truly realize the honour due to others, despite our own involvement. For instance, a person who worked hard in a group project can sometimes take all the credit and forget about the classmate who worked a week straight on the powerpoint presentation. Sometimes, we are the ones who worked a week straight, but yet fail to credit the classmate who contributed a good amount of work, too. The Torah way to go about honour is to flee from it. If a teacher tells you, "Wow, you did so much work. You deserve a lot of credit," the proper response should be, "I can't take all the credit. Look at what all my friends did, too!" This does not mean that internally we have to deny our involvement, or even lie about the work that we did to others. It does mean that we have to go about it modestly and try our best to shy away from taking all the honour. Hashem knows what you did, and that is really all that counts.

Regarding the lighting of the Menorah in the Mishkan, Rashi notes that the lamplighter had to hold the flame to the wick until a flame arose of its own accord (Bamidbar 8:2). Rav Shimshon Rephael Hirsch, quoted by Rav Yissochar Frand, explains this concept by means of a parable. A teacher cannot always hover over a student and tell him, "Remember, I was the guy who made you what you are," or, "I taught you everything you know." A teacher must be prepared to stand back, take himself out of the picture, and let the student go forth on his own. Likewise, the flame of the Menorah should arise on its own. A world where one person hogs the spotlight is a dark world, but a world where everyone is trying to let the flames of each other's souls burn bright on their own is a bright world indeed. Even if we deserve the honour, even if we were the ones who made it happen, we have to step back, and, like our great Rabbis, allow others to shine.

At face value, it seems odd to read Parshat Tetzaveh on the same week as Moshe Rabbeinu's yahrtzeit, but, in truth, it is a silent testimony to his stunning greatness.

For Glory and Majesty

By Elianne Neuman

"You shall make vestments of sanctity for Aaron your brother, for **glory** and **majesty**."

The phrase "for glory and majesty" refers to the priestly garments.

Sforno says that these items of clothing were for the glory of G-d, but that they would also reflect to the majesty of the Kohanim, as leaders and teachers of the nation.

The Malbim takes a different approach. He says that glory refers to a person's G-d-given abilities, while majesty refers to the fact that he is held in high regard because of his accomplishments. Thus, the glory given to the Kohanim was a result of their G-d-given abilities, and their majesty, their high regard, would result from their handiwork and their devotion to the Beit Hamikdash.

The Malbim's approach connects nicely with the first few verses of the Parsha, in which G-d instructs the Kohanim about the types of oil they must use to light the Menorah. The Menorah can only be lit with pure olive oil, "shemen zait zach." Ibn Ezra comments that the purity of the olive oil reflects the purity of the Kohanim, who must remain separate from the rest of the nation because they are the only people who can perform the priestly duty.

So according to the approaches of the Malbim and Ibn Ezra, the Kohanim take it upon themselves to maintain the Beit Hamikdash, and thus, they separate themselves from the rest of the nation. Their daily commitment to Hashem makes them pure, like the olive oil, and their rewards are a direct result of their handiwork, their efforts to perform their priestly duties.

I believe that there is a very important lesson we can learn from the Kohanim, their priestly garments, and the olive oil.

Whenever we do a mitzvah, we should perform it like the Kohanim: for glory and for majesty. By acting in the way of G-d, we continue in a path of the righteous, a path that allows us to devote ourselves to G-d through daily commitments, and thus we reap rewards that are a direct result of our handiwork.

Divrei Torah on **Shemot**

Blot Out My Name
By Michali Glasenberg

This week's Parsha is Parshat Tetzaveh. Moshe Rabbeinu's name is nowhere to be found in this week's Parsha. The reason for this is well known: when Moshe asked Hashem to spare the Jewish people from punishment for their involvement in the incident of the Golden Calf, Moshe said to Hashem, "And now please forgive their sin, and if not, erase me from the book You have written" (Shemos 32:31).

Moshe's actions work to save the Jewish people, but it resulted in his name being left out of this week's Parsha. As we learn from Yaakov Aveinu's inadvertent curses of Rachel in cursing whoever took Lavan's idols, the words of a Tzadik do not go ignored. Somehow, Moshe's words would come true. The Baal Haturim says that Moshe's name actually was taken out of the Torah by not being mentioned in this week's Parsha.

Elsewhere, the Torah speaks of another erasure: "Therefore, when Hashem your G-d grants you safety from all your enemies [...] you shall blot out the name of Amalek from under the heavens. Do not forget!" (Devarim 25:9). The opposite of Moshe is Amalek, whose essence is the belief that the world operates according to chance. This is an outright contradiction to Divine Providence. Amalek attacked the Jews in the desert to prove their vulnerability and to show that the Jewish people were not protected by Hashem.

Haman, a descendant of Amalek, also wanted to prove that he could destroy the Jewish people by chance. He cast lots to choose the most opportune time to destroy them. The Torah tells us to blot out the name of Amalek, destroying the essence of poisoning people's minds with the belief in chance.

This Shabbos, we read the Parsha of destroying the memory of Amalek, which is a Mitzvah Deorita. It is also the Shabbos before Purim, when we celebrate our victory over Haman and Amalek.

Spreading the Light
By Mindy Chapman

This week's parsha, Tetsaveh, is a long list of protocols concerning the Mishkan that is to be built and operated in the desert. The first commandment in this week's parsha says: "You shall further instruct the Israelites to bring you clear oil of beaten olives for lighting, for kindling lamps regularly… [to burn] from evening to morning before the Lord. It shall be due from the Israelites for all time, throughout the ages."

This is a wonderful way to open up this week's parsha, brimming with laws and rules, because it has many beautiful explanations that help teach us something about life. Similar to the Lubavitcher Rebbe's commentary, I interpreted the verse in the following manner: it is our duty, as commanded by Hashem, to spread light and goodness throughout this world, through the times of easiness and good outlook (comparable to "morning" from the text), and through the dark periods filled with uncertainty and evil (comparable to the text's mention of "night").

Today, we spread this "light", albeit somewhat inadvertently, through Tsedakah and Tikkun Olam. When you help somebody with his problems, you are spreading light throughout the world; and when you are raising money for a natural disaster relief fund, such as the recent forest fire in Israel, you are helping to spread light throughout the world. Every act of kindness that you commit, as well as helping others help the world, is spreading goodness and holiness to those who will then spread the good and help others themselves.

We are faced, every day, with the harsh reality that the world in which we live is teeming with problems, and, at times, it is a cruel place in which to live. Trying to illuminate the world with kindness makes it a better place for us to live in. By doing acts of Tikkun Olam, we are trading in some physical difficulties, as well as material things, for a greater spiritual reward that everyone will benefit from, just like the material oil that Bnei Israel would give to Aaron was traded in for a better, spiritual light, that the Israelites benefited from in this week's parsha.

Divrei Torah on **Shemot**

Ki Tisa • כִּי תִשָּׂא

Counting With a Pleasant Eye
By Idan Bergman

Parashat Ki Tisa begins with Hashem telling Moshe that if he should take a census of Bnei Yisrael, he should do so by counting the half-shekel donations each person gives. Moshe, He says, should count each single donation in the census instead of counting the people themselves. The problem here at first glance is why did Hashem decree for Moshe to count the shekalim instead of the actual people?

Rashi ("And there will be no plague among them," 12) explains the reasoning behind Moshe's counting: whenever a group is counted according to their "heads," according to who they are, "an evil eye can affect that which has been counted and pestilence can come upon them." Thus, Rashi holds that the reason Moshe was told not to count the actual people is because it provokes the evil eye and can thereby cause harm to Bnei Yisrael.

Rashi brings forth an example of this, in which Bnei Yisrael were counted improperly and were hurt for this. A census is taken in Eretz Yisrael during the time of David haMelech. David orders his general, Yoav, to count the nation by each individual person. After the numbers are returned to David, David realizes the mistake he has made of the way he conducted the census. Soon afterwards, a plague strikes Eretz Yisrael and seventy thousand people die. David and the prophet at the time, Gad, understand that this was not the way to count Bnei Yisrael, and for this the people were punished.

In general, the evil eye is the name given to harmful negative energy which is created by people gazing at others with envy, ill-feeling, or arrogance. We, as humans, possess supernatural powers, energy, or something simply beyond comprehension, that can physically cause harm in another person's life.

Now, how is the counting of individuals of Bnei Yisrael connected to the evil eye, and how does counting shekalim take away from the evil eye? The counting of Bnei Israel in the desert can be compared to the following: *a couple moves next door to a house with a large family with many children.*

When the large family comes to greet the new neighbours, the couple sees all the kids and, before thinking, asks the wife "How many kids do you have?" The answer, half-heartedly and almost robotically, comes back as "Twelve." The couple replies, "Wow! That is unbelievable; how do you do it? You must be a super-wife or something. You must have no time on your hands."

The obvious problem here is the fact that the couple knew the family had a lot of children, but that did not stop them from still asking how many children they have and demeaning and embarrassing the wife, who was only there to greet her new neighbours. The question posed to the wife can only be described as a form of the evil eye. It is a question not intended for informative purposes, but asked to degrade the wife, in order to feel superior that she, the neighbour, does not have to take care of twelve mischievous kids.

On a similar note, we know that Am Israel left in large numbers from Egypt and was a large nation in itself. When they were to be counted in this parasha, the numbers were sure to be large, but in reality, the exact number had no meaning. As such, shekalim were used to count the nation, to symbolize a "truma" or portion for Hashem, and to act as a form of atonement in order to not flaunt the numbers of Bnei Yisrael and create an evil eye amongst, for example, other nations, but rather to show that their numbers could contribute to something with unlimited magnitude, holiness.

Another Ten

By Becky Friedman

Several Parshiot ago, in Parshat Yitro, we read about how Bnei Yisrael received the Ten Commandments. In this Parsha, Ki Tisa, Moshe comes down from Har Sinai with the Two Tablets, presumably inscribed with those same Ten Commandments. Unfortunately, when he came down and saw the people committing idolatry with a golden calf, he dropped the tablets, which shattered. Moshe was obliged to go back up the mountain and re-write the Ten Commandments onto a second set of tablets.

But there's reason to believe that they weren't the same Ten. We all know the original Ten Commandments-- "I am G-d," "don't worship other gods," "don't take G-d's Name in vain," Shabbat, "honour your parents," "don't murder," "don't commit adultery," "don't steal," "don't bear false witness," and "don't covet." Strangely, these Ten Commandments-- or, more accurately, Ten Statements-- are never referred to as such. The one time the phrase "Ten Statements" (or "Ten Commandments") appears in the Torah is in reference to a different, though overlapping, set of Ten.

In Perek 34 of Dvarim, Moshe takes two tablets of stone upon which he will carve the Ten Commandments, and ascends the mountain. He asks G-d to forgive Bnei Yisrael (for the sin of the golden calf), and G-d declares that He will make a covenant with Bnei Yisrael. After a few tangential words about covenants, there follow ten distinct commandments. (These commandments also appear elsewhere, in a different order but otherwise unchanged, reinforcing the parallel between these and the better-known Ten Commandments, which appear twice in the Torah.)

The Ten Commandments as they were given in parshat Ki Tisa, from G-d to Moshe, are as follows:

1. Don't make idols.
2. Pesach
3. Pidyon haben (redeem the firstborn son of every animal).
4. Do not appear before G-d empty-handed.
5. Shabbat
6. Shloshet Haregalim (make a pilgrimage to the Beit Hamikdash 3 times a year).
7. Don't offer the blood of a sacrifice with leavened bread.
8. Don't leave the Korban Pesach over until the next morning.
9. Bring the first fruits to Beit Hamikdash.
10. Don't boil a kid in its mother's milk.

Immediately following these Ten Commandments, G-d instructs Moshe to write them down, explaining that His covenant with Bnei Yisrael is based on these very statements (or commandments). The text then says that Moshe "wrote on the Tablets the Statements of the Covenant: the Ten Statements" (Shmot 34:28). It cannot be clearer that these Ten are the Ten Commandments referred to as such.

As you can see, these are very different from the Ten Commandments we know and love.

Numbers one and five are familiar, corresponding to numbers two and four of the usual set.

Beyond that, numbers four, seven, eight, and nine are outdated, as commandments that can only be fulfilled in the days of Beit Hamikdash-- perhaps this sheds light on the question of why we *don't* generally recognize these Ten Commandments.

Number six could be said to belong to that group, too, though we still follow part of it by keeping those three holidays.

Of the remaining three, our views of them are extremely varied. Pidyon Haben, while it is still followed, is hardly thought of much; Pesach, on the other hand, is widely considered one of the most important mitzvot even by unobservant Jews. Kashrut, alluded to with "don't boil a kid," occupies some space in the middle. Those who take it seriously take it very seriously; those who don't range from those who pick and choose aspects of kashrut to those who disregard it altogether.

This is a sharp contrast from the better-known Ten Commandments, which are universally known, and, if not universally kept, then universally respected and acknowledged as important.

Who knows? In the days of the Third Beit Hamikdash, perhaps we will honour and remember these Ten Commandments as highly as the other Ten.

Reward and Punishment
By Teddy Kravetsky

In this week's parsha, Bnei Yisroel sin when they make a golden calf. After they make and worship it, Moshe comes down from Har Sinai and sees. He then breaks the two tablets, and G-d punishes Bnei Yisroel. As punishment, G-d kills many thousands of Jews and is infuriated at Bnei Yisroel.

But why is G-d so angry? Weren't Bnei Yisroel just trying to find another way to worship G-d? The answer to this is no. Bnei Yisroel worshipped the Golden Calf because they thought that G-d had abandoned them, as Moshe was delayed, or so they thought, in coming down the mountain. This led to their worship of "another god," or an idol. G-d punished them because they broke one of the very commandments they had just been given, being "Do not worship other gods." G-d punished us because we broke a commandment.

This incident can be compared to any situation in which we do something wrong, and whether it come from the school, a parent, etc., we will most likely get some sort of punishment. From this we can learn that we get these punishments for a reason. Parents don't enjoy punishing their kids; however, sometimes it's the only way to get them to listen.

Another reason that people get punished is because a lot of the time-- including the situation with the Golden Calf-- not only one person is affected, but others as well. For instance, the sin of the Golden Calf was so powerful that not only did G-d get upset, but Moshe, too, as he broke the two tablets that G-d had given him to give to Bnei Yisroel.

The other lesson that people should realize is that not only do the things we do affect ourselves, but our decisions also affect everyone around us, and although we may not realize it at the time, if we think long and hard about what we did, we can probably come up with someone else who suffered because of us. This cause-and-effect scenario can also have a positive turn-out-- meaning, if we do something good, we will be rewarded. Not only because of what we did, but also we must take into account that a lot of the time we are doing something good that will affect others as well, in this case in a good way.

Maybe this is why G-d punished Bnei Yisroel-- in order for them and future generations to learn a lesson or two: to think before they act, and that everything they do has a cause-and-effect result. As we see, our actions and words have a lot of power; therefore, my suggestion to everyone is to make good use of your position, strive to make good decisions, and realize that these decisions can affect and help countless others.

The Coin of Fire
By Matthew Goodman

Upon the completion of the building of the Mishkan and the inauguration of Aharon and his sons as Kohanim, Hashem commanded Moshe to take a census of the people. The Torah reads, "When you take a census of Bnei Yisrael according to their numbers, let each one give to Hashem an atonement for his soul when they are counted... This they shall give -- everyone who passes through the census -- a half shekel of the sacred shekel" (Shemot 30:12-13).

Rashi, quoting Midrash Tanchuma, tells us that Hashem showed Moshe a "coin of fire" weighing a half-shekel, and said to him, "Like this one they shall give." When Rashi comments on a pasuk, he usually addresses an inherent problem with the text. At face value, however, the text of the Torah shows no anomalies! Why did Rashi need to say that Hashem showed Moshe a "coin of fire?"

Rav David Halberstam of Krashnov z"l deals with this problem. He explains that Moshe Rabbeinu was exceedingly humble, as we learn, "Now the man Moshe was very humble, above all the men that were upon the face of the earth" (Devarim 13:3). In his deep humility, he could not understand why Hashem would bother to count people, considering how insignificant they are! According to Rav Halberstam, the "coin of fire" was meant to answer all of Moshe's problems.

Hashem was telling Moshe that he is, in part, correct. An individual alone is insignificant. However, the coin of fire teaches that there is a way for an individual to become an extremely powerful force. Fire cannot exist unless it's joined with another medium. Similarly, every single Jew is a spark of fire; alone, he is nothing, but when he is part of Klal Yisrael, his power is enormous. Moshe was meant to calculate the census through the half shekel. He would count the number of coins given to him, and thereby determine the number of people in Bnei Yisrael. Through a contribution, a single person is able to become part of the overarching entity that is the nation, just as fire becomes something when combined with a medium.

The coin of fire also teaches us the proper way to contribute to the community. The Chidushei HaRim asks: Why did Hashem show Moshe a coin of fire as opposed to a fiery metal coin? He answers that Hashem was not just instructing Moshe regarding the coin itself, but rather the state of mind that should accompany the giving. Being part of the Klal does not just require giving according to your obligation. The coin of fire represents the fiery zeal and passion that should accompany the giving. Similarly, the Kotzker Rebbe teaches that when a person performs even a modest act of charity with gladness, when he gives with the fire of passion and enthusiasm, then he indeed is giving a piece of his soul to the Klal.

The Chofetz Chaim, in his sefer Ahavat Chesed, explains this idea using a story:

Rabbi Bunim of Pshische spent his early years as a businessman. In his constant business travels, he used every interaction as a means to bring Jews closer to Hashem. On one such journey, he stopped at an inn on a cold, stormy night. The Jewish innkeeper found Rabbi Bunim to be a sympathetic ear, and told him all about his failing business. Peasants no longer came to him, vats of liquor sat untouched in the basement, and the landlord was growing impatient for his rent. Rabbi Bunim spoke to the man for a bit, and then sat down to learn.

In the middle of the night, there was a loud knock on the door. A traveler, drenched and freezing, begged the innkeeper to admit him, even though he had no money with which to pay for the stay. The innkeeper sighed at his misfortune. He finally had a customer, but he had no money. Nevertheless, he helped the traveller and let him in, giving him a room and a change of clothing. The traveller, still shivering, asked, "Could you bring me some vodka, please? I don't have any money, but I'm so cold!"

The innkeeper went to the basement to fetch the vodka. He didn't notice that Rabbi Bunim was there, watching him. What the Rabbi saw next struck him so powerfully that he told of the scene for the rest of his life. The innkeeper poured a cup of vodka, then shook his head firmly and smashed the cup to the floor. Once, twice, three times, four times he repeated this procedure, oblivious to the sin of wastefulness he was committing. Finally, after pouring the fifth cup, he happily proclaimed, "Now!" and brought the drink to his guest.

Rabbi Bunim asked the innkeeper to explain his strange behaviour. The explanation was touchingly simple. He couldn't serve the guest a drink he had poured with disappointment and resentment in his heart. He knew he had been handed a golden mitzvah, a chance to revive a shivering, hungry, poor man, yet his financial and business worries were clouding his ability to appreciate this gift. He tried and tried again, until he reached the Ahavat Chesed that was within him. Satisfied that he was doing the kindness with a full heart, he brought the man his drink.

As independent, single individuals, we really are very little. We can't accomplish, achieve, or attain significant to our fullest extent. However, when we combine ourselves with other people and give to them, we create a bond of Ahavat Chesed (lovingkindness) and Achdut (unity) so powerful and so strong that, together, anything is possible. The key is to give with fiery zeal. Hashem's coin of fire sent a clear message that the only way to truly combine with others is to give to them with passion, happiness, and a full sense of selflessness. This requirement permeates every aspect of our lives. We have countless opportunities to help and to give to other members of Klal Yisrael. Every day hands us new chances to perform golden Mitzvahs. Performing them with a full appreciation of the gift and a heartfelt smile ignites the true power and strength of Klal Yisrael.

Vayakhel • ויקהל

This Parsha has been generously sponsored by the Weisbrod family in honour of all the teachers and staff at TanenbaumCHAT, & Laurie Blake, in honour of her son, Joey Hadari

Wisdom in Their Hearts
By Yaron Milwid

This week's parsha is Parshat Vayakhel. In it, Moshe asks the children of Israel to make a donation to the Mishkan fund. The children of Israel make many donations, including jewelry, money, linen, and wood.

When it talks about the different types of cloths that were given, it says: 'And every wise-hearted woman spun with her hands, and they brought spun material: blue, purple, and crimson wool, and linen.' Then it says: 'And all the women whose hearts uplifted them with wisdom spun the goat hair.'

Now, there are two very interesting things about these psukim. Rabbi Zalman Sorotzkin deals with the first question in his comments on verse 2 of chapter 36. If the people were slaves in Egypt and had to spend all their time performing hard labor, how were they able to spin different types of cloth? Rabbi Sorotzkin explains, "G-d placed wisdom in their hearts." He takes this question a bit further, asking how G-d decided to whom He would give this wisdom. He explains that G-d inspired anyone who wanted to work on the Mishkan. He supports this with a quote from Tractate Shabbos which says, "If one sets out to be purified, G-d helps him."

Rashi addresses the second question raised by these two verses in his comments on verse 26. Rashi says 'This was a craft of special skill, for they spun it while it was still on the animals' backs.' This explains why these women were referred to as "women whose hearts uplifted them with wisdom," but one has to wonder whether it is a very realistic explanation for why these women are referred to this way. I do not believe that there would be any reason for the women to spin the wool while it was still on the goats' backs, and so I do not believe that Rashi was right in this case.

I think that, in order to understand why there is a distinction between the two jobs, one should go back to the verses. The verses present two possible reasons. The first is based on the concept that there is no order to the Torah. The verses are in the wrong order, and the second verse talks about the women who did the actual creative activity, while the other women only modified what these women created.

The second reason is based on the fact that the first verse includes colors and the second does not. This shows that the product of the second group of women was of such quality that it did not need the extra color. This explanation is similar to Rashi's explanation, in that it talks about the difficulty of the work, but, unlike Rashi, it provides a logical, qualitative difference.

How to Make Your Own Success Story
By Matthew Goodman

Everything that gets done in life is an achievement. Since the crux of our existence is task after task, test after test, and goal after goal, we need to be in a constant state of pursuing accomplishment, be it spiritually or materially. We need to be able to do well in school, fix a relationship after an argument, stop speaking gossip, raise good Jewish children, and so on and so forth. So many things need to get done, and they all require a tremendous amount of effort. Sometimes, it can seem to be tremendously difficult to accomplish something. At face value, we might tell ourselves that we are simply not suited for the task, that we are not skilled enough, or that it is simply too hard. Something in our mind tells us, "There is no way I, of all people, could possibly succeed at this. What's the point of trying?" This week's Parsha deals fantastically with this problem.

Parshat Vayakhel tells us that Moshe Rabbeinu gathered a team of artisans to build the Mishkan and its furnishings according to Hashem's specifications, detailed in the previous Parshiot of Terumah, Tetzaveh, and Ki Tisa. The pasuk states, "Moshe called Betzalel and Ahaliav and every wise-hearted man into whose heart Hashem had given wisdom, everyone whose heart lifted him up to approach the work to do it" (Shemot 36:2). The Torah's statement requires some explanation. Why do we learn that Moshe gathered men who were endowed with wisdom and uplifted hearts, as opposed to the actual skills required to complete the job? Would it not be more logical to write that Moshe called Betzalel and Ahaliav and all those who were master artisans or learned in craftsmanship?

The Ramban answers our question with a fascinating observation on the pasuk: "See, I have called by name Betzalel the son of Uri, the son of Hur, of the tribe of Judah" (31:2). He points out that no one in Klal Yisrael was trained in the crafts or skills necessary to build the Mishkan. Due to the conditions in Egypt, there were no Jewish artisans or craft-smiths. The Egyptians did not train them or even permit them to develop their talents for finer skills. Some, however, did have inherent natural ability, though unrefined. Therefore, the pasuk tells us that Moshe gathered all those who had a motivated spirit and inspired heart. Klal Yisrael were able to succeed in the task of building the Mishkan solely because they had absolute determination; their hearts lifted them up to approach the work and do it. They really wanted to help with building the Mishkan. Their hearts were yearning to be able to fulfill the Mitzvah. The Torah would be lying if it told us that Moshe gathered men of skill, so it writes instead that they were men to whom "Hashem had given wisdom" to complete their holy task.

According to the Ramban, since Klal Yisrael took initiative and put their hearts into the job, Hashem granted them the knowledge necessary to be successful. The Chofetz Chaim (Torat HaBayit, Perek 7 - footnote) also comments on this idea, but extends it even further. He writes that Hashem gave the knowledge and wisdom necessary to anyone who put his heart and desire into building the Mishkan. The pasuk (above, 36:2) does not say "<u>and</u> everyone whose heart inspired him," signaling a separate thought, but rather, "everyone whose heart inspired him," indicating a single matter. This means that anyone who agreed and decided in his mind to draw close to the task and whose "heart lifted him up" was given knowledge by Hashem. The Chofetz Chaim explains that this applies to any good thing, whether it is an action concerning a holy matter, which requires heavy contemplating, or whether it is a matter of learning Torah. If one decides in his mind to become an expert in some part of the Talmud or similar thing, and sees to it to review, pursue, and study it, Hashem will grant him knowledge in his heart and help him make his thoughts a reality.

The soul has the amazing ability to motivate, inspire, and drive our minds and actions to a point at which we actually yearn to be able to complete something. It is possible to be absolutely set on getting something done, and to entirely put your heart into the work. Anyone who has ever yearned to achieve a goal knows how true this is. Sometimes, however, we don't really have all the skills, knowledge, or ability to complete the task set in front of us. The Torah, therefore, teaches us that anyone whose heart lifted him up was given wisdom by Hashem. One who truly yearns to complete something will get Siyata Dishmaya (help from heaven). How, though, can we make ourselves motivated, and how do we properly act upon it? It may be inspiring to hear that one who yearns to achieve will, please G-d, achieve, but how can we actually put this into play?

A few lines are, unfortunately, not enough to deal with the whole issue of self-motivation, but I'd like to share one idea with you. A lack of motivation, for the most part, means that a person is too lazy to get things done. You don't need a tremendous amount of motivation to complete homework, but you certainly need a tremendous lack of laziness. As such, we need some inspiration in life to lift us up on our feet and get going! Shlomo HaMelech realized this and wrote in his proverbs: "Go to the ant, you lazy person! Note his ways and become wise... She prepares her food in the summer, and stores her food in the harvest time. How long will you sleep, O lazy person? When will you arise from your slumber?" (Mishlei 6:6-9). Why did Shlomo HaMelech choose an ant? What is so special about an ant that will incite us to wake up?

The Midrash (Devarim Rabbah 5:2) notes that the ant has an average life span of a short six months. In its entire lifetime, it only requires 1.5 grains of wheat to survive. Yet, the ant spends its life accumulating 300 kur (Talmudic measurement). While there is no exact modern equivalent to 300 kur, it is excessively more than the necessary 1.5 grains of wheat. The Midrash, wondering why, ascertains that perhaps the ant thinks that Hashem will grant her a long life and she'd better be prepared. This is the unbelievable drive and initiative of such a miniscule creature! This is what Shlomo HaMelech entreats us to emulate! We, who have so much to do in such a short amount of time, need to reap the opportunities to get those things done. There's no time to be lazy! Think about everything that you want to achieve in life, spiritually and physically, interpersonally and personally. All those things have to be done in the time you're given. There's no use procrastinating. Fully internalizing and understanding this fact is a certain motivator to pursuing our initiatives.

Once you're motivated, it's time to act. Rav Yerucham Levovitz zt"l, the famous Mashgiach Ruchani (spiritual supervisor) of the Mir Yeshiva (1873-1936), writes in his Sefer Da'at Torah (p. 348) that every rags-to-riches story has a common denominator: a desire to succeed where others have failed. He writes: "If one looks at the great people in the world, if one looks at those who have made financial fortunes, most, if not all such people, achieved their greatness through tremendous drive and initiative." Great individuals don't just have a will to accomplish their dreams. They take initiative. They never stop acting on them, while refusing to succumb to the voices of naysayers.

The Reichman family is a perfect example of this. Originally from the shtetl of Beled, Hungary, the family survived the Holocaust by moving to Morocco, and then resettled in Montreal. The Reichmans owned the biggest real estate company in the world, and gave a tremendous amount of money -- millions and millions of dollars -- to Tzedakah and Torah causes. Rav Yissochar Frand, Rosh Yeshiva of Ner Yisroel in Baltimore, in his weekly Dvar Torah, once shared part of their success story from a book he recently read about the family:

According to the book, the Reichmans had a tile business called the Olympia Tile Company, selling building material. As their business grew, they decided that they needed a bigger warehouse. They went to several different general contractors and gave their requirements for the building. The lowest bid that came back was $120 000. Mr. Reichman thought to himself, "I bet I can build a warehouse myself for far less than $120 000."

At the time, he didn't know the first thing about construction or building. He did, however, believe in himself, and firmly thought that he could successfully build a warehouse that would meet his needs for less than $120 000. He ended up building the whole thing for $70 000. Thinking that building wasn't too bad a business, the Reichmans started contracting one-story warehouses. From there, they moved to multi-story buildings. Eventually, they become so successful that their company, Olympia & York, became the largest property development and management firm in the world. This all came into actualization simply because of the Reichman family's initiative and drive to try and achieve.

They tried. They wanted to succeed, so they tried. That's really all we have to do. When you have a great yearning to accomplish something, and your mind is set on getting it done, you find that the moment you start working towards the endeavour, everything falls into place. If you are, for example, absolutely set on refraining from speaking Lashon HaRa (evil speech, i.e., gossip, slander, etc.), the moment you start actualizing the will through practical means, you will find yourself accomplishing more, and understanding what you need to do to achieve your goals. Hashem gives us the wisdom to realize what to do next and how to pursue our goal even further. If you stumble or trip a little bit on the way, that's simply part of the whole process. If, however, you find yourself failing, then you are obviously doing something wrong. Either you don't actually have the will, you're not putting in enough effort, or you fail to realize that you are not actually failing, but being tested in a way that will help you achieve.

The Midrash on Shir HaShirim (5:2) says: "Open for me an opening like the eye of a needle, and, in turn, I will enlarge it to be an opening through which wagons enter." When we take initiative and open up a little tiny hole, when we make the attempt to fulfill our potential, Hashem helps us to make it happen.

Pekudei • פקודי

Self-Sacrifice
By Michali Glasenberg

In Parshat Pekudai, we read that "Betzalel, the son of Uri, the son of Chur, of the tribe of Yehuda, had made all that Hashem had commanded Moshe"(38:22). Why was Betzalel's grandfather, Chur, mentioned in this Passuk?

Chur was murdered during the sin of the Golden Calf because he opposed making the calf. The fact that the Mishkan was constructed through Chur's grandson atoned for the guilt of Chur's death. Betzalel was also the great-grandson of Miriam, Moshe's sister. Miriam was rewarded with a descendant who possessed the necessary expertise, and was worthy of building the Mishkan, because her fear of Hashem allowed her to disobey Pharaoh's order to murder Jewish babies.

Both Betzalel and his ancestors possessed the personality trait of willingness to sacrifice oneself for Hashem. Perhaps Chur is mentioned to emphasize the great degree of self-sacrifice on Betzalel's part. Even though the Mishkan was to serve as an atonement for the sin of the Golden Calf, over which his grandfather was murdered, he did not hesitate to accept this position. He had no sense of revenge or resentment, but was able to apply himself fully to the service of the Mishkan, trusting completely in Hashem. That was true self-sacrifice and an aspect of his noble lineage, which was an inherent part of his personality.

Based on the commentaries by Rabbi A.L. Scheinbaum

Divrei Torah on **Shemot**

Required Blueprints
By Becky Friedman

The past few parshiot, up to and including Pekudei, read, for the most part, like a set of architectural blueprints, as do several of the corresponding haftarot. And, really, reading a set of architectural blueprints can't be that interesting, except perhaps for architects. Why, one might ask, does the Torah (and Neviim) contain such boring, unreadable segments, if we're all supposed to read Torah and enjoy it?

Well-- ignoring all the other excellent reasons delineated in other Divrei Torah for this and previous parshiot-- for one thing, they're useful. In the haftara we read about King Shlomo constructing the Beit Hamikdash according to G-d's plan. Although the Temple is constructed on a far grander scale than the portable Mishkan, the principle is the same; many of the descriptions in the Torah of the construction of the Mishkan probably aided in the construction of Beit Hamikdash.

That only answers half the question; why repeat the long, drawn-out blueprints in Sefer Melachim, then? Couldn't the book have just said in one verse that Shlomo built Beit Hamikdash?

Well, no, it couldn't (and, again, I am ignoring all the perfectly legitimate *internal* reasons for the entire blueprints to be spelled out). That was, of course, the construction of Beit Hamikdash *Harishon*, the First Temple. What about the second?

The Second Temple was, of course, modelled directly on the first, but it wasn't so simple. It was more than seventy years after the destruction of the First Temple that construction of the Second Temple even started; it wasn't like they had a building that just needed a few renovations. They had to start from scratch. And where could they start?

We know that in the time of the Rebuilding of the Temple they had access to the Torah, and we can infer that they had access to the stories of Sefer Melachim. We know this because in the books of Ezra and Nechemia, who spearheaded the reconstructions in Jerusalem, the people read the book of the Torah and lament how they have not followed the laws-- specifically, the law against intermarriage. The great leaders, denouncing the sin, refer to Shlomo, whose foreign wives led him into sin.

If they knew the one story of Shlomo-- that of his sins-- it is reasonable to assume that they knew, equally well, the other-- that of how he built Beit Hamikdash Harishon. Now we see the reason why it was detailed so exactly in the book of Melachim: without those blueprints, the returnees from the Babylonian exile may never have been able to build Beit Hamikdash Hasheni!

And, of course, the story isn't over. We ourselves are in exile, our Second Temple long since destroyed. We continually dream and pray of the day that we are returned to our land in its full glory and can rebuild our Temple as it was in the days of old.

But how can we build a Third Temple? How can we replace all the instruments that were necessary to its operation, that have been long since destroyed, stolen, or lost?

With our blueprints, of course! When Mashiach comes, we will be able to build the Third Temple, armed with the architectural and technical blueprints in Shmot and Melachim to guide us. And so we read this, every year (and, hopefully, more frequently than that!), to familiarize ourselves with the task that, please G-d, will be before us soon.

May we all see the day, soon in its coming, that we put this parsha to work in rebuilding our Temple. Shabbat Shalom!

The Best of Intentions
By Matthew Goodman

The topic of the Mishkan easily gets the most press in the entire Torah. The last five Parshiot in Sefer Shemot (that's almost 1/10th of the Torah!) painstakingly detail the whole process of its construction. The specifications for each element are carefully and clearly recorded, and then repeated again. In this week's Parsha, the building of the Mishkan is completed, and the Torah tells us, "In accordance with all that Hashem had commanded Moshe, so did the children of Israel do all the service. Moshe saw the entire work, and behold, they had done it -- as Hashem had commanded, so had they done. And Moshe blessed them" (Shemot 39:42-43).

These two psukim require a bit of explanation. Why was it necessary for the Torah to express the same idea using two different terms? The first pasuk tells us that Klal Yisrael did all the service (Avodah) according to Hashem's commands, while the second pasuk tells us that Klal Yisrael did all the work (Melacha) according to Hashem's commands. Furthermore, why was it necessary at all to repeat what is seemingly the same idea, and then add that when Moshe saw this, he blessed them? Why couldn't the Torah tell us that Klal Yisrael did all the work in accordance with Hashem's commands and that when Moshe saw this, he blessed the people?

The Alshich HaKadosh, HaRav Moshe Alshich (1508-1593), in Torat Moshe, explains that the term Avodah in regard to our pasuk connotes that Klal Yisrael built the Mishkan with the right Kavanah (intention) -- as a service to Hashem, and as a fulfillment of His command. They had no ulterior motive, and, therefore, theirs was an Avodat Ha'Lev (service of the heart). In the next pasuk, Moshe himself saw that they had completed the construction of the Tabernacle in its entirety, and knew that it had been built with the right intention; as Hashem had commanded, so had they done, and he blessed them as a reward for their Kavanah.

The Alshich HaKadosh's explanation reveals two important ideas. The first is that the intention behind an act is crucial to its overall success. The Mishkan was completed in its entirety, without any imperfections, only because every element was produced with the right Kavanah. This made the Mishkan a beacon of true holiness.

Sforno (Shemot 38:24) takes this concept further. He asks, which, of the Mishkan, the First Temple, and the Second Temple, was holiest? One could potentially conclude that the Second Temple, after its renovation by Herod, was clearly the holiest of the three. The building was unbelievably beautiful, and the amount of gold used to build it was incalculably more that the amount invested in either the First Temple or the Mishkan. The Mishkan, being the least physically beautiful and splendourous, was the least holy of the three. Sforno points out that, in fact, the opposite is true. The Mishkan was holier than the First Temple, which was holier than the Second. The key to its holiness was not its grandeur, splendour, or beauty. The people behind its construct were the intrinsic cause of its holiness. Betzalel, the man commissioned by Hashem to construct the Mishkan, was endowed with the spirit of G-d, and completed his task with the utmost Kavanah. Every material, part, and element was carefully made for the sake of fulfilling Hashem's command and creating a place where Hashem could "dwell amongst the people." The First Temple, on the other hand, was built by non-Jews, payed for their services (Melachim I 5:15-25), and the renovated Second Temple was built by the Romans. Sforno here clearly demonstrates the tremendous effect proper Kavanah has on the spiritual makeup and success of an endeavour.

The second idea relayed by the Alshich HaKadosh is that a product created with the proper Kavanah can be evidently recognized as such. For instance, the Torah tells us that Hashem told Moshe to tell the people: "And you shall speak to all who are wise-hearted, whom I have filled with the spirit of wisdom, that they may make Aharon's garments to consecrate him, that he may minister to me as a kohen" (Shmot 28:3). The Netziv, HaRav Naftali Tzvi Yehuda Berlin (1816-1893), the Rosh Yeshiva of Volozhin, in Emek Davar (Shemot 28:3), notes that the instructions in the pasuk are addressed in the plural, but the Hebrew suggests that only one person was "filled with the spirit of wisdom." That one person must have Aharon. The Netziv solves this problem by rendering an alternate reading of the pasuk: "And you shall speak to all who are wise-hearted; tell them: 'Aharon, whom I have filled with the spirit of wisdom, will know if they had proper intention.' They may make Aharon's garments to consecrate him, that he may minister to me as a kohen." When Aharon dons his priestly garments, he will be able to tell whether they were created with the right intentions and if they were, indeed, imbued with thoughts of holiness, or if they were created through a motivation to gain pride, fame, and glory.

These two points extracted from the Alshich HaKadosh are astounding, and are exceptionally relevant to all aspects of our life. Everything we do, any project or goal we undertake, requires significant effort to be placed in the process itself. We can't simply do whatever it takes to get it done. In order to truly create or achieve something marvelous and worthwhile, the intentions we have along the road need to be "right." Having proper intentions can drastically alter the end product, endowing it with a sense of purpose and holiness. And this is not just a truth that you can intellectually grasp. It doesn't just mean that in your heart you know that it was created with the right intentions. This is something that can actually be felt and recognized. Whatever the product is, be it a deed, achievement of a goal, or a physical creation, it emanates the intentions placed into it from its very conception. You can feel them and see them from the product's successes.

The Gemara (Bava Metzia 85b) tells a story that aptly describes this idea:

Once, Rebi Chanina and Rebi Chiya were arguing with each other over a certain matter. Rebi Chanina said to Rebi Chiya, "Why do you argue with me? If, Heaven forbid, the Torah was forgotten from the Jewish people, I could restore it through my deliberations!" Rebi Chiya responded, "Why do you argue with me?! I make sure that Torah is not forgotten from the Jewish people in the first place! What do I do? I go and I sew flax. Then I weave nets from the grown flax, and I trap deer with these nets, and I feed their meat to orphans. Then I prepare scrolls of parchment with their skins, and I write the five Chumashim of Torah on these scrolls. Then I go up to the village, and I teach five children each a different book of Chumash, and six other children each a different order of the Mishna. Then I tell them, 'During the time that I return to my place and come back here again, teach Scripture to one another and teach Mishna to one another.' In this way, I make sure that the Torah is never forgotten from the Jewish people." This is what Rebbi referred to when he said, "How great are the deeds of Chiya!" Rebi Yishmael, the son of Rebi Yose, said to him, "Even in comparison to your deeds?" Rebbi said to him, "Yes."

Rebi Chiya could have easily taught the children Torah, and thus accomplished his final goal, without having to plant his own seeds, make his own nets, catch his own food, and prepare his own parchment. He would have been able to teach Torah far more efficiently had he garnered all the above materials from local purveyors. HaRav Yaakov Kamenetsky zt"l (1891-1986), one of the Gedolei HaDor of the last generation, in Emet L'Yaakov on Sehmot 26:15 (in the name of the Gra; also see the Maharsha on Bava Metzia 85b), explains that Rebi Chiya was not preoccupied with the final product as much as he was with the path to achieving it. Rebi Chiya wanted the whole process, from start to finish, to be performed amidst purity and holiness. Every intention, from the making of the parchment from which to learn, to the making of the food to feed the students, had to be entirely sincere. In this way, Rebi Chiya was able to ensure that he would succeed in teaching the children Torah, and that the Torah would endure and stand by them forever.

There is even a fantastic modern day example of such an enterprise, undertaken in order to endow a project with the utmost amount of Kavanah:

In the 1980s, the fifth Belzer Rebbe, HaRav Yissachar Dov Rokeach, spearheaded plans to erect a huge Shul in the Kiryat Belz neighborhood of Jerusalem. It would be an enlarged replica of the Shul built by the first Belzer Rebbe, the Sar Shalom, in the town of Belz in 1843. When I was in Israel this summer, I went with a group to visit it. It is unbelievably enormous and beautiful. There is a giant main sanctuary which seats 6 000 people, multiple study halls, simcha halls, libraries, dormitories, and smaller sanctuaries used during the week.

The Belzer Chassid who showed us the Shul told us that the Belzer Rebbe managed all aspects of the construction and design. The Belzer Chassidim have a tradition that Eliyahu HaNavi relayed to the first Belzer Rebbe Kabbalistic secrets and Kavanot for building his Shul. The Rebbe made sure that all of the secrets and patterns and designs were used in the construction. He even appointed Chassidim to pour the concrete used for the structure, as he wanted the building itself to be infused with holy thoughts. *They were instructed to go to the Mikveh and recite Tehillim before working, and to maintain a deep sense of Kavanah during the work itself. The Belzer Rebbe obviously understood the immense effect having the right Kavanah has on any endeavour.*

In our own lives, there are multiple ways, on multiple levels, to bring this lesson into fruition. For instance, having the right intention while performing an act of kindness transforms the action. If you are performing the action in order to gain glory or honour, then your kindness will be lacking! How could you possibly display the most love and chesed possible if the intention behind the action is utterly vulgar? On the other hand, an action infused with the right intentions can be amazingly powerful. If you do something because you really want to help someone else, fulfill a Mitzvah, and bring a little bit more light into the world as an Oveid Hashem, a worker of Hashem, the action is elevated. You'll be able to give with more excitement and to smile with a bigger smile, and the person on the receiving end will be able to actually feel the fact that you are doing something completely altruistically.

We all need to be extremely vigilant of the intentions we put into our actions, as they can really mean the success or failure of our endeavours. If we want to fill the world with everlasting holiness, a tangible holiness that emanates from the Jewish people, we have to make sure that the work of our hands is infused entirely with altruistic, holy, and spiritual intentions that far surpass self-glorification, honour, and glory. "And may the pleasantness of Hashem our G-d be upon us, and the work of our hands establish for us, and the work of our hands establish it" (Tehillim 90:17).

Equal Opposites
By Aaron Goldberg

One of the main ways in which to stress an idea is repetition. Repetition. Accordingly, when reading the Torah, it is interesting to note certain phrases that come up time after time. In Parshat Pekudei, the reader is drawn to the many times it says "as G-d commanded Moshe." In reference to almost every section of the construction in this week's Parsha, the refrain "as G-d commanded Moshe" is added.

In order to understand this line, it is important to return to the oft-posed question: what is the purpose of the Tabernacle in general, and of the multiple vessels included therein? What role do they play for the Jewish nation, and why? Or to look at it from a different view, what difference would it make if we *didn't* have these things?

A classic answer is the following. When Moshe is up on Mount Sinai receiving the Torah, Bnei Yisrael build a Golden Calf. They do this not to rebel against G-d, but rather in order to achieve a physical connection to Him. In building the Calf, Bnei Yisrael attempt to make G-d tangible, with the innately human desire to worship Him in a more concrete manner. To understate the situation, one may say that G-d got angry. He was furious. To literally put G-d into a box is to limit G-d! This was obviously a mistake.

But G-d understood the human need for tangibility and compartmentalization. It is quite difficult to connect to an abstract concept, as G-d realized. When Bnei Yisrael demonstrated that they could not surpass this human limitation, G-d gave them another outlet – the Tabernacle. The Tabernacle epitomizes the marriage of the abstract and the concrete, by encompassing the most abstract of concepts-- G-d-- within the most tangible of concepts-- a box. Humanity requires a Tabernacle in order to worship G-d, so G-d gave us the Tabernacle to make.

If this is the case, what did the nation do wrong in building the Golden Calf? If G-d is willing to concede to human nature with the Tabernacle, then why not do the same with the Calf? The answer lies in the distinct difference between the two items. G-d was involved in the building of the Tabernacle, but not the Calf. About the Golden Calf, G-d relates that "they have strayed quickly from the way that I have commanded them," whereas about the Tabernacle, there is the constant refrain of "as G-d commanded Moshe." In almost every section, the Torah emphasizes this difference between the Tabernacle and the Calf – that while they may seem to be equal, the single discrepancy between the two makes them opposites.

This idea teaches a beautiful lesson. Up to a certain degree, it doesn't matter what you do. Just because there is a fork in the road doesn't mean that one way is better than the other. Each way could be the best way to go. What really matters is your intention. It is simple to make the 'worse path' better and vice-versa. All you need is to have the right outlook. By infusing your decisions with G-d, positive attitude, and a drive to succeed, it is nearly impossible to go wrong. With these in mind, every path can lead to your Tabernacle.

The First Tzedaka Box
By Becky Friedman

In the Haftara for Parshat Shkalim, which is this week, we read about the renovations that King Yoash did for the Beit Hamikdash. A bit of background-- Yoash had been hidden as a baby when his grandmother Atalia murdered all his male relatives and siezed the throne herself. When at last he regained his rightful place as king, Atalia had been ruling for seven years. The kingdom was in ruin.

Twenty-three years later, King Yoash discovers that people haven't been keeping the Beit Hamikdash in order like they should be; the money to do so does not exist. What does Yoash do? He makes a hole in the top of a locked box, which he places beside the altar; into this box is put all the money that people bring to Beit Hamikdash. Whenever the box got too full, it would be emptied out, the money counted up and used for the renovations of Beit Hamikdash.

What does this image of a locked box with a hole in the top remind us of? A tzedaka box! And that's exactly what it was, in the truest sense of the word.

This Haftara is specially chosen to go together with the reading for Parshat Shkalim, and not just because it's the closest thing the books of Neviim have to the donation of money for worship of G-d as detailed in the Torah Maftir reading for Shkalim. In fact, it could be argued that it's the other way around-- that the Maftir for Shkalim was chosen because it's the closest story in the Torah to *this*.

Purim's in a week, more or less (next week, Parshat Zachor, is the parsha immediately before Purim, so on any given year, Purim is anywhere from exactly one week to just under two weeks from Parshat Shkalim). In addition to Matanot Le'Evyonim, gifts to the poor, being one of the four cardinal mitzvot of Purim, it is generally accepted that Purim is a time for giving tzedaka. In fact, we learn that on a normal day, we should give tzedaka, but through reliable sources (i.e., check to make sure that the money we give is going to someone who actually needs it); on Purim, if anyone approaches us, asking for tzedaka, we should give him something, no questions asked. *That* is how powerful the mitzva of tzedaka on Purim is!

So this Haftara's message comes in a timely fashion to remind us of the importance of tzedaka. Yoash sets up the first tzedaka box, and all the money that fills it goes to G-d-- that is, to the renovation and upkeep of the Beit Hamikdash. Similarly, on Purim, we should have in mind that all the tzedaka we give-- be it dropped into a tzedaka box modelled after that of Yoash, or given into the hand of someone begging-- goes directly to G-d, metaphorically speaking. On Purim, we don't need to check up on the reliability of our method of charity, because we know that wherever it goes, it goes to G-d.

ויקרא אל משה וידבר יי אליו מאהל מועד לאמר דבר אל בני ישראל

Vayikra
ויקרא

This Sefer of Chumash has been generously sponsored by

The Bloom Family

In honour of Benjamin, Georgina, and Karly Bloom

Vayikra • ויקרא

The Need to Change
By Elianne Neuman

The verse says: "If one's offering is an olah-offering from the cattle, he shall bring a perfect male; he shall bring it to the entrance of the Tent of Meeting in accordance with his will, before Hashem."

Rashi comments: The words "he shall bring" teach us that he is forced to bring this offering. Thus, it would be reasonable to conclude that someone could be forced to bring an offering against his will. But this is not so because the verse says that he brings the offering "in accordance with his will." How can someone be *forced* to bring an offering, yet bring it *willingly*? He is forced to bring the offering until he says, "I am willing to bring it."

In effect, Rashi says that the only way that someone can completely atone for his sins and change his ways is if he is *willing* to do so. This is a very practical lesson.

If we want to change, we must recognize that we have a problem and be willing to take the necessary steps to modify our behaviour. If someone has a temper, he must willingly recognize that he has an issue, be open to changing, and then willingly resolve to take the necessary steps to ensure that he will not repeat his mistakes.

Contemplating Torah
By Matthew Goodman

"And He called to Moshe, and Hashem spoke to him from the Tent of Meeting, saying" (Vayikra 1:1)

Rashi, commenting on "And He called," wonders why the Torah is broken into different subsections through hafsakot/breaks. He answers that the purpose of these subsections was to give Moshe a pause to contemplate between one passage and the next, between one subject and another. And if this pause for contemplation was given to Moshe Rabbeinu when it was taught to him by Hashem, how much more necessary would it be for the ordinary Torah scholar to be allowed pauses between sections and subjects, to carefully contemplate and understand the material he is learning.

R" Menachem Mendel Taub Shlita, the Kaliver Rebbe, observes in "Kol Menachem" that in a typical year, the reading of Parshat Vayikra falls very close to the week in which most schools begin their Pesach breaks. He asks, what purpose do these hafsakot/breaks serve? They give time to review, reflect, and digest what one had learned in the preceding months.

Most of us are currently experiencing a couple of weeks of tests, projects, and assignments, all combined together at the same time. And during this period of time, we have the chance to study and review a great deal of material from the past few months. This review, however, is not at all like the level of reflection that Rashi or the Kaliver Rebbe are commenting on. Very few of us have the time to appropriately contemplate and consider our Torah education. Most of our review and study is spent for the sake of a test or quiz. Much of it is crammed. Very little of it is fully appreciated.

If you are receiving detailed instructions for performing a science lab, it would be very difficult to take it all in at once. You would need time to consider them and plan out your actions. It would be too hard to just run and start. So too, when receiving instructions for living, you have to process every word and sentence very slowly, carefully, and meticulously. Especially in these few weeks, it is exceptionally important to look back at all the study we have done, and to start to contemplate. Choose a topic in Tanach, Rabbinics, or Talmud that you find to be particularly interesting or intriguing. Try to apply it to your life. Sit back and contemplate it. The Torah was far too vast to be given all at once and without hafsakot, even to Moshe Rabbeinu. Even the Torah we learn at TanenbaumCHAT is simply too vast and overwhelming to be fully understood in a short period of time.

This message resonates particularly with the approaching chag of Pesach. Seder night encompasses the entire sweep of Jewish history, from Avraham Avinu to the future redemption. Pesach is filled with concepts that can go far over our heads and leave us very empty, when they should fill us with emotional charges. The only way to fully appreciate the chag, just like our Torah studies, is to take a step back, expand our usual narrow view, and let everything sink in.

Show the King Your Beauty
By Becky Friedman

In the Haftara for Parshat Zachor, which is this week, we read about King Shaul's failure to fulfill G-d's commandment. In the Torah reading for Zachor, we are commanded to remember Amalek and to wipe them out; Shaul, commanded by G-d a *second* time to wipe Amalek out, completely ignores this instruction and keeps Agag, the king of Amalek, alive.

Zachor, the parsha before Purim, is generally said to be connected intrinsically to Purim because Agag, the king Shaul failed to kill, became an ancestor of Haman; tragically, if Shaul had done as he was told, the Jews would never have been imperilled in the story of Purim.

But that's not the connection I'm looking at today. When the prophet Shmuel confronts Shaul about his failure to heed G-d's command, he tells him that G-d will take the kingship from Shaul and will give it to "your fellow who is better than you."

Now flip ahead in your Tanach from Sefer Shmuel to Megillat Ester. When Queen Vashti fails to appear before King Achashverosh as per his command, the king's advisor Memuchan (often identified with Haman) suggests that she be banished, and her queenship given to "her fellow who is better than her."

Of course, careless translators obscure this commonality, but there it is: but for tense changes to accomodate for the shifts from male to female and from second to third person, the exact words of what Shmuel said.

How do we explain this similarity? Do we just dismiss it as a coincidence? After all, it's highly unlikely that Memuchan had read Sefer Shmuel and chosen his words accordingly. Nevertheless, it's in the Tanach. Nothing is an accident.

Vashti is too often dismissed as a literary device to pave the way for Ester to become queen. She is often, also, used as a paragon of feminism, by those who interpret the king's request for her to appear in her royal crown as a request for her to appear in that *and nothing else*, which she admirably refused.

Then there's the third understanding of Vashti, also tossed around often enough, but worth repeating: Vashti as a metaphor for the Jewish people.

I know, I know, I'm crazy, she's the *non-Jewish* queen-- but please bear with me for a moment.

Megillat Ester is famous for G-d's name never appearing once, and because of that, people search for G-d everywhere in it. Add to that the historical context: while it's difficult to determine *exactly* when it took place, it's almost certain that it was *after* the Declaration of Coresh-- that is to say, Mordochai and Ester and all the other Jews in Persia *could* have gone back to Israel, but didn't. When the text introduces Mordochai, it goes to great lengths to explain that he ended up in Persia because he'd been exiled there, even using the word 'exile' three times. It starts to sound like an excuse.

Back to Vashti. So the king asks his wife to show everyone how beautiful she is. She refuses; he gets angry. Haman suggests that her queenship be rescinded, and given to her fellow who is better than her.

Now compare: G-d asks His people, via Coresh, to show the other nations how 'beautiful' they are in their worship of Him by returning to his land. The vast majority of them-- including Mordochai and Ester-- refuse. Haman tries to destroy them. Keep in mind, also, that throughout Biblical literature, G-d's relationship with His people is often compared to the relationship of a husband and wife.

Start to see it? There is, of course, one puzzle piece missing. One thing that will cement the allegory.

In sefer Shmuel, G-d asks Shaul-- as king, the representative of His people-- to show the world how 'beautiful' Bnei Yisrael are in their worship of G-d by completely destroying Amalek. Shaul refuses. Verdict: his kingship will be rescinded, *and given to his fellow who is better than him*.

As with Shaul, so too, with Vashti-- and so, too, with the nation of Israel. G-d calls, we don't answer. We lose out.

May we all show the nations our beauty in obeying G-d; may we all be the "better fellow" who receives G-d's reward.

Undeserved Cookies Are Tastier
By Matthew Goodman

The last Parsha in Sefer Shemot, Parshat Pekudei, relates that Klal Yisrael completed the construction of the Mishkan. The Torah tells us that "the cloud covered the Tent of Meeting, and the glory of Hashem filled the Mishkan. Moshe could not enter the Tent of Meeting because the cloud rested upon it" (Shemot 40:34-35). Our Parsha, the first in Sefer Vayikra, begins by telling us that, amidst this setting, Hashem "called (Vayikra) to Moshe, and Hashem spoke to him from the Tent of Meeting, saying..." (Vayikra 1:1).

If you look at the text of a Sefer Torah, the word "Vayikra" is written with a small aleph. This makes the word look like it's actually "Vayiker" rather than "Vayikra." As opposed to connoting a calling out to someone, "Vayiker," from the word, "Mikreh," happening, connotes an occurrence that happens simply by chance. It is used to describe the contact between Hashem and the non-Jewish prophet Bilaam (Bamidbar 23:16), who was given prophecy only because Hashem deemed it necessary to protect the Jewish people. Jewish prophets strive to build tremendously strong and powerful relationships with Hashem, and thus they are called to with love. Sometimes, however, it is necessary for Hashem to contact non-Jews, though the communication is one driven by necessity rather than relationship. It is nothing more than a happenstance.

It seems, then, that by using a small alef, the pasuk is attempting to downgrade Moshe's level of prophecy to that of Bilaam's. This is unbelievably odd! Moshe Rabbeinu was the greatest Navi to ever live. He talked to Hashem "face to face," a level of prophecy that no other prophet had in the history of the Jewish people! The Torah tells us, "Mouth to mouth do I speak to him, in a clear vision and not in riddles; at the image of G-d does he gaze" (Bamidbar 12:8). How could the Torah possibly insinuate that Moshe's relationship with Hashem was as base as Bilaam's?

Rashi seems to ignore this insinuation altogether, and says just the opposite. Hashem did, indeed, "call out" to Moshe. In fact, before all the utterances, all the sayings, and all the commandments that Hashem gave to Moshe, was a call. This calling is a term of endearment (Lashon Chiba), a language that the angels on high utilize. However, in revealing Himself to the prophets of the other nations, Hashem revealed Himself in a fleeting, impure fashion, as it says, "The Almighty happened upon Bilaam."

What does the pasuk really mean? What is it trying to teach us? How could Rashi explain that Moshe was contacted lovingly and endearingly, while the pasuk itself, with the little aleph, insinuates just the opposite?

The Rosh, HaRav Asher ben Yechiel (13th century), in his Torah commentary "Hadar Zekeinim", explains that Moshe Rabbeinu purposefully intended to write a small alef in the word "Vayikra." He felt uncomfortable to have his name appear right at the beginning of the Sefer. He pleaded with Hashem to indicate in the Torah that he felt uneasy about being called into the Mishkan. Thus, Moshe Rabbeinu wrote in a small alef, alluding to his fantastic humility. The Rosh's son, the Ba'al HaTurim (on Vayikra 1:1), adds that, by minimizing the alef, Moshe intentionally made the word seem like "Vayiker," downgrading his own level of prophecy. In this way, Moshe was able to downplay the fact that Hashem really called out to him with a tremendously loving and affectionate invitation to enter the Mishkan. Similarly, the Paneach Raza (on Vayikra 1:1) asks, Why is the aleph of the word Vayikra smaller than the other letters of the Torah? It answers that this is in order to show that, although Hashem called to Moshe, and although He showed Moshe tremendous respect by constantly speaking to him, Moshe always lessened himself before Hashem and before Bnei Yisrael.

Really, the pasuk was meant to read "Vayikra" without any abnormal augmentations, and it still stands to connote the fact that Hashem's call was one of love. The small alef was a compromise reached by Hashem and Moshe that retains that original meaning of the verse, yet subtly alludes to Moshe's humility.

I think, however, that there is far more to this explanation than what meets the eye. The Torah is not simply teaching us about Moshe's humility, which is, in fact, mentioned multiple other times. It's giving us a unique look into the relationship between Moshe and Hashem. Hashem loved Moshe, and Moshe loved Hashem, but he was very humble about it. This created an amazing relationship that was literally filled with light.

The Torah tells us that, after Moshe descended from Mount Sinai with the two tablets in his hands, "Karnei Or," beams of light, emanated from his face (Shemot 34:29). From that point on, Moshe would keep a covering over his face. Every time Moshe went to speak to Hashem, he would remove the covering, and his face would become radiant. When he repeated Hashem's words to the people, he would keep his face uncovered, so that the would see that "the skin of Moshe's face had become radiant," and then he would replace the covering.

The Midrash (Shemot Rabba 47) tells us that when Moshe finished writing the Torah, a drop of ink remained on his quill. He smeared the ink on his forehead, which resulted in his face becoming radiant with Karnei Or. The Midrash begs for explanation. How could there have possibly been extra ink on Moshe's quill? Wouldn't Hashem have been able to give Moshe exactly enough ink to transcribe the entire Torah? We can answer this question using our pasuk in Vayikra. Since Moshe compromised with Hashem to write a small alef as opposed to a normal-sized one, he had a bit of leftover ink. That ink caused his face to glow, and on every subsequent occasion that Moshe spoke to Hashem, his face would be filled with these Karnei Or.

Moshe's humility caused his face to be filled with light every time he talked to Hashem. Every single time! That one display of humility towards his relationship with Hashem greatly invigorated his connection with Him. This, however, is a difficult concept to understand. How did Moshe's humility achieve this? How did downplaying his spiritual greatness cause Moshe's face to light up when he spoke with Hashem?

Imagine if you had a societal right to receive a daily package of chocolate chip cookies. The Canadian government passed legislation that said, "Every Canadian deserves to have chocolate chip cookies every single day." For the first few days, you'd probably be quite excited at the notion, but this excitement would inevitably die down after a while. Furthermore, you'd most likely begin this new era of free cookies with a tremendous appreciation for the baked goods, savouring and cherishing each cookie given to you. Soon after, however, I'd suppose that your reaction and appreciation would be far more subdued. If society ingrained within you the feeling that you deserve cookies every single day, you would slowly but surely become less and less enthusiastic about them. It is a psychological truth that when we are used to something, to the point that we feel that we deserve it, our appreciation, love, and excitement for that thing are immensely diminished. On a mundane level, this certainly applies to physical items. Cookies, for instance. But on a far deeper level, it is just as evident that these truths apply to human beings, as well. And certainly to Hashem.

Now imagine, on the other hand, that, once a week, on, let's say, Shabbos, your mother bakes your family chocolate chip cookies. As opposed to something that you deserve, it is inherently a special treat baked specifically for a special day. It is a privilege, not a right, to get them. How much more delicious do you think they would be, compared to the cookies that you 'deserve' to get? How much more special, meaningful, and exciting are things when they come as gifts and privileges, as opposed to warranted rights? How much more thankful and appreciative are we of them?

Moshe's face radiated light, Karnei Or, every single time he talked with Hashem. Every time. And it was because Moshe approached Hashem with the utmost humility. His prophecy, as far as he was concerned, was completely and utterly undeserved. It was an amazing privilege to speak to Hashem, a rare and precious opportunity. To Moshe it was a fortuitous happenstance, as opposed to an expected phenomenon. This enabled him to have an unbelievably powerful and strong connection with his Creator. It was a privilege for him to have a relationship with Hashem, and, thus, his relationship was consistently filled with love and affection. This explanation fully answers our original question. The pasuk was able to insinuate that Moshe's prophecy was equivalent to the lesser status of Bilaam's, for, in Moshe's eyes, that was the case. Rashi, despite this insinuation, was able to point out that "Vayikra" is really a term of love and endearment -- a call to Moshe to come closer and enter the Mishkan-- as it was, indeed, just that.

Life has the uncanny ability to allow us to, unfortunately, take many of our relationships for granted, be they relationships between us and Hashem, or between us and family, friends, relatives, spouses, etc. This lesson from the Parsha needs to become a critical aspect of our overall outlook on life. We have to see absolutely everything as something that we don't deserve. That is the greatest tool to ensure that every single relationship we have is invigorated with a sense of appreciation and affection. When someone else is a part of our life or gives to us, and we are convinced that the presence or kindness is undeserved, then the presence or kindness can only be seen as a display of care and love. A child who expects to be waited upon by a parent cannot truly comprehend or appreciate the parent's affection. A child who feels his parent's care is a privilege, something completely undeserved, will have a much easier time realizing that his parent loves him very much. When relating to Hashem, if we deeply feel that all the good He bestows upon us is an act of immense kindness, we will become far more cognizant of His abundant love.

With a little bit of humility, we, too, will have our faces shine brightly when we connect with those whom we love and who love us back.

Tzav • צו

This Parsha has been generously sponsored by Pearl Schusheim and Moshe Ipp in honour of their children

Transcending Time
By Matthew Goodman

"And Hashem spoke to Moshe, saying: Command (Tzav) Aaron and his sons, saying, this is the law of the burnt offering; that is, the burnt offering which burns on the altar all night until morning..." (Vayikra 6:1-2)

"And you shall guard (U'shmartem) the matzot, for on this same day I brought your armies out of the land of Egypt, and you shall observe this day throughout your generations as a law forever" (Shemot 12:17)

Have you ever felt that you had so much to do and so little time in which to do it? Have you ever wanted to take some time out of your schedule for someone else, only to realize that you had no time to give? Have you ever wanted to do an act of kindness, but rejected the opportunity, simply because you had no time?

Time is a topic discussed in this week's Parsha. Rashi explains that the term "Tzav" (command) always denotes an urging to promptly and meticulously fulfill a commandment. The Talmud (Kiddushin 29a) also teaches: "The Academy of R' Yishmael taught: whenever "tzav" is stated, its only purpose is to denote an encouragement to quickness." Rashi has a similar understanding of the use of the term "U'shmartem" (found in the second quote above). One is meant to guard the matzot, so that they do not become Chometz. Rebbi Yoshia said, don't read the words as *Matzot*, but as *Mitzvot*. Just as you should not let the Matzoh become Chometz, you should not let a Mitzvah become spoiled. When a Mitzvah comes into your hands, perform it immediately.

The comparison between Matzot and Mitzvot is not immediately clear.

Matzah must be made in no more than 18 minutes, or else the water sits with the flour for too long and the mixture becomes Chometz. Therefore, the commandment to "guard" the Matzot requires speed. The Matzot are used for the performance of one Mitzvah which can only be fulfilled two nights each year, and only for a limited number of hours. Not all Mitzvot, however, have such time restrictions. For many, time has no effect, no specific urgency in their performance. Furthermore, a Mitzvah is an expression of love and creates a relationship with Hashem. Why would it be something that needs to be rushed through? It should be done meticulously, made to last, and performed with emotion. To think of a Mitzvah as something that has to be gotten out of the way is simply the wrong attitude!

The Maharal explains that a Mitzvah is really the link between the physical and metaphysical. Therefore, the performance of a Mitzvah with speed is an expression of a person's desire to leave the constrained confines of the physical world and enter into a spiritual plane of existence. Essentially, the physical world is defined by time. The spiritual is embodied by Hashem, who transcends time. A Mitzvah allows us to break through the limits of the clock.

Pesach is the holiday that transcends time. While enslaved in Egypt, Hashem gave the Jewish people multiple commandments, all time-oriented, before they became physically and spiritually free. The first Mitzvah Bnei Yisrael were given was to sanctify the new month. They were then commanded to guard the Paschal Lamb for a precise period, and instructed on precise times for its slaughter and eating. They were told to eat in haste. And obviously the Matzah itself was prepared rapidly. The entire Chag revolved around this concept of doing a commandment with speed. The reason is that doing a Mitzvah with speed is a demonstration that time does not matter. The Jewish people went from being a nation of slaves to masters of time itself.

Practically, what does this mean? Your performance of Mitzvot is not subjugated to the confines of time. Many have to be done according to timely specifications. All should be done the moment the opportunity comes into your hand. But no Mitzvah can be rejected because of time constraints. Even if you are the busiest person in the world, working 24/6, there is always time to do a Mitzvah, because the fulfillment of creating a connection to Hashem does not bow, unlike us, to the clock. The next time you say to yourself, I can't do this because I am too busy, I can't help someone because I am too busy, I can't give tzedakah because I am too busy, remember that busy has nothing to do with it. That word does not exist when it comes to acting according to the Torah.

The next time you have an opportunity to do a Mitzvah, relish it, and act. If Reuven comes up to you and says, "Shimeon, I really need help in math," and you have your own math test tomorrow, help Reuven. If Reuven asks you, "Shimeon, would you like to donate money to TanenbaumCHAT's UJA week fundraiser," and you are rushing to go somewhere, donate. And if your heart tells you, "Embrace Shabbos," and you have a ton of homework and very little time in which to finish it, embrace Shabbos anyway. A Mitzvah transcends time, so there is always time to do a Mitzvah.

Our Father, Our Master
By Zachary Zarnett-Klein

As we get ready to celebrate Pesach in just a few days' time, it is interesting to take a look at how the first two Parshiot in the book of Vayikra, which we read in the first two Shabatot of Nisan leading up to Pesach, relate to each other and to the holiday. These two Parshiot start off on different paths right from the beginning. Vayikra comes from the verb "to call". This gives a feeling of love and of G-d reaching out to the Children of Israel to give them his commandments. On the other hand, Tzav comes from the verb "to command". The quick transition from a softer call to a harsher one shows a different personality of the Almighty. This shift from a father, a merciful G-d who helps Israel through all hardships, to a strict master with tough rules to follow, is surely present throughout the Parshiot.

In the Haftarah for Vayikra, G-d does not hesitate to show his compassion and unconditional fatherly love for Israel. G-d expresses, "I fashioned this people for Myself that they might declare My praise." These words highlight G-d's desire for Israel to rejoice in his holiness by showing how he blesses them with the Mitzvot and beautiful traditions which we, as Jews, hold so dear.

Conversely, the qualities of a master and judge surface right at the beginning of the Haftarah for Shabbat HaGadol, which this year coincides with Parashat Tzav. It is written, "I will draw near to you for the judgement... against those who do not fear Me, says G-d, Master of Legions." Here, as in the Parashah, G-d shows his intolerance for rebellious behaviour. G-d teaches that while he is loving, caring, and pleasing to serve, all Israel must fear him and show proper respect and obedience to his commandments, so that we may all prosper in a fruitful relationship.

While it is intriguing to see these two personae of G-d, it is somewhat odd to see these diverse characters in Parshiot that are read one after the other. This is where the holiday of Pesach comes into play. The Children of Israel are slaves in Egypt, and in order to be set free, they must learn to find an admiration for G-d and follow his Mitzvot. Once they learn both these things, it is clear that they were subject to slavery in Egypt because of their stubborn ways, and they make the changes required for redemption.

This chase after G-d continues in the present day, and as we sit down at our Seder tables, may we all recognize that the qualities of being a Father and being a Master are what make this holiday, and every day for Jews, holy, meaningful, and special.

Shemini • שְׁמִינִי

Dancing Before the Lord
By Becky Friedman

In the Haftarah for Parshat Shmini, King David finally brings the Ark of G-d to Yerushalaim, and there is a big celebration. David himself dances wildly in commemoration of this event. When he comes home, his wife (one of the many), Michal, criticizes him for making himself look like an idiot in front of the people. David responds that he has nothing to be ashamed of, because he was dancing before G-d. At the end of this incident, the narration in Sefer Shmuel mentions that Michal had no children.

Doesn't that seem like a very harsh punishment for such a small reproof?! Moreover, the pasuk telling us this seems very abrupt, almost as if it were a non-sequitur.

In fact, it is not necessarily a punishment that Michal never got to be a mother. Perhaps the pasuk tells that to us as though it were unrelated because it is not a punishment. Nevertheless, the question remains: why does Michal have no children?

There are two answers: the pedantic one and the relevant one.

The pedantic answer is that it's just good politics. Michal was married to Palti ben Laish for many years, while David was on the run from King Shaul; any children she might have once she returned to David would always have their royal lineages suspect. People might think that these were the children of Palti and not David; better that she have no children, to avoid that type of confusion.

Then, of course, there is the relevant answer-- the better answer.

Michal could not stand the idea of David lowering himself in the eyes of their servants, even though he was at the same time exalting G-d. She deemed any sort of immature behaviour as innappropriate, regardless of context.

As we know, children are very difficult to take care of, and they are, by nature-- childish. If Michal disapproved of David when he was dancing before G-d, how much more would she be upset were the purpose not so holy!

Michal was not personally equipped to deal with frivolity, with immaturity. Should a woman who reproves her husband for dancing before G-d be expected to be a good mother? Michal's childlessness, though of course tragic in the abstract for people who love small children, was a blessing for her; she displays in this incident with David that she is not capable of dealing with a childish mentality.

In the parsha, it says that Aharon's two oldest sons, Nadav and Avihu, die after sacrificing a "foreign fire" to G-d. In reference to this, G-d says to Aharon, "Bikrovai Akadesh" (by those close to Me, I shall be sanctified); Aharon is silent.

These passages are very difficult, and have been interpreted in any number of contradictory manners. One way to look at it is to see it as the flip side of the Haftarah.

"Bikrovai Akadesh" could be seen as comfort or reproof. It could be meant as comfort, telling Aharon that G-d will be sanctified by Aharon's sons, who are now with Him. It could, on the other hand, be a warning, telling Aharon that G-d will be sanctified by those close to Him, and *not* by those, such as Nadav and Avihu, who insist on sacrificing foreign fire. Aharon's silence may then be understood accordingly, either calmed and more at peace, or unable to answer the implied challenge.

There is room for both interpretations to be understood together. Perhaps Nadav and Avihu were very wrong in sacrificing this foreign fire-- and yet, as tzaddikim in all other respects throughout their lives, G-d is now sanctified through them despite their grave error.

Nadav and Avihu were so excited to be sacrificing to G-d in the new Mishkan that they added their own "foreign fire" after the sacrifices they had been commanded to make (Sifra Shemini Mekhilta deMiluim 99:5:4). Like David, their intentions were for the best-- they, too, were dancing before G-d. Because of this, though they died, G-d was sanctified through them; this was the bereaved Aharon's small comfort.

Michal didn't know when it was appropriate to start dancing before G-d; Nadav and Avihu didn't know when to stop. As a result, Michal could have no children, and Aharon's sons died. Certainly not consequences on a level with each other, but certainly both tragic to some degree, greater or smaller.

Between the Parsha and the Haftarah, we must find some sort of balance, somewhere in between Michal and Nadav and Avihu. It is important, every now and then, to dance before G-d, in moderation: don't glare at the dancers, and don't go too far, get too caught up. And those who dance before the Lord, He will be sanctified through them.

May we all have reason to dance before G-d; may we all have a sense of balance in our dancing; and may we be close to Him, that He be sanctified through us all.

Divrei Torah on **Vayikra**

Tazria • תַזְרִיעַ

The Bright Side of Life
By Matthew Goodman

The Parsha of Tazria details a very interesting concept in Jewish law. Hashem spoke to Moshe and Aaron, telling them that if a person who saw on his skin a lesion called Tzara'at, he should be taken to Aaron or the Kohanim to be inspected. If the lesion turned white and was deeper than his skin, he would be pronounced "impure." He must then be isolated from the community for a period of seven days, and then undergo a process of purification to rid him of his *Metzora* status. Tzara'at can also infect inanimate objects, specifically clothing and homes, and the Torah likewise deals with the required methods to inspect and declare the Tzara'at and purify the object.

In regard to clothing, the Torah tells us that the garment has to be quarantined for seven days, pending further inspection. If the lesion does not spread after that time period, the clothing is washed and quarantined again. Finally, we read: "Then the Kohen shall look at it, after the lesion has been washed. And, behold, the lesion has not changed in appearance (hanega lo hafach et eyno), and the lesion has not spread; it is impure. You shall burn it in fire" (Vayikra 13:55).

The Chidushei HaRim, by the Gerer Rebbe, HaRav Yitzchak Meir Alter (1799-1866), changes our understanding of the pasuk by augmenting the meaning of the line "the lesion has not changed in appearance." As opposed to interpreting the word "eyno" as "its appearance", it can alternatively read "its ayin," as in the letter Ayin. The novel explanation of the Gerer Rebbe is rooted in the interesting relationship between the word "Nega," spelled nun-gimmel-ayin, meaning lesion or affection, and "Oneg," spelled ayin-nun-gimmel, meaning pleasure or enjoyment. The only difference between the two words is the placement of the Ayin, while the nun and gimmel remain in the same order. Thus, the pasuk is really teaching a far deeper and more spiritual lesson. "Then the Kohen shall look at it...And, behold, the nega has not changed its Ayin...it is impure" - the Ayin has remained at the end of the word, as opposed to being moved to the front. The Nega remained an affliction, and did not become an Oneg.

Rav Yissochar Frand, Rosh Yeshiva of Ner Yisroel in Baltimore, explains that the difference between seeing a Nega or Oneg simply depends on where one places the Ayin, which also means "eye." Your perspective determines whether something is truly good or bad, and a Nega, something that appears to be an affliction, can actually become an Oneg, if you have the right attitude. The pasuk homiletically means that attitude towards the affliction of Tzara'at did not change, and thus the garment remained impure. There existed, however, the potential to see the situation as an Oneg, and that type of attitude could have saved the garment from destruction.

This explanation incurs a very obvious question: How could Tzara'at possibly be seen as something positive? It was a gruesome infection that, if contracted on skin, separated a person from the entire community for a full week. It caused the bearer to become ritually impure, and required a whole purification process. Furthermore, everyone would find out that the afflicted person was sent to solitary confinement. How could such a tragedy be seen as an Oneg?!

In order to properly answer this question, it is crucial to understand the cause of Tzara'at. This infectious disease was no ordinary infectious disease. It was actually a miraculous affliction induced by a spiritual malady. The Talmud (Arachin 15b-16a) tells us that it served as a punishment for people who had transgressed certain sins, among them Lashon HaRa, speaking badly about others. One who committed such an atrocity would be afflicted with the condition. Since the primary cause of Tzara'at was sin, and not natural disease, the Metzora was not instructed to see a doctor. Rather, he was told to see a Kohen.

Rav Alexander Moshe Lapidus (1819-1906), in Divrei Emet, explains that the function of the Kohen was to guide the Metzora through the process of Teshuva, repentance for his actions. As such, the Kohen was instructed by Hashem to quarantine one who had a definite case of Tzara'at for seven days. Since his actions separated people in the community (by speaking Lashon HaRa, he had created rifts between individuals), he was consequentially punished by being separated himself.

How could this Nega be seen as an Oneg? Tzara'at was a public display of Hashem's providence that encouraged individuals and the entire Klal to do teshuva. It was a unique opportunity to have Hashem Himself point out your sins and give you a specialized Teshuva process. That certainly does not happen nowadays. It is clear, therefore, that Tzara'at was really a blessing from Hashem, and it is doubtful that one who went through it would not be thankful for the opportunity to become a better person. In order to realize this Oneg, however, it was incumbent upon one to change his perspective on the situation.

The lesson of the Gerer Rebbe is one that should be applied to our entire outlook on life. Everything has the potential to be seen as a Nega or Oneg, and the only divergence between them is our perspective on the situation. The Ayin could be placed at the end of the word, looking backward at the letter, but it could be placed at the beginning of the word, looking forward and seeing the big picture. If we look at the situation from Hashem's eyes, we can realize that it really is an Oneg, an opportunity to learn and grow.

Rabbi Leib Kelemen, a Rebbi at Neve Yerushalayim, a woman's seminary in Jerusalem, tells the following story about perspective. A secular woman once came to visit him at the seminary. She had come to Israel for a short while, and, while at the Kotel, had met Rabbi Meir Schuster, founder of the Heritage House, who reconnects secular Jews with their Jewish identity. He had asked if she would like to visit a seminary, and she, excited at the prospect, quickly took up his offer. Rabbi Kelemen was available at the time, and Rabbi Schuster brought the woman in to see him.

She sat down in his office and said, "Rabbi, in a few weeks, I am going to have an operation that will effectively close my womb and deny me from having children. I want to know what you think."

Rabbi Keleman replied, "Well, what do you think I'll say?"

She looked at Rabbi Kelemen and then burst out, "If you'll tell me that I'm wrong, then you are crazy! You are all crazy!!! How can you bring children into the world? How could I bring a child into the world? There's so much pain! There's so much suffering! There's not enough food, there's not enough resources! There's not enough love! How could I possibly give birth to a baby!"

Rabbi Keleman answered her with a parable: "Imagine that you have a dream -- you want to become a surgeon, and you'll do anything to achieve your goal. You spend four years of high school in the library, studying, reading, working, aiming for that 4.0 GPA. You work tirelessly to get into university, and then work tirelessly in university. In medical school, you stay up studying into the early hours of the morning, devouring and memorizing books. Finally, many years later, you prepare to enter through the doors of the emergency room as a surgeon. Before you go in, someone comes running out, crying, 'It's terrible in there! There's so much pain! There's so much death! There are maimed bodies and torn limbs!' You, however, go in and start to heal.

If you come into this world looking to take, you're right. It's a terrible place. There's not enough resources. There's not enough love. There's a lot of suffering. But if you come into this world looking to give, the world is a dream come true."

A few years later, Rabbi Keleman received a postcard from the same woman, announcing the birth of her first child.

There are many things in life that can be seen as a Nega. Unfortunately, throughout our lives, we have to deal with many types of problems and suffering, from death to illness and everything in between. It is difficult to live with so much hardship. A slight change of attitude, however, can bring a lot of light into the world. That does not necessarily mean that one should rejoice at sickness or pain -- that is too much to ask. It does mean that one should use suffering as a step-stool for growth, and that we should try our best to consider the positive aspects of the situation. You'll be surprised at what you come up with.

Nega and Oneg are a world away. One connotes affliction, while the other connotes pleasure. Despite the distance, it only takes a small change in perspective, a single Ayin, to turn the worst of situations into something positive.

Divrei Torah on **Vayikra**

Metzora • מצורע

This Parsha has been generously sponsored by the Hoffer family

Desperate Measures
By Becky Friedman

This week's Haftarah teaches us the value that can sometimes lie in desperation. Necessity, as they say, is the mother of invention; the desperate measures taken in desperate times can sometimes lead to wondrous results.

The Haftarah opens on four *metzoraim*, people afflicted with leprosy who lived outside of society. Now, at the time, Shomron, their city and the capital of the kingdom of Yisrael, was under heavy siege by the army of Aram. Inflation was raging, and there was barely any food left. People throughout the city were starving.

So not only were these four lepers starving, but they were also diseased, and, as such, outsiders. If the city of Shomron was hopeless, they were even more hopeless than the rest. In their hopelessness, they realized that death was inevitable no matter what: if they remained on the outskirts of the city, they would die from starvation and disease; if they entered the city, they would likewise die from starvation and disease. With nothing left to lose-- not their lives, not their health-- they figured that they may as well venture out to the Aramean army's camp. After all, if they were killed, they would be no worse off than before, and if they could find food, they would be considerably better off.

Act of desperation number one; without this, none of what followed could have been possible.

What the *metzoraim* didn't know was that soon before they arrived at the enemy's camp, G-d had frightened away the army of Aram, who left their camp and all their possessions in their flight from what G-d made them hear.

The lepers found the empty camp, and, after nourishing themselves from the pickings, were stricken with a guilty conscience. They reported to the officials in Shomron about the empty camp that they had found.

The king of Yisrael was suspicious; he assumed that the goods and so-called empty camp were a trap, meant to draw the Yisraelim into the open for an ambush.

Nevertheless, the city was desperate. Everyone would die of starvation if the situation continued for much longer. A servant of the king pointed this out; they were in such dire straits that it was worth it to check out the lepers' story. After all, he reasoned, so many of their men had died that they would hardly miss more, should the king prove right and the scouts be ambushed. What a terrible sentiment!-- And yet he was right, for in their desperation, they had little choice left.

The king's scouts found the story to be true, and the city of Shomron opened up to plunder the empty camp. Their siege was over, their fortunes restored; the prophet Elisha, who had foretold all this and been ridiculed for it, was vindicated.

When we have nothing left to lose, there is so much to be gained.

Divrei Torah on **Vayikra**

Acharei Mot • אחרי מות

Edible Food
By Idan Bergman

Of the few topics in this parasha, parashat Acharei Mot discusses the matter of the Jewish people's inhabitance in the Land of Israel. Without getting into any political controversies, the Torah itself makes it clear that the Jewish people have a divine right to live in *Eretz Yisrael*.

The parasha discusses certain abominations of "nakedness" or *ta'ava*, as well as worship of pagan deities just to name a few, which are all forbidden by *Halacha* and that we are to refrain from.

Not only are these forbidden acts, the Torah directly relates these transgressions to nations that once lived in *Eretz Israel* before the Jewish people and were expelled because of these actions; Hashem advises the Jewish people to "not become impure through any of these [abominations]," and reminds them that "through all of these the nations that I expel before you became impure" (Vayikra 18:24). The Torah then states that *Eretz Yisrael* "vomited out [these] inhabitants" because of their actions (18:25).

The Torah continues on to write that Hashem commands us "to safeguard [His] decrees and [His] judgments, and not commit any of these abominations" (18:26). Hashem then seems to promise unconditionally that "the Land will *not* vomit you out when you contaminate it as it had vomited out the nation that was before you" (18:28).

For this last pasuk, Rashi brings a parable: *This [pasuk] can be compared to a prince whom they fed something repulsive, which his stomach could not retain, and he vomited it out. So, too, Eretz Yisrael cannot retain sinners."* Here, Rashi compares the sensitivity *Eretz Yisrael* has for its wrongdoing inhabitants to that of a distinguished prince who was been fed inedible food.

Avigdor Boncheck, in his book *What's Bothering Rashi?*, highlights a question on Rashi. The parable seems to base being "vomited out" on whether the food is repulsive-- in other words, whether our, the Jewish people's, actions are worthy. Yet the pasuk, simply read, seems to make the *unconditional* statement that Hashem promises the Jewish people the land of Israel. This midrash then contradicts our pasuk!

With further analysis, the answer lies in the meaning of the first letter of the first word of the pasuk: *ve*, meaning "and". However, says Rabbi Boncheck, the word *ve* can have a number of different meanings, one of which can be "so that", and that is exactly the meaning in our pasuk here. When the Torah writes "And the Land will not vomit you out" (18:26), it is meant to also be read together with the prior pasuk: "To not commit any of these abominations" (18:24). When our pasuk is connected to this sentence, it now reads: "[Do] not commit any of these abominations... **so that** the Land will not vomit you out when you contaminate it."

Another question Avigdor Boncheck asks is how did Rashi know that this *"ve"* means "so that" and not "and"? The answer is quite evident, both from various texts in the Torah and from history. For example, there are parts of the *Shma* that warn and threaten us with expulsion from *Eretz Yisrael* if our actions are sinful. As well, it is a known fact that the Jewish people were exiled-- "vomited out"-- from *Eretz Yisrael* more than once in our course of existence. It is likely that, with these understandings in mind, Rashi knew, in hindsight, that a conditional inheritance to the land must have been the meaning of the pasuk, and that *Eretz Yisrael* does not tolerate abominable behaviour to happen in its midst.

May we all, unlike in the parable, be the *edible* food in the prince's belly!

Passover: A Story of Social Justice
By Elianne Neuman

This week, we read Parshat Acharei Mot, and we will celebrate the holiday of Pesach. While reading the Parsha, I noticed a sentiment which, I believe, connects the weekly Torah portion to this holiday.

At the end of the Parsha, G-d relates to Bnei Yisrael the necessity of maintaining the holiness of the land of Israel and the imperative to keep the mitzvot. The Torah states, "You should safeguard (*ushmartem atem*) my decrees and my judgements."

Why does the verse say 'you' twice (*ushmartem atem*)? It seems as though the second 'you' is superfluous!

According to the commentaries, the context of the verse is that G-d has now given the Jews a tremendous responsibility: to set up courts in the land of Israel and ensure that the society is moral and just. The Or HaChaim says that in order to encourage the Jewish people and assure them that this is a task they can accomplish, G-d specifically adds the superfluous 'you', to remind them that had escaped assimilation in Egypt; surely they could maintain purity in their own land.

Bnei Yisrael not only failed to assimilate into Egyptian society, they also became advocates for societal change, and stood up against the ruling powers in Egypt. How so? Before the tenth and final plague, G-d instructed every household of Bnei Yisrael to tie a lamb or a kid to their bedposts for four days, slaughter it, and spread its blood upon their doorposts. This Pesach offering was a revolutionary act in Egypt, for the Egyptians revered lambs and similar animals as gods. To treat a god in such a manner was unspeakable in Egyptian society; thus, the Jews were risking their lives by undertaking this act.

Bnei Yisrael performed the Pesach offering, despite the potential consequences. The Jews knew that the Egyptians would be infuriated to see their G-ds treated in such a manner, but every single household-- by partaking in the offering-- chose to show the Egyptians that they were wrong: the lambs that they revered were not gods. There was only one G-d. He was powerful and mighty. And He would take the embittered slaves from Egypt into freedom.

Now, in Parshat Acharei Mot, G-d instructs, "You should safeguard (*ushmartem atem*) my decrees." The verse's superfluous use of the word 'you' is not simply to remind the Jews that they had failed to assimilate into Egyptian society; it also serves to note that they had chosen to be advocates of change and openly refute the values of the Egyptians. They had been willing to establish a new moral code in Egypt; it is now incumbent upon them, as they enter their own land, to renew the vows they made on the night of the Pesach offering: to stand up for what is right, to pursue justice, and to safeguard the mitzvot.

This Pesach, I hope we will all reflect on the strength that the Jews had in Egypt, and the power it took for Bnei Yisrael to stand up and deny the values of Egyptian society. Hopefully, we will all commit ourselves to strive for true justice.

Chag Sameach to you and your families.

Kedoshim • קדושים

Word Power
By Rebecca Silver

"Great minds discuss ideas. Average minds discuss events. Small minds discuss people."
-Sign in a pizza shop, Miami Beach, FL.

In this week's parshah, Kedoshim, fifty-one mitzvot are given to B'nei Yisrael. One of the many mitzvot mentioned discusses the concept of lashon harah (gossip). The pasuk reads, "Do not be a *rachil* among your people" (Vayikra 19:17). The word *rachil* is difficult to translate. The Ra'avad translates it as 'gossipmonger' and compares it to the word *rochel*, meaning a merchant. Just as a merchant goes around to different towns buying and selling goods, a gossiper finds out information about people and spreads it to others.

Rebbetzin Esther Jungreis, in her book *Life is a Test*, shares that no matter what situation we are in, there is a parallel situation that occurred in the Torah to which we can relate. The key is to go to the source. The first occurrence of lashon harah in the Torah is found in Bereishit, when the snake convinces Chava to eat from the tree of knowledge of good and evil. The snake asks Chava if she is allowed to eat from any of the trees in the garden. Chava responds that she may eat from every tree except for the tree in the middle of the garden, the tree of knowledge of good and evil, for if she touches its fruit or eats from it, she will die. The snake responds slyly by saying, "You will surely not die; for G-d knows that on the day you eat of it, your eyes will be opened and you will be like G-d, knowing good and bad" (Bereishit 3:4-5).

The Midrash in Bereishit Rabba (19:4) explains that the snake was really speaking lashon harah about Hashem by saying that He ate from the tree of knowledge and was then able to create the world, and did not want Adam or Chava to eat from it, too, so that they would not be able to create their own worlds and compete with Hashem.

Since the snake spoke lashon harah about Hashem, all of mankind was punished with death; man was no longer immortal. As well, the snake's punishment follows the concept of Midah Keneged Midah (measure for measure): the serpent caused death; therefore, man seeks to kill him. This story exemplifies the significance of speaking destructive words. Lashon harah is so horrible and detrimental that it caused man to be mortal when the snake's gossip caused Adam and Chava to sin.

How do we know that lashon harah is considered to be so damaging? Rambam, in Hilchot Deot (7:4), warns that there are three sins that take a person away from this world and deny him a portion in the world to come: idol worship, forbidden sexual relations, and murder -- but lashon harah is equivalent to them all. It seems pretty obvious that murder, idolatry and forbidden sexual relations are all really awful sins that deserve major punishment, but it's hard to imagine that something as relatively small as gossip could be worse than all three of those combined!

It is odd that gossip is commonly practiced in modern society, when Judaism holds that it is so destructive. What can we do to change our behaviour in order to stay away from it?

Before we attempt to deal with these questions, let's define exactly what lashon harah is. Lashon harah is any derogatory or damaging statement against an individual. Rambam, in Hilchot Deot (7:5), gives a test to help us figure out whether what we say could be considered gossip: anything which, if publicized, would cause the subject physical or monetary damage, or would cause him anguish or fear, is lashon harah.

How can we apply this definition to our lives? There are two simple principles that, if followed, can lead to a much healthier and gossip-free life. However, it is important to keep in mind that these two suggestions are only the tip of the iceberg, and there are many more complicated issues involving lashon harah. There are numerous books that detail its intricate laws; for beginners, I highly recommend the book *Gossip: Ten Pathways to Eliminate it From Your life and Transform Your Soul* by Lori Palatnik and Bob Burg.

One way to eliminate lashon harah from your life is through speaking no evil. In order to achieve this, it is important to give people the benefit of the doubt (in Hebrew, *Dan et kol adam b'caf zchut*), so that we are not incited to speak badly about them. If you have plans to meet with your friend at a coffee shop at a particular time, and he doesn't show up after ten minutes, thirty minutes, even an hour and a half, it's very easy to be fuming and upset that your friend didn't even have the courtesy to call and cancel! Your friend wasted your time and should have been more thoughtful, right? In such a situation, we must judge him favourably. Maybe there was a car accident on the highway, causing bumper-to-bumper traffic for hours, and your friend forgot his cell phone at home in a rush to meet you on time. Or perhaps your friend had a family emergency, G-d forbid, and was in such a rush to get to the hospital that he completely forgot to call and cancel. There are many different ways to give someone the benefit of the doubt, and maintaining that mindset can not only really help you to think the best of others, thereby improving your relationships, but can also cause you to stop yourself from speaking badly about others. You'll have no reason to assume something negative about your friend, and therefore will have nothing destructive to share with others.

Another way to stay away from lashon harah is by hearing no evil. If you are standing in the hallway during lunch while talking to a friend, and the conversation suddenly turns towards the latest gossip, you can steer the conversation in a new direction-- for example, bring up a funny story that happened to your dog over the weekend-- that does not involve harmful information about others. If your friend still manages to move back to discussing other people, you can walk away and join another conversation.

Speech is an extremely powerful and influential gift that Hashem has given us. In fact, it is so powerful that Hashem created the world through speech. If words have the ability to create a world or to destroy a life, then clearly Hashem has given us a huge responsibility to treat this gift appropriately. Good Shabbos!

Emor • אמור

Hidden in Plain Sight
By Aaron Goldberg

There is a certain story in Parshat Emor that is clouded in obscurity. Not only does it seem out of place, but it is definitely a contender for being the hardest-to-find story in the entire Torah. At the very end of Parshat Emor, we find the story of the blasphemer. As the story goes, a man, who had a Jewish mother and an Egyptian father, gets into a fight with another Jewish man. The son of a Jewish mother and an Egyptian father curses G-d's name, and, as punishment, is stoned to death by all who heard him.

This story is so hard to find because it hardly seems to fit in with its surroundings. Immediately preceding the story are laws relating to the Festivals and the Temple, while immediately following the story are laws relating to the Sabbatical and Jubilee years. In fact, the closest narrative to this story can only be found after going back eight chapters. Clearly, there must be something special about this story that puts it in such a place.

Simply put, the answer is as follows. The previous sections describe how one is to worship G-d, and this story represents what happens when one goes against such. But this answer is much too shallow, and doesn't fully satisfy the question. Why *blasphemy*?

This last question may lead to the answer. Blasphemy is the epitome of rebellion against G-d. In blaspheming, the man not only publicly declares that he does not believe in G-d's commandments; he is waging war on the very idea of G-d! This man in effect reneges on all of the commandments surrounding this story!

But why? Why was he so opposed to mainstream society? The answer lies in the Torah's description of him – "The son of an Israelite woman... and he was the son of an Egyptian man." Time and time again, the Torah refers to him by his lineage, but never states his personal name. This implies that his family was to blame for his actions! The situation in which he was raised caused him to rise up against G-d, owing, no doubt, to the lack of certain morals imparted upon him by his family.

However, that is not all. What leads to this man's blasphemy? He gets into a fight in the camp with another man. His blasphemous feelings are provoked by the fight, which causes him to curse G-d.

From this we learn a valuable lesson. Yes, each person is responsible for his actions. But more importantly, Jews as a nation are responsible for the entire population's actions. If one person fails, it is a result of society's failure. Rather than blame one person, the entire Jewish nation must be blamed. Even further, the solution to this problem lies in the placement of this story. How would this incident have been prevented? By performing the commandments between fellow men in their proper fashion. By doing the little things that keep people moral, the blasphemer would never have felt the need to go against the entire nation. Maybe he would have kept those same thoughts, but he never would have used them against a people who displayed kindness inside and out. In making the pilgrimages for the Festivals, the Jews need to act as a *nation* of homogeneous morals. In observing the Sabbatical year, the Jews need to act with compassion in releasing their slaves. In all actions, every single person must strive to conduct himself with the utmost respect for his fellow people. Only once we prevent the incident of the blasphemer will we have truly carried out all of the commandments surrounding it.

Divrei Torah on **Vayikra**

Behar/Bechukotai • בהר/בחוקותי

Walking with Torah
By Matthew Goodman

"If you walk with My statutes and observe My commandments and perform them..." (Vayikra 26:3)

The Torah came in two forms. When Klal Yisrael was given the Torah for the first time on Har Sinai, it was given as the "Luchot HaBrit," tablets of the law, containing the Ten Commandments-- etched by the hand of Hashem on blocks of stone. At the end of Moshe Rabbeinu's life, the Torah was inscribed again, handwritten on parchment scroll.

The Ba'al HaTanya (Shneur Zalman of Liadi) explains that when something is written, the substance of the letters, namely, the ink that forms the very words, remains a separate entity. An addition to to the parchment, rather than part of the parchment. Engraved letters, on the other hand, are forged into the stone. The words are stone and the stone is words.

The name of the second part of this week's Parsha is "Bechukotai", meaning, "My statutes", stemming from the word "Chok," law. But "Bechukotai" can also mean "engraved," from the word "chakuk."

Torah can be understood partly as something "inked" on our soul. A concept we understand, something that can resonate with our lives, even become our lifestyle. It will always remain as ink on a page, an addition to ourselves. Yet it can also be compared to something that is "chakuk." There is a dimension of Torah that expresses an engraved bond with Hashem that is part of our very being. Rav Yosef Yitzchak of Lubavitch explains that every Jew is a letter carved in stone. At times, the dust and dirt may accumulate and distort, or even conceal, the letter's true form. But underneath it all, the letter remains whole.

The first pasuk of Parshat Bechukotai teaches us just how special Torah is, in that it is an intrinsic, innate part of a Jew's very soul. It is who we are. As such, the pasuk basically reads, "if you walk with this engraving..." which leaves us with a vividly clear question: why on earth are we meant to walk? If Hashem meant to say "observe My chukim," the pasuk would seem awfully redundant, as the next few words reads read, "and observe My commandments!" For some strange reason, Hashem is telling us specifically to walk.

Anything that is part of your spiritual being is going to grow as you grow. We constantly work on improving ourselves and on becoming kinder, more selfless, more respectful, and more spiritual people. It takes ridiculous amounts of time, energy, and introspection to even begin to achieve the changes we want to see in ourselves. Even at our young age, we have aspects of our personality that we seek to improve upon. However, especially at a young age, we tend to find these tasks to be unusually daunting.

It is excruciatingly hard to be able to look in the mirror, find something wrong with your personality, and change it. Many high school kids have a hard time even starting this process. But I am sure that we are not all perfect and that there are many aspects of ourselves that we wish to change-- even to change utterly and completely.

The Torah tells us that when we want to take something engraved in our souls, something that is part of who we are, and work on it, we have to pace ourselves. If we want to truly move and grow with those "chakukot," engravings, we have to walk. This is true for any form of lateral movement, whether it is becoming more observant, and embracing the engravings of Torah that are etched in our hearts, or working on our personality, and becoming better people-- for that, too, is growth in Torah.

Walking has to be taken very seriously. It means that we can only barely move at a snail's pace towards out destination, and we cannot, under any circumstances, run to the finish line. Every step forward is valuable. Every footprint leading in the right direction is in itself tremendous growth. Walk too slow and we will never be able to accomplish our potential distance. Run too fast and we will inevitably trip and fall. Take a look in the mirror, the Torah tells us, find one small thing that you can work on, set a reasonable goal, and start the journey.

Walk with your engraved Torah, and marvel at how far you can get.

Divrei Torah on **Vayikra**

We're Free! It's Jubilee!
By Zachary Zarnett-Klein

This week's Parashah, Behar-Bechukotai, begins by discussing the laws of Shemitah and Yovel. The Torah teaches us that we are permitted to work our land for six years, but in the seventh year we must let it rest and not grow anything. This practice is referred to as Shemitah.

A cycle of seven is used once again to determine when the Yovel will occur; Yovel is a year in which all Jewish slaves go free. The Yovel year is the year after a cycle of seven Shemitah years has been completed; in English it is called the Jubilee year. This event occurs every fifty years. Sound familiar?

We are also commanded to count seven weeks after the Omer offering is brought. The day after these seven weeks is known as Shavuot. Having just celebrated Lag B'omer this week, the commonality of numbers between these two events is key. How are they key, one might ask?

A Jubilee is an opportunity for immense change. A passage from this week's Parashah comprehensively explains the misfortunes that will befall Israel should they forsake G-d. This is followed up in the Haftarah by the prophet Yirmiyahu telling Israel that, should they refuse to rid themselves of the false G-ds in their midst, the world will meet complete destruction.

At this auspicious time of year, during the counting of the Omer, it is certainly the right time to evaluate our ways-- all the more so as we near Shavuot, the holiday on which the Torah was given to Israel. May we have the good fortune to find favour in G-d's eyes, with our renewed approach to life's challenges and an enhanced appreciation of G-d's miracles and mitzvot. We will then be able to truly rejoice, following the right path as described by the Torah and by the prophet Yirmiyahu.

Parent and Child
By Elianne Neuman

In this Parsha, Bnei Yisrael are presented with a deal: if we follow the ways of Hashem, we will be blessed, and if we neglect to uphold the Torah and the Mitzvot, we will be cursed.

The Torah describes the time that may come, when there will be so much sin that G-d will expel us from the land of Israel and the Jews will be "lost among the nations." But even then, G-d promises, no matter what happens, He will still remember the covenant with His people and will remember them.

This promise is immediately followed by the instructions for those who would like to bring voluntary contributions to the Temple. What is the connection between G-d's promise to the Jewish people and the laws on voluntary gifts to the Temple? Why would two such seemingly different topics be placed next to each other?

I would like to propose that this juxtaposition represents how G-d's relationship with Bnei Yisrael can be compared to that of a parent with a child. While G-d may be angered when Bnei Yisrael disregard the mitzvot and may even expel them from their land, He will always remember the covenant between them. Similarly, parents may be annoyed with children who don't follow their rules, and may even punish them, but they will always still have an attachment to their children.

G-d gives all the inhabitants of this earth a very precious gift: life. In return, G-d asks for a bit of recognition-- not because He is haughty, but because He wants us to understand that there is a greater power. So He instructs us in ways that we can show this recognition, one of them being the voluntary gifts that we can bring to the Temple. Similarly, parents give their children so much. They provide them with food and clothing, love and shelter. All they ask is for some affection and gratitude in return-- not because they are greedy, but because they want us to understand what they have done for us.

This is my last month at TanenbaumCHAT, and this is the last time that I will be contributing to the Shofar. If I could think of one last thought that I would want to write in this publication, it would be the message that can be learned from the juxtaposition of G-d's promise to His people and the instructions on voluntary gifts in this Parsha: G-d is like a parent, and He provides us with so much. Although there is suffering and hardship in this world, there is also a lot of good around us. Granted, that good may take a while to see, and it may take some time before we can fully appreciate it, but once we recognize all the good in this world, we should thank G-d as though expressing our appreciation to a loving and generous parent. Let us show our gratitude to G-d in return for all that He gives us.

וידבר יי אל משה במדבר סיני באהל מועד באחד לחדש השני בשנה

Bamidbar
במדבר

This Sefer of Chumash has been generously sponsored by

The Glasenberg Family

In honour of Akiva Yosef Dov Glasenberg,
who is enlisting in the IDF (Golani Brigade)

Bamidbar • במדבר

Where have the Leviim gone?
By Michali Glasenberg

This week, we start reading Sefer Bamidbar. The rabbis in the Talmud refer to Sefer Bamidbar as Sefer Pekudim, the Book of Counts, because of the two censuses that were taken in the desert, as described in Sefer Bamidbar. The first one was taken in the second year after Bnai Yisrael left Egypt, and the second one was taken in the fortieth year, just before they entered the land of Israel. The census counted every male over the age of twenty in each tribe. The Leviim, however, were counted by each male over a month old, as opposed to twenty years, adding up to only 22,000. Even counting the Leviim from one month and up, they were still less than any other tribe. The Ramban poses the question: why were the Leviim so few in numbers compared to the other tribes?

He gives two possible explanations. First, he suggests, based on what Chazal taught, that the Leviim were not enslaved in Egypt, and perhaps because of this, they only had a natural growth in population, unlike the other tribes. "And as they (Egyptians) persecuted it (Bnai Yisrael), so it grew and increased" (Shemos 1:12).

It seems as if the Ramban is not too comfortable with this explanation, so he brings a second explanation. The tribe of Shimon also had a low population compared to the other tribes. The Ramban wishes to suggest that, even though the population of Shimon was decimated by the plague in the incident with Moav as described in Parshas Balak, the population of both tribes were very low relative to the other tribes due to Yaakov's "curse" at the end of Sefer Bereshis, just before he died.

Today, we find that the number of Leviim are drastically fewer than even the Cohanim, yet when they entered Israel, there were many more Leviim than Cohanim, since the only Cohanim were the sons and grandchildren of Aahron. The phenomena of very few Leviim relative to the number of Jews today is even more mystifying than that described in the Chumash. We seem to have no logical explanation for this phenomena.

Divrei Torah on **Bamidbar**

Changing the World

By Matthew Goodman

"Hashem spoke to Moshe in the Sinai Desert" (Bamidbar 1:1)

An idealistic young man came to seek the advice of a great sage. "I want to change the world," he said. "I want to make it a better place. How should I start?" The sage smiled. "You remind me a little of myself when I was young," he said. "I wanted to change the world, but I discovered that I could not. Then I decided that I would at least change my community, but I discovered that I could not. Then I decided to change my family, but that, too, was beyond my ability. Finally, I tried to change myself, and that has been a lifelong struggle. Perhaps if I started earlier with changing myself, I might have been able to change the world, too."

Let's talk practically. How can we change the world? Parshat Bamidbar opens up by telling us that Hashem gave the Jewish people the Torah in a desert. Why would Hashem give something so beautiful and precious as the Torah in a place so barren and hostile as the desert? A place that is desolate and void of life. An expanse of arid land.

In fact, it is for those reasons that Hashem gave the Torah in the desert.

The world in which we live is not a perfect place. It can, at times, be a spiritual desert, lacking morals, ethics, and humility. We can find ourselves in situations in which we are subject to pernicious influences and peer pressure. Forces that try and turn us into people we simply do not want to be. How do we manage effective personal introspection and change in such a hostile environment? The Talmud tells us "a person should make himself into a desert" (Eiruvin 54a). We have to fortify ourselves and become a desert, isolating ourselves from the roadblocks to our personal growth and refusing to compromise on our cherished values.

We have to shut out the world around us and work on ourselves.

The Hebrew word for desert -- "midbar" -- shows a certain ambivalence. On one hand it, it indeed refers to isolation on remoteness. On the other hand, however, it resembles the word "medaber," meaning to speak or communicate, which is essentially the opposite of isolation.

First we have the task of becoming a "midbar." Afterwards, we have the equally difficult task of becoming a "medaber" -- one who spreads words of Torah. Once we successfully manage to bring Torah into our lives and light up our own souls, an interesting thing starts to happen. The flame that we have just started to build and tend starts to grow. Suddenly, a light spreads to our families, our friends, our schools, our communities, and eventually, our world.

It seems like a very unenviable job, but it can be simple and beautiful. It requires you to be the best person you can be. Do as much chesed and kindness as you can. Perform as many mitzvot as you can. Show as much ahava, love, as you can. Every time you give tzedakah, help your friend, put on tefillin, light Shabbos candles, or even compliment someone, you become a brighter soul. That light can illuminate the people around you and encourage them to become better people themselves. If you turn yourself into a role model for others, than you have effectively changed the world for the better.

Chazal tell us that when Hashem gave the Torah to the Jewish people, the desert bloomed and sprouted flowers. The job description of a Jew in this world is to take a desert-like world and make it beautiful. The way we accomplish that is through being an "oyr legoyim", a light to the nations, a role model for all people.

First change yourself, then change your family, then change your community, and then change the world.

A Gift from G-d
By Teddy Kravetsky

This week's parsha is Parshat Bamidbar. In the beginning, G-d tells Moshe to take a census of all males who are over the age of 20 in all the tribes except for one. The tribe that was not getting counted with the rest of Bnei-Yisroel was the tribe of Levi.

But why were they were to be counted separately and not with the rest of Bnei-Yisroel? Well, according to some commentaries, this was because they were considered to be at a higher spiritual level than the rest of Bnei-Yisroel. This goes back to the sin of the golden calf, in which all the tribes took part except for the Leviim. They had showed G-d their loyalty to him, and because of this, G-d rewarded them in many ways. One of the ways in which they were rewarded was by getting counted separately because of their heightened spiritual status.

A second way in which they were rewarded was in being given the honour of guarding, carrying, and taking care of the Mishkan (Tabernacle). The Leviim were also honoured in a third way, because they were now the tribe that surrounded the Mishkan with the rest of the nation around them. From this we see that loyalty can go a long way, as G-d rewarded the Leviim in three ways for this small mizvah!

So, what can we take from this? Well, the message that can be taken from this is that G-d rewards those who are loyal to him, not just in one way but in many. Therefore, if you are ever given the opportunity to do even a small mizvah, it might just be worth it, as you could end up reaping the rewards. Plus, you can feel good about what you did, knowing that you just helped someone.

Naso • נשא

This Parsha has been generously sponsored by the Glasenberg family in honour of Akiva Yosef Dov Glasenberg

The Nazir and Wine
By Michali Glasenberg

In this week's Parsha, we learn about the rules by which a man or woman could temporarily become a "nazir" (Nazirite), taking a vow to abstain from wine and grape-based products, as well as not cutting his hair, for a temporary period-- usually 30 days-- as well as to observe certain other restrictions. The Hebrew word "nazir" means "separation."

A person became a nazir to attain a greater degree of kedusha (holiness), to dedicate oneself more fervently and exclusively to spiritual issues for a fixed period of time. Even though this meant abstaining from certain physical pleasures, the Torah confirms that holiness is the result of this separation. "All the days of his abstinence, he is holy to Hashem" (Bamidbar 6, 8). The nazir does take on a different, elevated spiritual status-- as indicated by the halachic prohibition from coming into contact with a dead body during that time. In this respect, the Nazir becomes like a temporary Kohen, who must always observe that law.

However, a number of great Talmudic sages teach that becoming a nazir is most certainly not the ideal. The Torah alludes to this through a strange wording in Chapter 6, verse 11, when, while discussing another issue, it describes the nazir as "sinning against the person." The understanding is that the Torah means that the nazir is sinning against 'his own person,' by depriving the body of something it enjoys-- drinking wine. All the more so, it is considered a "sin" to afflict the body with excessive fasting.

Is a nazir holy or a sinner? Is he to be praised, for the desire to come closer to G-d through temporary abstinence, or chastised, for doing it through physical abstinence?

The Torah does not want us to be hedonists (i.e., to overindulge in physical pleasures for their own sake), but at the same time, it does not wish us to deprive our bodies of certain pleasures, enjoyed in moderation. The Rabbis decreed that Kiddush, the declaration of the sanctity of the Sabbath, should be made over a cup of wine or grape juice. We sanctify wine, by partaking of it in moderation, and by utilizing it to show our gratitude to Hashem.

The nazir is to be praised for taking a temporary respite from the usual pleasures of wine, to attain a higher level of holiness, or to repair a certain fault that he has. But he has to ultimately bring a korban, a sin offering, for temporarily abandoning the physical pleasures that Hashem has given us, and for partially removing/separating himself from society. Holiness needs to be a permanent state in society, as we are commanded in the beginning of Parshat Kedoshim, "Kedoshim tihyu, Ki Kadosh Ani Hashem Elokeichem."

(Based on Dvar torah from Rabbi Yosef Edelstein, Savannah Kollel)

◈ The Shofar's SHABBOS COMPANION ◈

🎵 Beha'alotecha • בְּהַעֲלֹתְךָ 🎵

> This Parsha has been generously sponsored by the Hubert-Chandler family in honour of their children, Ariel and Yael

Kvetch Much?
By Matthew Goodman

"We remember the fish that we will in Egypt free of charge, the cucumbers, the watermelons, the leeks, the onions, and the garlic" (Bamidbar 11:5).

In this week's Parsha, the Jewish people complain about the lack of meat in the desert. They nostalgically recall the "good old days" in Egypt, back in the time when they were slaves but fish was free!

There are two interesting points in the above pasuk that make it difficult to understand. The first is a question asked by Rashi. In Shemot, Pharaoh decreed that the Jews would not be supplied with their own straw: "Straw shall not be given to you" (Shemot 5:18). If straw was not given to the Jewish people free of charge, how on earth could fish be given to them free of charge? Obviously there was not free fish, or any other free commodity, in Egypt. What would lead the Jews to compare their situation to something non-existent? The second difficulty is grammatical. The pasuk says "zacharnu et hadagah asher nochal" - we remember the fish that we will eat. Why is the pasuk in future tense as opposed to reading "we remember the fish that we ate?"

Midrash Rabbah comments that if the Jewish people had known about the manna beforehand, they would have claimed to have already eaten it at Pharaoh's table. This concept is best understood with a story from Rav Moredechai Kamenetzky.

Yankel would spend a few of his precious kopeks (Russian currency) each week to buy a lottery ticket, and every week he would come home from work that much poorer. When his wife heard about his habit, she implored him to stop. She said that is efforts were futile and it would be impossible for him to win.

This, however, was to no avail. Yankel would keep on betting on the almost impossible odds that he would win the lottery. One day, his wife could not take it any longer. She schlepped him to the Rabbi and had him make sure that Yankel would no longer waste his money on lottery tickets.

When he finally acquiesced, his wife put her hands on her hips and declared her victory. "For the last five years, you did nothing but lose the lottery! I told you it would be a waste of money."

Poor Yankel shrugged. "My dear wife," he sighed, "you don't understand. Every night before the big drawing, I fell asleep dreaming about winning the lottery. And that, my dear, was surely not a waste."

People sometimes like to live in a world of dreams as opposed to the world that is. Like Yankel, they enjoy leaving reality and submerging themselves in the pleasure of the imaginary. The Jewish people dreamed up this concept of free fish in Egypt just so that they could complain about their situation in the desert. Had they heard of this food called manna, they would have convinced themselves that they had had manna in Egypt at Pharaoh's own table! They would have done this just for the sake of complaining.

While living in a world of the imaginary, they forgot about what they really had. Manna tasted like anything you wanted it to. They did not have to work to get it; it literally fell from the sky, and it came in ample amounts. And they complained about not having meat. The Jewish people made themselves think that their situation was worse than it actually was, and failed to appreciate and be grateful for what they did have in their lives.

I think it is safe to assume that almost every TanenbaumCHAT student is dealing with the most stressful and busy part of the school year: summatives and exams. This is a great time to apply a lesson from this week's parsha. I sometimes feel the urge to complain about the amount of work that we have to deal with in such a short time. Unfortunately, many of us can turn this into a highly stressful situation, and we turn it into a much bigger deal than it actually is. We are, effectively, living in a dream world, thinking that something is far worse than what reality holds it to be. We compare manna to non-existent free fish and fail to realize that there really is no reason to complain. There are, unfortunately, much worse things that a person could complain about, and B"H (Thank G-d), most of us do not have to deal with those problems.

Whenever you feel the need to complain, think about all the blessings Hashem has given to you and your family. Look at all of them as unmerited and undeserved. Appreciate them as gifts from Hashem, and try and fill yourself with gratitude. We are all fortunate enough to go to a Jewish High School; we live in beautiful Jewish community in a free, nondiscriminatory country. We have families and many of us have siblings, aunts, uncles, cousins, and Bubbies and Zaidies. We have opportunities for the future and strong support from our friends and our teachers. Do not try and live in an imaginary world where all the good in your life is overlooked and neglected. Live in reality, counting every blessing like it is a precious diamond, and try not to complain about narishkeit (silliness).

Zechariah's Prophecy
By Zachary Zarnett-Klein

The Haftarah for this week's Parshah is derived from the book of Zechariah, a prophet who prophesied during the time of the Return to Zion. How could anything from this time period relate to something in our Torah?

While it does seem strange, there are really many similarities between these two readings, specifically the Menorah, the Mishkan/Beit HaMikdash, and G-d's spirit. Parashat Behaalotcha emqhasizes the laws reagarding the Kohen Gadol kindling the Menorah each day. Zechariah, in his vision, sees the Menorah, and is bewildered. What could this possibly mean? Hasn't the first temple been destroyed and its utensils stolen and destroyed?

This is where the message of the prophesy comes into play. G-d is telling Zechariah here that the time has come for the Second Temple to be built. This directly links to the Parashah, in which Aaron is commanded concerning the Menorah soon after the erection of the Mishkan, G-d's sanctuary in the desert and in Israel until the First Temple was built.

But in Zechariah's day, the people are impoverished and all that can be seen are the ruins of the first temple. "Lo B'Chail V'Lo B'Koach Ki Im B'Ruchi Amar Hashem Tzvaot"-- "Not through valour and not through strength, but through my spirit, said G-d." It is Zechariah's duty to convey to the people that G-d is with them and that through His divine and holy spirit, the Temple CAN be built.

Despite the destruction and the unavailability of fancy building materials for the Temple, G-d's spirit will be with them and will guide them in rebuilding the Temple. G-d does not desire physical gifts and proclamations of belief, as much as He values internal belief in G-d's presence in the heart of every Jew. G-d's spirit will be the primary tool to build The Temple, and perhaps this is a lesson. To increase one's material wealth, belief in G-d is critical, and without this, the gaining of material riches is unachievable.

Miriam's Sin
By Elianne Neuman

In our torah portion, Miriam is punished for speaking Lashon Hara about her brother, Moshe. Miriam criticized Moshe for separating from his wife, Tzipporah, by stating that neither she nor Aaron—both of whom were prophets as well—had had to end their marriages. Miriam was stricken with leprosy and was removed from the camp for seven days because of her words.

The common interpretation is that Miriam sinned for speaking Lashon Hara, and thus this episode teaches us to guard our tongues.

Rabbi Chaim Soloveitchik has a different take on this incident.

At the end of our davening every morning, we recite the six remembrances: the Exodus from the land of Egypt; the commandment to keep Shabbat; the giving of the Torah at Har Sinai; the battle with the Amalekites, who had the audacity to attack us almost immediately after we left Egypt; the sin of angering Hashem in the midbar; and the incident with Miriam.

The incident with Miriam seems to be out of place here. The first five remembrances relate to some of the pivotal events and experiences in Jewish History— Yetziat Mitzraim, Shabbat, and Torah. Why is this story included in this list?

Rabbi Soloveitchik answers that we must look to Maimonides' thirteen principals of faith in order to better understand this.

One of the 'ani ma'amins' is the command to recognize Moshe as the "father of all prophets"—of both those who preceded him and those who followed him.

Miriam's sin was that she knew of her brother's greatness, his strength as a leader, his uncontested abilities as a prophet, yet she still thought that she was in the position to criticize him for separating himself from his wife. However, while Moshe was too humble to tell her that she had erred,

Hashem felt no such constraint. For if Miriam was to go unpunished, it would have opened the door for others to question Moshe's authority.

The incident with Miriam also teaches us that good motives do not justify Lashon Hara. Although Miriam only spoke badly about Moshe out of concern for his relationship with his wife, that was no excuse.

Miriam should have recognized Moshe's authority as a leader and as a prophet, and not contested his judgment. By doing so, regardless of her motives, she demonstrated that she lacked basic consideration for him, for his humility, and for his influence. She should have kept her thoughts to herself out of regard for her brother.

This is why the incident of Miriam is mentioned in the six remembrances. Miriam's sin sheds light on one of the fundamental concepts of Judaism: treat people properly, with kindness and respect. We are taught: "Veahavta Lereayacha Kamocha," or in English, "Love your neighbour as you love yourself." The avoidance of Lashon Hara is one of the most common—albeit the most difficult—instances in which we can put this principle into practice and learn to treat our friends with respect.

Ascension

By Becky Friedman

"Speak to Aaron and say to him: When you light the lamps, the seven lamps shall cast their light toward the face of the menorah" (Bamidbar 8:2)

The word "Behaalotcha" comes from the root ayin-lamed-hey, which means ascension. It is often used to refer to a spiritual ascension as well as a physical one. The word "Aliyah", from the same root, can mean both a general ascension and immigration to Israel-- because that is considered a great spiritual ascension. "Behaalotcha" means, depending on the vocalization, either *when you raise up* or *when you ascend*.

Unfortunately, though, "Behaalotcha" doesn't seem to be talking about some grandiose spiritual ascension-- it's used in the context of describing how the Menorah should be set up.

Let's take a closer look, though.

After the details about the Menorah, Mishkan, etc., the parsha goes on to detail Bnei Yisrael's departure from Har Sinai-- the next leg of their Aliyah to the Promised Land.

The perek after that details complaints about food-- well, that doesn't seem very exalted! But the perek that begins with complaints ends with the Elders gaining prophecy; not only does it describe their spiritual ascension, but the perek itself undergoes a structural ascension, from complaints to prophecy, from complaints to ascension.

After that is Miriam's Lashon Hara. That is surely not an example of heightened spiritual levels! But by the end of the perek, not only is she healed from her leprosy, but the people waited for her to heal before travelling-- displaying, in doing so, just the sort of heightened spiritual level appropriate for the perek's title. Again we experience an elevation, an ascension from base insults to pure consideration and absolution.

This is, if anything, more evident in the Haftarah. Zechariah, prophesying a rapidly approaching Messianic/ utopian age, describes the spiritual ascensions first of the city of Yerushalaim, then of the high priest Yhoshua-- with a physical ascension of rags to purified priestly robes as a metaphor for his ascension-- and finally of the king-to-be Zrubavel, again using the metaphor of a physical ascension, this time saying that a mountain will be as a plain before him-- that he will tower above the mountain, not in height, but in his spirituality.

"Who are you, O great mountain? Before Zerubbabel you sink to a plain! He will bring out the stone of the main architect, with shouts of grace, grace to it" (Zechariah 4:7).

The parsha, aptly named, is all about ascensions, and I hope we take its message to heart. From any situation-- even mundane rules, even base complaints, even nastiness-- we can ascend to another level and become closer to G-d.

As we move on towards new experiences and new opportunities, may we follow in the example of Parshat Behaalotcha-- may we always ascend.

Respect and Kindness
By Teddy Kravetsky

This week's parsha deals with a number of topics, from Bnei Yisroel's travels in the desert all the way up to right before G-d sets the 40-year decree. One of the topics has a small section in which Moshe invites Jethro, his fathe-in-law, to join the nation and lead the Jews into Eretz Yisroel in three days (if it hadn't been for the 40-year decree). From this small act of kindness, Jews-- and everyone-- all over the world today can learn many valuable lessons.

The first lesson we can learn is the fact that we should treat everybody with respect and kindness even if they are not our friends and family. We also learn this mitzvah partially from the stork, which in Hebrew is called a chasidah, which means kindness. Rashi asks why it's on the list of birds that are not kosher if it's a kind bird; non-kosher birds are generally vicious and cruel. He then answers that it's only kind to its friends and not to others around it, and therefore it's really a cruel bird. From this, the lesson to be kind really shows. The Torah doesn't even consider someone who's nice to only his friends as kind; the Torah wants us to go a step further and be kind to everyone.

The second lesson we can learn is the fact that we should treat people the way we want to be treated. Moshe treated Jethro with as much respect as he would get on a day-to-day basis; therefore, we should do the same with our friends, family, etc.

Remember that no matter how much you dislike someone, you should still treat him with the same respect and kindness that you would want to be treated with, whether you're at camp, working, or doing something else this summer. As well, realize that treating people with this high a level of respect and kindness is one of the fundamental principles of Judaism!

We Shall Do and We Shall Listen
By Rabbi Yisroel D. Goldstein

The Torah portion "Bamidbar" is always read on the Shabbat before Shavuot (Tosfot, Megila 31,2), which is no coincidence, given the fact that the Torah was given "Bamidbar" (in the desert). What is the significance of the fact that Torah was given in a wilderness, in a barren and infertile desert, not in a civilized terrain, nor on soil conducive to human living and nature's blessing? Why did G-d communicate His blueprint for life and enter into an eternal covenant with the Jewish people in the aridity and desolation of a desert?

There are several answers given: 1. The Torah was given on soil not owned by any particular people or community, to signify that the Torah belongs to every single Jewish soul. 2. The giving of the Torah in the wilderness represents the idea that Torah is not a product of a particular culture and genre. It enriches all cultures, but transcends them. 3. The function of Torah is to confront and refine the "barren wilderness" within the human psyche and the world.

The Torah relates that when Moses presented the covenant before the Jews, they responded, "We will do and we will listen" (Exodus 24:7). This expression has always been a source of wonderment and surprise to rabbis and a refutation of the anti-Semitic portrayal of Jews as calculating and self-protective. "We will do and we will listen" implies a commitment to observe the covenant even before the Jews heard its details and understood its ramifications.

The Talmud (Shabbas 88b) tells a story about a Sadducee who once saw one of the great Talmudic sages, Rava, so engrossed in learning that he did not attend a wound in his own hand. The Sadducee exclaimed, "You rash people! You put your mouths ahead of your ears [by saying "we will do and we will listen"], and you still persist in your recklessness. First, you should have heard it out. If it is within your capacity, then accept it. If not, you should have rejected it!"

His argument was logical. The Jews declared that they were ready to embrace a life-altering covenant, even before they had heard all the details and knew what Judaism was all about! Why? How? Rava answered the Sadducee with the words, "We walked with our whole being."

What Rava meant was that, by definition, a relationship with G-d cannot be created on our terms; it must be on His terms. If there is something called Truth, if there is something called Reality, we cannot define it; it must define us. We cannot accept it on condition that it suits our senses and expectations. On the contrary, we must realign our conditions to it. Once the Jewish people knew that G-d was communicating with them, they did not want to fit religion into their imagination; they had no preconditions for a relationship with truth. It was in the desert that the Jews could declare, "We will do and we will listen."

To receive the Torah, we must have the courage to walk into a desert; we must strip ourselves of any pre-defined self-identity. Torah is not merely a cute and endearing document filled with rituals, to satisfy nostalgia or tradition. Torah demands that we open ourselves up with our whole being and declare, "We shall do and we shall listen!"

Korach • קורח

This Parsha has been generously sponsored by the Markman family in honour of all the students at TanenbaumCHAT

Religious Authority
By Samuel Buckstein

One of the more common inferences about Judaism from Parshat Korach is an authoritarian heirarchal society that should not be challenged. The argument for this is that Korach and his 250 leaders of the congregation confronted Moses and Aaron, saying that they were monopolizing the spiritual connection to G-d. As a result of their opposition, G-d opened the ground beneath their feet and swallowed Korach and his dissenters.

However, this is the wrong lesson to learn. Judaism is not a religion that censors anyone or any thought that challenges its hegemony; in fact, quite the opposite. Many prominent Jewish theologians, including the revered Maimonides, openly encouraged Jews to challenge established rules and authority, even G-d's. The reasoning behind this is that the theologians did not want Judaism to comprise a mindless, unintelligent, and strictly obedient congregation. These great men realized that ideas only improve if they are constantly challenged and reevaluated.

So what did Korach do that was wrong? He was belligerent and combative. There is a right way and a wrong way to challenge authority. After all, his concerns are just. Korach lamented that it is unjust that Levites and Kohanim are the only ones allowed to perform the spiritual services to G-d, much like how Catholic priests are the only people who can communicate with G-d. Korach's first mistake was that he confronted Moses and Aaron openly, in front of the entire people of Israel, and with the support of all the leaders of the congregation. An open confrontation challenged Moses' leadership. To remain in control, Moses needed drastic measures.

The second mistake was that he directly attacked Moses and Aaron by saying 'you'. They charged Moses and Aaron of elevating themselves above the congregation unnecessarily, since all Jews are holy. By evoking an ad hominem attack, they personally insulted Moses and Aaron. A more proper way would have been simply to voice their complaints, saying that all Jews are holy and that there was no need for priests. For his insolence, Korach and his supporters died.

Now that that issue has been addressed, I will examine Korach's claim, which appears legitimate. To revisit the Catholic priest analogy, there is a significant difference between Kohanim and Levites in Judaism and clergymen in Catholicism. Catholicism maintains that only priests are capable of communicating with G-d, so as a result, all the congregation's pleas must travel via the priest. In Judaism, the Kohamin and Levites are only the representatives of the people. Can all people connect with G-d? Yes; that is the concept of personal prayer three times a day. However, animal sacrifice is a very holy spiritual ritual, and people have to be in the right spiritual state of mind to be worthy of performing this ritual. The solution for this problem was to assign to one part of the people the responsibility of performing sacrifices on the behalf of all the people. The benefit of having a designated sect of priests is that the worries of everyday toils do not interfere with their priestly work. Indeed, Kohanim had to spiritually cleanse themselves in order to be worthy of performing the sacrifices, even though they did not work!

Kohanim are not better that everyone else, and to distinguish them as such is a misinterpretation of what was intended. This is another major lesson to be learned from Parshat Korach: that in the eyes of Judaism-- and G-d, for that matter-- we are all equal.

Chukat • חֻקַּת

A Mystery Inside an Enigma
By Mr. Jeremy Cohen

Shabbat: a time for rest and spiritual growth. Though Shabbat is our primary means of connecting with G-d, there used to be a second way. Our sages refer to *zman v'makom*, time and space. The 'space' connection was through the Beit Ha Mikdash, the Holy Temple, which fell in the year 70 A.D. But *zman*, time-- specifically, Shabbat-- remains, and makes Shabbat even more significant in our relationship with G-d.

By extension, the weekly portions help us to connect with G-d by learning what He wishes to teach us. In theory, this should be simple, but the more we learn, the more sophisticated our efforts need to be. It's like deciding to improve your sleep habits. You decide you need more than four or five hours per night. Try as you will, it's not easy to sleep that many hours. After further investigation, you purchase a quality spine-supporting mattress and memory foam pillow with speakers that emit white audio that emulates the sounds of surf on the beach. You evaluate your sleep and conclude that there is some improvement, but extended, restful sleep remains elusive. You investigate medical journals to grasp the complex puzzle of sleep. On it goes…

And so it is with Torah. The texts we read offer a range of messages – some obvious, some not. To understand, we need to dig deeper. Like getting better sleep, understanding Torah replenishes us after we have done our ever-deepening work. With this mindset, we can now look at parshat Chukat.

The Torah portion opens with *'vzot chukat haTorah.'* 'This is the decree from the Torah.' Our laws are divided into those that are logical and fully explainable, known as *mishpatim*, and those that have logic, a logic that remains elusive, referred to as *chok, chukim*, or our parshah's name, *chukat*. An example of a *chok* is the red heifer, an animal that was used to purify those who had become impure.

This difficult concept was addressed by the greatest mind in Jewish history, King Solomon. He is described as having possessed a level of understanding that was unique among all people (1 Kings). However, when he studied the laws of the red heifer, he said, "All this I tested with wisdom. I thought I would be wise, but it is far from me" (*Kohelet* 7:23). Even King Solomon could not decipher the meaning of the heifer. Consider what a shock this must have been for him, as he was able to explain all the other chukim.

When we study a chok, our initial logic might be challenged. Our natural flow of logic is interrupted. When we study Torah laws that are chukim, we require a deeper level of commitment – more study and analysis. If we skip these steps, we are left confused, at risk of losing the chok's message, and, as such, we also lose the ability to interpret. For the person striving to grow, a questionable or inconclusive logic is a poor foundation for building a deeper relationship with G-d. In an extreme situation, it could foster doubt in our texts, in our spiritual leaders, and even in G-d.

But in the case of divine and prophetic text, as the Torah is, there may be the other lessons to be learned. Not all that we read now will be understood now. Remembering King Solomon and how he was stymied should give us license to concede that some things are, at least for the moment, incomprehensible. When we encounter this-- and we will encounter this-- the problem is not inconsistency in the Torah, but our reliance on immediate proof-logic. We never imagine that we may not yet have achieved the necessary insights into the Torah. A psychotherapist might suggest, 'It's not about the things out there, so much as the things inside of us.' What we don't understand speaks to our limitations, not a limitation of G-d or G-d's Torah.

The chukim in our lives challenge our understanding and practice of Judaism. They challenge us to have a deeper understanding of Torah and greater faith in the One who created us. May we all be successful in directing the physical and emotional replenishment that Shabbat offers so that our spiritual growth is unencumbered, unending. Shabbat Shalom!

Balak • בלק

Balaam's Motives
By Yaron Milwid

In his comment on verse 5 of Parshat Balak, Rabbi Zalman Sorotzkin says that Balaam was a renowned sorcerer who "instead of bringing sanctity and fear of G-d into the world [...] sought honor and wealth for himself, and brought about an increase in witchcraft and immoral practices." Based on this comment from the great rabbi, it seems incongruous that Balaam would ask Hashem's permission before going with Balak's messengers to curse the Jews. Rabbi Sorotzkin mentions in his comment on verse 8 that Balaam knew that Hashem would come talk to him because it was in relation to Hashem's chosen people. Perhaps this can shed some light on why Balaam thought that he would not be able to curse the Jews.

If Balaam suspected that G-d would not allow him to curse the Jews, and Balaam was so selfish as to do anything to increase his reputation-- even being dishonest; as Rabbi Sorotzkin mentions in relation to verse 6, Balak said that "only if a person is already blessed do you agree to bless him, so that your words have the appearance of producing results"-- why would he give the impression that he could not curse the Jews? After all, he could just refuse and not mention that he was afraid that G-d would not allow him to curse the Jews. This would save his reputation.

I think it is possible that he knew that if he just said no, Balak would assume that he was scared of Moses. This is because Balaam was known as greedy, and so, if he was not willing to curse the Jews for all of the money of the Midianites and Moabites, he must be scared of the Jews.

At that time, one who did not believe in the gods was considered crazy. Therefore, if he gave G-d as his reason for not cursing the Jews, rather than making him look bad, it made him keep his good image. Therefore, in doing what would seem to be a G-d-fearing act, he is truly being selfish.

Divrei Torah on **Bamidbar**

Pinchas • פִּינְחָס

This Parsha has been generously sponsored by the Segal family in honour of TanenbaumCHAT

Why Marry Jewish
By Samuel Buckstein

Parshat Pinchas is a very troubling and bloody chapter in the book of Bamidbar. To give a brief synopsis, the people of Israel begin to intermarry with Midianites, and, as a result, begin to turn away from G-d in favour of idol worship. G-d becomes very angry and jealous, and decides to wipe out the people of Israel for what seems like the umpteenth time. At the last minute, Pinchas, the grandson of Aaron the high priest, skewers a Hebrew, Zimri son of Salu, and his Midianite consort. This limits the heavenly plague to *only* twenty-four thousand people, who die as a result. At the end of the story, G-d encourages the Israelites to exact retribution on the Midianites.

What is so troubling about this Parshah? The large excesses of death sort of detract from the perceived image of the Torah as a holy book of right and wrong. Instead, G-d outright sanctions mass xenophobic reprisals against a people whose sole crime was to marry Jews. Does the Bible encourage crusade-like persecution of any and all that differ from our religion? No.

Many commentators suggest that the Midianites were sinisterly attempting to sway Jews away from G-d. Their impetus was that they felt a threat from the appearance of a new, strong, large, and united people in their lands. Due to the debacle of intermarriage that follows, this Parshah is essentially the basis of the argument used by Jewish parents to prevent their kids from marrying non-Jews. As illustrated by the opening Psukim, assimilation will destroy any minority belief, including Judaism.

Judaism is a unique society/religion that is unlike any other on the Earth. It is arguably the world's first religion based on reason and education, which, as a result, spawned two other major religions and became the foundation of much of Western society. For this reason, it is worth preserving. That does not mean that our religion is better that all others. We are not the only religion that preaches humility, generosity, and community involvement. Although this is a minority view, I'm going to go with the argument that the phrase 'light onto the nations' means an example to follow, not a superior model to adapt.

In summary, Judaism is a crucial addition to a tolerant and free society and is a beneficial resource of intellect and morality for the rest of the world. As a result, it is worth preserving, which means that Jews of all religious affiliations should be greatly encouraged to marry other Jews in order to continue a four-thousand-year-old tradition of morality.

Matot/Massei · מטות/מסעי

Can-do Attitude
By Becky Friedman

In Parshat Matot, the tribe of Ruven, the tribe of Gad, and half the tribe of Menashe have a strange request to make of Moshe. Those two and half tribes in particular have a lot of flocks, and they find that the land on the east side of the Jordan-- land that they had just won from Sichon and Og, the foreign kings who had made war on Bnei Yisrael-- is the perfect land for flocks. They want to make their homes there, rather than cross the Jordan into the Land of Israel.

Now, there are two ways this request can go-- two ways they can approach it-- and, in fact, one of those ways has been done before. Moshe himself brings up that incident, preemptively warning the two and a half tribes not to try it. He talks about the story from Parshat Shlach, when the ten spies subverted the will of Bnei Yisrael, spreading lashon hara about the Land of Israel.

But Ruven, Gad, and Menashe take the other option. Rather than go on the offensive, they have a can-do attitude. They see what they want, and they pick the most mutually beneficial way of getting it. They suggest to Moshe-- to prove that their intention is *not* to subvert the destiny of Am Yisrael-- that they fight in the first ranks of soldiers, and only return to the lands that they have requested once all of Am Yisrael have inherited their portions in the Land of Israel.

This idea is acceptable to Moshe, and the two and a half tribes build their cities in the land they have chosen before moving on with the people on their way to the Land of Israel.

Similarly, at the end of Parshat Masei (and the end of Sefer Bamidbar), part of the tribe of Menashe comes to Moshe with a problem. Last Parsha (in Pinchas), the five daughters of Tzlofchad successfully bargained for portions of their father's land among his brothers. Now, though, the men of Menashe are worried that when the women marry, their lands will be lost to their husbands' tribes, once again subverting the just apportioning of the tribal lands in the Land of Israel.

Moshe's response (instructed by G-d) is that the daughters of

Tzlofchad have-- once again-- two options. If they marry outside the tribe, they cannot inherit lands, as they insisted they must, because lands must not pass from tribe to tribe.

Rather than lose what they fought for, the women cooperate with their tribe, marrying their cousins to retain their inheritance.

It's often very tempting to insist that we can't do something, when it seems very difficult. "I couldn't figure out that math problem." "I can't write my essay for English class." "I can't do this." "I'm too young/ short/ stupid/ tired/ etc. to understand."

You won't be the first one to say it. In the haftara for Matot (which is not read when the parshiot are combined), Yirmiyahu uses the same excuse. He tells G-d, "I don't know how to speak [to Am Yisrael] because I am [only] a young man" (Yirmiyahu 1:6). But G-d won't let him off that easy. G-d tells him, "Don't say 'I am [only] a young man,' [...] for I am with you" (1:7-8).

Later in Sefer Yirmiyahu-- in the haftara for Masei, which we do read-- he despairs of Am Yisrael's defeatist attitude towards repentance: "You say, 'it is useless; no'" (2:25). Rather than taking the attitude of the two and a half tribes and the five daughters, and finding a workable compromise, Am Yisrael insist that they have no hope of doing tshuva, simply because it seems such a daunting task.

This week's double-parsha reminds us, over and over again, that it's never "all or nothing". We should never think that just because something is difficult, it can't be done; we should never give up without trying. All we need is a can-do attitude, and the rest will work itself out.

Don't say "I can't," for G-d is with you.

אלה הדברים אשר דבר משה אל כל ישראל בעבר הירדן במדבר

Devarim
דברים

This Sefer of Chumash has been generously sponsored by

The Weiss Family

In honour of their beloved father and grandfather,
Leon Weiss Z"L

Va'etchanan • ואתחנן

This Parsha has been generously sponsored by the Opler family in honour of Arielle Opler, & Mark and Naomi Satok in honour of their children, Josh, Ari, and Jordana

Love and Rejection
By Rabbi Jay Kelman

Jews of faith, when faced with imminent death, have departed this world with the words of the Shema on their lips. Perhaps the most famous example of this is the tragic death of Rabbi Akiva, one of the ten martyrs we read about on Tisha B'Av. As he was being tortured by the Romans, Rabbi Akiva gained a measure of comfort, as he could now literally fulfill the mandate "And you shall love the Lord your G-d with all you soul -- even when He takes your soul" (Brachot 54a).

The importance of the Shema is such that it is the only Biblical text which we are required to say on a daily basis, and the only mitzvah which is fulfilled twice each day. The Mishna, the foundation of the Oral law, begins with the laws of the Shema, opening with the question of when is the earliest one may say the evening Shema.

Yet, strangely enough, this mitzvah only appears in the Torah in Sefer Devarim. Why were the words of the Shema not included with those heard at Sinai? The Talmud teaches that the *kabbalat ol malchut shamayim*, the acceptance of the yoke of heaven, found in the first paragraph of the Shema, is the foundation stone that must be accepted prior to the yoke of the commandments. Surely we should have expected the Shema to appear when G-d made His covenant with us.

The focus of Sefer Devarim is Moshe's preparation of the Jewish people for entry to the land of Israel. Most of the mitzvoth recorded here are those relating to the nation of Israel, such as appointing a King and a Sanhedrin, laws of social justice, laws of war, and even the concept of communal repentance. Moshe exhorts the people time and time again not to follow in the corrupt ways of the nations currently in the land, and warns against the dangers of intermarriage. The fear of excessive materialism-- brought about by the blessings of the land-- leading to forgetting G-d can be heard throughout Moshe's words.

Perhaps the Shema, with its acceptance of the yoke of heaven and the command to love G-d, is, in many ways, one that is dependant on the land. Only in Israel can we fully accept the yoke of heaven which serves as the basis of the Shema; only in the land can many of the mitzvoth be fulfilled. Even more fundamentally, the land of Israel is the central dwelling place of the Divine Presence. Those who love G-d would want to be near Him in the land of Israel. The all-embracing nature of our relationship with G-d that is the hallmark of the Shema can only be fully implemented in the land of Israel.

Loving G-d is a very difficult mitzvah to observe in the best of circumstances. In times of tragedy, when we cannot fathom the injustices and suffering we see around us, the mitzvah becomes doubly difficult. Conquering and settling the land of Israel is a mitzvah that, our Talmudic Sages warned, would only occur through *yisurin*, pain and suffering. It will take great faith to love G-d in the land of Israel. It will take even greater faith to believe that G-d truly loves His people and suffers with us.

I do not believe it is coincidental that G-d emphatically rejects Moshe's pleas to enter into the land of Israel in the same *parsha* as the Shema. Love of G-d cannot be dependant on G-d answering our prayers. Even-- especially-- when G-d acts in a way that seems unfair to us, we must display our love toward Him. We do so by continuing to observe His commandments, by learning His Torah, and by studying the beautiful natural universe that G-d created for our benefit.

Parshat Vaetchanan is always read on the Shabbat following Tisha B'av. After tragedy, we enter the period of *Nechama*, comfort, reading 7 special haftarot of comfort as we prepare for the Rosh Hashanah season. Let us pray and perhaps even demand that, after close to 2,000 years of Jewish pain, the time for comfort has arrived. May G-d's love of the Jewish people manifest for all to see.

Re'eh • ראה

This Parsha has been generously sponsored by the Friedman family in honour of Elisheva Friedman

A Surprise Test
By Rabbi Jay Kelman

How can you tell if somebody loves you? We understand that words alone are hollow and that actions are what count. Even so, it is not always easy to understand the actions of others. Misreading one's intentions in this sensitive area can have disastrous consequences. Imputing noble motives when none exist is no less dangerous than falsely accusing someone of nefarious intentions. While the latter is liable to lead to tensions, the former can lead to death. Testing someone's love, trying to snare someone, seems a little immature and outright dangerous. What if your beloved fails the test? Yet it appears that this is what the Torah tells us that G-d may do to the Jewish people.

"When a prophet or a person who has visions in a dream arises among you: He may present you with a sign or a miracle; do not listen to the words of that prophet or dreamer. G-d your Lord is testing you to see if you truly love your Lord" (13:2-4). Apparently, G-d is going to allow a prophet to correctly perform wonders to see whether or not you will then listen as he tries to lead you astray. Will you be wowed by his truly amazing feats, or will you have the strength to look deeper into his true character? Why is G-d putting you in such a situation? What kind of love is this?

A test of G-d is like no other. It is not meant to determine if we will pass or fail; G-d needs no test for that. Rather, a test is to challenge us, to enable us to use resources we were not sure that we had. G-d did not test Abraham to see whether he was willing to sacrifice his son; rather, G-d enabled Abraham to reach the level of love of G-d that he was willing— not yet understanding that that this is in reality abhorrent to G-d—to sacrifice everything for the love of G-d. It is no coincidence that it is Abraham who is called "My beloved." The first aspect of love is challenging us, giving us opportunities to fall, because then we can rise that much higher.

While we cannot fathom the ways of G-d, the many tests we all face —some, tragically, involving great pain and suffering—can and must serve to strengthen us. We are bidden to ask not *lamah*, why, but *lemah*, for what purpose. Strange as it may seem to modern man who equates love with pleasure, Judaism sees no contradiction between pain and love (just ask a mother in labor). Judaism has, thus, taught the complex concept of *Yisurin shel ahava*, afflictions sent to man that actually express G-d's love towards us.

There is an even more fundamental lesson here. G-d does not want us to observe the mitzvoth because they are 'in' or 'cool' or we are 'blown away' by them. Miracles can never have a long-term effect on people's behaviour; their impact wears off after a few short days. We need look no further than the generation of the desert, who, despite witnessing the greatest miracles of all time, were a stiff-necked, complaining lot. We observe mitzvoth because they are G-d's command, not because we are influenced by some charismatic leader. For this reason, the one trait that *Moshe Rabbeinu* surely lacked was charisma. His total lack of oratorical skills would, in modern times, have doomed him to political oblivion, yet Moshe was the greatest of prophets. The role of a prophet is not to be a great speaker, but rather a great spokesperson, relaying G-d's message to His people and beyond.

With the destruction of the first Temple, the period of prophecy came to an end. While this is, on the surface, to be lamented, it can be viewed much more positively. During our early formative years, we needed G-d's constant guidance - expressed through miraculous events and righteous prophets. Without these constant reminders of the Divine presence, the nascent nation born from slavery would have been stillborn. However, as we developed and "matured" as a people, especially with the development of the oral law, the centre of authority shifted to our rabbinic leaders. Torah is not to be found in heaven - we humans must interpret the Divine will. While there is greater uncertainty, there is also greater struggle and greater involvement with Torah. Just as a parent must wean a child from total dependence, so, too, our Father wants us to take responsibility for the development and implementation of Torah. We must see the divine manifestations in history, even-- especially-- when they are not obvious. We are not to be swayed by charismatic false prophets, but rather by the serious words of Torah.

Simcha Be'Artzecha

By Elisheva Friedman

Our Parasha has a disproportionate amount of "simcha" in comparison with the rest of the Torah. Of the 8 or so times the root "Sameach" is mentioned in Devarim, about 6 of those are in Parashat Re'eh. Bereisheet, Shmot, Vayikra, and Bamidbar each contain a single instance of this combination of letters. And of those, only Vayikra and Devarim present it as a command—always in connection with the Land.

Parashat Re'eh starts off by presenting us with a choice, delineating the ensuing consequences of each-- blessings if we follow the mitzvot, and curses if we don't:

> *"Behold, I set before you today a blessing and a curse. The blessing, that you will heed the commandments of the Lord your G-d, which I command you today; and the curse, if you will not heed the commandments of the Lord your G-d, but turn away from the way I command you this day, to follow other G-ds, which you did not know."*

The extension of the first part of Re'eh (about the brachot and klallot and Har Grizim and Har Eival) comes a few parshiot later, in parashat Ki Tavo. In Devarim 28:45-47, in the middle of the litany of klallot (curses) that may come about, an interesting reason is given for the harsh implementation of the klallot:

> *"All these curses will befall you... And they will be as a sign and a wonder, upon you and your offspring, forever, because you did not serve the Lord, your God, with happiness and with gladness of heart, when [you had an] abundance of everything."*

The Torah seems to say that we evoke wrath by not serving G-d with simcha!

Simcha (joy) is a funny idea. Why should we have to be joyful while doing the mitzvot, or a job, or offering a sacrifice? Why should our state of mind matter, as long as we get the job done? Don't we believe that our ma'asim matter more than our thoughts?

Interestingly, we find that, according to the Rambam's Mishneh Torah, Hilkhot Yesodei haTorah 7:4, to achieve a state of readiness to receive nevuah, prophecy, neviim had to be in a state of simcha. (Examples are found throughout Shmuel Alef and in Melachim Bet 3:15.)

Studying Navi, we observe that neviim played musical instruments to try to induce a state of nevuah, ostensibly by way of simcha from the music.

To prepare to confront the Divine, they had to be joyful—not just fearful, pure, and in a "holy" frame of mind. They had to work themselves up to a state of euphoria.

Many are familiar with Rabbi Nachman of Braslav's famous teaching: "mitzvah gedolah lehyot besimcha tamid." Infusing every part of our lives with kedusha and G-dliness mandates always finding simcha in serving HaKadosh Baruch Hu.

In the Gmara, on Brachot 31a, we find that proper tfilla, prayer, comes not from sadness, lightheadedness, or other attitudes, but from "simcha shel mitzvah."

If we carry out the mitzvot mechanically, or recite tfillot monotonously and with our minds elsewhere, we miss out on a crucial aspect of this opportunity-- connecting with HaKadosh Baruch Hu. Even if we focus on what we are doing, but carry it out joylessly, we are forgetting about Hakarat Hatov, and don't achieve the full potential of our encounter with G-d.

Depression is energy- and attention-consuming; Simcha is energizing and motivating. Apathy is destructive, and allows for people to "stray from the derekh." We must fight lethargy—simcha helps achieve zrizut and "getting more done." So, in the end, simcha improves efficiency and helps keep our focus where it should be.

When we sing "Ivdu et Hashem Be'simcha", we need to be trying to stir ourselves into a state of joyful, ecstatic fervour, constantly recognizing the Source of the good that we have, as we are energized for our avodat haBorei and full kiyum of the miztvot.

Simcha in our parasha comes largely in the context of enjoying the produce of Eretz Yisrael as we spend time in the vicinity of the mikdash or on chagim that involve aliyah la'regel.

> *"And you shall rejoice before the Lord, your God, -you, and your son, and your daughter, and your manservant, and your maidservant, and the Levite who is within your cities, and the stranger, and the orphan, and the widow, who are among you, in the place which the Lord, your God, will choose to establish His Name therein."*

We are commanded to rejoice-- with our families and with the more vulnerable members of society, with our produce and on our chagim, in our Land, before Hashem. In other words, we rejoice in sharing with am Yisrael as we follow Torat Yisrael in Eretz Yisrael. We are being makir tov during our time off from farming, when we finally have time to enjoy—quite literally—the fruits of our labours, which we acknowledge as a gift from G-d. "Kosi Revayah"-- Happy people are motivated to "pay it forward," spreading the love, letting their joy spill over to those around them. Enthusiasm is infectious. Being able to share our bountiful produce as we give ma'aser allows us to further appreciate the gifts G-d has given, especially as we enjoy the ma'aser in Yerushalayim, or a holiday that allows for time to reflect and appreciate the goodness that we have.

Simcha seems to be very connected to the mikdash. Psukim 12:5-13 emphasize rejoicing with our produce, which G-d has given us and which we return to Him in the Beit HaMikdash.

> *"But only to the place which the Lord your God shall choose from all your tribes, to set His Name there; you shall inquire after His dwelling and come there... And there you shall eat before the Lord, your God, and you shall rejoice in all your endeavors you and your households, as the Lord, your God, has blessed you... And it will be, that the place the Lord, your God, will choose in which to establish His Name there you shall bring all that I am commanding you: Your burnt offerings, and your sacrifices, your tithes, and the separation by your hand, and the choice of vows which you will vow to the Lord... And you shall rejoice before the Lord, your God you and your sons and your daughters and your menservants and your maidservants, and the Levite who is within your cities, for he has no portion or inheritance with you."*

The portion in Re'eh about the chagim (Perek 16) also emphasizes "And you shall rejoice before Hashem" and "the place that Hashem your G-d will choose."

> *"And you shall rejoice in your Festival-- you, and your son, and your daughter, and your manservant, and your maidservant, and the Levite, and the stranger, and the orphan, and the widow, who are within your cities... Seven days you shall celebrate the Festival to the Lord, your God, in the place which the Lord shall choose, because the Lord, your God, will bless you in all your*

> *produce, and in all the work of your hands, and you will only be happy."*

After the Mikdash was destroyed, Chazal (the early Rabbis) discuss diminishing our simcha. While we do not experience the level of simcha inspired by the sight of the Beit HaMikdash up and running, we also cannot eradicate all simcha from our lives. Simcha is a necessary component of our well-being, and, moreover, of our Avodat Hashem.

May we soon see the day when Am Yisrael can truly fulfill Mizmor 122 in Tehilim: *"I rejoiced when they said to me, 'Let us go to the house of the Lord.'"*

The Shofar's SHABBOS COMPANION

Shoftim • שׁוֹפְטִים

The Pursuit of Happiness
By Teddy Kravetsky

This week's parsha is Parshat Shoftim, which begins by explaining how Bnei Yisroel will establish a court system in the land. It explains the role of judges-- they can't accept bribes, can't be unjust, and can't favour any one person-- but what it says next is very peculiar, as it seems like a repetition of the points just mentioned. It says, "Righteousness, righteousness shall you pursue, so that you will live and possess the land that Hashem your G-d gives you."

Here is a major grammatical problem with the text. First, it repeats the word 'righteous' twice; and second, it repeats that a judge must be righteous, which is already known from a previous Pasuk.

So, to answer this problem in a simple manner, one could say that the repetition is just for emphasis on the word, and that a judge must be absolutely righteous. However, I believe that, like with many other Pasukim from the Torah, there is a deeper meaning to this line.

First of all, an interesting commentary here by Rabbi Bunam interprets the reason for the same Pasuk to say the word 'righteous' twice. He explains that this means that a righteous judge must achieve his position through righteous means, and not by improper ways, as this would contradict what he is trying to do. This is a very interesting conclusion, as, in order to elevate one's holiness, he must do so through righteous means.

I think that this makes perfect sense, but only if it's looked at in the right frame of mind. It says the word twice because this commandment from G-d is not only meant for judges, but for all Jews trying to achieve righteousness.

This leads me to an even better conclusion on why the word is mentioned twice. It is to teach everyone, not just judges, a very valuable lesson: that, in order to go through life properly, one must elevate his holiness through righteous means-- this is according to Rabbi Bunam.

However, in order to fully understand what the Rav is saying, you must now apply this concept to your entire life, and to everything that you are trying to pursue. This is not to say that when you're going for a trip, you have to do so righteously; it is saying that in order to achieve a higher success in life, you should pursue your goals in a righteous and honest manner. Achieving financial success is great, but if it's done through being a dishonest businessman, then how much have you really learned in life?

This message, to me, is very powerful, as it takes one's goals and provides them with a moral base to achieve success, whatever that may be. This, in turn, can provide the person with a much better sense of morality, as well, in their pursuit to happiness; maybe this is the key. This suggests that the pursuit of happiness begins by being righteous in all decisions.

So, next time you're thinking of a way to start your pursuit of happiness and success, look no further than being righteous, and, beyond that, following the many great mitzvoth that the Torah has laid out. Soon after coming to these realizations, I think you'll find yourself with a much better outlook on life.

כי תצא · Ki Teitzei

הורים וילדים – חובות וזכויות
הרב איתי מוריוסף

"כִּי יִהְיֶה לְאִישׁ בֵּן סוֹרֵר וּמוֹרֶה אֵינֶנּוּ שֹׁמֵעַ בְּקוֹל אָבִיו וּבְקוֹל אִמּוֹ וְיִסְּרוּ אֹתוֹ וְלֹא יִשְׁמַע אֲלֵיהֶם" (דברים כא:יח).

התורה מגדירה בן סורר ומורה כמי ש"איננו שומע בקול אביו ובקול אמו." אמת נכון שחייבים כל בן ובת לשמוע בקול הוריהם. לחובה זו ישנם שני היבטים:

האחד הוא הכבוד. כבוד להורה על עצם קיומי (אלמלא ההורה לא הייתי זוכה לחיים - הוא שילד אותי). כבוד על שגידל אותי ומילא את מחסורי הפיזי והנפשי. וכבוד על נוכחותו בחיי, יום יום ושעה שעה, כך שאוכל למלא את שאיפותיי (ולא רק את צרכיי).

השני הוא היראה. היראה, שלא ככבוד, איננה הכרת הטוב ואמירת תודה. היראה היא ההכרה שאני כבנם של פלוני ופלונית תמיד אהיה מושפע מהם. לעולם לא אוכל לברוח מלהיות בנם. לעולם - אופיים, יחסם אליי, והדרך שבה גידלו אותי בתוכייהיו נוכחים. זה בהחלט מפחיד לחשוב על כך, שהוריי הותירו בי חותם בל ימחה. כזה שלעולם לא אוכל להתכחש אליו או לברוח ממנו.

על שני ההיבטים הללו - הכבוד והיראה - מצוה התורה שני ציוויים שונים: "כבד את אביך ואת אמך" (שמות כא:יא; דברים ה:טו), ו-"איש אמו ואביו תיראו" (ויקרא יט:ג).

אולם, האם חובתי כילד לכבד את הוריי ולירא מהם מוחקת את זהותי העצמית? האם לי - כילד - אסור להשמיע את קולי הפרטי, האישי, האינדבידואלי? מתי אני חייב לשמוע בקול הורי ומתי אני פטור מכך?

אציין רק דוגמא אחת: ר' משה איסרליש כותב בחיבורו המפה על שולחן ערוך (יורה דעה רמ:כה): "אם האב מוחה בבן לישא איזו אשה שיחפוץ בה הבן, אין צריך לשמוע אל האב." כלומר: אין חובה לבן לשמוע לאביו או לאמו כאשר הם מכריחים אותו להתחתן עם אשה שאינו רוצה. כמובן, ראוי שהבן והבת יקשיבו לעצת הוריהם, ברם אין להם חובה לעשות מה שהוריהם אומרים להם לעשות בענין. ומדוע? יש החלטות שאדם צריך לעשות בעצמו ורק הוא ישא באחריות להחלטה זו. משום כך אין אף אדם זר, ואפילו לא ההורה, רשאי להתערב בהחלטה כזו.

Ki Tavo • כי תבוא

Ma'aser and Bikurim

By Zachary Zarnett-Klein

Ki Tavo is a very intriguing Parashah on many levels. It has a number of points of interest, including the offering of the first fruits and the offering of the ma'aser. The Parashah starts off by commanding the Israelites to bring their first fruits to the Temple and offer them in front of the Kohen when they arrive and settle in the Land of Israel. While there, they must recite a passage acknowledging G-d's might, and all that He has done for Israel, from the time Lavan oppressed Yaakov, to the exodus from Egypt, to their arrival to the Land of Israel.

This whole ceremony evokes the question: what is the big deal about first fruits? Also, what is the significance of bringing the Bikurim, and why is it necessary to make this declaration?

The act of bringing the Bikurim to the Temple symbolizes a person's dedication of all he has to the service of G-d. The declaration, on the other hand, is said to remind the individual that the Bikurim could never have been produced had it not been for G-d and the miracles He performed for the Israelites. Therefore, the first fruits are a very significant part of Jewish life, and it is commanded that one celebrate the Bikurim with the entire household, together with the Levites and proselytes in one's midst.

Next, the Torah commands a person to donate a ma'aser, a tithe, of all his produce, every three years. He makes a declaration at his home that all that he has done was in accordance with the law. This time, the declaration highlights the fact that G-d's commandments have been followed by the individual without transgression, and that the individual has shared his gifts from G-d with the Levites, proselytes, orphans, and widows in his midst. The declaration concludes with the request that G-d bless Israel and continue to preserve the Land of Israel and all its greatness.

One may ask: why is the declaration of the Bikurim about giving thanks to G-d, when the declaration concerning the ma'aser takes the form of a confession?

To answer this, one must first understand that Sefer D'varim is divided into three parts. The first is a review of what has happened to the Israelites since they left Egypt. The second half is a compendium of laws, which ends in the chapters which discuss the Bikurim and ma'aser. The third part is an affirmation of the covenant between G-d and Israel.

There is a very important reason why these two laws were included right before the text discusses the covenant. On the one hand, the land is already ours, as promised to our forefathers, and we have the ability to live there and do things such as grow produce. On the other hand, we must continue to keep the covenant which G-d has presented to us in order to keep the land, and we must treat it as holy so that we may continue to reap its benefits in the future. This also explains why the declaration of the Bikurim is associated with praise, since it offers thanks to G-d for fulfilling His promise.

On the flipside, the ma'aser deals with our continued sanctification of the land and our future in Israel, which is contingent upon the specific actions we take and whether we honour the covenant. Furthermore, the declaration of the Bikurim takes place in the Temple because it deals with praise that all of Israel gives to G-d, since G-d did all the miracles discussed for the entire nation. The Temple is the only place where all Jews can be seen completely as equals, and therefore this declaration must be made there.

However, the ma'aser's declaration is made at home because it highlights the personal connection we share with G-d and is directly linked to the prosperity which G-d has granted us as individual, and therefore it is only appropriate that this declaration is made from the home.

The relationships between the Bikurim and the ma'aser are critical to life in the Land of Israel, and they can also be applied to many other aspects of Jewish life. May the entire Jewish nation be blessed to return to the Land of Israel once and for all, and may we all have the opportunity to make these declarations again in the near future.

Nitzavim/Vayelech • נצבים/וילך

This Parsha has been generously dedicated by the Dunn family L'iluy Nishmat HaRav Nachum Yehudah Eliyahu ben HaRav Shmuel Eliezer Z"L
"Beautiful is the study of Torah with Derech Eretz" (Pirkei Avot 2:2)

Listening to Hashem
By Matthew Goodman

Parshat Nitzavim is always read on the Shabbos before the start of Slichot davening in Elul, the Shabbos before Rosh HaShana. A particular pasuk teaches us a lot about teshuva and what Hashem expects from us on the Yamim HaNoraim: "And you will return to Hashem your G-d and hearken to His voice" (Devarim 30:2).

As the pasuk states, the first step to Teshuva is to listen to the voice of Hashem "v'shma mata b'kolo." But this seemingly simple statement could perhaps refer to something other than listening to Hashem's mitzvot and fulfilling them, as we would normally assume. Perhaps it indeed means that when Hashem speaks, we need to pay attention. But how is this done? When Hashem speaks through natural or historical events, we must listen.

The Talmud in Brachot 59a states that when a person hears a clap of thunder and flinches, the experience may give him a pause. The Gemara states a number of various opinions regarding what causes (according to the Rashba's understanding) thunder: the tears of Hashem, Hashem clapping, stamping His feet etc. A number of achronim ask a very obvious question. The Gemara is clearly conveying a deeper message than the literal meaning of its words. How do we understand the Gemara?

Rabeinu Chananel explains that the Gemara is teaching that loud noises express Hashem's dissatisfaction with the fact that the Jewish people are in exile. He wants to redeem the Jewish people, but the time has not yet come. The Rashba adds that even though thunderclaps during storms seem to be no more than a natural occurrence, in the times of the Beis ha'Mikdash, when the Jewish people fulfilled the will of Hashem, fierce storms did not occur. This does not mean that storms occurred unaccompanied by thunderclaps. Rather, it means that rain came in a timely and tranquil manner, such that tempests were uncommon. Fierce thunderstorms occurred only when the Jewish people were not fulfilling the will of Hashem. The thunderclaps that accompanied those storms, like the thunderclaps nowadays, were meant to arouse the Jewish people to repent, "to straighten the crookedness in our hearts."

For this reason, when the Chofetz Chaim, zt"l, heard thunder, he would ask "What does Father want? Vos vill der Tatei?"

In fact, there is Gemara in Yevamot 63a that states that no misfortune comes to the world unless it is for Israel -- unless it is for the sake of sending a message to Israel. This fascinating Gemara is stating that every earthquake, tsunami, disaster, war, every happening in the earth that could be considered as bad misfortune, exists only for the Jews. Rashi explains that it is in order to tell Israel to be chazer b'teshuva.

There's another story about the Chofetz Chaim that relates to this Gemara. He once heard of an earthquake in Japan and his talmidim said he turned white and began a fast. They could not understand his actions at all. They had barely heard of Japan and there were no Jews living there, so why did their Rebbe care so much? The Chofetz Chaim then pointed out the Gemara in Yevamot and said that Hashem is sending us a message and it is our job to listen.

In Avodah Zara 18a, Rabbi Chanina ben Teradion asked Rabbi Yosi ben Kisma "Am I destined to go to Olam HaBa?" Rabbi Yosi responded, "Did you ever do anything special?" Rabbi Chanina responded, "I once had Purim money for my meal that go mixed up with money for charity. So, I gave the entire sum away to poor people." Rabbi Yosi replied, "If that is the case, may my portion in Olam HaBa be as great as your portion. You are destined to go to Olam HaBa!"

This Gemara is very peculiar and strange as to what it is trying to say. What did Rabbi Chanina merit by giving the whole sum of money? What mussar did this show?

Rabbi Chanina ben Teradion saw in this incident that the Almighty was trying to tell him something. The Master of the Universe was sending him a message. The message was that really, this money that he had set aside for his Purim meal should be given to charity. Rabbi Chanina ben Teradion was so sensitive and so open and receptive to Hashem's messages that in that small, almost trivial incident, he recognized that "the Almighty is trying to tell me something." Rabbi Yosi said, "If that is the case-- if, in such a small little incident, you see and hear the Hand of G-d, I can be confident that you are destined for the World to Come. It is obvious that you go through life in a way that when Hashem merely taps you on the shoulder, you hear it and you get the message. The story of Rabbi Yosi and Rabbi Chanina is telling us that natural and historical happenstances as explained in Yevamot and Brachot are Hashem's way of reminding us that He rules this world, and the man who merits Olam HaBa is he who can establish that this happenings are for Israel to be chazer b'teshuva. In fact, a man surely merits Olam HaBa if he can accept and listen to these messages when they come in very small forms. This is what the pasuk in this week's parsha means when it states "And you shall hear His voice."

This idea is so important that it is the first step of teshuva. It is also an idea repeated in the prayers of the Yamim HaNoraim. In Unetaneh Tokef we say: "And with a great shofar blast He shall blow and with a small silent voice He shall be heard!" What does this paradox come to teach? Why is it that Hashem gives a big tkiah and we only hear a small voice?

It teaches us the nature of people. That Hashem could give us the a huge catastrophic event and we will only hear a small voice. What we need to do is pay attention. What we need to do is to do something! What we need to do is have the ears and eyes to pay attention to what is really going on and hear a loud message for what it is: a loud message! Vos vill der Tatei? What does Father want? Being able to ask that question alone when the times call for it is enough to merit Olam HaBa.

Haazinu • הַאֲזִינוּ

This Parsha has been generously dedicated by Laurie Blake in honour of her daughter, Rachelle Hadari

The Voice of Teshuva
By Matthew Goodman

The great Amora Reish Lakish distinguishes between two types of Teshuva, the act of returning to the heart's true purpose of love and kindness and reforging a relationship with Hashem. One is called teshuva me'yirah, and is motivated by awe and fear. It reduces the severity of the transgressor's sins. The other is called teshuva me'ahavah, and is motivated by love. It turns all sins into merit and good deeds.

Rav Yosef D. Soloveitchik, zt"l, expounds upon these two types of "return." The Rambam in Hilchot Teshuva describes a teshuva of sudden change, of total catharsis, through which a sinner, who was but yesterday despised by Hashem, becomes a close friend of Hashem. This form of teshuva is tikun hara, repairing the evil.

The other form of teshuva is not instantaneous; it is part of a process rather than totally abandoning the past. In this form of teshuva, the sinner does not assume a new identity. Instead, he takes a new road in life, utilizing all of his skills to gradually develop a new relationship with Hashem. The Rav refers to this move as ha'alat hara, elevating the evil.

Likewise, Rav Avraham Y. Kook, z"tl, contrasts teshuva pisomit, sudden change, with teshuva hadragit, gradual change. Sudden change is the equivalent of tikun hara and can be identified also with Reish Lakish's teshuva me'yirah. It can not wipe the slate perfectly clean because little effort was put into the defining moment of repentance. Gradual change, however, is the equivalent of ha'alat hara and can be identified with teshuva me'ahavah. This form of , the result of a long cleansing process, transforms the energy of sin into merit.

We are currently nearing the end of the Ten Days of Repentance, and it strikes me as bothersome that we are given ten days to do teshuva. How can we be expected to perform a full teshuva in such a short period of time? We don't even have a chance to preform a gradual teshuva and receive the merits of doing so. This problem teaches us a very important message about the High Holidays and how to obtain a teshuva hadragit.

It is very hard to just change. Even when it is a gradual change, it still needs to start somewhere. It starts with a little voice in our heads that tells us that something is wrong. This voice is alluded to in this week's Shabbat Shuva parsha, Haazinu. The first word of Moshe Rabbeinu's song is 'Haazinu,' listen. The Torah, at many times, stresses the importance of listening. The Mishna tells us that there is an echo of Sinai that may be heard every day of our lives. In order to hear that echo of holiness and purpose, we need to listen out for it. The voice of Sinai, like the voice of Haazinu itself, is an inner voice that emanates from our souls and consciences. It instinctively tells us what is morally right and what is wrong; reminding us to always strive to better people.

Parshat Haazinu tells us something very important about teshuva, and it is very fitting that this is told in a time of the year in which we only have a few days to do something BIG. The Eseret Yamai Teshuva is not about a long gradual process of change. It is about beginning the change by listening to the voice inside our heads. Haazinu! Listen! And if we listen, we will have the koach to begin with a teshuva pisomit, a sudden change. A tikun hara. A lessening of the severity of our sins. The very change that makes us aware of the path that needs to be followed in order to turn all our sins into merits with a teshuva hadragit. Tikun Hara and Ha'alat Hara should not always be seen as two standalone ideas; nor should teshuva me'yira or me'ahava. They can be very powerfully conjoined and make us aware of profound insights into the human heart.

"Some acquire the world to come in an instant," the Talmud declares. Whether we do teshuva instantly or gradually, whether we are motivated by fear and awe or by love, there is always time and opportunity for us to obtain forgiveness and develop ourselves and our relationship with Hashem. But something has to get us to start. Something has to set us on the right path. Something sudden has to make us click. And it comes from listening to the voice of teshuva.

Swansongs

By Zachary Zarnett-Klein

Even though the regular Haftarah portion for Haazinu is replaced by a special reading for Shabbat Shuvah, I will be discussing the regular Haftarah portion for Haazinu. Haftarat Haazinu is derived from "The Song of David," found in Shmuel Bet, Chapter 22, Verses 1-51. This is quite a fitting Haftarah for Parashat Haazinu, seeing as Haazinu is the "Song of Moshe." However, there is a very significant difference between these two songs. In "The Song of Moshe," he sings about the many emotions that he has experienced during his time as leader of the Israelites, embodied by a feeling of impending death.

On the other hand, David sings a song of praise to G-d for saving him from probable death and from his strong enemies. One must ask oneself why G-d would spare the life of a youth, while he would take the life of Moshe, a man who had taken care of his children for forty years in the wilderness, reminding G-d of this in his song. To find the answer, we must first take a look at the mind frames of these two men. David, in his song, thanks G-d for supporting him and defending him against his enemies at a time when his physical strength was not great enough.

This teaches us that no matter one's strength and agility, without the sustainment of G-d, one cannot survive on this Earth. On the other hand, Moshe, one of the greatest leaders ever of the Jewish people, cries out to G-d, reminding him of all he has done over his period as leader to ensure the vitality and development of the Jewish nation. Moshe ends his song almost in an admission of defeat, and, like all men, at the mercy of G-d. Although our Parashah predominantly deals with the notion of death, and the Haftarah with the sense of security through the salvation of G-d, perhaps there is a connection between these two thoughts. Indeed, finiteness, as the Parsha maintains, is part of what it means to be human. Yet as the Haftarah reminds us, there are times when sickness, fear, and even death can be overcome. In those moments we should remember, as does David, that such human resources as courage, strength, and determination are best revitalized, and nourished, through prayer.

Holidays
חגים

Sukkot • סוכות

HaUshpizin HaKedoshim
By Matthew Goodman

"You shall dwell in booths seven days; all citizens in Israel shall dwell in booths, that your generations may know that I made the children of Israel to dwell in booths when I brought them out of the land of Egypt. I am Hashem your G-d" (Vayikra 33:42-43)

On Pesach, we are very lucky. Eliyahu HaNavi himself visits our seder table every year. On Sukkot, we are extremely lucky. Every night of the seven nights of Sukkot, a very special and holy guest joins our table. In fact, as we sit and enjoy our Yom Tov meals, we are privileged to have in our company seven of the undisputedly greatest leaders of Klal Israel of all time.

On one level, the act of inviting these guests into our Sukkah is reminiscent of the supreme importance of having guests, especially those less fortunate then us, to share the joy and simcha of the Yom Tovim with us. The Rambam tells us that any kind of physical enjoyment which is not shared with the poor or less fortunate is viewed by Hashem as "alien" and only enjoyment of our physical beings. When it is shared, our celebration is raised to the heights of Avodat Hashem, Service of Hashem.

Three of these seven guests are our Avot, Avraham, Yitzchak, and Yaakov. We also welcome Moshe Rabbeinu, our great teacher, and his brother Aaron HaKohen, along with Yosef the Righteous, son of Yaakov, and the "sweet singer of Israel," King David. Each of the seven endured difficulties and overcame the struggles of exile with the constant protection and watch of Hashem, and this idea will help introduce us to a much deeper understanding of our Ushpizin Kedoshim.

Avraham was commanded, "Go forth from your homeland, from your birthplace, and from the house of your father, to the land that I will show you" (Bereishit 12:1).

Yitzchak left Caanan for Gerar; "And there was a famine in the land, in addition to the one that occurred in the days of Avraham, and he went to Avimelech, King of the Philistines in Gerar" (Bereishit 26:1).

Yosef was sold as a slave to Egypt. Moshe and Aaron wandered the desert for 40 years and never got to set foot in Israel, and David was forced to flee from his enemies and from the wrath of Saul into the Desert of Judea.

In all these situations, our ancestors taught us how to retain complete emunah and bitachon in Hashem, despite their challenges and troubles, and despite the great adversity that, at times, threatened their very existence. How interesting that these are the guests we invite into our Sukkah, a portable home reminding us of our journey in EXILE. Even more interesting is the fact that we invite these guests into a Sukkah which should really be seen as a shelter of Hashem's protection.

When we leave our home to live in a Sukkah, we don't do that just because for 40 years Bnei Israel lived in the same sort of structured portable house. By swapping our permanent house for a temporary one, we are in fact affirming that we are under the supervision of Hashem, professional mashgiach.

The Vilna Gaon explains that the Jewish people forged a unique relationship with Hashem that made them subject to divine protection. However, it almost disintegrated at the foot of Sinai with the sin of the golden calf. Sukkot marks the day that the Divine Presence of Hashem returned to rest upon the Jewish nation, and was confirmed with the instruction to build the Mishkan. The celebration of Sukkot is a 'zman simchateinu' because the Ananei HaKavod, Clouds of Glory, that protected the Jewish people in the desert, returned to them once more.

The Talmud tells us that it is no coincidence that the time of year that we celebrate our trust in G-d is the fall. The timing of Sukkot seems almost arbitrary. After all, our stay in the desert took place over forty years, rather than a particular week in the year. The timing of Sukkot, no less than the physical structure of the sukkah, is an integral statement of our identity. We are not leaving our homes for relief from the heat of summer; we are leaving our homes to experience our vulnerability.

Every time we walk into a Sukkah, every time we eat in a Sukkah, every time we sing about, celebrate, or enjoy the Sukkah, we are affirming Hashem's protection over us. The same protection that guided our seven holy Ushpizin when they suffered exile.

On January 16th, 1996, then-President of Israel Ezer Weizmann gave a speech to the joint house of the German parliament, in Hebrew. He said:

"I am a wandering Jew who follows in the footsteps of my forebears. And just as I escort them there and now and then, so do my forebears accompany me and stand with me here today."

We are indeed very very lucky to have seven very special, very meaningful forebears join us every Sukkot. And we stand beside them under the shelter of Hashem, and between us lie thousands of years of history and millions of Jews who merited to enjoy the presence of the same guests, and the same protection. How else could the wandering Jew exist for so long, and survive through so many tragedies, if not under the Sukkah?

Chanukah • חֲנוּכָּה

Reminders of Home

By Elianne Neuman

Chanukah commemorates a Jewish revolt which took place over 2,000 years ago —a revolt prompted by opposition to Greek oppression, as well as by a determination to resist assimilation.

Upon becoming the King of Greece, Antiochus Epiphanies embarked on a campaign: to pressure the Jewish people to abandon their religion and to embrace Grecian culture as their own. This worked to a limited extent. Frustrated by Jewish resistance, Antiochus looted the *Beit Hamikdash*, engaged in a murderous campaign against the Jewish people ,and essentially outlawed the practice of Judaism.

Understandably, many Jews were outraged by Antiochus' attack on their institutions and religion. A zealous group of Jews banded together and started the Maccabean revolt. After a hard-fought campaign, the Maccabees, a relatively small force who fought fearlessly against the tremendous Greek armies, were able to rededicate the *Beit Hamikdash* and secure the freedom of the Jewish people.

While there are many miracles of Chanukah, in my opinion, the Maccabee's struggle to regain the *Beit Hamikdash*, the epicentre of *Eretz Yisrael*, the Jewish homeland, and the centre of Jewish sovereignty, is the most wonderful miracle of all.

By recapturing the *Beit Hamikdash*, the Maccabees restored both Jewish self-determination and a sense of national purpose, thereby enabling Judaism to flourish

and the Jewish nation to prosper once again. And by standing up to oppression, the Maccabees provided us with a prime example of Jewish survival throughout the ages.

Although we have been without the *Beit Hamikdash* for close to 2,000 years, we adapted to its absence by building alternative, sustainable institutions which are conducive to ensuring Jewish continuity. Our homes, our synagogues, and our *Torah* have become the epicentres of Jewish life, because they provide us with spiritual and physical sustenance and they enable Judaism to blossom.

By acknowledging the extraordinary measures taken by the Maccabees to become the masters of their spiritual home, the *Beit Hamikdash*, and their physical home, the land of Israel, Chanukah challenges us to reflect on our commitment to ensure that the synagogues and the homes we build maximize our ability to embrace *Torah* and to maintain our Jewish identity.

In so doing, Chanukah challenges us to re-evaluate the environment which we have created for ourselves, because it ultimately affects our values, our personalities, and our abilities to perform *mitzvot*. On Chanukah, we should ask ourselves what sacrifices we would be prepared to make in order to preserve our religion and our identity. And on Chanukah, we should strive to create warm, welcoming surroundings which allow us to feel connected to *Torah* and *Am Yisrael*.

Sukkot

By Becky Friedman

I know what you're thinking, if you just read the title. Succot? What has that got to do with Chanuka? Succot was months ago! But bear with me for a moment: there may be more in common between the two holidays than you think.

As you know, we light the chanukiah in accordance with Beit Hillel, adding another candle each day. But Beit Shammai's opinion-- the one we ended up not using-- suggests *starting* with eight candles and removing one each day. Even though we don't follow this practice, there must be a reason behind it. But why would he have such a crazy idea? After all, according to Hillel, "we rise in holiness, not diminish"! The answer can be given in one word: Succot.

By now I'm at risk of losing my audience, so I'd better cut to the chase. Why is Chanuka called Chanuka? Because of "Chanukat Hamizbeach"-- the Rededication of the Temple. And Succot was the time of the original "Chanukat Hamizbeach"-- the Dedication of the First Temple in the time of Shlomo. Not only that, but in the book of Ezra, it is mentioned that the people celebrated Succot at the time of the Dedication of the Second Temple. Those who made Chanuka a holiday wanted very much to evoke comparisons to Succot.

As was mentioned before, Shammai wanted to remove one candle each day, in order to emulate the Succot sacrifices, in which one less bull is sacrificed each day. Although this practice wasn't adopted, there are several other striking similarities.

Why is Chanuka eight days long, the only holiday with that number of days? Why not seven? After all, the miracle of the oil was only a miracle for the latter seven days that it burned, and not for the first, when it was expected to burn-- and seven is a common number of days for a Jewish holiday. Or why not one day? Why drag it out? Why eight days? Succot. Succot (in Israel) is seven days, but that becomes eight if we include Shemini Atzeret, the added eighth day of celebration following Succot.

By December, it's too cold to even think about living outside in a Succah, but as you light your chanukiah-- adding candles, rather than subtracting bulls-- it might be worth your while to reflect on Succot anyway-- that was the intention.

Jewish holidays aren't random; they are deeply interconnected. The Shalosh Regalim and Yamim Noraim come from the Torah, but what about the others? They are there, too. Chanuka is hinted at by the segments in the Torah discussing both Succot and the dedication of the Temple, just as Purim is hinted at by Yom HaKiPURIM. I myself have complained that Chanuka gets undeserved stage time just because of its proximity to the major Christian holiday of Christmas, while the Shloshet Regalim are our 'real' holidays, but in fact, Chanuka is as legitimate a holiday, as divinely ordained a holiday, as-- as Succot!

Chanukah's Relevance

By Idan Bergman

Chanukah is one of only two celebrated religious *chagim* not mentioned in the Torah. Nevertheless, it is probably one of the most celebrated *chagim* in any Jewish household. But we know that each Friday night, only 36% of Jewish households light Shabbat candles. You may then ask the question: why is lighting one set of candles more popular than lighting another set? Why do we favour one act over another, similar, act? In addition to this, an even more concerning phenomenon is our lack of observance of the rest of the *chagim*--the G-d-given *chagim*. It can be said, sadly, that in general, the *chagim* commanded to us by the Almighty G-d are those that we observe the least, and the *chagim* decreed to us by the Rabbis are those that we observe the most.

Let us first inquire into the strength that Rabbinical and Biblical teachings have. Moshe Rabeinu proclaims in the desert that the Rabbinic teachings after his death must be observed, no matter their absurdity. He tells Israel that *"You shall do according to the word that [the Kohanim] will tell you...You shall not turn from the word that they will tell you, right or left. And the man that will act with willfulness, not listening to the Kohen...that man shall die and you shall destroy the evil from among Israel" (Dvarim 17:10-12).* Evidently, much strength is given to Rabbinic Law as well, and it may seem that Judaism regards Rabbinic Law with the same authority as Biblical Law. What is Biblical Law's authority? Hashem commands us in Parashat Eikev to *"observe the commandments of Hashem, your G-d, to go in his ways and fear Him" (8:6),* and if this is forgotten, Hashem will *"testify against [us] today that [we] will perish" (8:19).* Surely we can see here that Biblical Tradition and Oral Tradition share similar punishments for misuse.

Nevertheless, when it comes to establishing *chagim*, any person can agree that a *chag* declared by G-d has more force than one declared by people. So although, according to the Torah, Rabbinic and Biblical *teachings* or *laws* are equal in their importance, we must agree that Rabbinically established *chagim*, which do not affect our actual observance of the law, are less significant. With this said, our question of why Chanukah, a Rabbinically established *chag*, is observed more than an equally or more important *chag* still stands.

The Jewish people have forever been blessed with *nissim*, miracles, from the time that they became a nation unto itself. However, most of the *nissim* they encountered affected single people, or relatively small groups of people. A "public *nes*" that actually saved the people has only occurred twice in our history: Purim and Chanukah. And even these two *chagim* are different kinds of "public *nissim*," whereby in Purim the Jewish "body" was saved, and in Chanukah the Jewish *"ruach,"* the Jewish "soul" was saved. To elaborate, the story of Purim details the Jewish people's fight for their actual lives, and by defeating their enemies, they were saved from extermination. On the other hand, in the story of Chanukah, the Jewish people are exposed to an intimidating "shiny and modern" culture, and have to overcome their temptations by force in order to save their spiritual connection with Judaism.

To apply this, "shiny cultures" should not sound so foreign to your ears. The Jewish people have been exposed to the "outside world" for thousands of years, and this exposure ,and what it can entail, is exactly why the Rabbis decided to proclaim Chanukah a holiday. They came to warn us of the every-day Chanukah, the Chanukah in which our connection to Hashem is challenged and our observance weakened. Even though in the story of Chanukah, thousands of Jews were eventually exiled and killed and had their *"guf,"* their *"*body," threatened by Antiochus, all this was only a result of their initial assimilation into a foreign culture which resulted in their loss of interest in Hashem.

Another interesting point is that to overcome the Greek threat, the Jewish people, led by the Hasmoneans, fought against all odds in numbers and in power. Unlike most wars in history, the Jewish people fought for their *spiritual survival* and not for their bodily survival. Therefore, we can interpret that to say that our spirituality is our way of survival, and when threatened, we must take these threats seriously.

An example of our struggle for survival that is relevant to today is that it is not only the fight against the denial of Judaism's legitimacy; rather, it can also be that of Israel's legitimacy. The spiritual and emotional connection we have with the land and state of Israel are deeply-rooted in our bones. Thus, any propaganda that solely tries to spread hatred of Israel to others should spark a physical action from us. Whether putting up signs defending Israel, or informing people about the facts, or writing letters to important parties of power on the issue, any action which can combat the spiritual attack on us is essential for our existence.

Now, one may say that the Jews of our time are losing faith and are losing belief, but if this is true, why do they burden themselves to light the Chanukah candles? Should they bother with any *chag* at all if they have lost faith long ago? My answer is no. Chanukah is a symbol of our response to the hardships we face amongst the nations, and to the temptations we have toward their culture. The very fact that some acculturated Jews light the Chanukah candles means that the goal of Chanukah is being fulfilled. We as a people have not yet lost our will to fight for our *emunah* in Hashem, and we thank the Rabbis for providing for us a miraculous and also relevant example to which we can relate in our lives.

We Are Miraculous
By Matthew Goodman

"The sea saw and fled" (Tehillim 114:3)

When the Jewish people came to the Red Sea, the sea saw Yosef's coffin that was being carried with them, and fled. In merit of the one who withheld and did not succumb, the sea split for Israel. It fled in honour of the one who fled.

Rav Yissochar Frand explains that in this week's parsha, Vayeishev, the term "vayanos hachutzah," and he fled outside, is repeated four times.

The same terminology was previously used in Lech Lecha, during the Covenant Between the Pieces. Hashem took Avraham "hachutzah," outside, and the Midrash explains that Hashem told him, "Go out from your constellation." Go out from what is normal. Go out from what is natural. Avraham, at his age, would not naturally have children. Yet he did, and Yitzchak was born to him.

The term "Vayotze oto hachutzah" means to do what is usually abnormal. In Vayeishev, we learn that Yosef did something that was certainly "yotze" from what is normal. Every assumption would suggest that Yosef would have succumbed to Potiphar's wife. However, Yosef overcame temptation. He fled and ran out of the house.

Therefore, when Yosef's coffin arrived at the Red Sea, it split in his merit. It fled before the one who fled.

The Sefer HaPardes, as Rav Frand points out, explains that there are 112 pesukim in this week's Parsha. All but eight of those pesukim begin with a vav. The Shemen HaTov, by Rabbi Dov Weinberger, suggests all the incidents in the parsha are one big vav. "And this happened, and this happened, and this...and this...and this."

This may be the way things work in the "normal" world. History is one thing inexplicably leading to the next. Jews, however, are a little different. The eight pesukim that do not have a vav teach us about the entire parsha. None of it is one big vav. Nothing in Jewish history is just cause and effect.

Just as the last eight pesukim are all "Yotze dofen," abnormal-- all are, essentially, "vayanos vayetze,"-- so, too, are the next eight days "Yotze dofen." On Chanukah we celebrate a grand miracle -- an absurdity of nature. A small jug of oil that burned for eight days. A small army of Jews who achieved great victory in battle against foes immeasurable.

Those miracles are in no way everyday occurrences, but they happened, because the Jewish people have a miraculous existence.

By the normal course of history, we should have been swept away in the dust after our vast expulsion and exile into Babylon. There we should have rotted and died out, never to revisit the Promised Land.

By the normal course of history, we should have slowly dissolved into the Hellenistic superpower of thought and culture that consumed the Mediterranean, like all the other countries the Greeks saw fit to conquer.

By the normal course of history, we should have been washed away by the Romans and spread far across the earth, blown away like sand, and never returned again, after the first revolt. And certainly after the second revolt.

If everything went the way it "should," we would have been dissipated long before any Crusade, Inquisition, or Holocaust. Hashem only knows why we were not. Indeed, Hashem only knows.

This Shabbos, as you stand around your Chanukiah and your Shabbat candles, with your family beside you, and you celebrate the miracles that we are now so used to, look into the flames. Stare at them and remember all that they remind us of. Stare at them and remember how we have always survived. Just like Avraham, just like Yosef, just like Parshat Vayeishev, just like our ancestors, we Jews are all miraculous.

Purim • פורים

The Difference
By Becky Friedman

Whenever I read Megillat Esther, it reminds me distinctly of Yetziat Mitzraim, and not just in the general, Jewish-Holidays-that-start-with-a-P sort of way. In both stories, the Jewish people, after a shift in the balance of power, find themselves in peril, and are ultimately saved by one, maybe two, people in high places, with, of course, the help of G-d.

Megillat Esther begins with the banishment of Vashti-- this, I contend, is on a par with the death of the Pharoah who knew Joseph, as setting the stage for regime change. In chapter two, Esther becomes queen, just as in chapter two of Shmot, Moshe is taken in by Pharoah's daughter-- in each, chapter two places our eventual saviour in a position of power *before* sowing the major conflict. True, in Egypt the people were already at that point suffering as slaves, just as in Megillat Esther the people were in exile, but the worst was yet to come.

And then, once these preparations were set in place, along comes another regime change: Haman is given a new high status in Achashverosh's court, and in Egypt a new Pharoah ascends the throne. With the latter, the people of Israel cry out to G-d, signifying that their suffering was worse under him than under his predecessors. With the former, conflict arises in the form of Mordochai's refusal to bow to Haman, and Haman's resultant decision to destroy the Jewish people.

In each story, in reaction to these seeds of conflict, our hero-- Esther and Moshe, respectively-- is told by an authority figure-- Mordochai for Esther, and G-d (lehavdil) for Moshe-- to speak to the king on behalf of the Jewish people. Each reluctantly agrees, after a lengthy negotiation, and speaks to the king.

But there, at a little bit before the halfway point, is where the similarities end, at least until we jump further ahead and find the deaths of the wicked Haman and the evil Pharoah, and the redemption in each case of the Jewish people, coupled with the destruction of many of their enemies.

What causes the two stories to diverge? In what way do they become so different? There are many answers, many different approaches to this question.

I could give the simple answer: G-d's name is not mentioned once in the story of Esther, while He is ever-present in the story of Yetziat Mitzraim. But while that answer works on one level of understanding, after all this build-up, it fails to satisfy me. After all, Esther spent three days fasting, along with Mordochai and all the Jews of Shushan, prior to approaching the king. If that isn't an appeal to G-d, I don't know what is! And it's believed that Esther's fast days coincided with Pesach: if I accept this answer, the stories become even closer!

Another difference between the stories is the reaction of the king: Pharoah adamantly refused, while Achashverosh promised to grant Esther up to "half his kingdom". Yes, this is true, but I'm still not satisfied. Keep in mind that Pharoah is doing double duty as both the villain and the king; at this point in Esther's story, Haman is still plotting the evil he will cause the Jewish people.

My answer is our hero's outlook on the people's predicament. Moshe clearly wants Pharoah to release the people; he unleashes upon him the ten plagues, and while the Jews were immune to most of the plagues, the implication is that he will risk whatever loss of life necessary to effect their freedom.

Esther, on the other hand, puts her people's lives above all else. "If only as slaves and maids we had been sold, I would have been silent," she declares. Now, curiously, this passage is one which, for me, *most* evokes the story of Yetziat Mitzraim. After all, there are few enough examples of the Jewish people being "sold as slaves and maids." But what is Esther saying here? She is saying that if she had been in Moshe's place, she would not have bothered-- or at least that, comparatively, their predicament in her time is far more serious.

Esther is saying that Purim is much more important than Pesach. Or is she?

Pesach is a serious holiday, to a point; we celebrate our freedom. We spend a night or two feasting, recounting history, and praying, but we stop for a minute to show pity to our oppressors. Pesach is a holiday of freedom, so we are solemn.

Purim is a far less serious holiday, whimsical, even; we celebrate our lives. We spend a day in festive costumes, feasting and drinking and retelling the story in a state of high energy. Far from mourning our enemies' deaths, we curse them, we make noise when we hear their names. On Purim we celebrate a narrow escape from death; we have no thoughts to spare for any but ourselves.

When your enemies enslave you, but let you live, they are still deserving of pity; when they want you dead, it is a mitzva to kill them first. On Pesach, we became a people. But now, on Purim, we have salvaged our right to remain one.

So let us rejoice.

Spreading Awareness
By Teddy Kravetsky

Every year, Purim comes around, and we do the same things, such as read the Megilah and give tzedakah. Although these are very important mizvot instituted by the rabbis, there is something else that I think many of us ignore completely: the topic of anti-Semitism and the role it plays in the story of Purim.

In order to understand why the story of Purim happened, it is vitally important to learn about how anti-Semitism played a role in it and to spread awareness so that it may never happen again. In the story of Purim, one of the factors leading to the rise of Haman comes from his supporters, who are clearly anti-Semitic, as they show a hatred for Jews based on what Haman tells them.

This can teach us two valuable lessons that Jews even today can learn from in order to help prevent future anti-Semitism from happening. The first is that one should always have the facts straight; skewing or misunderstanding what someone else is saying is a major cause for anti-Semitism, as a lot of the "facts" that anti-Semites hear are false. This is important, because misunderstanding facts turns them into rumours and, as many have experienced, a false rumor can lead to a world of unnecessary suffering.

The second lesson is that spreading awareness is vital in order for an idea to live on in the memories of future generations. This is not to say that spreading awareness is always a good thing; in fact, in the story of Purim it's the exact opposite. In the Purim story, Haman spreads awareness of anti-Semitism, which obviously works, as he gains many supporters for his plan in all 126 provinces under the king.

However, the concept of awareness can also be used as an advantage to the Jews, to spread the word about anti-Semitism being a bad thing to those who believe otherwise. This can be just as useful-- if not more so--

than spreading anti-Semitism, as it brings awareness to those who have never learned that Jews really aren't evil people. This is why spreading awareness is so important in today's society, where information can be sent to millions of people at the click of a few buttons.

In order to truly make a difference, the words being spread have to be true, and not skewed to reflect one's own views. I encourage and challenge everyone who reads this article to spread the word about anti-Semitism and to get as many people as you can to realize that it's wrong and should never be viewed as okay. This is just the start, though, of the fight against it. In order to really wipe out anti-Semitism, we need bright young leaders to step up and speak out against those bad-mouthing Jews, as this is the only way that anything will be done to completely destroy this evil sentiment that many still have today.

The Hidden Face of Hashem
By Matthew Goodman

The Talmud (Ta'anit 25a) relates a story about miracles. Rav Chanina ben Dosa was known for his extremely dire financial straits and for the blatant miracles which followed him. Once, on Erev Shabbos, he noticed that his daughter was upset. He said to her, "My daughter, why are you sad?" She replied, "The oil can got mixed with the vinegar can, and I lit the Shabbos lights with the vinegar." He said to her, "My daughter, why should this trouble you? He who commanded the oil to burn will also command the vinegar to burn!" Just as Rav Chanina said, the vinegar burned, and remained lit the whole of Shabbos.

Rav Chanina did not say to his daughter, "Want to see something amazing? Look at this miracle!" To him, vinegar burning was no more spectacular than oil burning, even though it is not the nature of vinegar to burn. They are both, in fact, miracles. If a miracle can be described as Hashem's intervention in the world, then everything is a miracle, and nature is simply a curtain that shields the workings of Hashem. Many times, however, we don't bother to look beyond what we see. We often have a little Wizard of Oz on our shoulders who says, "Pay no attention to the man behind the curtain."

Out of the 24 books of the Tanach, Megillat Esther is the only one to never mention the name of Hashem once. It seems like He is completely absent from the entire narrative! Chazal teach us that Hashem is definitely not absent. Rather, Hashem is hidden. The Gemara (Chulin 139b) asks, "Where was Hashem in the story of Esther?" Rav Matna replies, "Veanochi Haster Astir panai bayom hahu" - And I will surely hide my face on that day (Dvarim 31:18). The name Esther comes from the word "Astir" which connotes concealment, showing that Hashem was merely hidden in the narrative.

The Bnei Yissachar explains that "concealment" conveys the essence of the Purim story. On Chanukah, Hashem defied the laws of nature to save us, while on Purim, salvation came from within a series of coincidences. It seemed like Hashem's hand was not at work, but really, it was. We just had to notice it.

The Megillah is filled with examples of secret Divine Providence interfering with the narrative. One particularly deep insight into the story summarizes the necessary outlook we should have when considering the events of Purim.

King Achashverosh signed an edict that all the Jews were to be killed. Mordechai asked Esther to intervene on behalf of the Jews, but Esther was hesitant. Anyone who entered the court of the King without permission was put to death, unless the king held out his golden scepter. Esther instructed Mordechai to gather all the Jews of Shushan, and they, along with her and her attendants, fasted for three days, and then she went to the King.

Ibn Ezra points out how unusual Esther's actions were. A person who fasts for so long will obviously become weak and look weak. Esther would be jeopardizing her beauty by fasting. The King chose her for her particular beauty. How could she diminish the assets that made her favourable before the King? Furthermore, why would she tell Mordechai about the fast?

The Talmud tells us that Esther was not really so attractive, but Hashem gave her enough charm to appeal to Achashverosh. Esther realized that her fortune was because of the hand of Hashem, and knew that here she could not rely on her physical beauty. In order to build up that trust with Hashem, she decided to fast, knowing that it would diminish her beauty, because her success would be 100% in the hands of Hashem anyway. If she was meant to succeed, then she would, and vice versa. She revealed her plans to Mordechai so that the Jewish nation would be forced to trust in Hashem. They would hear that Esther was jeopardizing her beauty, the asset they thought was so critical, and become distraught. They would not be able to rely on anything other than Hashem's countenance.

On Chanukah, Hashem came down to the Jews, displaying His providence with grand and exquisite miracles. On Purim, the Jews brought Hashem down to them. They realized that what could be considered at face value as coincidences, politics, or natural events, were actually all the hand of Hashem. Yes, the name of Hashem is not mentioned, but Hashem was still there. He was simply behind the curtain.

One has to realize how important and amazing it was for the Jews of Shushan to "pay attention to the man behind the curtain." The Sefat Emet explains that the deep understanding of Divine Providence manifesting itself in the natural course of history gave that particular generation the privilege to seal the unification between the Jewish people and the Torah and make it complete. The Talmud (Shabbat 88a) says that the Jews accepted Torah two times. Once at Har Sinai, where they had no choice, and a second time in the days of Achashverosh, where Jews re-accepted Torah out of their own free will. The realization of Hashem in the story of Esther was amazing enough to have been a second Kabbalat Torah! The fact that the Jews of Persia were able to reveal Hashem's presence despite the lack of an emblazoned signature was a tremendous thing.

Rabbi Mordechai Kamenetzky tells the following story that beautifully summarizes this whole theme:

It was a sweltering August day when the Greenberg brothers entered the posh Dearborn, Michigan offices of the notriously anti-Semetic carmaker, Henry Ford. "Mr. Ford!" announced Hyman Greenberg, the eldest of the three, "we have a remarkable invention that will revolutionize the automobile industry!" Ford looked skeptical, but their threats to offer it to the competition kept his interest piqued. "We would like to demonstrate to you in person." After a little cajoling, they brought Mr. Ford outside and asked him to enter a black car that was parked in front of the building.

Norman Greenberg, the middle brother, opened the door of the car. "Please step inside, Mr. Ford." "What?!" shouted Ford. "Are you crazy?!!! It must be two hundred degrees in that car!" "It is," smiled the youngest brother, Max, "but sit down, Mr. Ford, and push the white button."

Intrigued, Ford sat down and pushed the button. All of a sudden, a whoosh of freezing air started blowing from vents all around the car, and, within seconds, the automobile became quite cool. "This is amazing!" exclaimed Ford. "How much do you want for the patent?"

"The price is one million dollars," stated Norman. Then he paused. "And there's something else," he said. "We want the name 'Greenberg Bothers Air Conditioning' stamped right next to the Ford logo." "Money is no problem," retorted Ford, "but I will not have a Jewish name next to the logo on my cars!"

They haggled back and forth for a while, and finally they settled. One and one half million dollars, and the name Greenberg would be left off. However, the first names of the Greenberg brothers would be forever emblazoned upon the console of every Ford air conditioning system. And that is why today, whenever you enter a Ford vehicle, you will see those three names clearly defined on the air-conditioning panel: *HI - NORM - MAX*.

Hashem may not have been as present or distinguishable in the story of Esther as in the story of the Exodus. Hashem may not be as present or distinguishable today as He was in Biblical times. Unlike the Greenberg brothers, his signature is not usually vividly emblazoned across his deeds, serving as a testament for all times. There is no doubt, however, that His hand is ever-present in the world. His face is hidden, but it is still there. We just have to be able to find it.

A Day Like Purim
By Elianne Neuman

You may have noticed the similarity in the names of two Jewish holidays – Yom Hakipurim (the Biblical name for Yom Kippur) and Purim. This similarity could indicate that these two holidays are connected to one another. But how could these two days – one which commemorates the most solemn day in the Jewish calendar and the other which celebrates the most jovial – be associated?

Rabbi Yitzchak Luria observed that this similarity is not just by chance. The Biblical name for Yom Kippur, the Day of Atonement, can be read as Yom *Ke*purim – a day that resembles Purim. According to Rabbi Luria, notwithstanding the very different ways in which we mark these two events, namely, that Purim is a celebratory day whereas Yom Kippur is not, they are closely related to one another. But how can this be? How can Rabbi Luria's statement, that Yom Kippur is like Purim, be reconciled?

Before this question can be meaningfully addressed, another one must be posed.

In Pesachim 68b, Rabbi Yehoshua stated that every holiday has two essential components: one being physical, and the other being spiritual. To illustrate his point, Rabbi Yehoshua observed that Shabbatot and Festivals should be spent in eating and drinking, to satisfy the physical component, and in studying Torah, to address the spiritual.

The exception to this rule occurs on Yom Kippur and on Purim. Yom Kippur is a completely spiritual day, which is celebrated by fasting and praying. Purim, however, is a purely physical day, which is celebrated by feasting and partying. How is it that these two holidays violate Rabbi Yehoshua's dictum?

The Vilna Gaon explains that Yom Kippur and Purim are meant to be opposites in order to fulfill the other holiday's deficiency. According to the Vilna Gaon, our spiritual efforts on Yom Kippur are meant to balance our physical endeavours on Purim, and vice versa.

So, according the Vilna Gaon, Yom Kippur and Purim complement each other. But is one—namely, the spiritual or the physical day—holier than the other?

It would be logical to assume that the Day of Atonement, the spiritual holiday, the day of affliction, is a holier day than Purim, the day of indulgence. But this is not necessarily so. According to Rabbi Eliyahu Kitov, holiness which is a result of celebration is more meritorious than holiness achieved through suffering or sadness. Rabbi Kitov writes:

> *If one attains holiness through affliction, and another attains holiness through indulgence, who is the greater of the two? It may be said that the one who attains holiness through indulgence is greater, for the attainment of holiness through indulgence requires an infinitely greater degree of striving and effort.*

There is a very important lesson to learn from Rabbi Kitov's statement.

Purim is the holiday that compels us to eat, to drink, and to be merry. But it challenges us to do more than just that. Purim, properly celebrated, is a day of holiness resulting from celebration and thus, it encourages us to be reflective: to think about the mitzvot we do, how they sanctify the mundane, how it is that they help us connect to Hashem, and how it is that they influence us for the better. This is a formidable task, but it is one well worth undertaking.

Mishloach Manot

By Idan Bergman

The story of Purim, with all its miracles, has both sadness and happiness-- fasts, feasts, annihilation, and redemption. When it came to finding a way to establish the modes of remembrance for the holiday for future generations, Mordechai and Ester decided to take both aspects of sadness and happiness into account. In terms of sadness, they required the Jewish people to fast on the day before Purim, Ta'anit Esther, but in terms of happiness, *simcha*, Mordechai chose three mitzvot: "days of feasting and gladness, sending portions one to another, and gifts to the poor" (Esther, 9,22). The reasons are more clear for the mitzvot of feasting and charity. First, the feast we conduct, with food and wine, helps us rejoice in the miracle of Purim just like on other holidays. Second, charity to the needy, is a tradition commanded to us in the Torah, and is one in which we perform before the other holidays as well on a regular basis. But what is the reason for the third mitzvah, sending portions to another-- giving *mishloach manot*?

The Rabbis ask this question, and provide two answers.

Rabbi Israel Isserlein, author of the "Trumat Hadeshen", explains that *mishloach manot* is directly connected with the mitzvah of the feast-- *seudat Purim*. While knowing that not all people have the means to prepare enough for their own Purim feast, the concept of *mishloach manot* was thus imposed in order to help those needy people who do not have the resources for the feast, and, as a result, to allow for all of Am Israel to sit and feast in commemoration of the miracles of Purim. We can assume from Rabbi Isserlein's interpretation that *mishloach manot* are only intended for the needy Jews who are not able to finance their own *seudat Purim*. If this is true, though, shouldn't Mordechai have emphasized that only the *rich* gave? Why, then, does the megillah require that *all* give *mishloach manot?* The Chatam Sofer answers, explaining that the mitzvah is for all to perform because of an ethical aspect, that klal yisrael not embarrass the needy or less fortunate by only giving *them* the portions, but rather that each person, rich or poor, provide for each other's feasts.

The other opinion brought forth for the reasons for *mishloach manot* comes from the author of the poem Lecha Dodi, Rabbi Shlomo Alkabetz. He explains that the mitzvah of *mishloach manot* contains an aspect of connectivity and unity between Am Israel, which was lacking at first in the time of the megillah, but was later regained to an extent which led to Haman and his aides to fall. We therefore perform the mitzvah by visiting friends and colleagues and greeting them with warm smiles and kind gifts in order to dismiss Haman's curse on us which was that we are "a people scattered abroad and dispersed among the peoples" (3,8), and so that our love for one another could always shine and help us overcome our hardships as a nation as it did in the time of Esther and Mordechai.

And so, there are two purposes for *mishloach manot*, one physical and one spiritual. One to assist in the feast so that all Klal Yisrael could perform it, and one to unite Am Israel and create peace amongst our nation.

Pesach • פסח

The Bread of Freedom
By Matthew Goodman

The holiday of Pesach commemorates the awesome redemption of the Jewish people from Egyptian bondage by Hashem Almighty. The obvious focal point of the festival is the Pesach Seder, occurring each night of the first two Yamim Tovim. Despite the implication of its name, literally meaning organized sequence or order, the Seder is far from straightforward. Compiled by the Sages, retelling the narrative of the Exodus while delineating the rituals and blessings intrinsic to the observance of the holiday, the Seder holds many hidden secrets, that, when uncovered, reveal tremendous teachings. Many of these lessons are buried deep within complications, problems, and questions that arise from the texts of the Haggadah or the aspects of the rituals. Our attempts to answer these problems make the Seder a truly marvelous and illuminating event.

I heard the following question from Rabbi Jay Kelman. One of the most striking questions in the entire Haggadah has to do with the depiction of the Mitzvah of eating Matzah. The Torah clearly tells us that there is a requirement to eat Matzot during the holiday. The reason for the Mitzvah, as brought down in the Haggadah, however, is seemingly dichotomous. At the beginning of Magid, the section in the Haggadah that relates the story of the Exodus, we lift up the Matzah and recite the declaration "Ha Lachma." The first line reads: "This is the bread of affliction that our ancestors ate in the land of Egypt." The Maharsha, Rabbi Shmuel Eidels (1555-1631), explains that the Matzah was the food that the Jewish slaves ate in Egypt, and thus Matzah reminds us of our slavery.

Later on in Magid, we quote Rabban Gamliel from the Mishna (Pesachim 10:5), who says: "This Matzah which we eat, what does it mean? Because the dough of our fathers did not have time to become leavened before the King of kings, the Holy One, blessed be He, revealed Himself to them and redeemed them; as it is said: 'They baked unleavened cakes of the dough that they had brought forth out of Egypt, for it was not leavened, because they were thrust out of Egypt and could not tarry...' (Shemot 12:39)." It seems that Rabban Gamliel views Matzah as the bread of redemption, the food that Klal Yisrael ate after the had been redeemed from Egypt.

This dichotomy is likewise presented in the verse that commands us to eat Matzot. The Torah tells us, "You shall not eat leaven with it; for seven days you shall eat it Matzot [unleavened], the *lechem oni* [bread of affliction], for in haste you went out of the land of Egypt, so that you shall remember the day when you went out of the land of Egypt all the days of your life" (Devarim 16:3).

Rashi comments that Matzah is called "the bread of affliction" as it reminds us of Klal Yisrael's anguish in Egypt. Similarly, the Ramban equates this mention of "lechem oni" to Ha Lachma's description of Matzah as "lachma anya," the bread of affliction that our ancestors ate in the land of Egypt. The Abarbanel, Rabbi Yitzchak ben Judah Abarbanel (1437-1508), on the other hand, points out that since Matzah is equated with the haste in which we left Egypt, it actually reminds us of our redemption.

What does Matzah really symbolize? How could it possibly embody two such opposing ideas, affliction and redemption?

The Maharal, Rabbi Yehudah Loew (1520-1609), deals with our question in his work on Pesach, Gevurot Hashem (Ch. 36). He begins by explaining that the understanding of "lechem oni" as a reference to the fact that the Egyptians fed the Jewish people Matzot as slaves is an incorrect interpretation of the text. There is no source that says that the Jews ate Matzot as slaves. Furthermore, equating Matzah with redemption and emancipation means that Matzah was not eaten during times of slavery, but rather, during times of freedom!

"Lechem oni" is actually a description of the Matzah. The unleavened bread itself is bread of poverty. The Maharal explains (as translated by Rabbi Shaya Karlinksy): "A poor person, who lacks money and possessions, has nothing besides himself and his body, the basic minimum for existence. His being and identity, as a poor person, are independent of anything outside of himself and his essence. Matzah, too, has nothing besides the basic minimum for making up the dough, flour and water. If it has yeast or any leavening, this adds something to the dough beyond the bare minimum, and it is no longer Matzah, no longer the bread of poverty."

Chazal refer to Matzah with additives such as eggs, oil, or other sweeteners as "Matzah ashira," rich bread, which does not adequately fulfill the Mitzvah of eating Matzah. (Pesachim 36a; see *Shulchan Aruch, Orach Chaim* 462:1). Matzah made from only flour or water, without yeast or sweeteners, is called "Lechem oni." Similarly, the Gemara (Shabbat 79a) explains that the meaning of Matzah is something simple. For instance, a totally unworked piece of animal hide is called Matzah.

Matzah is quintessential bread -- it is the intrinsic raw essence of what bread is. There is no dichotomy within the Haggadah or the Torah in regard to Matzah. It was never eaten in slavery and then eaten in freedom. Rather, it was eaten at the time of the redemption, and the idea of "Lechem oni" is actually a fundamental reason why Matzah is a symbol of redemption and freedom.

The Maharal goes on to explain that the physical world is one of tremendous complexity and interdependence, in which everything is connected to everything else. The spiritual world is simplistic and independent. Redemption means connecting to the essential truths of the spiritual world. A slave is not independent, as he is owned by his master. A rich person is not independent, as he can easily be controlled by his possessions and wealth, and identify himself with them. A poor person, having nothing but himself, separate and independent from anything physical outside of himself, is the epitome of freedom. He is his essence. He is nothing but himself. The Maharal is obviously not advocating a life of shunning the physical, nor is he advocating a life independent of human interaction. To do so would be antithetical to Torah values. Rather, he is using Matzah to explain what real freedom is, and his conclusion is stunning. Freedom is knowing who you are at your very core. Freedom is connecting to your essence.

The most dominant theme in the entire holiday of Pesach has to be the idea of freedom, yet the concept is unbelievably difficult to comprehend, and the word itself has the ability to be terribly misused. The Maharal's explanation of Matzah, however, provides us with the key to understanding this elusive concept.

The type of slavery endured by the Jewish people in Egypt was far more virulent than a physical one. It was inherently spiritual. The Hebrew word for Egypt, Mitzrayim, comes from the root, "Metzar," meaning narrow or constricting. Egypt was a place where people were spiritually enslaved by all sorts of physical taskmasters. They allowed their inclination to appease their bodily yearnings run rampant. Thus, the very name of the Egyptian leader, Pharaoh, is rooted in the word "Parua," meaning wild or untamed. The Rambam (Mishna Torah, Hilchot Avodah Kochavim 1:3) explains that the Jews "learned from the Egyptians' deeds." They adopted Egyptian values and worshiped Egyptian gods, eventually becoming enslaved by the spiritual vacuum that was Egyptian culture.

The redemption from this slavery is epitomized in the message that Hashem instructed Moshe to give to Pharaoh. The Torah relates: "And you shall say to him: The Lord G-d of the Hebrews sent me to you, saying, 'Send forth My people, so that they may serve Me in the desert'" (Shemot 7:16). At first glance, it seems that the Jewish people went from slavery to... slavery! The pasuk clearly states that the purpose of the redemption was to bring the Jews into Divine service. How is the yoke of Divine service, Mitzvot, and Torah observance considered to be freedom? These obligations literally envelope our entire lives!

The truth of the matter, however, is that the purpose of Torah observance is not to place a heavy burden on our shoulders, nor does it mean to serve Hashem. In actuality, the whole fundamental reason behind the Torah is to connect us with "Lechem oni" -- the truth. The quintessence of our being. That is to say, Torah allows us to be ourselves. It helps us become less of a body and more of a soul. It gives us purpose, meaning, and understanding of our existence. This idea is ratified by a pasuk in Shlomo HaMelech's Mishlei: "Take fast hold of Musar (morality/ethics), do not let it loose; guard it, for it is your life" (Mishlei 4:13). The Vilna Gaon asks: how could Musar be our life? Torah is our life! Mitzvot are our life! He answers by explaining that the whole point of Torah is really to make us better people. Mitzvot are a means to an end, and the goal is human transformation, to the point that we are fully connected to our spiritual essence.

Freedom is the state in which one's essence, the soul, is in complete control of every single action. That is "Lechem oni." You are nothing but yourself. This is achieved through the intricate and detailed process of Torah observance. Any exterior force outside of the soul that manages to influence your being, such as the body, is a form of spiritual slavery. The Gemara tells us that Hashem gave us the Yetzer HaRa, the evil inclination that tempts us towards wrongdoing. In response, Hashem gave us the Torah, the antidote that ensures our freedom from the binds of the Yetzer HaRa.

Pesach adds another dimension to our quest to achieve the state of "Lechem oni." One of the central aspects of Seder night is the question-and-answer framework that is replete throughout the Haggadah. In fact, Chazal tell us that there is a requirement to ask questions at the Seder, and, for that reason, young children sing "Ma Nishtanah." The Maharal, commenting on the importance of questions, explains that a question is an admission of some lack. By asking a question, a person admits that he is lacking knowledge in a certain respect. This creates an "empty space" within a person that needs to be filled with new knowledge and new ideas. Thus, every single question asked the Seder table yields the potential for tremendous growth.

In order to connect to our essence and achieve the freedom expressed in this fantastic holiday, it is necessary to begin the process of growth through questions. This Pesach, try to illuminate your experience with these ideas. Try to answer some of the "big questions." What is our purpose? Why are we here? What are the things that hold me back in life? What are my inner "Egypts" that block the connection between my actions and my soul?

The Matzah on our tables, a simple combination of flour and water, symbolizes this pursuit. As "Lechem oni," it is nothing but the bare bones of bread. It is simply the truth.

Bringing Us Back
By Becky Friedman

It's said that sometimes, we need to do things in a different way from the norm, in order to keep our brains exercised, and to gain new perspective on what we are doing. For example, if you normally write with your right hand, try writing with your left; or try reading a book you've read many times, but this time back-to-front instead of front-to-back.

Of course, when we're reading the Torah reading or the Haftarah in shul, and when we're conducting the Pesach seder, we have to hold to a very specific structure-- we can't just go doing it backwards in order to see things differently. That's why we should *always* be reading the Torah and the Hagaddah, even when it's not the prescribed time. That way, we have the chance to start at the end, and work our way forward.

At the end of the seder, we joyously proclaim: L'shana Haba'a B'Yerushalaim! Next year in Jerusalem! Coming from the front, this seems straightforward enough; we know that it should be our goal to make aliyah, so that our next seder is conducted in the Holy Land.

But, in fact, there's one word more to the phrase, often not included when it's quoted out-of-context. L'shana Haba'a B'Yerushalaim Habnuia. Next year in the *rebuilt* Jerusalem. What-- is Jerusalem not built? Last time I visited, it was a thriving city! No; the word rebuilt is referring to the Beit Hamikdash. We end our seder, a night of talking about g'eula, redemption, with the hope that we will soon be redeemed from our own exile, and see the coming of the Mashiach and the rebuilding of our Temple.

More about that soon.

At the seder, we drink four cups of wine, each one corresponding to one of the "leshonot hag'eula"-- the words of redemption. These words are "V'hotzeiti, v'hitzalti, v'ga'alti, v'lakachti." *I will remove you [from Egypt]; I will save you; I will redeem you; I will take you [as My people].* Each of these four words is a quote said by G-d in the book of Exodus, referring to the stages by which He will redeem Bnei Yisrael from slavery and bring them to the Land of Israel. In Judaism, wine represents celebration; we commemorate each of these words of redemption with a cup of wine to show our joy at G-d's salvation.

In fact, there is one more prescribed cup of wine at the seder: the cup of Eliahu. In some traditions, this cup is connected with a fifth word of redemption, v'heveiti. *I will bring you [to the Land of Israel].*

Why is the cup of Eliahu so important at the seder? We make a place for Eliahu at several important Jewish events, including the seder and the brit mila; this can be explained through certain stories of Eliahu. He grew very disillusioned with the people of Israel in his time, and believed that they had wholly turned from G-d. Thus, when we attain levels of great observance, as is common at the seder-- many Jews with few other observances continue to make or attend seders-- we invite Eliahu, to show him that there is still hope for the Jewish people.

But that doesn't explain everything. It doesn't, for example, explain why his cup of wine is associated with the Jewish people being brought to the land of Israel. To understand that, we will have to turn to the Haftarah for Shabbat Hagadol-- the Shabbat directly before Pesach, read this Shabbat.

The penultimate pasuk of the Haftarah-- repeated after the end, so that it is the last thing we hear-- discusses Eliahu. *Behold, I will send to you Eliahu HaNavi before the coming of the great and terrible day of the Lord* (Malachi 3:24). G-d promises us that we will be warned of the coming of the Mashiach by Eliahu HaNavi, who will arrive shortly before the day of g'eula.

Suddenly, all the pieces seem to fit together. Eliahu's cup is the one about *bringing* us to the Land, because, when he comes that final time, that is exactly what he will do; he will bring us to the Land of Israel to witness the coming of the Mashiach and to join in the rebuilding of our temple.

We save a place for Eliahu at our seders not only for his benefit, but for our own, for we live in hope that this time, when Eliahu comes, it will be not only to drink of our wine but also to bring us the good news of the coming of the Mashiach-- to tell us what we usually have to tell ourselves: next year, in the rebuilt Jerusalem!

Finally, I work my way backwards to the beginning of the Haftarah for Shabbat Hagadol. The first pasuk in the Haftarah sends us the clearest message of all. *The mincha of Yehuda and Yerushalaim shall be pleasing to G-d, like in the days of yore and in the earlier years* (Malachi 3:4). Just as in the days of the temple, once we rebuild, and make our sacrifices, G-d will accept us again.

May this be the year when Eliahu finally brings us to the rebuilt Jerusalem.

The Beauty of a Question
By Ben Welkovics

What is a question? Is it a symbol of ignorance or of wisdom? Is it a device used to appease curiosity or to provoke thought? Is it a means of learning or of teaching?

For each individual, questions hold a unique significance. In the life of a high school student, questions, for the most part, are obstacles we must overcome in order to pass tests and quizzes. We are asked to display our knowledge and understanding of a subject by answering questions related to the subject. Rarely are we required to ask questions about the subject. Furthermore, we are never evaluated on the questions we ask. But is this the best way to learn? Shouldn't we be required to question our opinions and beliefs rather than blindly accept them? If we don't question our beliefs, how can we support them?

In the Yeshiva world, the highest compliment a student can receive from a teacher is praise for a good question. Why? Because "to ask is to grow" (Rabbi Jonathan Sacks). This beautiful quote means that when one asks a question, he/she shows a passion to grow and to gain understanding. One can be familiar with the answer to a question without being interested in the material. However, when one asks a question there must be an interest in or a fascination for the subject being questioned.

The stimulus behind any question is ignorance. Questions are asked because ignorance exists. Every human being has questions and therefore lacks understanding in certain areas. If one were to know everything, questions would be unnecessary. Therefore, we must be humble and recognize that there is much to learn. The only reason scientific advancements are made is because questions are asked about old theories. Scientists recognize that there is much to uncover and learn, and are therefore never satisfied with what they know. Scientists seek what they don't know, and eagerly work to expand their knowledge base.

According to Rabbi Jonathan Sacks, "questioning is at the heart of Jewish spirituality." Judaism is a religion full of perplexing concepts and challenging ideas. It is therefore essential that one ask questions. To simply accept thoughts, ideas, and opinions without questioning would prevent growth. If you disagree with someone's opinion, challenge it. If you hear a new concept at your seder table, question it.

It is therefore my hope that each of us chooses to ask good questions at our respective seders this Pesach in order to enhance the experience and to spread passion and growth.

The Gift and Responsibility of Freedom
By Elianne Neuman

Pesach is the time of year when we remember our people's ordeal of slavery and exile in Egypt, which ultimately resulted in our redemption and the birth of our nation. With the hand of G-d and with His mighty miracles, we were able to escape the bondage of slavery and start a new chapter. At this time of year, we celebrate our deliverance, as well as our becoming a great nation.

We are instructed in the Haggadah to remember the Exodus from Egypt as if we, ourselves, had seen this great miracle. By doing so, we must think about our freedom, and reflect upon our fortune.

Freedom is a gift which must be guarded, cherished, and protected.

Freedom can be regarded in two ways. There is a physical aspect to freedom, which can be characterized as *"freedom from,"* that is, the liberation from oppression and bondage. But there is also a spiritual aspect of freedom, stemming from the responsibility to exercise our G-d-given free will through the making of moral choices.

The story of the Haggadah documents our struggle to achieve *"freedom from"* Egypt. Once G-d liberated us, He gave us the Torah, which provides us with the blueprint to maximize our success in discharging our responsibilities that are associated with freedom.

The Talmud recognizes the responsibilities of freedom when it describes true freedom as being part of following the Torah and its values. This is so because Torah teaches us to be moral, upstanding, and kind. However, when we abuse our freedom, we become slaves to our evil inclinations. We lose our focus and our ability to take advantage of one of the greatest privileges that G-d has offered us.

The responsibility associated with freedom is a very delicate gift. If this obligation is properly exercised, it holds the promise of successfully achieving our full potential as responsible, moral beings -- but, if neglected, it can lead to very severe consequences. Because of the great risks associated with it, freedom is very much like a beautiful, delicate glass bowl, which deserves to be admired, but must, at the same time, be carefully handled.

Part of the responsibility which comes with freedom is the obligation to teach moral behaviour to others. Our tradition encourages our children to fully participate in the Seder in order to teach them about the miracles of the Exodus. Since freedom is a major theme in the Haggadah, we are, on a deeper level, also educating our younger generations about the gift of freedom, and the responsibilities that come with it.

Wishing you and your families a Chag Kasher Vesameach, I hope you will be able to partake in this wonderful Mitzvah and, in so doing, celebrate both the beauty and the responsibilities associated with the G-d-given gift of freedom.

An Act of Faith
By Becky Friedman

One of the most perplexing aspects to the story of Pesach is the commandment to slaughter a lamb and coat our doorposts with its blood on the night before leaving Egypt. The lamb I understand; it is to be eaten as the Passover sacrifice. But the blood?

"And Hashem will go over to smite Mitzraim, and He will see the blood on the lintel and on the two doorposts, and Hashem will pass over the opening and He will not allow the destruction to come to your houses to smite" (Exodus 12:23).

Moshe explains the commandment of putting blood on the doorposts by saying that when G-d sees the blood on the Jews' doorposts, He will pass over their homes, and the plague of the firstborn will not affect them. And I should be familiar with this reason-- it is, after all, the reason behind the name of the holiday Passover, or Pesach.

But it doesn't make any sense.

Think for a moment: why are we putting the blood on the doorposts? So G-d will see and know that Jews live there, so He'll know not to smite that house. But that's crazy! Shouldn't G-d, being omniscient, already know where the Jews live? Why does G-d need to see blood on our doorposts in order to know not to smite us?

Ah, but-- contrary to our common interpretation of the passage-- Moshe doesn't actually say that G-d will pass over the houses on account of their inhabitants being Jewish. "He will see the blood... and Hashem will pass over the opening"-- G-d already *knows* which homes are Jewish, but it isn't enough. The blood isn't for G-d, it's for you, and the blood itself, not what it signifies, is what saves those homes.

What G-d is asking is for something I called crazy just two paragraphs earlier. What He's asking for is that we put blood on our doorposts despite thinking it shouldn't matter if we do or not. What He's asking for here, really-- is faith.

When the Jews put blood on their doorposts, they were signifying to G-d not that their family was Jewish, but that they were willing to follow this commandment, willing to trust in G-d to save them, willing to make a public declaration of their faith. And when G-d 'saw' that act of faith, He passed over those homes because their inhabitants were truly worthy of belonging to the Jewish nation.

So it is with almost every aspect of our lives.

Why pray? G-d already knows what you're thinking. But when you pray, you're showing G-d that you're willing to make that extra effort, to take that leap of faith and formulate what G-d already knows into words. Why keep kosher? Why keep Shabbat? G-d already knows what's in your mind.

Even more so for Pesach, when we spend a little more than a week operating under a much more stringent set of rules, many of which we don't and won't understand. Why do we bother, when it would be so much easier to just say, "I don't need any of these crazy rules; G-d already understands my intentions"? Because G-d asked us to. And He asked us to show a little faith.

May your faith this Pesach be as strong and as fruitful as the faith of those who coated their doorposts in blood.

The Shofar's SHABBOS COMPANION

Sefirat HaOmer
By Idan Bergman

The Torah commands us to count seven full weeks from the second night of Passover until Shavuot. Counting begins on the second night of Passover, since this was the night on which the omer (new barley offering) was brought to the Beit Hamikdash, and it continues for forty-nine days, until Shavuot-- the day that the Jewish people first gathered at Har Sinai after leaving Egypt, and received the Torah. Hence the name *sefirat haomer*, counting of the omer.

Many rabbinical sources, such as the "Ran", Rav Nissim ben Reuven, explain that the purpose of *sefirat haomer* is to prepare us for Shavuot, when we celebrate our receiving of the Torah and our devotion to all that it represents. Shavuot demands we purify ourselves of sins and rise to a higher spiritual level than we were at before. The Torah therefore ordered us to *count* the omer, so one could numerically see himself rise up. As the Jew counts, and the number of days rise one by one until Shavuot, he is able to parallel the rising numbers to his rising spiritual level accordingly.

As explained earlier, the days of the *Omer* are ones in which we prepare for the celebration of Shavuot, and one can assume, as such, that they are joyful days, as well. Over the generations, however, the nature of the *Omer* has changed entirely. The Gemara, in masechet Yevamot 62b, tells us that Rabbi Akiva had twelve thousand pairs of students, who, in the days of the *Omer*, died a terrible death because they did not conduct themselves with respect towards one another (*"Lo Nahagu Kavod Ze la'ze"*). The question comes up as to how disrespect towards each other led so many G-d-fearing students, students of the great Rabbi Akiva, to die. The Iyun Yaakov adds some insight to this. He suggests that, whenever a great sage leaves this world, his passing is meant to inspire the living generation to take note of his deeds and to try to improve their own. The still-living are to look at the situation and think, "If such a great sage has been taken from this world, a sage who is greater than me in all aspects of Torah and Emunah, then I should be in fear that I will be quickly taken from here, as well. As such, I will review my actions, and the Rabbi's actions, and try to improve my conduct with my peers, and my relationship with G-d."

However, the Iyun Yaakov explains that the students of Rabbi Akiva must have not taken much notice of the death of one of their great colleagues, and did not engage in the necessary introspection the *Iyun Yaakov* speaks about. The students, as the Gemara in Yevamot tells us, did not have respect for one another, and, for this reason, did not see eachother as "something special." When they saw one of the students die, they did not feel that they had lost anything great. They neither gained any inspiration nor refined their own characters at all. And, since the students lacked respect for each other, they came to lack a vital component of Torah. The Maharasha therefore explains that, since they lacked this component, they could not fulfill the pasuk, "Because [Torah] is your life, and that which lengthens your days" (Dvarim, 30), and could not gain a lengthening of days. Rather, their days were shortened, and all ended in the time of the *Omer*.

The tragedy of the students of Rabbi Akiva comes hand in hand with the persecution of the Jews of Europe throughout the Middle Ages, also in the time of the *Omer*. With these tragic events events in mind, the rabbis in the Middle Ages felt that the nature of the *Omer* should be a harsh one, despite the Torah's approach that sees it as a time of joy. It is a time of mourning and self-reflection, and for this reason, the Rabbis instated that marriage, shaving, dancing, and instrumental music are all prohibited during these times.

This time of mourning nevertheless comes to an end, even before Shavuot, on the thirty-third day of the *Omer*-- Lag Ba'omer. This day commemorates the *yahrtzeit* (anniversary of passing) of the great second-century Rabbi, Rabbi Shimon Bar Yochai. Rabbi Shimon was the first to publicly teach the mystical aspects of Judaism, known as *Kabbalah*, and is the author of the Holy *Zohar*. We Jews are joyful on this day because we celebrate Rabbi Shimon's life and revelation of the mystical dimensions of Torah, and an end to the dying of the students of Rabbi Akiva. For the latter reason, the theme of *Ahavat Israel* and respect towards a fellow Jew is focused on even more on this day.

May we, the Jewish people, always channel our efforts to respecting one another.

In Every Generation
By Mindy Chapman

This week, we observe Passover, the celebration of our freedom from Egypt. One of the amazing things about Passover is that it is impossible not to take a few moments of your time to really think about what the holiday is about and how it relates to your life. There are uncountable uses of symbolism at the Seder and in the Haggadah. You read things that tell you that you must remember the story and how it affects your life.

In every generation, we must look at ourselves as if we had come out from Egypt! In preparation for Pesach, every year, I have always taken it upon myself to try my best to do just that. This year, I realized something interesting. At the very same moment that you are having your Seder, there are more than thousands of other people who are doing the exact same thing, and that is only in your time zone!

With this in mind, it is also interesting to consider how much the Seder has evolved over the years. We no longer make sacrifices, nor do we take any animals into our home prior to this sacrifice, and now we have a "manual" for conducting the Seder, the Haggadah, which itself has changed. Somehow though, despite all these changes, we are all on the same page; we all follow the same rules, and we all follow the same order when we proceed with our dinners. Even though different cultures do have different traditions, we still follow the same basic laws, though many of these universal Pesach traditions were created and edited long after the Torah.

This knowledge certainly puts things into perspective and gives us a sense of how united all of the Jewish people, all over the world, are. After the Exodus from Egypt, we were taken into the desert and isolated, and we became one united nation. When we got to the promised land, Israel, despite being separated into tribes, we all came to the Beit HaMikdash for three different holidays, one of which is Pesach. Now, although we have no more Beit HaMikdash and we are scattered all over this earth, we remain one people, with the same morals, values, and Jewish traditions. We are all one people, celebrating the same holiday in the same way, just as we did when Hashem brought us out of Egypt.

Divrei Torah on **Chagim**

The Seder Plate: A Mystic Centerpiece
By Zachary Zarnett-Klein

Flowers, balloons, even chocolate fountains did not make the cut to become the esteemed centerpiece of the Seder table. Seder plates, with their incredible symbolism, represent the many aspects of the holiday of Pesach. Pesach is a holiday with many layers, and the items that we find on the Seder plate each have a special significance to the history of Pesach and ourselves today.

There are 5 items on the Seder plate: Maror, Z'roa, Karpas, Charoset, and Beitza.

First, the Maror appears on our Seder plate, to symbolize the bitter lives of the Jews in Egypt, who were subject to harsh and cruel slave labour each and every day. The Haggadah states, "And they embittered their lives with hard labor, with mortar and with bricks and with all manner of labor in the field; any labour that they made them do was with hard labour" (Exodus 1:14). One asks: what is the problem with "hard labour"? Isn't that what we do each and every day at school? However, there is a very fine line between the type of labour performed by the Jewish slaves in Egypt and the work we do each day.

Our people, at all times in our history, have consistently proven themselves to be hard workers, who will not quit, and who constantly stand up for their morals and principles. The issue with the Jews in Egypt was the fact that the Jews had lost hope, and, therefore, their work had lost all meaning, causing them to simply perform each miserable task out of compulsion. This lack of reason to our work is what we attempt to avoid today, by finding our interests, and pursuing our unique goals that make us feel self-fulfilled and reassure us that we are on the right track. The Maror is on the Seder plate as a reminder not to resort back to this meaningless work, and to continue to push forward as an ambitious nation.

The Z'roa represents the *Korban Pesach*, which was the special sacrifice made on the night of the Seder in the Mishkan, and then in the Temple. It is important to note that it is customary not to point at the Z'roa when reading the portion about this item in the Haggadah. In fact, it is customary not to even touch the Z'roa throughout the evening. This is to acknowledge the fact that we are unable to perform the Pesach offering, since the Temple in Jerusalem is destroyed. Despite the unification of the Halachah that took place at Yavneh, there is definitely a part that is noticeably missing from Jewish life today. Without the Temple, there is no single place that Jews can come together and worship, and, therefore, we are still in a state of destruction. Just as it is customary to break a glass at weddings, the Z'roa represents the small portion that we must take away from our happiness, since our Simcha is not complete without the Temple.

The Karpas embodies both the pain felt by the Jewish slaves and the springtime, the time of year during which Pesach is celebrated. Another interesting reason offered by some Rabbis as to why we have Karpas on our Seder plate is to symbolize Joseph's colourful tunic, which was dipped in the blood of a lamb after he was thrown into the pit by his brothers. The reason we perform the ritual of dipping the Karpas into salt water closer to the beginning of the Seder is because this event started the ball rolling, and eventually led to the Jews' descent to Egypt and their subsequent enslavement. This serves as a symbol to us today that "what goes around comes around," and teaches us to never act with cruelty towards anyone else, because it will eventually lead to our own demise.

The Charoset represents the mortar used by the Jewish slaves to build the storehouses in Egypt. As it is written, the Jews "built the store-cities of Pitom and Ramses" (Exodus 1:11). Life in Egypt began to become especially tough when Pharaoh stopped giving the Jews straw to make the mortar, and they were forced to go out into the field and collect their own straw. However, the salvation came at the time that the straw was taken away. This teaches us to never lose hope; even if a situation seems incredibly dire, with no possible shift to a brighter future, faith must be retained, because, as Hannah says in her prayer to G-d, "G-d makes poor and makes rich; He brings low and lifts up" (Samuel 1 2:7). Even when times are tough, it is important for us to keep our belief in G-d, because the tide can turn at any moment, as proven by the Jews in Egypt.

Finally, the Beitza is the only item on the Seder plate that is not formally used in the Seder, and it symbolizes the Korban Chagigah, an offering made in honour of the holiday. Despite this sacrifice being a meat offering in the Temple, it is embodied on the Seder plate in the form of an egg. How odd!

In Egypt, the Jews were deprived of their fundamental rights as humans, and were subject to difficult lives, left to mourn the days of their ancestors which had passed ever so quickly. Similarly, eggs are the first food eaten by mourners after a funeral. On the Seder night, we are commemorating the difficult times that our people faced throughout our history. However, the egg gives us a glimmer of hope, representing the roundness of life, the cycle of life, and the wish that the Temple will be built speedily and in our days, as we sing in Adir Hu.

Hopefully, we will all look towards our Seder plates this Pesach as more than a random centrepiece, but rather as a facet of our rich past, our powerful present, and our promising future.

Shavuot • שָׁבוּעוֹת

Visions of G-d

By Becky Friedman

The haftorah for the first day of Shavuot is from the beginning of Yechezkel, in which he describes his visions of angels and G-d. Now, the first question that rises up in our heads-- that rises up in my head-- is: how is this connected? How does this relate to Shavuot, the holiday on which we celebrate our receipt of the Torah, or to the Torah reading for that day, which is about the giving of the Torah and the Ten Commandments?

Haftarot are specifically chosen to "match up" to the corresponding Torah reading, or, on occasion, the time of year, so it's always a sensible question to ask. Nevertheless, in this situation it cannot be more fitting. Yechezkel's detailed and, in a lesser man, possibly ludicrous descriptions of how many wheels the angels had and what each of an angel's four faces resembles seems to bear no relation to Shavuot or the Shavuot Torah reading. How does this connect? Surely there is something more apt.

But it is Yechezkel's message, more than his exact words, from which we should learn on this occasion. Yechezkel begins, "It was in the year thirty, in the fourth [month], on the fifth of the month, and I was among the exile at the river Kevar, that the skies opened up and I saw visions of G-d" (Yechezkel, 1:1).

While Yechezkel's writing, in general, is far inferior to the poetry of some of his fellow prophets, the language here is striking for the perfectly captured contrast between the mundane and the divine. He begins, in his usual pedantic way, with an exact date, further delineating exactly where he was-- and suddenly the first half of the verse comes crashing to the floor with his lofty declaration that "the skies opened up" and here he is, seeing visions of G-d.

In the Torah reading from Shmot, Bnei Yisrael had advance warning. They had known for a long time that they would receive the Torah, and Moshe warned them three days in advance to purify themselves in preparation for Matan Torah. When they had their encounter with G-d, they were ready.

But life isn't usually like that. That is, yes, of course, it's *never* like that, because we don't have divine revelations anymore. But when we do have spiritual, transcendental experiences, we don't usually know in advance. More often we're like Yechezkel, wallowing amidst an exiled people, when suddenly the skies open up.

We are like Yechezkel, that is, in situation, but in how we react we are each one of us different. This is where we can learn from Yechezkel, because while he had no warning whatsoever, he did not act shocked; he did not argue, or complain, or try do deny his Shlichut-- as did *many* other prophets, up to and including Moshe Rabeinu-- but rather, he obligingly recorded everything he saw.

If you read further in the book of Yechezkel, he appears to be one of the most mundane figures of the Tanach. He is positively driven by G-d; in all or nearly all cases, he must be ordered by G-d exactly what to say or be carried by the spirit of G-d to exactly the right place in order to fulfill his missions.

Nevertheless, when the skies opened up to him, he accepted the vision. In all other cases, perhaps, he received strict instructions from G-d, but here, in his first divine encounter, he took the initiative to write it all down. Although he had had no warning, he was ready.

And yes, we will not have literal visions of G-d, but each one of us has a life made up of a curious marriage of the mundane and the divine. We must, like Yechezkel, accept our spiritual experiences when they come and as they come, and learn how to balance them with our everyday activities.

On Shavuot, we celebrate the receiving of the Torah, but in many ways, each day we receive the Torah. On Shavuot, we know the holiday is coming, and, like Bnei Yisrael at Matan Torah, we can be prepared. But the rest of the time, we must still be always ready, like Yechezkel, for visions of G-d.

May we all find that perfect balance; may we all see the skies open up.

Made in the USA
Charleston, SC
08 May 2011